ADVANCE PRAISE FOR **Imagination**

"This collective volume might have been titled the primacy of the imagination—it elaborates, articulates and almost perfects a theory of the creative act as imaginative re-creation. The contributors raise a wide variety of issues focused around imagination as social practice within the confines of contemporary societies as knowledge economies. For the three authors, the act of creative imagining is a self-perpetuating paradox which institutes new meanings and novel codes of signification. The act of imagination re-structures the human mind in order to face its creative performance and objectifying output. The writers quite firmly assert that imagination does not simply free the mind from the restrictions of the known and its social conditions, but it expands the limits of the known itself and institutes human presence as an act of continuing self-definition. From the ancient Greeks and Plato to the Romantics and the postmodern capitalist economies, this book explores the deep interaction between the need for novel ways of seeing and new practices of creative action. This is a meticulous, passionate and original exploration that simply redefines the parameters of the question."

Vrasidas Karalis, Associate Professor of Modern Greek, University of Sydney

"Who would want to demur from the sentiment that imagination is a marvellous thing? Do we not live in the age of creative industries, knowledge economies, cyberspace and post-industrialism? Romancing our *zeitgeists*, and believing in new signs and wonders is a perennial pastime of human societies. Much harder work is to think about imagination, collective forms of creativity and knowledge production. This is the signal achievement of *Imagination*. Its three authors do the hard work for us and in three different registers: first in foundational terms, that of thinking about imagination and creativity as collective knowledge innovation and production; second, by interpreting the history of imagination as the cumulative production of knowledge across cultures and ultimately as a global process; and third, in the age of cyber capitalism, understanding the transmission of knowledge via digital production and open sourcing of property. This kind of thinking is hard work but good writing that produces lucid critical insight. Murphy, Peters and Marginson demonstrate that critical analysis and foundational thinking can also be written with panache. This book is not only good to think with, but is also a pleasure to read."

Trevor Hogan, Senior Lecturer in Sociology, La Trobe University

Imagination

PETER LANG
New York • Washington, D.C./Baltimore • Bern
Frankfurt • Berlin • Brussels • Vienna • Oxford

Peter Murphy, Michael A. Peters,
Simon Marginson

Imagination

Three Models of Imagination
in the Age of the Knowledge Economy

PETER LANG
New York • Washington, D.C./Baltimore • Bern
Frankfurt • Berlin • Brussels • Vienna • Oxford

Library of Congress Cataloging-in-Publication Data

Murphy, Peter.
Imagination: three models of imagination in the age of the knowledge economy /
Peter Murphy, Michael A. Peters, Simon Marginson.
p. cm.
Includes bibliographical references and index.
1. Imagination—Social aspects. 2. Information technology—Economic aspects.
3. Intellectual capital. I. Peters, Michael A. II. Marginson, Simon. III. Title.
BF411.M86   303.48—dc22   2010011400
ISBN 978-1-4331-0528-9 (hardcover)
ISBN 978-1-4331-0529-6 (paperback)

Bibliographic information published by **Die Deutsche Nationalbibliothek**.
Die Deutsche Nationalbibliothek lists this publication in the "Deutsche
Nationalbibliografie"; detailed bibliographic data is available
on the Internet at http://dnb.d-nb.de/.

FSC
Mixed Sources
Product group from well-managed
forests, controlled sources and
recycled wood or fiber

Cert no. SCS-COC-002464
www.fsc.org
©1996 Forest Stewardship Council

The paper in this book meets the guidelines for permanence and durability
of the Committee on Production Guidelines for Book Longevity
of the Council of Library Resources.

100011527

TABLE OF CONTENTS

PREFACE

In this, the third of a series on creativity in the age of the knowledge economy, we focus on the dimension of imagination. Intellectual interest in the subject of the imagination has ebbed and flowed across the past three centuries. From Addison's 'The Pleasures of the Imagination' (1712) the topic passes to Burke and Hume and then to Lessing and Kant—and finally segueing via the latter two to Coleridge's *Biographia Literaria* (1817). The next significant surge of interest occurs in the 1930s, with the closely timed production of Dewey's *Art as Experience* (1934), Sartre's *The Psychology of Imagination* (1936), and Collingwood's *Principles of Art* (1938). The cachet of the term imagination ensures that it is mentioned now in passing often and with a certain casual awe. But as quickly as it is mentioned, it is dispensed with. Everyone seems to admire imagination and to reckon that being imaginative is a marvellous thing. The 'creative imagination,' which may be a tautology, is also highly rated. Nevertheless, actual explanations of what is the imagination are quite rare—and the whole business of creativity remains a bit of a puzzle.

In the first volume of this series, *Creativity and the Global Knowledge Economy*, we observed that the mind is a force of production. That which is discovered in the arts and the sciences is applied to economic and social processes—sometimes with spectacular effect. In many ways, as we noted, modern capitalism at its leading edge has become an aesthetic and scientific mode of production. The prototype of this, though, as we also pointed out, was already in place in the nineteenth century. From works in engineering and architecture to chemistry and biology to educational and social policy, the advancement of the arts and sciences is central in a modern society. The most talked-about entrant into the club of economic modernity today is China, who along with India, Brazil and a number of others is forging a second-tier of international economies. In the year 2000, the Chinese government made a decision not only to continue expanding its schools and universities, but also to commit large resources to develop internationally competitive research universities. That latter would seem to be practical proof of the centrality of knowledge creation in a modern economy.

Yet is it? In *Imagination*, we raise some doubts. A point that was made in *Global Creation*, the second volume of the current series, is returned to in the present work. This is that while it is all well and good to talk about knowledge economies and post-industrialism, it is not clear that knowledge *by itself* creates the kind of dynamism and energy typical of advanced societies at their most ebullient. Put another way—knowledge is a function of something deeper. Consequently, we should ask ourselves the question: where does knowledge come from? It is not evident that resources alone can create knowledge. Building institutes and campuses, and hiring staff, doesn't guarantee the creation of knowledge. Rather the source of knowledge is much more intangible. Knowledge is a function of imagination and thinking, not resources—even if it is true that a certain amount of free time and stimulating surrounds is required for sustaining both imagination and thinking.

After the recent 2008 world financial collapse, the Chinese government looked hard at its economic base and asked itself what kinds of industries should it encourage for the future. The answer was cultural and creative industries, that is, post-industrialism. Even with a still very low per capita income base across much or most of China, the government can see that economic and social prosperity requires going beyond brutal cheap industrialism. However, the phrase 'cultural and creative industries' invokes two very difficult words—culture and creativity. We know full well that art and science— or culture and creativity—can be industrialised, once they exist. When a film is created, it can be distributed. When a powerful or seductive film is made, it can attract an audience, and with that audience, it can generate an economy. But the question of how a film that is interesting and attractive is created in the first instance is a much more troublesome matter. For such film making requires more than money and more than time. It requires imagination and thought. In short, it calls for 'creative imagination.' These are words that roll very quickly off our tongues, and easily become flippant clichés. But, as we point out in *Imagination*, while these are words that may be easily spoken, they are words that are very difficult to practice. The reality is that the number of genuinely creative artefacts or processes or works is very small. To bring them into the world is arduous. Very few people can do it. Likewise, the number of places or institutions capable of doing so is a tiny handful. To create a creative economy is not a matter of policy. It is not a matter of resources. It is not even a matter of knowledge. For sure, policies, resources, and knowledge help at the margins. But are they the decisive factors? No, they are not.

Which factors matter is what we turn our attention to in this book. Broadly speaking, we single out three aspects: (a) the capacity of a society to manage deep cultural ambidexterity even to the point of systemic paradox, (b) the ability of a society to avoid scientific or cultural path dependence, and thus be able to make the kinds of genuine intellectual leaps that create knowledge rather than just transmit, reproduce, or distribute it, and finally (c) the capability of a society to create ways, styles, and kinds of thinking. The latter might be described as the aesthetics of thought. Styles of thought emerge in time, and disappear. But in doing so, they allow societies—for a period—to manage their ambivalences in interesting ways, and to gather sufficient intellectual power to create formidable art and science. The difficult thing is to bring these into existence, rather than to simply parcel out what already exists. Collective creativity is what permits a society to be intellectually productive. Societies that lack the factors of ambidexterity, gymnastic capacity and the aesthetics of thought lack imagination. They are not creative, or they confuse creativity with the accumulation, reproduction, and distribution of what is already in hand. This is what we think many contemporary 'creative societies' are doing. On close inspection, they are a lot less creative than many of their historical forbears, and it is this that makes us wonder whether much of the contemporary talk about 'world class universities' and 'knowledge economies' might not in the end be bravado in the face of a shrinking real capacity to animate institutions of knowledge with the kind of awe-inspiring art and science that is the expression of genuine intellectual power. One is left with the impression that today—despite some impressive achievements—we are surrounded by too many hollow institutions filled with too many hollow men and women doing too many meaningless things.

—PETER MURPHY, MELBOURNE, DECEMBER 2009

The authors, collectively and individually, want to thank a number of people. First at our publisher Peter Lang, there is Chris Myers and Bernadette Shade who have been very supportive and very efficient. Peter Murphy extends his warm thanks to John Carroll for conversations over many years about innumerable interesting subjects, some of which are echoed in the present volume. Peter is also very grateful for the thought-provoking exchanges with Simon Marginson about the issues tackled in this volume, and for Michael Peters' collaborative prowess which has made the work of co-authorship a delight. In recent years, Peter has had the chance to collaborate with a variety of scholars working in cognate areas. This work has stimulated not a small part of what the reader finds here, so heartfelt thanks also to Eduardo de la Fuente, Peter Snow, Anders Michelsen, Dimitris Vardoulakis, Trevor Hogan, Xin Xin Deng,

Elizabeth Coleman, Vrasidas Karalis, Ken Friedman, Andrew Dawson, Janine Burke, Markus Locker, Dominique Bouchet, Stuart Grant, and David Roberts.

Michael Peters would like to express his sincere gratitude to his two Australian co-authors who have been a dream to work with and prove that trans-Tasman academic partnership is possible and necessary. He would also like to acknowledge the useful conversations with his colleagues at the University of Illinois: Tina Besley, Bill Cope, Fazal Rizvi, and Nicholas Burbules. He would particularly like to acknowledge PhD students at the University of Illinois that he has had the opportunity to work with over the last few years, including Daniel Araya, Rodrigo Britez, Garett Gietzen, James Thayer, Huseyin Essen, Rushika Patel, Ergin Bulut, David Ondercin, Tze-Chang Liu, Mousumi Mukherjee, Brett Grant, Lucinda Morgan, John Jones and Lucinda Morgan.

Simon Marginson also has thanks. Michael Peters negotiated this group of three volumes that have been beautifully published by Peter Lang (*Creativity* 2009, *Global Creation* 2010, and *Imagination* 2010). Michael's range, penetration, inclusiveness and productivity are inspiring. Collaboration with Peter Murphy has been immensely fecund and opened the way to writing on a range of topics—including planetary history and evolution, the ancient Rome and Maya, Japan, the pre-history of human cultures, problems of modernity, and music—connecting these to older preoccupations in political and social theory, political economy, universities, knowledge and policy. To list all those who have helped in imagining the global would be impossible. Much is owed to the scholars cited in the chapters, including David Held, Arjun Appadurai and Manuel Castells who helped in shaping early understandings of globalization. Work on the books has been assisted by stimulating and happy discussions with Fazal Rizvi (especially), Rajani Naidoo, Glyn Davis, Richard James, Mark Considine, Marijk van der Wende, Aki Yonezawa, Hugo Horta, Roger King, Brian Pusser, Imanol Ordorika, Ken Kempner, Allan Luke, Phan Le Ha, Dang Kim Anh, Jane Kenway, Johanna Fahey, Chris Ziguras and Ravinder Sidhu. Simultaneous collaborations on international education with Chris Nyland, Erlenawati Sawir, Helen Forbes-Mewett, Gaby Ramia, Jenny Lee and Sophie Arkoudis suggested ideas about global agency. Thanks to Kazuhiro Kudo who kindly read and corrected Chapter 6 on Japan. Special thanks to three education managers who make it possible to be a scholar: Vice-Chancellor Glyn Davis, Dean Field Rickards and Director of the Centre for the Study of Higher Education Richard James. Sincere thanks also to Director Shinichi Yamamoto, Futao Huang and Jun Oba at the Research Institute for Higher Education at Hiroshima University in Japan where the readings for the *Imagination* chapters were completed in July-October 2009.

ACKNOWLEDGEMENTS

Chapter 8, 'Thinking' originally appeared as 'Kinds of Thinking, Styles of Reasoning' in *Educational Philosophy and Theory*, 39:4, 2007: 350–363; and Chapter 10, 'Practice' appeared as 'Personalisation, Personalised Learning and the Reform of Social Policy: Prospects for Molecular Governance in the Digitized Society' in *Policy Futures in Education*, 7:6, 2009: 615–627. Both have been edited and rewritten for this book and appear with permission of the copyright holder (the author) and journals.

Introduction

PETER MURPHY

Prologue

Imagination is the third volume in a series. It follows *Creativity and the Global Knowledge Economy* (2009) and *Global Creation* (2010).[1] The previous volumes explore the social and intellectual impact of the global knowledge economy, and some of the central socio-economic and spatio-temporal aspects of digital capitalism. In this, the third volume of the work, we turn our attention to the imaginary dimension of cybernetic capitalism. It is this, the symbolic aspect, which lends contemporary society its immaterial aura. In that, it is not unique. All material systems have their immaterial aspects. All social orders have symbols and representations. Images and the manufacture of imagery are rampant in contemporary life. But if this is the case, it is only because human beings are conspicuously drawn to symbolic and imaginary things.

Among the most important things that human beings create for themselves are symbols. They love something that represents something else. In a way, this is what meaning is, and all artifacts that social systems create, even the most material of things, and sometimes most especially the most material of things, have a symbolic dimension. The attraction to symbols is deeply embedded in the nature of humankind at the core of its species-being. Consequently, all societies produce symbols, and all societies have an imaginative dimension. In this volume, we ask what is the nature of this imaginative dimension, and how does it manifest itself in the digital age? All knowledge has an imaginative aspect. In our time, in the age of the knowledge economy, in an era that will pass as all previous eras have passed into the oblivion of time, we ask whether the power of the imagination plays a particularly pronounced role in social life? Has the production of symbols now, today, become an observable animating economic force in contemporary society? Do we live in a world of Imagineering? If so—are contemporary societies then more creative than their forbears? Or are they just better at distributing the symbols and signs and other kinds of imaginative artifacts? Is the Internet first and foremost a medium of distribution or a means of production? And what do the answers to these questions tell us about the nature and dynamics of imaginative creation? Where, as the young child reasonably asks, does it come from, why does it exist, and what does it do?

(Looking) Around Corners

The imagination allows us to look around corners. The advantage of this to the human species has been remarkable. For our distant ancestors, to be able to anticipate the sudden turn of prey was close to miraculous. It provided an edge in the tough struggle to survive. And survive, it did—for ours is a species that not only sees what there is to see but it sees itself in the mirror in reverse, and in its mind's eye it sees in converse. It also sees what is not there at all, and it sees affinities and connections between things that are completely unexpected. But a note of caution: the idea that the imagination 'sees' is a metaphor. Every characteristic that we attribute to the imagination, just like every connection between things that the imagination 'sees' or 'draws,' is a metaphor—just as the attributes of all things are metaphorical, even if most of them are long dead metaphors. No need to belabor the point much more—but a 'dead' metaphor is itself a metaphor, as is the 'laboring' of an argument and the 'point' of a contention. There is no escaping the infinite circle of metaphor. Correspondingly, we can invoke any of the senses, and much else besides, to describe the imagination. Our imagination can hear and touch, as well as see. Someone somewhere long past cast the imagination in olfactory terms. There are perfumed ideas and acts of artistic direction that have the stench of decay about them. But, equally, we 'paint' the imagination in both cognitive and emotional 'colors' as well. There are hot and cold imaginations, just as there are cutting and probing imaginations. The imagination is a mix of feeling, sensing and thinking. From each of these sources, a torrent of descriptors pours forth.

So whenever we talk about the imagination, we can only ever talk about it in imaginative terms, even if we habitually have to resort to the dried-up imagination of cliché. We cannot escape the circle of imagination. That circle, and what it condemns us to, is the human condition. We are the imaginative species that lives metaphorically. This is a strange condition. What it means is that human beings 'act' in pursuit of meaning, rather than 'react' out of instinct as other species do. The imagination is the obverse of animal instinct. Where the imagination is reflexive, instinct is a reflex. Instinct is a response to internal and external stimuli. It is true that some basic human feelings (such as affects like anger and fear) are reactive. They are, in some sense, a residue of the instincts. But human beings are not only reactive in their behavior. In the course of their natural history, and its eventual peculiar interweaving with social history, human beings developed cognitive feelings.[2] These feelings regulate human interventions into the world. They animate the human ability to create a second nature. This second nature, humankind's own constructed environment, does not replace first nature but rather exists sometimes happily and sometimes not so happily in tandem with it. Cognitive feelings draw human beings into shaping and directing, constructing and re-constructing, and on occasions destroying the world around them. Cognitive feelings are bound up with choosing, deliberating, deciding, calculating, risk-taking, and so on.[3] Such feelings have a sizable imaginative component.

Cognition requires in each of us the capacity to run scenarios, to think about alternatives, to model situations based on assumptions, and then to change the assumptions. To think 'what if?' and to plan 'if, then' requires imagination. So also does the human capacity to make friends and fall in love. Beyond the level of simple affects, human attraction relies on imagination. We never think of others as they are, nor do they think of us as we are. For who we are, is always who we are not.[4] Human beings have public and private sides, open and secret lives. They commit and betray, and love and hate, in the same breath. They are actors, they wear masks, and they perform roles. They are themselves and yet at the same time someone else also. Because of this, they surprise and excite us—and keep us interested and on our toes.

Humankind has an altogether unusual capacity for imaginative transport. It imagines itself in places before it goes there. Sometimes, some individuals even prefer to travel in their imagination rather than actually go places. The imagination often is more interesting than everyday reality. Even staying home, some human beings roam far and wide. Without the imagination, the ascent of the species out of Africa, and its vast journey across the face of the globe and beyond, would have been impossible. It is not that human beings have managed to occupy several ecological niches successfully. Rather they created their own artificial ecology, a built world.[5] They invented their own second nature. This second nature inevitably has complicated and tensile relations with the first nature that human beings are eternally part of. Human beings have occupied lands and seas, coasts and interiors, shores, mountains, plains, estuaries, and forests. They belong everywhere and nowhere. They inhabit an uncanny zone located in-between nature and society, biology and history. They are a peculiarly double-coded species. The human condition of being in between nature and society is perhaps, speculatively, a reason for the imagination. The imagination is an outgrowth of this bifurcated condition, and at that same time it underscores it. The imagination is the human faculty that copes best with the double-coding of human existence. In a way, it relishes the double nature of human existence. Conversely, the imagination turns everything that it sees, hears, and touches into something else.

For human beings, everything is 'as if' it was something else.[6] As Michael Peters observes in chapter seven ('Thinking'), Wittgenstein famously imagined language as a 'game.' Nobody conceived of language in such terms until Wittgenstein drew the connection. In drawing the connection, he engaged—profoundly—in an act of thinking. He 'showed' (as he liked to put it) how one important thing (a game) was like another important thing (language). This happens in all human discoveries and inventions, and in all generation of new meanings. They 'show' how one artifact 'is like' another artifact—how one thing 'is' something else. Take for instance the case of the ancient Greek temple. In certain key design aspects, the temple was 'as if' it was a wooden hut, and the hut in turn took its cue from the sheltering canopy of trees. Since antiquity, endless building types, from houses to banks, have been inspired by the Greek temple form. Everything that we encounter is 'like' something else. Human beings see everything around them as a metaphor. Mostly these are dead metaphors, itself a metaphor. So, mostly, the imagination leaves only a very slight trace upon the world. Yet there also comes moments when the imagination has powerful effects. It transports us. Before cars, boats, and even our humble legs, comes the imagination. It is the single most effective means of transportation that we have. Metaphor, in ancient Greek, is a word for transport.[7] Everything that we hear, see, taste, and touch, all of our cognitive processes, our choices, evaluations, and decisions, are subject to our imagination at some point, even if only peripherally. Our reason also, as Peters remarks on in chapter seven, has a history because of this. Different metaphors—different styles—frame our thinking. Different eras, different epochs, have a penchant for different metaphors for thought. These styles of thinking pass into and out of use.

The species whose mind has the remarkable power to transpose and transport everything it encounters into something else simultaneously has the equal and opposite capacity to transpose and transport itself around the world, and beyond. This is an adventurous, exploring species. It cannot help itself because it is so constituted. If it cannot explore outer space, then it turns to the nano-level of creation. If it cannot go abroad, it explores the landscape of its inner psychological world. Soon it finds that its inner explorations are conjoined with its outer explorations, and one form of exploration becomes the metaphor for another kind.

The metaphorical power of 'as if,' the power to imagine one thing as another, makes the human world a virtual one. Our own contemporaries are very aware of the virtual aspect of the imagination because of the spread of digital technologies. The impact of these is assayed by Michael Peters. The book is transformed into the electronic reader, community migrates online with LiveJournal and Facebook, currency notes turn into electronic credit transactions, and physical mail is replaced by electronic mail. Images become words, and words become images. Games look like movies, and films mimic games. Prolific acts of 'as if' re-mediate the media of the world. This is an effect of our species' unusual capacity for metaphorical translation. Such translation allows us to turn what is different into what is similar, and yet retain dramatic contrasts in the very midst of those fertile likenesses. The transmogrifying of the horse-drawn carriage into the automotive car is typical of the inventive consequences of the analogical mind-set of human beings. As Simon Marginson observes in chapter six, Japan translated Chinese premodernity and Western modernity into a successful and idiosyncratic civilization. In borrowing, it created anew.

It was once popular to conflate the imagination with dreams. Twentieth-century philosophical painters like René Magritte and Salvador Dali depicted unusual juxtapositions and revealed the hidden affinities of things in dream-like or surreal landscapes. This had a partial validity. A part of the imagination does work in sleep. Anyone who has had to solve a problem can testify to the power of sleeping on it. Yet the imagination is not simply reducible to dreaming. More particularly, it ought not to be confused with fantasy. For the imagination is deeply rooted in reality, even if it utilizes dreaming and other kinds of free association as a way of experimentally making unusual conjunctions of things. It is notable that highly imaginative people are also often very practical and grounded. Shakespeare, who epitomizes the poetic imagination, was an exceptionally capable businessman. Because the imagination is practical, and is grounded in reality, it has profound social consequences. If we look at modern economies, as we do in this volume, we find that the most successful ones, measured by the normal indicators, are also highly inventive. Gross domestic product and per capita registration of patents and copyright are strongly correlated. Invention is powered by the analogical imagination. Things 'come to be'—that is to say, they 'come into being'—through metaphor and its material applications.

We may speculate about a root metaphor of all things, but a root itself is a metaphor, as is the well-spring, the origin, and the source of creation, as indeed is the very notion of creation itself. This does not mean that the explanation and the interpretation of things are fruitless or regressive, or that meaning is ultimately meaningless. Rather what the phenomenon of imaginative transportation implies is that meaning is paradoxical. Namely, everything meaningful turns into its opposite. Creation, as Peter Murphy describes it, is a paradox. It is out of such paradoxes—which are seemingly semantic impossibilities—that new meanings arise. Metaphors turn the impossible into the possible, and thereby new meanings emerge. Meanings created in this fashion are not only linguistic in nature. Social meaning is produced in a similar way.

The production of new social meaning is akin to what Michael Peters describes in chapter nine. The bureaucratic industrial system of the twentieth century was remarkably successful for many decades. It generated the institution of the business firm and flagship companies like General Motors. Then it fell into systemic decline. The result is that once mighty companies became supplicants before governments. When events of this kind happen in a social system, crises of meaning are generated. Crises, if they are resolved, are followed by a renewal of meaning. The renewal of meaning is achieved through creative media such as those of metaphor. In 'Practice,' the final chapter of *Imagination*, Peters reviews a concrete, micro-logical example of such a stirring of renewal. He describes the phenomenon of 'mass customization'—the development of models of service delivery that combine personalized characteristics with standard characteristics, and in doing so bridge in a paradoxical manner between industrial and non-industrial, mass and custom, personal and standardized models of production and delivery. In a semantic sense, this is how meaning is created.

The production of meaning, as much as the production of goods and services, has a social dimension. Not only does it have a social dimension, but different societies are better and worse at producing meaning. This is because societies are more and less imaginative. At different times, and in different places, societies display greater and lesser powers of imagination. When societies open the flood-gates of the imagination, it is for short periods of time. In the present volume, we observe at close quarters the way in which the species-capacity to imagine becomes a social and historical force. Imagination is not just an individual and psychological capacity, though it is that. It is not just a faculty that belongs to us as a species, though it is that as well. Imagination is also a collective, social, economic and historical capacity. The creators of the modern firm helped sweep away centuries of feudal behavior. But they did so analogically by reinventing the idea of hierarchy, translating the idea of the highly personalized status hierarchy of the feudal era into the de-personalized procedural status hierarchies that we are familiar with from the organizational era of modern capitalism. Corporatism was replaced by the corporation. Hierarchy did not disappear in the modern age of equality. Rather it assumed some remarkable new expressions.

Three Models of the Imagination

The invention of the procedural hierarchy—the key form of modern organization—highlights the ironic field of tension that the three authors of Imagination deal with. Each one observes the twin imperatives of imagination and institutionalisation, and the paradox of imaginative powers that create institutions and the institutional forces thus created that then inhibit the imagination.

Model One: Collective Creation

The first model of the imagination that is presented here emphasizes the role in creation that is played by common cognitive forms (such as paradox and analogy) and by common aesthetic forms (such as proportion and symmetry). These are the pervasive media of creation—and are widely deployed in diverse acts of creation. Conversely they are the building blocks of the human imagination. But not in an inward-looking sense—for the media of creation are public and social in character. Indeed some of them are sewn into the very fabric of first nature.

Chapter one, 'Imagination,' discusses collective acts of creation. Many of these, such as the European Renaissance or the Age of the Knowledge Economy, are epochal in scale and impact. They all draw on a deep background of persistent aesthetic forms and enduring cognitive and metaphysical patterns that shape nature, society and human selves. Human beings draw endlessly on these forms and patterns. They constitute a creative commons available to all social actors who recast them in adaptive, inventive and innovative ways, and apply them to surprising ends. Developments in the sciences and the arts, innovations in economic and social institutions, and new types of political behavior and existential character owe much to the generative power of these forms. Yet these same forms and patterns, no matter their unorthodox applications, have an immutable or recurrent nature. The chapter reflects on the paradoxical relationship between change and continuity in creation—and speculates that in fact it is appositions and paradoxes of this kind that drive or constitute the very act of creation.

Chapter two, 'Creation,' expands the discussion of the collective or social nature of creativity. What is highlighted is the role of non-discursive phenomenon such as intuition, figure, and shape in the creative process—as opposed to discourse, logic and argument. Creative media, it is suggested, are primarily pre-linguistic in nature. That is, the unsayable is the primary medium of creation. That is true even when we speak and write. This directs our attention to the way in which large-scale collective creation works. The architecture and design of cities shows us how the inarticulate 'design principle' of creation operates. Great cities are a kind of commons. They are works of indescribably complex yet intuitively graspable cooperation that is inspired and put in motion by splendid forms and ingenious patterns. From Athens and Rome to Renaissance Florence and Venice, Elizabethan London, nineteenth-century Paris, New York and Chicago from 1860 to 1960, mid-twentieth-century Tokyo, and, thinking about the future, Shanghai and Houston tomorrow— all these are cities in their golden age (or what might prove to be a golden age).[8] Most of the great examples of human invention have come from a handful of mercurial cities in very concentrated time periods.[9] No-one can really explain why this is. It is as though a collective rapture subsumes places for a time, and then, all of sudden, passes on, leaving them contemplating their own stolidly uninventive navels. Creation is fascinating and often inexplicable. So is the faltering of creation. The latter can happen catastrophically—as in the case of Detroit after 1960. It can also take a less visible form, say of drift, which is evident, as Simon Marginson discusses in chapter six, in Tokyo today. Surfaces may glitter for centuries, as in the case of Venice, but in the depths of the mercurial city the machinery of creation can unwind, generating in its wake fascinating tensions and social self-delusions.

Our own age—the age of the knowledge economy—widely advertises itself as imaginative. It loves metaphors of the imagination. At the close of the twentieth century, many advanced economies had become enraptured with the idea that they were creative economies run increasingly by creative classes of technologists, artists and the wielders of signs and symbols.[10] As in the case of all dominant social self-conceptions, there is more than an element of truth in that assertion. Yet it is also an exaggerated truth. Chapter three 'Discovery' looks at the contemporary inventive capacity in the arts and sciences, and asks whether it is greater or lesser than in comparable societies and periods in the past. The conclusion, here, is that we do exaggerate our own capacities. Contemporary creativity, measured in real terms, is less today than it was a hundred years ago, and is less impressive when compared with a number of major scientific and cultural periods from the Renaissance onwards. Whether we are talking about cultural and creative industries or about basic research in universities, the picture of the last twenty-five years has been one not of the growth of creative power in real terms but rather the relative decline of such power. It is not unusual in human history that decline is matched by assertions of the opposite.

This does not mean that the digital age does not have its remarkable inventions. It does, just as the digital age in effect re-invented capitalism. That extraordinary calculating machine, the computer, has deeply transformed economic, social and intellectual behavior. It is difficult to find any area of human behavior that is not now in one way or another mediated by computing in one guise or another. Cybernetic, digital and knowledge capitalism is a significant social phenomenon with the distinctive features that Michael Peters delineates in the present volume and which we have discussed at length in *Creativity and the Global Knowledge Economy* and *Global Creation*. From open source property to distributed organizations, the managerial and technological inventiveness of the digital age is significant. But the question of the degree and depth of that invention, and how it will stand up in the long-term, remains nagging. The research universities, for example, have come to a moment of self-consciousness in recent times, as Simon Marginson observes. Yet, as he also suggests, the power of invention of those key cultural and scientific institutions may be today less in the arts and sciences in the traditional sense, and more in the field of management and strategy, as these great universities re-invent themselves as global institutions separated from their metropolitan origins and their twentieth-century national settings.

Model Two: Global Imagination

In Model Two the lens is the global imagination. The global dimension has a planetary materiality but global vision and relations are human practices. Chapters four to six by Simon Marginson are about imaginings of the world as a whole; about the imagined global dimension of action, and the map of actions and strategies emerging in universities in the wake of contemporary communicative globalization; and about what is happening to imagining and creativity in this contemporary global dimension. They also talk about the collision between the global imagination and more bounded fields of thought that is becoming increasingly apparent. These chapters continue the exploration of globalization, creativity and the field of higher education in Marginson's chapters in the second volume in this series, *Global Creation,* and extend the discussion of the university and creativity that is opened by Peter Murphy's chapter three in this volume.

Chapter four, 'World,' opens with a history of the global imagination. It begins with Earth, the eco-sphere itself, and the emergence of the vision/mobility coupling in animal species. More than 540 million years ago at the opening of the Cambrian period the ubiquitous trilobites, the dominant species of their day, were the first to achieve vision, enabling them to instantly apprehend the environment around them as a single relational space. The decisive achievement of vision generated a tremendous wave of species innovation and ecological transformation, the Cambrian radiation. Vision and mobility together enabled successive animal species, including human societies when they emerged, to move closer towards the reflexive apprehension of the interdependent world as a zone of action. The ancient Greeks knew that the world was round, and science in India and Persia was able to measure its circumference in abstract, but it was not until the sixteenth-century European world empires' astronomy and navigation that the notion of the world as a sphere became lodged in popular awareness. Even then the round world was not visible to the eye. In the twentieth century air travel and the visual apprehension of the curved Earth brought a sense of the global closer. Then came the leap into space. The decisive breakthrough into the global imagination was the vision of the Earth floating against the blackness of space transmitted back to earth by the astronauts and cosmonauts in the 1960s and 1970s. At that point the form of the iconic sphere and the notion of the 'global' moved to a central place in the human mentality. The ecological movement, the cheapening of air transport, the Internet and the roll out of global communications followed, bringing into practical form a global dimension already lodged in the imagination as the common home of humanity.

Chapter four draws together the dynamics of global space in the age of the knowledge economy, including the de-severing of distance, the flourishing of synchronous relations across borders, place and identity, positioning strategies and global flows of knowledge. With the emergence of the global dimension to a central role in human imagining, relations and action, global sub-systems have developed rapidly. The focus of chapter five, 'University,' is the global space of higher education and research and the imaginings that are building it. In the universities a novel global architecture is being made and the pace of change is remarkable. After discussing the university forms and strategies of the last two decades, the period of communicative globalization, the chapter moves to data gathered in a set of interviews with university leaders from twelve countries. The university presidents expound their visions and fears; their acts of enterprise, daring and timid by turns; the productions of the 'World Class Universities' over which they preside; and the openings, hierarchies, inequalities and closures they see. At a time when the university form has become truly ubiquitous, university strategy-making has become a key site of creation. The landscape of the global knowledge economy is dotted with the pyramids erected by latter-day pharaohs: the networks and consortia, the would-be education hubs and offshore campuses, and the citation engines, the concentrations of science power. University rankings and other comparative performance indicators monitor executive action. Every president wants to preside over the next Harvard. Yet it seems that building global presence and status in the k-economy is not the same as hosting major intellectual achievement. The capacity of the modern university-city to generate really great works in the arts and sciences is in question (chapter three). Does this means the locus of creativity in universities has shifted from scholars and researchers to university executives? Are the methods of research management used to lodge the university form in national political economies, at the same time as universities are colonizing the new global spaces, somehow inimical to those leaps of thought in which heterogeneous or opposing qualities are cast into creative relations, and questions of the utilities of research remain open rather than inherent in pre-managed research design? Is the simulated 'research economy' and its performance indicators crowding out stellar creativity and diminishing rather than enhancing the potential for intellectual breakthroughs? The chapter draws on evolutionary theory to discuss patterns of innovation in the knowledge economy, and organizational sociology to investigate the standardization of university forms in this period. It reviews archaeological findings in the hundreds of ancient Mayan city sites in Mesoamerica, contrasting the Mayan patterns of commonality and diversity with those apparent in the global university sector today. A key element in the emerging global university space is the tension between national and global ways of seeing. The modern university is the product of the high time of the nation-state of the last two hundred years. It continues to be nationally regulated and funded. Yet its global imaginings and actions push beyond national borders and the pre-global notions of international competition, internationalism and multilateralism whereby states define and limit the world.

Chapter six, 'Nation,' expands on the discussion about globalization and the national imagination. It crosses the Eurasian landmass in time and space from the western to the eastern extreme, passing from Ancient Rome to emerging Japan and then Japanese universities today. The core inquiry is into different ways that bounded national identity and wider engagement are combined, the costs and profits in those strategies—and also what happens when national and global imaginings conflict. Rome enfolded its prolonged engagement with Greek culture and the reciprocity between 'romanization' and 'hellenization,' and its tolerance of local languages and agency, into the process of identity formation. The climax of this feat of multiplicity was the remarkable pre-industrial modernization of the emerging empire of Augustus. At the heart of the revolution was a renovated Roman tradition, which, in a sharp break with the exclusive forms that sustained the republic, could be progressively extended so as to encompass all of the free inhabitants of the empire. The successive and contrasting modernizations of Japan that followed from the Tokugawa Shogunate at the beginning of the seventeenth century, and the Meiji 'restoration' of the power of the emperor in 1868, likewise drew much of their authority from a malleable and potent national tradition that was remade in the process of modernization. But in other respects Japan's solution could not have been more different. Instead of a porous and extendible boundary a firm wall was created. Despite the derived nature of many of Japan's icons such as Buddhism and script and the emperor system, *Nihonjinron*, the world of constructed 'Japaneseness,' was closed to outsiders. Challenged by foreign technology, language and culture in the nineteenth century, the method was not to embrace multiplicity on national terms as in Rome, but to do as Japan had always done, to produce a sanitized hybridity, in which foreign motifs were 'translated' into Japanese ones and then absorbed safely into the national sphere.

Led by a top-down nation state which retains a close hold on many aspects of social and cultural life, the Meiji approach to the world continues. The resilience of a distinctive and also bounded Japanese zone of imagining is notable. The price is that within the protected shell only some kinds of innovation are possible; in a more global era in which loose networking and multiple identities maximize strategic flexibility, the two-step character of engagement emerges as a handicap, and unlike its neighbour China, Japan seems unable to shape the emerging global order. This might explain the apparent paradox of universities in Japan. Global research universities favor common language and the loose coupling of plural selves, and like creative cities they draw much of their edginess from the strangers in their midst. Despite the brilliance of Japanese systems and products in many spheres, and the often stellar character of Japanese science, university strategies are under-developed, academic cultures seem to be closed and conservative, and there is vexed confusion about 'internationalization.' The case of Japan also illuminates in stark relief the national-global tensions that are an endemic feature of the global knowledge economy. Those tensions especially show themselves in sites such as higher education where global imaginings are part of the core business of research universities, but many of the conditions of possibility of higher education, including funding and regulation, continue to be shaped by nation-states. Nations and national cultures will not disappear in a more global era, whether associated with nation-states or not, and in all kinds of practical ways University and Nation are necessary to each other. But it is a case of 'same bed, different dreams,' because nation-states often have other imaginings to those of 'their' universities. Paradoxically, universities are only really valuable to the nation-state when they are 'disloyal' to it—when they place global relationships and systems, such as the formation and sharing of knowledge, and the free cross-border border movement of people, above the interests of the nation-state. Universities engaged in the global dimension are able to open up opportunities for the nation to learn from global sources, and also to take the nation's agenda into the world. National cultures that are unable to become proactive within the global conversation are likely to lose ground in the longer term.

Model Three: Re-imagining Education

Part of this global conversation is about the kinds of institutionalisation relied on by contemporary societies. Almost four decades ago Ivan Illich in *Deschooling Society* (1973) drew attention to the impossibility and contradictory nature of education through schooling within modern economies in the West.[11] The institutionalization of education leads to, and is a paradigm example of, the institutionalization of society—one might also say the 'institutionalization of the imagination.' Illich provided a trenchant critique of educational modernization: in the style of a present-day Rousseau, he explained the corrupting and psychological destabilizing effects of institutions on the individual that robs people of their initiative and imagination, standardizing personalities and encouraging an unhealthy dependence on the school that as an institution confuses process and substance, teaching with learning, grade advancement with education, and competency with imagination. Like Carl Rogers before him, Illich pointed to the fact that there is no necessary relation between teaching and learning, that freedom is necessary for people to flourish, and that, indeed, the position of teacher or administrator is no more than an authority that actually prevents learning. (Illich talks of the 'disabling professions' in a critique of 'expert culture.')[12]

The process of schooling for Illich is an example of mass institutionalization that produces conformity, undermines confidence, breeds 'psychological impotence' and kills conviviality as the source of imagination and new ideas. Illich's deschooling critique is also fundamentally a critique of the commodification and standardization of education related to the production and marketing of knowledge, where learning itself inevitably becomes a commodity. Illich's deschooling thesis is a generalized critique of institutions and the processes of institutionalization—a thesis that predates Foucault's 'power/knowledge' and his studies of the effects of the clinic, the school, the prison and the factory. The deinstitutionalization thesis gelled with the antipsychiatry movement of the 1970s and the attempts to reform the large centralized mental, prison and hospital institutions that existed at that time. Illich's critique must be seen ultimately as a critique of modernity and, perhaps, his central question is how do we create convivial rather than manipulative institutions that encourage 'creative intercourse' among persons where modern technologies serve 'politically interrelated individuals rather than managers' enabling the choice of a life of action over a life of passive consumption.[13] In education he advocates 'learning webs' as convivial institutions where skill exchanges and peer-matchings could take place and references to educational objects, processes, and education-at-large may occur within a decentralized, facilitative network.

Illich's critique and his advocacy of convivial institutions and in particular 'learning webs' made well before the advent of the Internet in 1992, and the new P2P networks and self-regulated learning platforms that developed progressively since the 1990s, was entirely prophetic. In one sense we can see Illich's essay on deschooling as a plea for the freedom of the imagination and of a set of decentralized and convivial solutions to the encouragement of imagination and action as the raw materials for a lifelong 'learning society.' It is in this context that 'personalization' as a policy discourse and practice emerges—as a generalized solution to the problem of the overburdened, 'big' centralized state and as the prospect of more open and molecular government both at the national and institutional levels. In chapter nine, 'Practice,' Michael Peters argues that personalization makes use of new open technologies and forms of social media (the technological imperative) to devise architectures of citizen participation and collaboration in 'prosumer' open governance systems with an emphasis on co-production of public goods tied to democratic action (the social democratic imperative) that harnesses high levels of individual motivation through use of social networking and utilizes rational choice making with the aim of promoting personal identity and autonomy (the psychological imperative). He then interprets these imperatives as the basis for the new personalization learning revolution on the horizon and reviews recent policy initiatives in the United Kingdom in this light.

In chapter seven, 'Thinking,' Peters develops a parallel or 'sympathetic' argument that centrally addresses 'thinking' and the cognitive rationalist paradigm that has dominated philosophy-as-epistemology,[14] and the Western tradition in education since the time of Plato. He argues that the contemporary tendency in education to treat thinking in isolation from imagination is reinforced by cognitive science that approaches thinking a-historically and a-culturally, as though physiology, brain structure and human evolution are all there is to say about thinking that is worthwhile or educationally significant. The movement of critical thinking also tends to treat thinking a-historically, focusing on universal processes of logic and reasoning. Against this trend and against the scientific spirit of the age, this chapter presents a historical and philosophical picture of thinking motivated by a Wittgensteinian interpretation—where 'thinking' is defined by the ability to make imaginative 'moves' in the 'language game.'[15] By contrast with dominant cognitive and logical models, the chapter emphasizes 'kinds of thinking' and 'styles of reasoning.' It grows out of interests primarily in the work of Nietzsche, Heidegger and Wittgenstein, and in the extension and development of their work in Critical Theory and French poststructuralist philosophy, and draws directly on some of this work to argue for the recognition of different kinds of thinking (explored with reference to Heidegger) and also for the significance of styles of reasoning (explored with reference to Wittgenstein and to Ian Hacking).

In chapter eight, 'Image,' Peters examines the new environment of social media—based on the radical concordance of image, text and sound, and the development of new information and knowledge infrastructures—in order to ask: What new subjectivities are constituted through social media and what role does image control play in this process? What new possibilities do the new media afford students for educational autonomy? What distinctive forms of immaterial labor and affect do social and image-based media create? And what is the transformational potential of new image-based and social media that link education to its radical historical mission?

Imagination's Model One concerns collective creation—'collective intelligence,' 'wisdom of the crowd,' the co-created production of symbolic goods and the 'collective unconscious,' often driven by the storehouse of accumulated pattern-forms. Model Two details the global imagination based on the 'open' university within processes of globalization. Model Three, motivated by readings of Wittgenstein and Foucault, modulates themes of both 'openness' and 'control' to provide both a picture and a story of education that is based on the liberation of the imagination from standardized processes of mass educational production and the transition toward new, networked, self-regulated, autonomous environments of co-creation as a means of promoting a new personalized 'education of the imagination.' This is a model of application that brings together both technological and moral orders in order to analyze the new conditions of the manufacture of imagination and to question the continuing ocularcentralism of the twenty-first century and the persistent hegemony for example of the screen image that drowns us in an overflow and repetition of visual images. With any shift of paradigm or model, there are new dangers: with the increasing dominance of visual images over text, we need to ask whether visual culture can deliver on its promises of a pedagogy that exposes the deep bias of screen images and their inherently ambiguous nature?

The Critique of the Bureaucratic State

As Michael Peters narrates in chapter eight, the twentieth century opened with the rise of the cinematic imagination. It closed with the rise of the digital imagination. The former mode of imagination is primarily visual; the latter is as much tactile-kinetic as it is visual.[16] One produced industrially, the other in cybernetic mode. Between the beginning and the end of the twentieth century, the cinematic imaginary underwent a series of transitions culminating in a kind of oblivion. In the course of this, the epistemological function of the image shifted dramatically. The cinematic image moved from being a reflection of reality to a mask of reality to masking reality to bearing no relation to reality. The sad end-point of Hollywood as an infantile sand pit of reality shows and celebrity disconnection from life is a perfect illustration of the terminal state of this historical process. Intellectually, when the image became simply an image of another image, the cinematic age had arrived at the post-modern dead-end. At that point, it had lost its metaphoric and consequently its artistic power. There is no doubt that, socially, the visual image triumphed. But in the end, with society awash with such images, it was a triumph of vacuity. From the moral summit of Michael Curtiz's *Casablanca* (1942), we have spiraled down to the clever inconsequence of Quentin Tarantino's *Inglourious Basterds* (2009). No set of encyclopedic allusions can take away the ultimate emptiness of the image that is the image of another image.

Cinema was the great art form of the twentieth century. It is not so in the twenty-first century—far from it, as Murphy notes in chapter three. The audience for cinema has declined, and so has cinema's artistic quality. The number of great films as a percentage of the total film production has shrunk dramatically and probably irreversibly. It is interesting to observe what has paralleled this development. As the visual-cinematic imagination has lost traction culturally, so, almost in lock-step, has the industrial mode of production and social confidence in bureaucratic forms of hierarchy. It is uncertain what will prove to be the great art form of the twenty-first century. It will not be cinema. Its day has past. We are coming to understand that—just as we already know that computer-mediated production is now more significant than mechanical-driven production.

The third key social dimension—after that of representation and production—is organization. In the modern age, bureaucratic hierarchy replaced feudal hierarchy. Michael Peters, in the final chapter of *Imagination*, traces the growth of the critique of bureaucracy through the second half of the twentieth century. In the years when the procedural ethos was at its peak of self-confidence, its first critics were developing cutting critiques of its nature. The criticisms have proliferated with time. Peters' narration of this culminates in a detailed discussion of one contemporary social democratic version of this current, coming out of the United Kingdom. He also notes though that the critique of bureaucracy has been prevalent across the political spectrum from left to right. There have been many versions of it. Iterations have ranged from deinstitutionalization theories to proposals to replace the state with the market to the creation of bureaucratic pseudo-markets. Some of these critiques forensically distinguish desirable public goods from the undesirable bureaucratic state. Others do not. How it is possible to deliver public goods without the wasteful absorption of time, energy, resources and judgment in witless bureaucratic labyrinths remains far from certain, though ingenuous definitions like mass customization continue to percolate to the surface.

The incidence of the critique of bureaucracy on the left and the right of politics is notable. For example, on the left of centre, the philosopher Cornelius Castoriadis (1991, 1997a, 1997b, 2007), whose work is discussed in chapter one, was a trenchant critic of bureaucratic capitalism. He proposed various ideas of self-organization and social autonomy in opposition to it.[17] Yet we find, on the right of centre, distinguished market liberals like Friedrich Hayek (1960) and Milton Friedman (2002), and major conservative intellectuals like Roger Scruton (2000), have all written eloquently against bureaucracy.[18] It is equally notable that, despite all of this, bureaucracy flourishes. It appears unstoppable. It might be that citizens, customers, and clients are ill-served by bureaucracies. Yet the modern state acts through bureaucracy. It is the principal medium of the state. It is also the principal medium of large companies and of large non-profit and non-governmental organizations and foundations. Therefore to act to solve a problem means, today, primarily, to create a policy and a set of paperwork and bureaucratic criteria for implementation, which is why, as Simon Marginson notes ironically, some of the most creative work of universities comes out of managerial and strategic action that creates new positions, new policies and new paperwork. Contemporary research universities worldwide are in process of globalizing their operations. National measures of research performance and national systems of research management are being in part displaced by global indexes of performance and comparison. Yet the bureaucratic structures of twentieth-century mass society and its cumbersome multiversity struggle to cope with these imperatives. Most national governments still run national research management schemes that do not align with international measures of performance. Most measures of creativity build in procedural assumptions that define many of the chief salient characteristics of creativity out of the measures of creativity.

We can happily live with irony. Still these ironies have a downside—for, as Peter Murphy observes in chapter three, the universities are less creative today than they were a hundred years ago. Overall the empirically measurable level of creativity in leading societies is less today than it was a century ago. The emphasis on bureaucratic management, and in a more general sense on procedure and procedural ideologies, is part of the reason for this. Yet despite this being so, and in spite of the critique of bureaucracy and the attempts to define public goods without a procedural incubus, bureaucracy continues to grows, and it has very determined defenders. Equally, there is no agreement between left of centre and right of centre critics of the administered society. Indeed, there is generally unmitigated loathing between the two. Procedure remains the default way of dealing with social issues. In a procedural world, no one is personally responsible for its failings. It is always 'the system,' so fix the system, which means in the end more system and more paperwork. In the paperless society, paperwork flourishes. Part of the problem is that there are also many unpalatable alternatives to the administered society. Neo-patrimonies, feckless patronage systems, collegial fawning, neo-feudal feather-bedding, and indulgent license are just a few that come immediately to mind.

So we begin the twenty-first century with a conundrum. We know we inhabit Max Weber's iron cage.[19] We want out of it. But we can't figure how to. We would like to think that human inventiveness will enable us to find a way out. Yet we are also aware that invention is paradoxical. We reach out for what is hot only to find that its heat is generated by the freezing cold. The composer John Cage made the point that silence is noisy, and that noise is ultimately indistinguishable from music.[20] Another composer, Roger Waters, the deviser of Pink Floyd's *The Wall* (1979), was a socialist who made brilliant dystopian musical theatre out of post-war state socialism's sour experiments in education. Within the space of such strange contradictions, we all live, happily or unhappily.

Notes

1. Peters, Marginson, and Murphy (2009); Marginson, Murphy, and Peters (2010).
2. Heller (1979).
3. Murphy, 'Living in a Kitsch World' (2009); 'From Information to Imagination' (forthcoming).
4. Murphy, 'I am not what I am' (2010).
5. Murphy and Roberts (2004).
6. On Adam Smith's penchant for the analogical 'as it were,' see Ford (2010).
7. The Greek *metaphero* (to 'transfer') from *meta* ('between') and *phero* ('to bear' or 'to carry').
8. On the interesting counter-intuitive (but for that reason very interesting) case of Houston as a global city of the future, see Joel Kotkin (2009).
9. A classic account of this is Lewis Mumford (1961).
10. Classic accounts of this include Florida (2003) and Howkins (2001).
11. Ivan Illich (1973).
12. Ivan Illich (1977).
13. Ivan Illich (1975).
14. As a counterpoint, Michael Peters points to Richard Rorty who addresses these issues in his *Philosophy and the Mirror of Nature* (1980) where he suggests that phi-

losophy must become 'therapeutic rather than constructive, edifying rather than systematic' and adopts a conversational model based on Gadamer's philosophical hermeneutics as a means both to release us from the cognitive paradigm of philosophy-as-epistemology and its foundational, analytical and representational impediments that have held us captive. Rorty—as the leading American neopragmatist who bases himself on Dewey—is one of a group of thinkers along with Nietzsche, Wittgenstein, Peirce, Heidegger, Derrida, and Deleuze who make room for imagination in philosophy by inventing new concepts, new vocabularies, new strategies in the 'language game' and edge us toward a new game or, perhaps, a new openness in the game. In 'Pragmatism and Romanticism,' he restates Shelley's argument in 'Defense of Poetry' claiming that at the heart of Romanticism was the idea that reason can only follow paths that the imagination has first broken: 'No words, no reasoning. No imagination, no new words. No such words, no moral or intellectual progress' (see Rorty, 2007). A more sceptical reading of Rorty is given by Peter Murphy in chapter two.

15. In this regard, see Peters and Marshall (1999) and Peters, Burbules and Smeyers (2010).
16. Murphy (2009).
17. The work of Castoriadis' long-time associate, Claude Lefort, was also notable for its sustained critique of bureaucracy. See for example Lefort (1986).
18. In the francophone world, see also the strong current of neo-DeTocquevillean liberal-conservatives such as Raymond Aron (1968), Jean-François Revel (1977) and Pierre Manent (1998).
19. On Weber's metaphor of modernity as a cage, see Murphy and Roberts (2004).
20. Cage typifies the mystical approach to the human imagination. On this, see Fuente (2010).

References

Aron, R. (1968). *Democracy and Totalitarianism*. London: Weidenfeld & Nicolson.
Castoriadis, C. (1991). *Philosophy, Politics, Autonomy*. Oxford: Oxford University Press.
Castoriadis, C. (1997a). *The Castoriadis Reader*. Oxford: Blackwell.
Castoriadis, C. (1997b). *World in Fragments*. Stanford, CA: Stanford University Press.
Castoriadis, C. (2007). *Figures of the Thinkable*. Stanford, CA: Stanford University Press.
Ford, T. (2010, forthcoming). Rythmus and the Critique of Political Economy. *Empedocles: European Journal for the Philosophy of Communication*. P. Murphy (ed.) Special Issue on Paradox and Communication.
Florida, R. (2003). *The Rise of the Creative Class*. New York: Basic Book.
Friedman, M. (2002). *Capitalism and Freedom*, Fortieth anniversary edition. Chicago and London: University of Chicago Press.
Fuente, E.D.L. (2010, forthcoming). Prophet and priest, ascetic and mystic: The twentieth century composer and the question of modernity. E. Fuente and P. Murphy (eds), *Philosophical and Cultural Theories of Music*. Leiden: Brill.
Hayek, F. (1960). *The Constitution of Liberty*. London: Routledge and Kegan Paul.
Heller, A. (1979). *A Theory of Feelings*. Assen: Van Gorcum.
Howkins, J. (2001). *The Creative Economy*. London: Penguin.
Illich, I. (1973). *Deschooling Society*. Harmondsworth: Penguin.

Illich, I. (1975). *Tools for Conviviality.* London: Fontana.

Illich, I. et al. (1977). *Disabling Professions.* London: Marion Boyars.

Kotkin, J. (2009). Blue State Exodus: Why the middle-class are fleeing for the hills. *Forbes.com.* 2 November. http://www.forbes.com/2009/11/02/blue-state-middle-classexodus-opinions-columnists-joel-kotkin.html accessed 5 November, 2009.

Lefort, C. (1986). *The political forms of modern society: bureaucracy, democracy, totalitarianism.* John B. Thompson (ed.) Cambridge, MA: MIT Press.

Manent, P. (1998). *The City of Man.* Princeton: Princeton University Press.

Marginson, S., P. Murphy, & M. A. Peters. (2010). *Global Creation: Space, Mobility, and Synchrony in the Age of the Knowledge Economy.* New York: Peter Lang.

Mumford, L. (1961). *The City in History.* Harmondsworth: Penguin.

Murphy, P. (2010 forthcoming). Paradox and Indirect Communication: The Case of the Comic God and the Dramaturgical Self. *Empedocles: European Journal for the Philosophy of Communication.* P. Murphy (ed.) Special Issue on Paradox and Communication.

Murphy, P. (2009). Living in a Kitsch World: An Aesthetic Anthropology of Contemporary Infantilism. *Aesthetics: An International Colloquium on Art, Aesthetics and Imagination.* Social Aesthetics Research Unit, Monash University, December 7.

Murphy, P. (2009). The N-Dimensional Geometry and Kinaesthetic Space of the Internet. Margherita Pagani (ed.) *Encyclopedia of Multimedia Technology and Networking* Second Edition Volume II. Hershey, PA: Information Science Reference,1042-1047.

Murphy, P. (forthcoming). From Information to Imagination: Multivalent Logic and System Creation in Personal Knowledge Management. G. Gorman and D. Pauleen (eds) *Knowledge Management: Preparing for Inevitable Change.* Aldershot, UK: Gower.

Murphy, P. & D. Roberts (2004). *Dialectic of Romanticism: A Critique of Modernism.* London: Continuum.

Peters, M.A., N. Burbules & P. Smeyers (2010). *Saying and Doing: Wittgenstein as a Pedagogical Philosopher.* Boulder: Paradigm Press (paperback with new Preface and Postscript).

Peters, M. A., S. Marginson & P. Murphy (2009). *Creativity and the Global Knowledge Economy.* New York: Peter Lang.

Peters, M.A. & J.D. Marshall (1999). *Wittgenstein: Philosophy, Postmodernism, Pedagogy.* Westport, CT. & London: Bergin and Garvey.

Pink Floyd. (1979). *The Wall.* United Kingdom: Harvest Records/EMI.

Revel, J.F. (1977). *The Totalitarian Temptation.* Garden City, NY: Doubleday.

Rorty, R. (1980). *Philosophy and the Mirror of Nature.* Oxford: Blackwell.

Rorty, R. (2007). The Fire of Life. *Poetry Foundation.* 18 November. http://www.poetryfoundation.org/journal/article.html?id=180185 accessed 16 March 2010.

Scruton, R. (2000). *England: An Elegy.* London: Continuum.

MODEL ONE:

Collective Creation

1. *Imagination*

PETER MURPHY

Creativity and Personality

We know a surprising amount about the nature of individual creativity. During the twentieth century, the empirical cognitive psychology of creation established a comprehensive list of attributes of creative personalities.[1] As a result, we can say with some confidence that creative individuals are a mirror of the nature of creation. Creation is best described as a union of opposites. This is its most enduring hallmark. As F. Scott Fitzgerald put it: 'The test of a first-rate intelligence is the ability to hold two opposed ideas in mind at the same time and still retain the ability to function.'[2] Creative personalities are the literal embodiments of this universal trait of creative action. They are often walking contradictions. They combine enthusiastic energies with the capacity for quiet concentration. They are predictive and insightful while displaying naïve even credulous wonderment at things. They are playful but disciplined, imaginative but grounded, responsible and irresponsible in turns. They mix extroverted and introverted, sociable and anti-social traits. Creative individuals are often lacking in courtesies and social manners, yet have close long-term intellectual friends and peers to whom they relate on the most generous and intimate terms.

About their own work, they are both humble and proud. They treat it with enthusiastic reverence and dispassionate, even brutal, objectivity. They are persons of wide interests and expansive curiosities yet they are persistent even obsessive about pursuing defined intellectual goals. Creative personalities are adventurous, even thrill-seeking, but for a point. At the highest level, 'the point' is to bridge apparently unbridgeable divides. The ambition, say, to unify Einstein's theory of relativity with quantum mechanics is a classic example of this. Creative personalities are persistent in the face of the 'it cannot be done' response to the difficult even recalcitrant nature of creative problem solving. Persistence, when translated into social situations, can take the shape of stubbornness and uncooperativeness—and the working of long, anti-social hours. Persistence in creation requires mental discipline, concentration, and focus. The flip-side of this concentration is forgetfulness. The memory that drives creation is so often absent-minded.

It is not uncommon that creative personalities are also careless and disorganized about whatever they are not working on. Yet about matters that command their attention, they always have a profound sense of order. For intuitions of order are the way in which the unbridgeable is bridged, and unions are created out of opposites. Ordering and creating are analogous actions. Ordering, it must be stressed, is not the same thing as rule-making or rule-following. Creative personalities are interested in order, not in rules. Rules are a by-product of order, but they are not a substitute for order. Often rules create the chaos or the inertness that high-level creative order overcomes. Creative personalities have a great tolerance for complexity and ambiguity. But they don't regard either complexity or ambiguity as a social or cognitive ideal. Their motto is 'keep it simple.' Order is a kind of simplicity. Order eliminates chaos. It lends the materials of the world an elegant and lucid structure. Creative persons are at home with complex intrigues and baroque labyrinths. But this is because they can see emergent patterns where most individuals only see murk. While they are at home with complexity, they delight in simplicity and parsimonious structure.

Creative individuals, as a type, tell us something about the nature of creation. What they excel at is unifying what is divergent, and harmonizing what is dissonant. The Latin verb *cogito*, signifying the act of thinking, literally means 'to shake together.' This is a perfect description of creatorship. Such shaking together is apparent even in sexual orientation. Creative personalities tend to a kind of androgyny. The impulse to unify opposites is also evident in their humor. They are often very witty. This is no accident. Humor works because it combines contrary thoughts. The punch-line of a joke takes you to the opposite place you expected. Indeed, it often takes you to a place you didn't want to go, and you smile all the while. Where the 'logical' mind sees a contradiction between the vertical and the horizontal, the quick-witted mind sees them as a 'whole' not bound by discursive logic but by the unifying force of opposition. The connection between the opposites A and X is analogical. The connective force, though, is such that the simile or metaphor or aspect of comparability (A is 'like' B, X is 'similar' to Y) is so powerful that A in some ways *is* X. All of the world *is* a stage. Difference via likeness becomes identity, opposites become the same. If adhesives are equated with strength, the creative mind says 'let us try a *weak* adhesive.' The notion of a 'weak adhesive' sounds at first take to be a contradiction in terms but it is exactly 'the power to connect the (seemingly) un-connectable' that constitutes the power of creation. This is not a 'logical' process. It is an imaginative process.

Collective Creation

Although we understand a fair amount about the nature of individual creativity, we still understand relatively little about the role of creation on a collective level—that is, creativity as an emergent property of large-scale social systems. This is so despite the very evident fact that creativity clusters in specific historical times and social spaces. Put simply—certain societies in certain historical periods are exceptionally creative. The principal examples in history have been ancient Greece, Renaissance Florence and Venice, the Île-de-France, the Low Countries, Southern England since the Renaissance, the Scottish Lowlands in the eighteenth and nineteenth centuries, nineteenth-century riverine Europe, and the various Seaboards of the United States.[3] These societies, in their golden epochs, are responsible for most of the human species' artistic, literary, political, economic, scientific, and technological inventiveness. They are, quite literally, amazing times and places.

Because inventiveness clusters in this way, it is also quite evident that creation is not just an individual attribute. Indeed, there is good reason to think that individual creativity, no matter how impressive, leans heavily on collective social creativity. There are exceptional individuals with high levels of innovative capacity but these exceptional individuals also cluster in a remarkably small number of times and places. How can we explain this?

The most important attempt hitherto to explain the collective scale of creation is the work of Cornelius Castoriadis.[4] Castoriadis' contribution to the theory of collective creation can be summarized thus:[5]

1. Societies create themselves. They emerge in collective acts of creation from chaos. They give themselves form or shape—from which norms and rules are derived. Castoriadis called this self-organization and self-legislation 'autonomy.'
2. Having created themselves, most societies arrest the process of creation. They replace the autonomous process of self-organization and self-legislation with heteronomous behavior.[6] They ascribe their own acts of creation to extra-social or transcendental sources. In other words, most societies create themselves as un-creative societies—whose forms are more or less fixed.

3. Heteronomous societies reproduce themselves through the repetition and recurrence of the same forms underscored by appeals to authority that lies beyond the mundane realm of society—to culture heroes and gods.
4. A small handful of societies have an unusual form: a form calibrated to create forms. Castoriadis called these societies 'autonomous.'
5. All of these autonomous societies belong in the slip-stream of Greco-Western history. They include the ancient polis, the Renaissance city-states, the burgher cities of Europe, and the American Republic.[7]

On this account then, creation is a collective process that operates on the largest social scale imaginable. All societies are formed through acts of creation—no matter how occulted such acts might be or might become. At the same time, collective creation as a permanent rather than arrested process is very rare, and is typical of only a small handful of societies in history.

All of this is of more than casual interest because, since around 1820 (at the point when the industrial revolution became institutionalized), social success, indeed social viability, has become massively linked to permanent innovation in the arts and the sciences, the humanities and technologies. The cost now of not having permanent creation in economies and polities—and in integrative (solidaristic) and technological systems—is to live a kind of collective social death that is historically unprecedented. Castoriadis was at pains to point out that much about the condition of 'permanent innovation' is illusory. Most 'creative' formation in practice is derivative. It is an elaboration of, or inference from, one or other existing social patterns. In contrast, the most far-reaching kinds of innovation suppose the social ability to generate forms that are not produced or deduced from pre-existing patterns. Thus in practice what is 'original' or 'innovative' mostly is an extrapolation or derivation. Such derivation creates 'difference' but, as Castoriadis put it, not the 'alterity' or 'otherness' typical of the kind of maximal creation that is not derivative.[8] A technological or aesthetic form that is rationally deducible from an existing template may appear at first glance to be 'different' from the social form that inspired it but, at the end of the day, it is still determined by that inspirational form. With the passage of time, this becomes increasingly obvious.

To make sense of the distinction between derivation and creation, Castoriadis insisted on the existence of radical, that is, un-determined or a-causal, creation.[9] This is the least compelling aspect of his theory of social creation. It is unconvincing because it is untrue. Acts of creation do not arise out of nothing. As we'll see shortly, the human imagination has available to it a common stock of form-generating media. The human imagination is exquisitely adapted to the use of such media. Such media play a crucial role in the determination of social forms. These form-generating intermediaries are not media in the sense of tone or stone—i.e. materials that convey meanings. Yet they are not full-fledged socio-cultural forms either in the sense that the sonata form or the Greek temple form, the republican form or the feudal form are. Rather they lay half-way between the sensuousness of materials and the meaningfulness of explicit forms. Proportion and harmony are examples of creative media. They shape tone and stone into recognizable, transmittable and reproducible forms. But they are not actually forms themselves.

Neither are they discourses or arguments, or parts of syllogisms. The self-reporting of leading creative figures strongly suggests that the primary media of the human imagination is not linguistic in character, and the workings of the imagination cannot be modeled after language. The imagination is not some kind of deep grammar of creation. The self-assessment by Albert Einstein is typical of what high-achieving creators say about their own imaginative processes. Asked to explain his working methods, Einstein observed that: 'The words or the language, as they are written or spoken, do not seem to play any role in my mechanism of thought.'[10] He described the elements of thought as 'physical entities' and the process of thinking as the 'combinatory play' of these elements. This process is pre-logical and pre-communicative. The elements of thought, Einstein noted, were 'signs' or the 'more or less clear images' of a *visual* or *muscular* type. The combination of these visual-muscular elements, the 'essential feature in productive thought,' takes place 'before there is any connection with logical construction in words or with other kinds of signs which can be communicated to others.'

One way of understanding pre-logical creative imagining is to think of it as a shaping process, hence Einstein's emphasis on the visual and muscular aspects. Shakespeare captured this tactile-shaping sense of the imagination when, in *A Midsummer Night's Dream*, he gives this beautiful account of poetic creation:

> The poet's eye, in a fine, frenzy rolling,
> Doth glance from heaven to earth, from earth
> to heaven;
> And as imagination bodies forth
> The forms of things unknown, the poet's pen
> Turns them to shapes, and gives to airy nothing
> A local habitation and a name.

The image created in the imagination is much more physical, almost tactile in nature, than it is linguistic or language-like. While his view of creation as radically under-determined is on the whole too romantic, Castoriadis was on surer ground when he criticized rationalists who equate the genesis of social forms with communicative reasoning or discursive interaction—or with logic and language. Castoriadis was skeptical of claims that reason is capable of positing or revamping the forms of society. The many delirious follies of intellectuals suggest such skepticism is warranted.[11] From the Jacobins to Pol Pot and Sayyid Qutb, their behavior over the centuries has turned numerous societies into charnel houses. As Castoriadis points out, reasoning rests on non-linguistic presuppositions. Thus, the first terms of any discourse are intuitive and figurative. They are the products of *nous*, not *logos*. The intellectual's vice is to think that *logos* can do the work of *nous*. But discourse left to itself is pitiless and destructive. Logical language, disconnected from figurative *nous*, is a violent medium. The way discursive logic moves, from premise to conclusion, is ruthless and implacable. For sure, as Castoriadis (1987) remarks, this is not physical violence, but it is destructive all the same. To stand in the way of the logical torrent is to risk being swept aside. To question the premises of torrential discourse is to risk excommunication—and worse. In this manner, rationalist discourse 'inevitably destroys discourse itself' (350). Once this happens, it is actually a short step from the violence of discourse to the force of arms.

Castoriadis equates 'reason' with communicative or discursive reason—the logician's reason.[12] When he talks about reason he means chains of reasons that rest on discursive principles and that are logically organized. The nature of such reasoning is distinct from the intuitive-figurative nature of social forms. Forms precede words. Of course once they are in existence, forms can be represented by language—i.e. they can be put into words and turned into the premise of an argument or discourse. Inferences and conclusions can be drawn from such premises. However, while reasoning is logico-deductive, form creation is not.

New forms emerge through images not words.[13] This was one of Castoriadis' most important presuppositions. New forms emerge from society's collective aural, visual and haptic-tactile imagining. The work of the imagination does not just represent 'what is absent.' It also posits objects that otherwise would not exist. This occurs in the first place through the creation of the image of the object. This is an act of figuration: the 'positing of figures and the relations between and to these figures.' (204) The creative or radical imagination, capable of bringing into being the image of something that has not existed before, does so by positing figures or models.[14] Although these models and figures may be represented by words, they are not created by words. This is despite the fact that 'writing' is often taken as a model of the creative process. It is widely assumed, not least by writers themselves, that creation in general has features that we readily associate with language, logic or discourse. 'Text,' 'textuality,' and 'inter-textuality' became very popular metaphors in the second half of the twentieth century to explain a large variety of cultural and artistic phenomenon. This echoed the influence of linguistic philosophy and linguistic models in twentieth-century cultural theory. Not only is there reason to think that the creative component of culture is not structured on the model of language but that acts of imagination in fact look more like object creation and design, than speaking and writing.[15]

Ironically, this is true of speaking and writing as much as it is, say, of painting or sculpture. The imagination involves a process of object creation. Imaginative writing, whether in the arts or the sciences, is closer in nature to an act of sculpture or work of design than it is to a speech act or a discursive text. Classical theorists of rhetoric understood this. For them the good use of language depended on *taxis* (arrangement). *Taxis* allows speakers and writers to communicate through figures. Figures of speech are resonant traces of figures of thought. They share structural characteristics and semantic architecture in common. Classical rhetoric stressed that schemas of balance, repetition, word order, presence and omission, and proportion are key aspects of this architecture. Great speakers and writers are masters of such schemas. They build their words using repetitions of alliteration, assonance and anadiplosis. They orchestrate plateaus and climaxes. They balance phrases and clauses, make calculated omissions (ellipsis), and create flexible word orders (parenthesis). Speakers understate and writers exaggerate—they play with the proportions of words and the (dis)proportionate relation of words to things and events. Most interesting of all is the kind of word architecture that creates relations between things that are seemingly unrelated. Metaphor and simile are classic ways of doing this. So is the drawing of comparisons or the arranging of words and phrases in opposition. There is also a *taxis* of stacking that allows for the creation of orders of superior and inferior, higher and lower, genus and species. Words, like tones and stones, also can be turned upside down. When we invert words, we create relations of irony and paradox. Whatever the techniques used, and however they are deployed, the overall power of words depends on the underlying *taxis*.

Taxis provides incipient structure for visible and audible words. *Taxis* arises in the imagination. Hence Castoriadis' view that linguistic-type axioms, criteria and rules are suspended in acts of imagination.[16] They are suspended by being over-determined by figures, models, and diagrams.[17] Figures, models, and diagrams are the common media of *taxis*. On an individual and collective social level, figuration occurs through the imagination's power of organization. Correspondingly, this power of arrangement operates through figures that take shape via the imagination's mastery of form-generating media like hierarchy, balance, parallelism, repetition, similarity, and proportion. The formation of an image involves the positing of elements and the bringing of those elements into a relation.[18] Whether the material is tone or stone, words or the physical matter of the universe, form-generating media play a crucial role in all kinds of creation.

This account of the emergence of forms through non-linguistic organizing media parallels certain conceptions of the pre-Socratic thinkers from Greek antiquity. The pre-Socratics recognized that whatever it is that brings contrary pairings into a meaningful relationship permits the generation of order out of chaos.[19] The impetus toward such pairings is a force or *phusis* built into the universe and mirrored in the human mind. *Phusis* is shaping/forming. It does not just permeate nature. It *is* nature, including physical, biological and human nature. The biologist, Andreas Wagner, observes how cells at the molecular level interact through the medium of bio-chemical shapes.[20] Molecular chemical 'signals'—or more precisely, *shapes*—transmitted from one kind of cell trigger the shaping or re-shaping, the morphogenesis, of other kinds of cells.[21] As Wagner notes, meaning and matter—shaping and substance—are equally implicated in the universe. Meaning emerges through the shaping of matter. Plato, Aristotle, da Vinci, and Goethe—whatever else may have set their accounts of nature apart—agreed on this. Nature is meaningful—and meaning arises through order, pattern and form. In this tradition, from the Greek pre-Socratics onwards, *phusis* is one of the names given to the distinctive force of organization that creates the lucid, sustainable, contrary pairings of elements, the force that gives shape to things. Already in Greek antiquity, it was observed the key role that abstract media—like rhythm, balance, equilibrium, proportion, harmony, and symmetry—play in the generation of order out of chaos. These form-producing media, when mobilized, function as powers that bring otherwise unconnected elements into a relationship that constitutes meaning. In doing so, these powers create objects, and amongst them social objects, but also physical and biological objects.

Castoriadis distanced himself from the pre-Socratic account of creation in one very crucial respect, though. Its notion of contrary pairings was, in his view, a-historical.[22] It thereby set the stage for Plato's assertion that forms of the cosmos are unchanging.[23] Castoriadis instead veered rather close to Plotinus' view of a universe of forms involved in a constant activity of morphogenesis. In Castoriadis' eyes, a universe of structural pairs was a universe of spatial 'difference' rather than temporal 'otherness.' It did not distinguish spatial boundary from temporal line. Repeatedly, he stressed that time was the key dimension of the radical imaginary of creation. His social physics was relativistic in Einstein's sense. Time was the crucial medium in which 'other' figures emerged. It was an indispensable medium for the 'otherness-alteration' of these figures.[24]

Nous and Logos

The history of Greek-Western thought can be divided into two strands. One is pre-Socratic. The other is Socratic. The pre-Socratics judged that what was most fundamental in the world was non-discursive. Socrates considered that what was most fundamental was speech and argument. One can think of this as the difference between *nous* and *logos*. In the dominant strains of philosophical thought since the seventeenth century, Socratic discursiveness trumped the pre-Socratics. This was so even though the oral spontaneity of Socratic speech gave way to the congealed language of 'the book' as the principal mode of discourse.[25]

There have always been dissenters of course—those who challenged the presumptive primacy of discourse. (Hobbes was a notable critic.) But, especially through the twentieth century, the idea that language was the principal medium for the generation of social relations was dominant in social self-understanding. Many philosophers—ranging from Ayer and Eco to Heidegger and Habermas—endorsed this view. The upshot was the vast over-estimation of the objectivating power of discursive language, and at the same time the underestimation of how important the making of objects, including social objects, is to knowledge.[26] Discursive reason in itself cannot create objects. It cannot do this because by its very nature it cannot posit the non-verbal patterned forms around which social objects coalesce. Reason can explore the implications of objects—or rather the implications of statements we make that represent those objects. But even this has its limits.

Words are not very good at representing objects—let alone at positing them. This is why Wittgenstein in his early philosophy thought that any hope for logic lay in picture languages—which was a good intuition.[27] Non-figurative languages misrepresent as much as represent social objects. Discourse is often touted as a therapy for this. The propositional statements that we make about objects can be subjected to discursive treatment—ending in falsification or verification. Yet these discourses, while sometimes impressive, are often found wanting. We can make deductions from, inferences about, and establish analogical relations amongst propositions. But discursive reason rests on the law of non-contradiction. If I accept that law, then I am bound to accept that my statements should not contradict the principles (the major premises, in effect) that I rely on. This, however, tells me nothing about the coming-into-being or invention of these principles—such as, say, the 'self-evident truths' of the American Declaration of Independence. Such invention is an act of creation that occurs through aural rhythms, visual pictures, and plastic-haptic shapes—that is, through images not words. The very expression 'self-evident truths' betrays this. Self-evidence is the evidence of the eyes. We *see* these principles. We see them before we say them. In such 'vision,' we grasp the shape—the outline—of a social form. We construct social forms through visual-spatial, bodily-kinetic, plastic-mathematical, and aural-musical cues.[28]

In the most far-reaching cases, such acts of creation suppose the emergence of what Castoriadis called 'alterity' or 'otherness.' His account of this, though, rested on an intellectual tension. On the one hand, he argued that such acts, and their resulting forms, were un-determined. They were generated out of nothing, *ex nihilo*.[29] On the other hand, he maintained that they were products of the imagination—formed through acts of figuration. This latter implied that the crucible of creation was not 'nothing' but in fact a process with explicable—though not discursive—painterly, aesthetic, diagrammatical, graphical, and like, qualities. When Castoriadis spoke of forms arising out of nothing, his clear intent was to preclude any thought that there were only a limited number of social forms. He contended that in history—that is, in social time—new forms emerge that are incommensurable with any prior existing forms. Put simply, modern bureaucratic capitalism does not emerge out of feudalism, even if feudalism precedes it chronologically. The process of History is not like a logical argument. Contra Hegel, History is *not* Reason. New forms may mean the appearance new discursive principles—but discursive principles do not create new forms. Creation is figurative. In historical time, there is a first tribe, a first bureaucracy, and a first sonata. These are things that previously had not been conceived, and thus could not have been logically deduced.

The ABA form of the sonata is figurative, not discursive. At the core of feudalism and bureaucracy is the picture of a hierarchy. In one case it is a personal hierarchy, in the other case an impersonal procedural hierarchy. This begs the question, though: where do such figures come from? Castoriadis described creation as a process of figuration figuring itself.[30] While this description has a certain dramatic quality, it is circular, and thus not particularly explanatory. Nonetheless it supposes one very important thing: *viz.* that new forms appear through some kind of a figurative medium. What is this medium like? Well, argued Castoriadis (1987), it is not impressionable material. The emergence of forms is not determined by sense impressions of something that already exists (301). Neither does figuration 'refer' to an extant world or object. It is not denotative. But neither is it symbolic (143). Figures don't 'stand for' something else that already exists. So, if figuration is not impressionable, referential or symbolic, then what is it? Having dismissed impression, denotation and symbolism, Castoriadis concludes that figuration is the generation of purely circular meanings of social signification,[31] and, as such, figuration figuring itself must start 'from nothing' (300).

Castoriadis acknowledged that existing forms *condition* the emergence of new forms.[32] But what he also supposed was the incommensurable nature of forms—their radical 'otherness.' This meant that their genesis, of logical necessity, is anchored in nothingness. If forms are incommensurable, then they must be un-determined. Forms thus emerge in the passage from nothingness to being.[33] How can something that is determinate apparently not have determinations? How can something that comes into existence not be deducible from something else that already exists?

Castoriadis' theory actually provides an implicit answer to these questions. As already noted, he stressed how important 'figures' of the imagination are to creative action. If we take this one step further, we can avoid the difficulties posed by the idea of creation 'out of nothing' without relinquishing any of the more compelling aspects of Castoriadis' theory. If we suppose that—both individually and collectively—the imagination is composed of form-generating media, then we do not have to assume that there is any numeric limit on the number of forms ever to be posited. Yet, at the same time, we do not have to assume either that forms appear 'out of nothing.' Rather, and more simply, they are brought into being by the figurative media of the *nous*. This is not a discursive process. There exist 'graphic' words of course—those forged, for instance, by rhyme or accent schemes—that conjure up images, just as shapes exist in music, and reason can be the attribute of an action or a person's character not just of their words. But the imagination is not structured like an argument, a dialogue, a conversation, logical reasoning, or any other discursive utterance.

Reasoning is a linguistic phenomenon, and it is in the realm of discursive reason that we see the manifest limit of words. All language-based models of society fall foul of this limit. There is no way of them escaping such limits. There is no linguistic solvent for them. This means that a 'rational society' based on collective discursive competence cannot posit its own foundations. Reasoning, no matter how 'unconstrained,' cannot create the shape of a society. Debate, argument, logic, and discussion all require a starting-point, the prime unmoved mover of discourse. Words cannot provide this, but the shaping power of form can.

Words thus are a secondary phenomenon in contradistinction to forms. Indeed words possess their greatest force when they are organized as forms—when they appear as genres of philosophy or science, or as novel and libretto, rhetoric and drama. Societies likewise acquire their efficacy and their lucid sense of themselves because they are organized as forms—as tribal, feudal, capitalist, or bureaucratic types. Forms rise and fall, gain impetus and lose force. Each genre, type or form is irreducible to any other. Feudalism does not produce capitalism. The chronicle does not produce the novel.[34]

The creation of these forms is an imaginative act. Imagination relies on individual and social capacities to mobilize abstract—schematic—media. Such media generate patterns. Such patterns shape bodily, kinetic, physical, aural, visual and other materials—including words. Thus it is rhyme schemas not words that elicit textual shapes. A word can give a name to a shape, but it can't posit a shape. Names without rhymes or other schemata are like colors without a painter's intuition of the contrastive complementarities of the color wheel. They can't order the divergent materials, whether of color or language, and turn them into lucid structures.

Phusis

Castoriadis was always tempted by the notion that forms are created 'out of nothing.' He once described this as 'figuration figuring itself, starting from nothing.'[35] No matter how much he denied it, this was a romantic-existential theology of creation. Much more interesting though than the idea of creation out of nothing was Castoriadis' recuperation of the Greek idea of *phusis* as the engine of creation.[36] If we think about creation as an act of *phusis*, it gives us a way of thinking about the creation of objects, not least of all social objects, as both 'other' (i.e. as not derivative) but also as not created 'out of nothing.' Castoriadis described *phusis* perfectly. It is nature pushing-toward giving-itself-form.[37] *Phusis* is the irresistible push of being that gives itself form in order to be. *Phusis*, nature, is self-making or self-constituting. *Phusis* forms itself. In doing so, nature moves itself and changes itself. The end of its self-movement and self-alteration is the positing of form. *Phusis* moves towards new forms and alters old forms in the process. Change, in the strongest sense of that word, is the emergence of new forms.

The nature of anything, including the nature of society, is the irresistible push of that being to give itself a form in order to be. Nature forms itself, and society organizes itself, by giving itself form and by destroying and replacing forms that it has previously given itself. Part of this destruction-creation process is to turn existing forms into the material of creation, to be pressed into the service of originating new and distinctly 'other' forms. In this process—we can speculate—*phusis* consumes existing forms as matter, and reworks them as fundamentally new forms. Thus epic poetry in the sense of Homer may become the material for the invention of James Joyce's modernist epic novel. The American Founders ransacked history for the material they used in the invention of a radical new political form.[38] They took material from ancient Greeks and Romans, modern Dutch and Anglo-Scottish Whigs, Deists and dissenting Protestants, and reshaped this form-turned-material in a massively distinctive manner—creating a sui generis form ('only in America') yet one whose historical materials, or more particularly the building blocks of creation that give such materials their shape, are quite evident even at a cursory glance.

We are all familiar with these building blocks. We recognize them. They are part of the common stock of creation. These building blocks are the determination of form generation. They are implicit in all form creation. They are what *phusis* contributes to creation. The building blocks are *the commons* of all creation. They are common to personality, society and external nature. These building blocks include the shaping powers of rhythm, harmony, equilibrium, and symmetry. There is potentially an infinite array of concrete forms that such media can usher into existence. So even if we recognize the building blocks of a form, that form may still be 'radically different' from what our experience has prepared us for.

'Radically different' does not mean radically incommensurable in Castoriadis' sense. We can see why this is so, if we again look at the case of America. The constitutional balance of powers or the workings of market equilibrium in the United States are abstract patterns that have a long history. Yet many visitors to America today, some five hundred years after its first settlement, are still puzzled about how that society works. The degree of puzzlement may be seen in the elementary mistakes foreigner observers habitually make about American institutions and mores. Thus the social form of America ends up being both familiar *and* unfamiliar. Outsiders recognize it, and yet they are confused by it. This is not the same as saying, as Castoriadis does, that great social forms are incomparably 'other.' Rather America is both 'other' *and* 'the same'—radically distinctive but still recognizable. An absolute 'other' in contrast would be unrecognizable.

There are many secondary reasons for it but the root reason for the 'familiar strangeness' of great forms is that the act of imaging that lies at the root of the making of social objects draws on a common fund of creation. This common wealth—the common wealth of the imagination—is constituted by the tacit organizing media of nature. Hierarchy, rhythm, symmetry, proportionality, and so on have countless expressions and assume endless guises but are themselves recurrent. These organizing powers, when deployed, give rise to an infinite variety of explicit forms both social and non-social. These forms are 'familiarly strange' when they are compared with each other. They can initially appear 'shockingly new' and yet because the human mind (as part of nature) readily recognizes organizing forces like rhythm and symmetry, they remain intelligible, coherent, and meaningful—especially once the subjective psychological 'shock of the new' has worn off. To cite just one simple example: both the works of Raphael and Cézanne are constructed around fascinating painterly balances but, in each case, these and other organizing powers deployed by the artists gave rise to very distinct aesthetic forms. In Cézanne's case, it took at least fifty years for the forms that he posited to be embraced by mainstream art audiences. But no matter how difficult these forms were to understand at the beginning, they were in the end comprehensible, and so much so that they eventually eclipsed the more popular works of his time.

Immanence and Legislation

How deliberate—how calculating—is the creation of forms? Joyce and Cézanne had a deep, not to say obsessive, idea of what they were doing. The same can be said of Thomas Jefferson and John Adams. But such precocious invention does not take place in a social vacuum. It may encounter intense social and political hostility, but that's not the same thing as saying that creation is the heroic work of romantic genius. Whether we are talking about modernist Irish letters or the forging of the American Republic, the greatness of its personalities is invariably matched, indeed over-determined, by an upsurge of collective invention. Lonely genius is a romantic myth. Creation is a collective process. But this is not to say that it operates through the scripts of groups, communities or committees. Quite the contrary is the case.

Creative action flourishes where there are porous social ties.[39] Porosity exists where psycho-social-linguistic ties are weak. This does not mean that all ties between social actors in creative milieu are weak. In fact, creative action occurs under conditions of 'anti-social sociability'—where weak psycho-social-linguistic ties are matched by strong ties between strangers mediated by art and science. This reflects the fact that—at the level of the human personality—creation is often marked by a-social traits, but that, at the same time, creation operates on the largest social scale imaginable. 'Anti-social' creators cluster in the same periods and places. Kant's formula of 'unsocial sociability' may be one way of summing up this paradox. Whatever name we give to this state of affairs, it is quite enough to suggest that creation is not a *deliberate* process that works through collective social discussion—regulated by social norms. Castoriadis (1991) rightly called creation an anonymous process. The power of social creation is the power of nobody (150). It is not individuals but *phusis* that deploys itself through forms (147).

No matter how accomplished he was, Thomas Jefferson didn't 'invent' America. He himself quite happily attributed that invention to nature. That was not false modesty. Jefferson knew that the 'balance of powers' and other devices of the new republic were, at a deep tacit level, a mimesis of *phusis*— brilliant copies, unprecedented copies, paradoxical copies but still copies of nature's forms achieved by the deployment of the collective media of creation.

What applies to politics also applies to art. Cézanne was exceptionally gifted but his ability to render the cubic-like structures of nature in two-dimensional planes was an imitation of nature's forms in the same way that Raphael's use of perspective was. Look at great painting and you'll see nature's geometry. Look at a great society, and you'll see the same—a balance of powers, a hierarchy, a harmony, a cluster, a constellation, a field of coordinate relationships, or some such pattern/*eidos* around which it is constructed.

Castoriadis perpetrated a curious contradiction. He insisted (rightly) that discursive reason did not create social forms—but he still shared the intellectual prejudice in favor of critical discourse. He thought that the handful of societies in which form generation had become systemic and recurrent were characterized by cultures of critical discourse.[40] Yet it was not critical discourse but rather constructive ability that made Jefferson, Madison, Adams and the other American 'founders' able to act as mediators coaxing the tacit media of creation into an explicit social form. Linguistic acts—whether they be prophecies, bureaucratic prescriptions, tokens of mutual understanding, unlimited questioning or unconstrained discourse—don't explain this phenomenon. If anything these acts end up being reasons for the enervation of creation, not vice versa. They foster illusions of creation. A large part of the reason for this is that the genesis of forms is *not discursive*. Communicative reason *follows* form. It does not precede it. *Form emerges in non-discursive figures, shapes and patterns.*

Despite this, most societies in most places and times have an aversion to weak psycho-social-linguistic ties. Their self-appointed representatives are forever complaining about the 'absence of community' incumbent upon such weak ties. Castoriadis tirelessly pointed out that the vast majority of societies in history have attributed creation of all kinds to extra-social or transcendent authorities. ('This is the word of Allah.') It may very well be that this is a compensation for the weak power of social scripts. One of the curious things about language is that it is constantly in need of support. Often when we use a proposition we feel a need to 'justify' or 'explain' ourselves. The weaker the script is, the more the author or speaker goes on and on. Transcendent authority for speech thus is very handy. It gives the illusion of being able to bring speech to a conclusion—just as the parent in response to the child's incessant 'why?' says 'that's just the way it is.' Being able to anchor the weak power of social language in an extra-social language—the commandment of God, for example—seemingly negates this weakness. This also has the effect of turning later acts of human creation either into the work of heretics or into 'reruns' of some mythical golden age when social actors unselfconsciously obeyed 'the transcendent word.'

But no matter what *fatwas* are issued in the name of God, these cannot guarantee the certainty of language. Doubt plagues the religious mind whose belief is based on 'the word,' for all words beg questions. That is as much true of religious words as it as of secular words—and vice versa. All stabs at maintaining truth grounded in speech or text ends in failure. This has two consequences. Some people will conclude then that all there is, is 'nothing.' Others will conclude that only violence can back up 'the word.' Often these two positions coincide in the one person. Yet trading in the transcendent word for the secular word does nothing to get rid of the weakness of language. In fact it often only exacerbates it. We see this in the case of modern intellectuals who try to write the scripts of secular societies.[41] These scripts are often very unconvincing, especially when they rely on the tacit premise 'if we, the righteous, say it is so, it must be true.' Hence we end up with the ground-less authority of the modern intellectual who loves to tell others what to do, and the massive resistance of those others to such authority-less and frequently ridiculous injunctions. Mostly nobody cares what the intellectuals say, but that doesn't stop them saying in a dogmatic manner what they nevertheless imagine to be 'critical and reflexive.' This vicious circle somehow seems built into the nature of language—and its impossible quest for a certainty that it can never attain.

The weakness of language stands in sharp contrast to the strength of images—what might be called the strong iconography of nature. It is its understanding of this that sets Castoriadis' social philosophy apart. Noteworthy in particular is the role he ascribes to the figure or *ikon*. There is a latent subtle Byzantine quality about this.[42] It has echoes of neo-Platonism.[43] Similarly, Castoriadis' understanding of creation as *phusis* resembles at times the immanent cosmology of the Stoics. This is not to say that he was either a neo-Stoic or a neo-Platonist. He was not. But his thought does have in common with them a desire to articulate what cannot be articulated—the non-discursive, holistic, intuitive, kinetic and figurative aspects of thinking. This leads invariably to theories of creation that emphasize imagistic immanence in opposition to scriptive legislation. Creation, on any level, is not the fruit of deliberate linguistic acts—be they the acts of a legislator God or a charismatic speech maker. To think it is, only encourages the delusions of those political intellectuals who produce endless volumes of 'writings' that recommend single-minded action based on pitiless consistency with discursive principles. Whether these principles happen to be divine commandments or foundation-less assertions of moral righteousness makes little difference. Without exception, this kind of uncompromising consistency ends in poisonous deeds or murderous conclusions. Discursive principles by their nature exclude contradictory statements. But the world, the ordered world, is not logically consistent. Thus when decent politics is defined as the art of compromise, the following is meant: any politics that is not mad or empty is like iconic art. It reconciles contradictions by deploying the silent connective powers of *phusis*. Beauty, not logic, is the enemy of tyranny. What erases arbitrary and despotic inconsistency from human actions is the graceful aesthetic melding of incongruous powers. Consistency in action models itself on the smooth, lucid, flowing—in a word, the graceful—quality of the beautiful image. In contrast, the fanatics' desire for the world to be consistent with discursive principles—a result of propositional language pushed beyond its proper limits—is exceedingly destructive and results in arbitrary, despotic and irrational deeds. The end result of fanatical rationalism in love with discursive principles is the creation of chaos, not the *kosmos* or pattern of creation.

The attempt to 'restore' the world or re-make the world 'anew'—by bringing it in line with discursive principles—has repeatedly failed. The result often has been horrible conflagration. This has not stopped intellectuals from touting ever newer, more absurd, and crueler scripts though. In contrast to this destructive impulse, a handful of societies in history have found ways of turning collective social creation into a permanent and constructive process. The evidence for this is continuing high levels of artistic, scientific, political, economic and technological creativity in these societies over sustained periods combined with manifestly high levels of social well-being and political happiness.

To have institutionalized creativity in such a manner may once have been considered good fortune, and nothing more. Since around 1820, however, social success—measured in terms of social well-being—has become massively linked to permanent innovation in the arts and humanities, and in science and technology. A society that exempts itself from the collective processes of creation—and some do quite willfully in the name of Allah or the Supreme Leader or the Tribe—now live a kind of social death that has no historical precedent. There are two kinds of escape from this kind of living social death. One is to institute a regime of permanent innovation. Such societies scour for, absorb and disseminate discoveries that are made elsewhere. The second, rarer, society is a regime of persistent form creation. Its reason for being is the creation of durable shapes, figures, types, and genres. The paradox of the creation of durable forms is that they come into being through new ideas, industries, firms, markets and institutions. Discovery is both the revelation of something new and the finding of something old. It is doubtful whether one can be separated from the other in the act of creation.

Highly creative societies at their peak make a series of discoveries in a short period of time. This should not be confused with Castoriadis' favorite image of a magma flow—the continual spewing forth of creative acts from the collective and individual radical imagination. This image suggests that every moment of existence is creation, which is implausible. Doubtless, low-level background creation is pervasive in human experience. Endless incipient forms appear and as quickly disappear for want of recognition or viability. A kind of creative action is also implicated in the relentless everyday micro-scale replication, adaptation, imitation and translation of existing forms. Even the most traditional society must be inventive in this sense, otherwise it will not survive. On the other hand, even the most creative society cannot produce the kinds of strong forms that define or re-define the essential shape of a society without enormous difficulty. One of the greatest of these difficulties is the question of stability—the persistence of forms in existence. Castoriadis was right to say that forms emerge in time, but Plato was also right to say that forms defy time.

Time has a penchant for destruction. It erodes and destroys forms—not least incipient forms. Time mocks weak forms. Heteronomy is one of the great defenses against destructive time. It defends social and existential forms by precluding further experimentation in form making. To avoid the petrifaction of tradition, autonomous societies reduce their reliance on external authorities.[44] Yet, in order to stabilize themselves, these societies have to deal with the doubled-sided problem of persistence. This is the problem of how to combine ongoing experimentation in form making with the durability of forms thereby created. If this problem is not satisfactorily dealt with, creation becomes indistinguishable from chaos. Castoriadis suggested—many times—that self-limitation was the way that autonomous societies stabilized themselves. Self-limitation suggests a society that can draw its own boundaries. This is a society that, knowingly, gives itself shape. This is plausible. It is certainly more plausible than the neo-romantic assertions of those who proselytize 'change for its own sake.' 'Creation-as-change' is indifferent to the form-endowing quality that lies at the heart of any great creation, and to the defiance of time by forms so created. Change as a social ideal confuses time's onward march with creation. It falsely equates 'the new' with 'the formative.'

Time Out of Mind

If Castoriadis is right, then society (in the singular) creates societies (in the plural). Society in the singular is self-altering. It acts—in time, through history—to posit social forms. These forms are durable, but not imperishable. Each form is exceptional; each is radically 'other.' This idea compares in interesting ways with the model developed by the great Swiss historian Jacob Burkhardt. Burkhardt proposed that the birth of social forms is closely connected with the renaissance or re-birth of forms. At first glance it would seem that Castoriadis' idea of the radical emergence of social forms and Burkhardt's notion of the re-emergence of forms are totally at odds. However, as we know, things are often not what they first appear to be. In fact there is a lot of common ground between Burkhardt's and Castoriadis' ideas. If there wasn't, there would be no way to explain Castoriadis' frequent invoking of what he called 'Greco-Western' societies. That hyphenated concept clearly suggests that emergence involves some kind of re-emergence. But what kind—that is the question?

Castoriadis used the phrase 'Greco-Western societies' as a synonym for creative societies.[45] In a loose empirical sense, he was right. The vast majority of high-achieving human creation to date has been the product of this band of societies. But the term 'Greco-Western' is also misleading. Without question, creation clusters in certain times and places. 'Greek antiquity' is foremost among these. Ancient Athens produced a staggering intellectual legacy with what was by modern standards a modest population of some 150,000 Athenians (about a third of them citizens), 100,000 slaves, and 50,000 alien residents. In contrast it is not so clear that 'the modern West' is as useful a designator of peak creation as 'Greek antiquity.' Take the case of Burkhardt's home city of Basel. Like Athens, nineteenth-century Basel had a modest if rapidly growing population and its citizen rulers made up about a third of the population. Despite the fact it was no London or Berlin, the Basel city-state domiciled not just Burkhardt, who was probably the greatest historian of the nineteenth century, but also Nietzsche, the greatest philosopher of that century.[46] That's quite an achievement. Yet this kind of extraordinary creative attainment is by no means evenly distributed across the West. Indeed it is much less evenly distributed across the West than serious accomplishment was evenly distributed amongst the hundreds of ancient Greek city-states.

In simple terms, the West is a bit of misnomer. Basel in the nineteenth century may have been an exceptional city of the mind, but it was also that because it was part of a larger creative constellation. There were geographic, social, and institutional factors that mediated its accomplishments. Basel was a major portal city on the Rhine and sat at the apex of one of a handful of 'creative inland islands' in Europe—in this case, the triangular area of Baden-Württemberg bounded by the Rhine and Danube Rivers that has Stuttgart at its center. If we compare such 'creative inland islands' with the rest of Western Europe, we find that many of the other regions of Europe (past and present) are lackluster, backward, or downright lethargic by comparison.

It is notable today that the non-Western societies that show distinct if still inconclusive signs of joining the company of the systemic form-generating societies are principally the island, archipelago, peninsula, and coastal societies of East Asia—Japan, South Korea, Taiwan, Hong Kong, the South Coast of China, and Singapore.[47] There is an interesting parallel between this littoral cluster and the first, second, third, fourth and fifth-stage institutionalizations of intensive creation. The first institutionalization occurred in the ancient Mediterranean, the second in the late-medieval and Renaissance Mediterranean, the third around the North Sea and Baltic rim of Europe, the fourth in the riverine arteries of Western Europe, and the fifth in the littoral powerhouses of the North American and Australasian settler societies.

In the annals of human creation, without question, the first institutionalization of intensive creation—the Greek breakthrough—was astonishing. Castoriadis' instinct always was to link the concept of 'Western modernity' to the peculiar space-time of 'Greek antiquity.' Even if we replace 'Western modernity' with the notion of 'littoral modernity,' which is an empirically stronger concept, there remains no question that there are, and there remain, extraordinary parallels between the antique and modern cases. Castoriadis proceeded to draw these parallels with great care. Any talk of the twinning of 'antiquity and modernity,' and of the collusion of 'Greeks and Moderns,' has obvious risks. One is that it plays out as nothing more than a kind of nostalgia—in short: a backward-looking Hellenism. Whatever criticisms might be directed at Castoriadis' work, there is nothing 'backward looking' in it. Yet his work does not belong to the 'forward looking' progressive genre either. Castoriadis was aware that backward and forward looking senses of time were personal or psychological in nature—and that creative 'works and objects' redolent with marks of this psychological time never outlive their authors' death. For anyone, like Castoriadis, interested in explaining the most adventurous acts of creation, this is important to note. Time is the ultimate judge of creative acts, and few things survive time's withering judgment.

In his theory of creation, we see Castoriadis carefully demarcate the temporal schemata of acts of creation from the subjective-psychological time of memory, attention, and expectation.[48] This, incidentally, is not an easy thing to do. Memory, attention, and expectation are normally the way that we apprehend time. Time in the three dimensions of retention, attention and protention is categorical for the human mind. These three dimensions are fundamental to what Castoriadis, after Augustine, called the stretching of the mind—the *distento animi*. This animus of the mind is capable of three activities or postures. It remembers, it pays attention, and it expects. All of these are subjective approaches to time. It is individual human subjects who remember, attend, and anticipate. Human beings of course try to project subjective time schemas onto institutions. They talk, analogously, of 'institutional memory' or 'collective expectations.' Sometimes there is a rough correspondence between subjective time and group expectation or archival memory. But it is only a very rough approximation.

What Castoriadis does that is interesting is to suggest that the most significant social acts of creation are not played out in subjective time. They are not enacted through memory, attention, or anticipation. What he raises, correspondingly, is the idea that there is a common or public time—an ontological time dependent neither on recollection, interest, nor promise. What kind of time is this? It is the time of anonymous creation.[49] This is the kind of creation that escapes being over-determined by human subjectivity. The footprint of subjectivity makes most speeches, novels, paintings and melodies read, sound or look excruciating once they are placed out of their own time. In contrast, non-subjective time is a time outside of mind—it is not the kind of time through which the human mind is 'stretched' forwards, downwards or backwards. Mostly we inhabit this personal-psychological time of 'stretching'—but not always. Sometimes we experience time out of mind. We do so when we encounter a 'classic.' This happens, for example, when we come across an artwork or a social object that may have been produced in time but that is not easily classifiable as an object of memory, attention or expectation. We are unsure in fact whether it belongs to the past, the present, or the future.[50]

Anyone who builds a social philosophy on conceptual pairs like 'ancients and moderns' or 'Greece and the West' risks producing a memory-saturated theory of society. This is work that is elegiac, sorrowful, funereal, or grief-stricken. Nostalgia is a paradigm instance of such memorial time. It is time filled with memories of loss. Such loss can be projected onto a world historical stage. The attempt to find redemption through the past is invariably destructive. Far from being enamored with the past—with 'what was'—Castoriadis if anything was 'guilty' of the opposite. He persistently argued that the social creation of forms was un-determined. His view was that maximal form creation occurred 'out of nothing.' Neither the past, nor the present, could logically be the causal determinant of any future form that was 'unprecedented' in the strong sense of that word.

This thesis profoundly affected Castoriadis' understanding of the relationship of 'Greeks and Moderns.' He saw them as a pair but reiterated on many occasions that the link between the ancient polis and the modern West was non-causal. Greek antiquity did not 'produce' the West. Rather it was the case that Greek and Western societies coincidentally shared a massive capacity for reflexivity. They were not causally or genetically related, but they had an uncanny family resemblance. Both were defined by their readiness for self-interrogation, self-critique, and internal dissent. These societies regularly questioned their own laws. They were not in thrall to extra-social validation. They critiqued their own presuppositions, axioms and foundations. They were able to suspend their most basic criteria and rules on their own recognizance.[51]

While there is some truth in this, reflexivity—on whatever scale—is not sufficient to explain the emergence of forms. Critique is a function of words, and words even if they are critical words play a remarkably low-level role in acts of creation. Words come after the fact of creation. They are ciphers for what we already know, not for new knowledge. Words at most offer the possibility of being syllogistically deducted from discursive principles. As Castoriadis often noted, such communicative reason cannot explain Europe's transition from agrarian feudalism to civic capitalism, the Roman and American replacement of kingship with republicanism, or the Greek and Western replacement of aristocracy with democracy. Nobody deduced the American Revolution or England's Glorious Revolution. Indeed large-scale attempts at social deduction have invariably led to terrorism and the triumph of chaos over cosmos. The French Revolution established the modern template for this. It confused the violent negation of form with the radical emergence of form. The intellectuals who devised Japan's Shinto fascism or Syrian-Iraq-Lebanese Baathist fascism or the strains of homicidal suicidal totalitarian Islamism all appealed to discursive principles whose logic led directly into the thanatocratic abyss. Principles without form, words without figuration, quickly become an incitement to social destruction because of their inherent chaotic drive. They portend destruction without creation.

As Castoriadis constantly reiterated, creation is a function of form—and, as the very idea of 'form' suggests, creation is figurative not linguistic. The medium of the act of creation is figure, shape, and pattern. There may be something built into the nature of the cosmos—into the nature of nature, or the nature of being—that conditions this. There are figures, shapes, and patterns—symmetries, scales, and rhythms—built into the building blocks of nature (e.g. super strings). The human mind and human society draw freely and recursively on these in form creation. In this sense, form follows nature. Reflexivity can amplify form—it can focus attention on it. It can link subjective and ontological time. But reflexivity cannot in itself create form.

Nature, *phusis*, is the key to understanding what Burkhardt meant when he talked about the renaissance of social forms. We all know that the cities of the Italian Renaissance 're-discovered antiquity.' Curiously, in doing so, they also forged an ebullient type of modernity. Their re-search or re-discovery of the past produced a social form that was not in any sense a shallow imitation. This was because what the very inventive inhabitants of the great Renaissance cities did was not 're-discover the past' in the sense of 'where we have come from' but rather discover (and discover they liked) societies (Greco-Roman societies) that had a powerful sense of form. What made the Romans secondary to the Greeks, and the Italian Renaissance secondary to the Romans and the Greeks, was not a feeble desire of one to copy the other as a child traces the outline of a picture it likes, but rather a deep desire to replicate what happens in only a very few social times and places—*viz.* an incredible upsurge of form. Mimesis is the force that drives such upsurges. But it is the mimesis of *phusis*, and of society's engagement with time out of mind, rather than any lame repetition of what has come before. When Einstein taught himself mathematics using Euclid's handbook, he did not think that geometry ended with Euclid. What he was developing was a strong sense of mathematical form. Euclid was a 'classic' for Einstein in the same sense that Europe's last great period of form-giving—the era of Braque, Stravinsky, Cavafy, Mondrian, and Minkowski—will one day be a 'classic' period for a future epoch.

From this standpoint, Castoriadis' assertion that socio-historical worlds are self-contained, and irreducible to each other, is both right and wrong. It is perfectly true that French Revolutionary attempts to duplicate Greek and Roman rhetoric, festivals, funeral ceremonies, and names were a silly pantomime. They—notably—had no impact on the revolutionary laws of the period.[52] While the effects of the French Revolution were massive, its Greco-Roman self-understanding was superficial—at least measured by its outcomes, which were remarkably unstable. From the time of the Revolution to the Republic of De Gaulle, France suffered persistent regime crises and collapses. Contrast this with the Italian Renaissance and the American Revolution. The Italian city-states certainly had their share of atrocious government, but, like a lot of the most creative states, a powerful underlying sense of self-organization neutralized the corrupting effects of much of this. Italian anarchy was not lethal. While in the American case, the Greco-Roman tradition produced a much more visible sense of order in government—synonymous with long-term stability and development.

Either way, and in both cases, Greek and Roman models served as instructive examples of the way in which some societies are able to draw on the common wealth of form-generating media, allowing them to enact socio-historical world making in ontological time. What explains the massive constructive surge of the great Renaissance cities and the American Revolution was their collective capacity to engage time out of mind. This was time out of mind in the sense that it was not the time of past, present or future. It was an ontological time in which the ancient appeared to be contemporary, and the contemporary looked and felt ancient. Human beings are born, and they live, in the subjective time of regret, awareness and expectation. This is an inescapable part of the human condition. However, human beings are also drawn to another kind of time. This time is timeless. Everyone has intuitions of it. Déjà vu is an uncanny psychological version of it. Plato's notion of forms that exist outside the flux of ordinary social or personal time is a great philosophical treatment of this timeless time—just as Cézanne's definition of nature as composed of cones and cylinders is a great aesthetic invocation of it. What Cézanne was getting at was that an artwork that is radically un-determined by previous artworks is nonetheless determined by the artist's encounter with forms whose time is ontological not personal. The forms of a Cézanne painting are unmistakable. They can be imitated but they are not an imitation of another artist's work. Nonetheless, they are mimetic. The paradox is that they are a radiant imitation, and yet they are not pedestrian copies. They are a mimesis of *phusis*, not a copy of existing artworks.

What applies to the great artist, also applies to great societies. Some societies, usually for short historical periods, encourage excursions into ontological time. The importance of the artistic masterpieces of these societies resounds across all times and periods. The forms that constitute the skeletons of these masterpieces are not 'new,' are not 'old,' and are not 'now.' They evade entirely the categories of subjective time. Ontological time instead compounds subjective time into the time of a 'new order of the ages.' This time and its forms are not exhausted—nor are they even particularly well represented—in discursive thought and speech. The normal 'train' of argument and discussion finds it difficult to extricate itself from the force of memory, or from the pregnant now, or from hope and expectation. Those extensions of the human mind, after all, are keys to the ordinary apprehension of time. We find it difficult, though not impossible, to bracket memory, attention, and hope. Such bracketing requires an exceptional toughness of mind.

Form creation—represented by a 'new order of the ages'—is not discursive. Discursive thought or communicative reasoning relies on the law of non-contradiction. If what I say is consistent, then it is true. Chains of reasoning are valid if the major and minor premises, and the conclusion, of the reasoning are consistent. If witches are bad, and supporters of policy Y are political witches, then witch-hunting these supporters is legitimate. Or, as Hegel once put it, they are many good reasons for doing bad things. Forms, in contrast, are composed out of contradictions. They are ruled by the law of contradiction. Forms are unions of opposites. They meld master and servant, sovereign and subject, hot and cold, hard and soft, steel and glass. Forms unite such divergent parts through pattern media. Patterns are the ordered—and ordering—coalescence of contrasts. Commonplace forms that organize patterns include hierarchies, harmonies, scales, rhythms, and proportions. This is not to suggest that the social appropriation of forms is always benign. Dark, violent, dissonant, crushing forms that turn towards formlessness are as common as elegant, beautiful forms. Human beings are hugely fascinated by the dissolution, ruin, and melt-down of forms as by their creation through renaissance.[53]

The renaissance of forms occurs principally through images—not discussions. The renaissance of forms is the intense but rarely lasting encounter of a society with ontological time. The most common images associated with the invention of social forms are conceived out of visual-diagrammatical, rhythmic-aural and kinetic-plastic patterns. Words can be material for harmonies, scales, and for rhythmic explorations, but social invention as opposed to social dissemination rarely relies on the discursive train of thought but rather on the figurative images of the imagination, which, in their turn, rely on universal form-hatching media like symmetries, clusters, and hierarchies.

Linguistic genres such as stories and dramas are relatively late-arriving evolutionary additions to this human repertoire of order-making—and notably what the masterpieces of these genres do is to transform subjective time into the time of epic, tragedy, and comedy. They turn human expectation into destiny, necessity, or comic reversal.[54] In contrast, memory, attention and expectation are social crutches—unavoidable but at times unhelpful. Castoriadis was therefore right to stress the importance of tragedy in the first great reflexive upsurge of human creativity—the Greek polis. The polis was fueled by the most unsparing inquiry into the *phusis* of personality, society, and cosmos. This emerged in various ways, but no more enduringly than in its epic song, its tragic drama, and its comedy. All pointed beyond the human vanity that subjects create social worlds out of their hopes and memories into the deep ontological layers where society and *phusis* meet and where creation unfolds.

The Crucible of the City

We can be confident that collective creation does exist because we know that a handful of societies in a number of specific times and places have engaged in massive acts of creation and re-creation for extended periods of time. In other social times and places, this simply hasn't happened. So, if collective creation exists, how can we explain it? It is no good saying that such societies are an aggregate of individual creative personalities. As Castoriadis rightly insisted, personalities lean on their society. What seems to be the case is that some societies are very hospitable to creative personalities—the cities of the Italian Renaissance are a classic example. In talking about Greco-Western societies, Castoriadis most often refers to the 'ancient polis' or the 'burgher city' as their spring.[55] This is an important observation. *The city is the most important condition of human creation. It is not the only condition of human creation but it is the most crucial one.* All of the great moments of Greco-Western creation are centered on specific cities: Athens, Rome, Venice, Florence, Amsterdam, London, New York, Chicago, and San Francisco among them.

Why is the city, the polis, so important? In a circular sense, we can say that in certain times and places the city is unusually hospitable to creative personalities. It accommodates their traits. But why is this so? One of the most powerful reasons is that the city, like the imagination, is a figurative-aural-plastic medium. All human society begins with the making of marks on the earth. Eventually this evolves into the kind of spiritual geometry that was achieved during the Greek break-through—and that is the most potent recurring sign of concentrated creative human achievement. The city is the most intensive expression of the work of humankind in creating an artificial environment for itself—be it a track, a field, or a street. The city is primarily defined not by words or language or textual signs but by architectonic forms, distributed networks, social geometries, and relational schemas. It is through such media that societies forge a union of opposites. What are logical contradictions from the standpoint of discursive language are harmonies and symmetries in sound and figure and touch.

We can give the name of the commons to these collective patterns. The commons is the primary medium for the imaging activity of the individual mind. Minds imag(in)e forms. Mainly these are familiar forms. They are replicated and adapted from what we see and hear and feel around us. But some, a much smaller number, are unfamiliar—or rather more exactly they are uncannily familiar. They are replicated from *phusis*. They are modeled on the forms of nature that the *nous* tacitly, already, always recognizes. These forms are both unfamiliar and yet somehow very familiar. Some of these 'unfamiliar familiar' forms are eventually embodied in the city. They inspire further mental imaging. The figures of the city correct for the idiosyncrasies of the individual mind. The forms of the city are (necessarily) collective. The images that they inspire are pre-disposed to collective recognition.

If that is so, then why are most cities creative dead-waters? In the last two centuries, much of the human population has moved into urban areas. But in the main, with very few exceptions, a small number of Western cities have remained overwhelmingly—and measurably—the dominant creative centers. At the first level, the answer is that only some cities develop strong architectonic forms. This is not just a matter of wealth, but of ambition and instinct as well. On a deeper level, this is because only a very few cities develop as open systems. This is a crucial condition of permanent form creation—even if it is not the only condition.

In most cases the principal sites of collective creation have been stranger cities—cities filled with aliens, visitors, travelers, exiles, migrants, settlers, and people from elsewhere. The enigmatic case of twentieth-century Japan—a very ethnocentric society—provides a partial exception to this proposition. But it is an exception that proves the rule—for the Japanese attempt to innovate in the sense of 'form create' under conditions of social closure reaped a terrible price. The Japanese resort to the use of scripts, notably the script of anti-

Western nationalist ideology, to steer a society struggling to reconcile 'change and tradition,' proved catastrophic. The anti-Western Shinto fascism of Japan's inter-war period ended in complete disaster. Yet, as with other littoral and seaboard societies, Japan is a society where form innovation has reached significant levels. Notably the key driver of this achievement has been non-discursive aesthetics—for example miniaturizing arts—and mathematics. But there always remains the question of how much aesthetic power alone, without the collusion of strangers, can sustain high-level creation?

A classic example of the importance of the stranger is Burkhardt's Basel. They may have been perpetually excluded from Basel citizenship but Protestant refugees from France, Flanders and Italy, who poured in during the sixteenth and seventeenth centuries, were crucial to the development of the industrial base of the city and its long-term success. The enduring model of the exo-city is the ancient polis—not least of all Athens in the sixth, fifth and fourth centuries.[56] In classical Athens, huge numbers of resident aliens had a very powerful influence on the character of the city. Why is the stranger city important? It is important because it tends to unleash the aural-pictorial-plastic imagination. Such creative imagining emerges under conditions of *porous social ties*. The stranger city is an ecology of such porous ties. It is the via media of unsocial sociability. Paradoxically, strong social forms emerge where society is 'weak' in the sense that its linguistic norms, rules and authority are feeble. Under conditions of weak linguistic interaction, figurative schemata, visual thinking, musical and plastic-haptic forms come to the fore. This occurs because the noise of language is reduced. Opinion, rhetoric, propositional judgments, verdicts, and convictions are all treated skeptically. The reasoning of debate, which can never escape conventional premises, is set aside. *Logos* and *doxa* are downplayed along with dogmatic, moralizing, and righteous assertions. Through the graphical, schematic and pictorial media of the imagination, new forms (shapes and figures) emerge.

Shape implies order—cosmos in contrast to chaos. Everybody has experienced the impulse to replace chaos with cosmos when we say: 'Let us meet where there is a whiteboard. I think more clearly when I can sketch things out.' Sense can be made out of the fog of a messy situation when we can sketch a solution. Just as there is individual and group sketching, there is also a social whiteboard. It is not language. Language is not the house of being. The house of being—being that pushes towards giving itself form—is the city. In cities, more than any other social medium, human beings outwardly (via the media of their external constructed environment) represent aural, visual and haptic forms to themselves. Cities allow considerable scope for experimenting with new shapes and patterns. Some experiments are idiosyncratic and quickly die. Most experiments repeat (with minor differences) what already exists.

Successful forms by definition are repeated. It is notable just how quickly compelling forms are picked up and replicated in cities. While repetition is a key
aspect of any form creation, it is not repetition per se that defines the creative
city. It is emergence. Emergence stands on contrariness: the capability to
unify what is divergent: 'out of many, one.' This is not the negative capability of social critique. It is the musical capacity to harmonize the discordant.
What contrary minds do on an individual level, great cities do on a collective
level. The city in this sense is the site for experiments that turn existing forms
into the materials out of which new forms emerge. This poietic activity turns
the past into the future, memory into expectation, and history into that which
is new and unexpected. Out of this compounding of time, it creates a 'new
order of the ages.'

Notes

1. This tradition is epitomized by Mihaly Csikszentmihalyi (1996). Other key contributors to the tradition include Francis Galton, Catharine Cox, Graham Wallas, G.
   P. Guilford, Arthur Koestler, Jacques Hadamard, R. A. Finke, Keith Dean Simonton,
   Robert Sternberg, and Charles Murray.
2. F. Scott Fitzgerald, 'The Crack-Up' (1936) in Fitzgerald (1956).
3. More recently, the Japanese archipelago and the Australasian littoral have shown distinct signs of joining these historic leaders. For a quantitative historiometric analysis of key locations of innovation in the arts and sciences, see Murray (2003). The
   term 'riverine Europe' is an allusion to four key post-1800 centers of creative achievement: (a.) the triangular region bounded by the Elbe and Salle Rivers that includes
   the cities of Freiburg, Jena, Halle, Bayreuth, Weimar and Prague; (b.) another triangular region bounded by the Maas (Meuse) and Rhine Rivers that includes the city
   of Cologne; (c.) the triangular area of Baden-Württemberg bounded by the Rhine
   and Danube Rivers that has Stuttgart at its center and that converges at its southern
   tip on Zurich; (d.) the line of the Danube that stretches between Budapest and Vienna
   and into Bavaria. As Murray notes (356), cities like Prague, Munich, Vienna,
   Cologne, and Stuttgart produced a huge concentration of highly creative talent after
   1800. Their geographical settings have distinct parallels with the older creative
   node, the Île-de-France, the inland peninsula that is delimited by the Oise, Seine,
   Ourcq and Marne rivers, which has Paris at its heart.
4. For an overview of Castoriadis' life, politics and philosophy, see Murphy (2005a).
5. See in particular, Cornelius Castoriadis, 'The Social-Historical: Mode of Being,
   Problems of Knowledge' [1987], 'Individual, Society, Rationality, History'
   [1987–1988], 'Power, Politics, Autonomy' [1978–1988] in Castoriadis (1991); 'The
   Institution of Society and Religion' [1978–1980], 'Phusis and Autonomy' [1986]
   and 'Time and Creation' [1983] in Castoriadis (1997a); 'Radical Imagination and
   the Social Instituting Imaginary' [1994] and 'Culture in a Democratic Society'
   [1991–1994] in Castoradis (1997b).
6. Simon Marginson, in chapter six, discusses how the Augustan settlement in Rome
   and the parallel Tokugawa/Edo settlement in Japan constitute brilliant examples of
   a stage 1(self-creation) that is engineered to become a stage 2 (arrested creation).

7. Castoriadis frequently made allusions to the constituents of this list—a list which is remarkably close to that of Charles Murray's empirically-derived inventory of creative places though Castoriadis' geography of creation understandably is not as minutely detailed as Murray's.

8. This is the 'irreducibly new,' the 'radical alterity' of creation. See 'The Institution of Society and Religion' and 'Time and Creation' in Castoriadis (1997a), 320, 329.

9. 'Radical Imagination and the Social Instituting Imaginary' and 'Culture in a Democratic Society' in Castoriadis (1997b).

10. As reported to Hadamard (1947), 142.

11. Castoriadis was unswervingly critical of the endless procession of intellectuals who identified with despotic and murderous regimes. In one very typical passage, he observed the magnetic appeal that even the creepiest kinds of 'revolutionary power' had for intellectuals of his generation. Whenever one of these ugly powers appeared, '[then] begins the golden-age of fellow-travelers, who were able to afford the luxury of an apparently intransigent opposition to a part of reality—reality 'at home'— by paying for it with the glorification of another part of this reality—over there, elsewhere, in Russia, in China, in Cuba, in Algeria, in Vietnam, or, if worst came to worst, in Albania. Rare are those among the great names in the Western intelligentsia who have not, at some moment between 1920 and 1970, made this 'sacrifice of conscience,' sometimes (the least often) in the most infantile kind of credulity, other times (most often) with the most paltry sort of trickery. Sartre, stating in a menacing tone: 'You cannot discuss what Stalin is doing, since he alone has the information that explains his motives,' will remain, no doubt, the most instructive specimen of the intellectual's tendency to look ridiculous.' ('Intellectuals and History' [1987] in Castoriadis, 1991, 10.)

12. Cornelius Castoriadis, 'Logic, Imagination, Reflection,' *World in Fragments* (1997a), 256, 265.

13. Castoriadis (1987), 321, 329; 1997, 258. Castoriadis remarks '...abstract thought itself always has to lean on some figure or image, be it, minimally the image of the words through which it is carried on,' 'Radical Imagination and the Social Instituting Imaginary' in Castoriadis (1997b), 329. He observes that radical imagination involves 'the incessant emergence of the other in and through the positing (*Vor-stellung*) of images or figures...' Castoriadis, 329.

14. Castoriadis (1997a), 269. The shape, pattern and form of imagination is akin to what John Locke set out in his treatise of 1690 *An Essay Concerning Human Understanding* (Woozley (ed.) 1964: 117). Locke distinguished three sorts of qualities in bodies, primary, secondary and tertiary. Primary qualities, associated with the imagination, are the bulk, figure, number, situation, motion or rest of bodies. Secondary qualities are the power of these insensible primary qualities to operate on the human senses. Tertiary qualities are the powers of any body, by virtue of its primary qualities, to alter the primary qualities of another body.

15. The Australian poet John Tranter, in his poem 'Pride', depicts the waking nightmare of the linguistic theorist:

> he woke from a bad dream choked with simulacra
> and cried out: 'Theory! I nurtured and raised you!
> But had I wished to trip you up through
> the defect of your initial faulty premise -
> cultural formations are "like languages", they

> have a "grammar" - why not "like roles", they
> interact with other "roles" constituting
> a "narrative" of social interaction? - why not
> "like a circuit", interacting choices which
> summed in Boolean groups constitute
> a variable and cybernetic current of meaning? -
> faulty, plausible simile - from which everything else
> extends like a cantilevered road to nowhere -

16. Castoriadis (1997a), 268.
17. The great English mathematician Roger Penrose observes in the concluding parts of his *The Emperor's New Mind* (1999 [1989]), 541–550, that the most creative thought is non-verbal. At the highest levels of insight, the sense of beauty plays the crucial role in thought. Penrose cites the self-reflections of Albert Einstein ('The words or the language, as they are written or spoken, do not seem to play any role in my mechanism of thought. The psychical elements which seem to serve as elements of thought…are, in my case, of visual and some muscular type.'), the geneticist Francis Galton ('I…waste a vast deal of time in seeking appropriate words and phrases…'), and the mathematician Jacques Hadamard ('I insist that words are totally absent from my mind when I really think…'). Penrose says of himself: 'Almost all my mathematical thinking is done visually and in terms of non-verbal concepts…'
18. Castoriadis (1997a), 259.
19. That makes a pair out of what otherwise has no relationship or else simply an accidental relationship.
20. Wagner (2009), 19–39.
21. Wagner (2009) overstates the metaphor of 'language,' characterising the interaction of cells and organisms as a kind of communication or conversation. What is more important, or primary, is that all conversations or communications, including human communication, from which the root metaphor derives, occur through the abstract medium of shapes. That a human sentence has a shape is central to the production of linguistic and social meaning. Both the fact and the act of meaning, though, ultimately derives from the larger shaping or form giving that goes on throughout nature. Human meaning is a subset of this much more comprehensive process. John Locke, in his treatise of 1690 *An Essay Concerning Human Understanding* (Woozley ed. 1964: 117), drew attention to the process of one body shaping another.
22. Castoriadis' view was conditioned by his palpable aversion to twentieth-century structuralism, an aversion in part explained by the hot-house politics of French intellectual life in the second half of the twentieth-century. This aversion to the structuralists, and its flow-on to Castoriadis' interpretation of pre-Socratic thought is somewhat ironic given his close friendship with the French Hellenist-structuralist classicists Vernant and Vidal-Naquet. Some labyrinths we should never try sort out.
23. One of the touchiest matters of all in contemporary social theory is the question of whether there is anything that is timeless or unchanging. In *Imagination*, the first model of the imagination assumes that there are unchanging forms. The second and third models assume the contrary. This more or less neatly sums up the division of contemporary views. Readers can make up their own mind. Irrespective of where anyone stands, the debate—for and against timelessness—is a genuinely interesting one.

24. Castoriadis (1987), 193.

25. This happened when printing made the production and distribution of the book so cheap and easy.

26. On this, see Murphy (2005b).

27. This is elaborated in Murphy and Roberts (2004), 127–136.

28. For this reason, then, Castoriadis' insistence that the imagination is the capacity to posit an image 'starting from nothing at all' is wrong. See Castoriadis (1997a), 269.

29. Creation manifests itself 'by the enormous diversity of social forms as well as in their historical succession. And this creation is *ex nihilo*: when humanity creates the institution and signification, it does not "combine" some "elements" that it would have found scattered about before it. It creates the *form* institution, and in and through this form it creates *itself* as *humanity* (which is something other than an assembly of bipeds.)' Social form, forming, formation arises out of nothing, even though this does not happen in and through nothing. '"Creation ex nihilo," "creation of form" does not mean "creation cum nihilo," that is to say, "without means," unconditionally, on a *tubla rasa*...all historical creation takes place upon, in and through the already instituted...This conditions it and limits it, but does not determine it...' Castoriadis (1991), 64.

30. 'The social-historical is radical imaginary, namely, the incessant originality of otherness that figures, and figures itself, is in figuring and in figuring itself, giving itself as a figure and figuring itself to the second degree.' Castoriadis (1987), 204.

31. Circularity—the circle—it should be noted in passing is a commonly recurring social geometry, and one that we find, for example, in the Renaissance, that is often invoked against hierarchical figuration. On the circle in Renaissance figurative politics, see Murphy, 2001a, 177.

32. 'Time and Creation' in Castoriadis (1997a), 392, 397; 'Radical Imagination and the Social Instituting Imaginary' in Castoriadis, 1997b, 322. Castoriadis observes that 'this creation is *ex nihilo*...'Creation *ex nihilo*'...does not mean creation '*cum nihilo*,' that is to say, without 'means,' unconditionally, on a *tabula rasa*.' 'Individual, Society, Rationality, History' [1987–1988] in Castoriadis (1991), 64.

33. Castoriadis (1997a), 321.

34. Schumpeter made a similar point about industrial innovation. It is always new firms in new industry sectors who pioneer new generations of technology. The new firms arise independently of firms in existing industries.

35. Castoriadis (1987), 300.

36. Castoriadis wavered in his attitude to *phusis*. In '*Phusis* and Autonomy' [1986], Castoriadis, 1997a, he had it moving of its own accord to create social forms. This indicated that, in a strong sense, society had a nature—an encompassing ordering that generated social forms. The problem is that he also held that societies closest to *phusis*—i.e., the autonomous societies—were highly reflexive, meaning that social actors looked on the laws of those societies as conventions (*nomoi*), not as *phusis*. (See, for example, Castoriadis, 'The Social-Historical: Mode of Being, Problems of Knowledge' [1987], 38.) It is perfectly possible to resolve the apparent contradiction between these views, by simply indicating that norms and laws are secondary manifestations of social form. But in practice Castoriadis couldn't do this because he made a strong equation between law and form.

37. 'Phusis and Autonomy' [1988] in Castoriadis (1997a).

38. This is discussed at length in Murphy (2001a).

39. This is elaborated in Peters, M. A., P. Murphy & S. Marginson (2009) and Murphy (2001b).

40. Typical of this are statements such as 'the rise of unlimited interrogation creates a new socio-historical *eidos*' (1991, 163), 'Greece is the first society where we find the explicit questioning of the instituted collective representation of the world,' 'the question of what a just law is, what justice is—what the 'proper' institution of society is—opens up as a genuine, that is, interminable, question.' Castoriadis, 'The Greek *Polis* and the Creation of Democracy' (1991), 102, 114. 'Politics, such as it was created by the Greeks, amounts to the explicit putting into question of the established institution of society' (1991), 159.

41. As Agnes Heller observed, in the twentieth century 'the task of creating meaningful world-views' increasingly became 'the prerogative of professionals.' Heller (1985), 181.

42. Castoriadis is not alone in this. A Byzantine neo-Platonism permeates the extraordinary cinema of Theo Angelopoulos. In Angelopoulos' case, the comparison is often made between his films and the 'Orthodox tradition of icon painting.' See Horton (1997), 27. This is perfectly true, though, as also in the case of Castoriadis, the iconography of the icon/figure is the visible rendering of invisible figures of form, alluding always to the way in which figuration figures itself. What happens at the 'point' of creation is very difficult to understand of course. Angelopoulos' ability to induce the contemplative stillness of the moving picture is a remarkable imagining of the time out of mind of creation, in which—through the iconic moment—past, present and future is suspended, just like 'the suspended step of the stork' (the title of Angelopoulos' great 1991 film).

43. Plotinus emphasized the non-discursive nature of the intellect—paramount in its contemplation of beauty and order. See, for example, the Eighth Tractate of Plotinus' *The Enneads* (1991). As part of that discussion, Plotinus (416–417) draws a very revealing analogy between the intellect and archaic Egyptian picture language. 'Similarly, as it seems to me, the wise of Egypt—whether in precise knowledge or by the prompting of nature—indicated the truth where, in their effort toward philosophical statement, they left aside the writing-forms that take in the detail of words and sentences—those characters that represent sounds and convey the propositions of meaning—and drew pictures instead, engraving in the temple inscriptions a separate image for every separate item: thus they exhibited the absence of discursiveness in the Intellectual Realm. For each manifestation of knowledge and wisdom is a distinct image, an object in itself, an immediate unity, not an aggregate of discursive reasoning and detailed willing.'

44. Agnes Heller describes the transition from external to internal authority in *The Power of Shame* (1985).

45. On the centrality of Greco-Western societies in creative action, see '*Phusis* and Autonomy' in Castoriadis (1997a), 339; 'Culture in a Democratic Society' in Castoriadis (1997b), 345; 'The Social-Historical: Mode of Being, Problems of Knowledge' (37) and 'Power, Politics, Autonomy' (144) in Castoriadis (1991).

46. And also Bachofen and Overbeck.

47. These states have done so under the impetus of various kinds of Anglo-American cooperation, hegemony, or incitement—sometimes welcomed and sometimes not.

48. 'Time and Creation' [1991] in Castoriadis (1997a), especially 379-383.

49. The idea of anonymous creation does not sit well with the self-image of modern lib-

eral societies precisely because it is not a 'self' image at all, but a 'collective' one in which society (not the self) is the primary and nameless agent—and medium—of creation. Despite this fact, and somewhat ironically, as was pointed out in *Global Creation* (the companion volume of the current work), it is often self-regarding individualistic societies like the Anglo-American ones that acquit themselves most spectacularly in acts of anonymous creation. The collective histories, personalities and mind-sets of London and New York City are cases in point. They act and they create, but without us being able to attribute action or creation to any individual or specific set of individuals. As Thomas Ford (2010 forthcoming) notes, this paradox is implicit in the work of Adam Smith, whose late-career writings were suggestive of the way in which aesthetic rhythm provides the paradoxical but nonetheless real collective foundation of highly individualized capitalist societies. A similar point is made in Murphy (2001c). In short, capitalism is the product of an ironic communism, while the disaster of communism was that its morbid collectivism produced highly atomised human beings frequently terrorised into states of extreme anomie.

50. Exactly the same applies to any kind of maximal creation. Works of maximal creation are not revivals. They are not contemporary chic. They are not millenarian—'about to be born.' It is this bracketing of subjective time incidentally that makes Castoriadis' own work a 'classic.' It transcends his personal identification with the hypertensive 'now' moment of 1968 and the social movements of the 1960s. It escapes the millenarian expectation of 'coming into being' that periodically surfaces in his work. He quells his own fascinated expectation of 'what is to come' with a deep respect for great social forms. Finally—and not least because of his abiding and deep admiration for great forms—his is a body of work that never looks back, with sickly nostalgia, at past social achievements.

51. Castoriadis (1997a), 267–268.

52. This is observed by Pierre Vidal-Naquet in his essay 'The Place of Greece in the Imaginary Representations of the Men of the Revolution' in *Politics Ancient and Modern* (1995).

53. Castoriadis (1997a) in 'The Institution of Society and Religion' observed that social forms are stretched rather thinly over the abyss of chaos and groundlessness. There is a nihilistic streak in the human psyche that is fascinated by the abyss, and its thanatocratic nature. Social dissolution and death—the death of forms—is often interpreted as a kind of dark beauty that attracts as much as the lucid beauty of ascendant forms. On this, see Murphy (2001a), chapter eight.

54. Wit is arguably the highest form of creation in the sense that it rests entirely on the undoing of expectation—a mode of subjective time—through turning what we expect into its opposite.

55. See, for example, 'The Movements of the Sixties' [1986] in Castoriadis (1997a), 56; 'The Crisis of Culture and the State' [1986] in Castoriadis (1991), 230.

56. This is discussed in greater detail in Murphy (2001b).

References

Castoriadis, C. (1997a). *World in Fragments*. Stanford, CA: Stanford University Press.

Castoriadis. C. (1997b). *The Castoriadis Reader*. Oxford: Blackwell.

Castoriadis, C. (1991). *Philosophy, Politics, Autonomy*. New York: Oxford University Press.

Castoriadis, C. (1987 [1975]). *The Imaginary Institution of Society*. Cambridge: Polity Press.

Csikszentmihalyi, M. (1996). *Creativity: Flow and the Psychology of Discovery and Invention*. New York: HaperCollins.

Fitzgerald, F. S. (1956 [1936]). The Crack-Up. In *The Crack Up*. New York: New Directions.

Ford, T. (2010, forthcoming). Rythmus and the Critique of Political Economy. *Empedocles: European Journal for the Philosophy of Communication*, P. Murphy (ed.) Special Issue on Paradox and Communication.

Hadamard, J. (1947). *The Psychology of Invention in the Mathematical Field*. Princeton, NJ: Princeton University Press.

Horton, A. (1997). *Theo Angelopoulos: A Cinema of Contemplation*. Princeton: Princeton University Press.

Heller, A. (1985). *The Power of Shame*. London: Routledge.

Locke, J. (1964 [1690]). *An Essay Concerning Human Understanding*. A. D. Woozley (ed.). London: Collins.

Murphy, P. (2005a). Cornelius Castoriadis. In G. Ritzer (ed.) *Encyclopedia of Social Theory Volume 1*. Thousand Oaks, CA: Sage, 82–83.

Murphy, P. (2005b). Communication and Self-Organization. *Southern Review* 37: 3.

Murphy, P. & D. Roberts. (2004). *Dialectic of Romanticism: A Critique of Modernism*. London: Continuum.

Murphy, P. (2001a). *Civic Justice: From Ancient Greece to the Modern World*. Amherst, NY: Humanity Books.

Murphy, P. (2001b). Architectonics. In P. Murphy & J. Arnason (eds.) *Agon, Logos, Polis*. Stuttgart: Franz Steiner Verlag, 207–232.

Murphy, P. (2001c). Marine Reason. *Thesis Eleven* 67, 11–38.

Murray, C. (2003). *Human Accomplishment: The Pursuit of Excellence in the Arts and Sciences, 800 B.C. to 1950*. New York: HarperCollins.

Penrose, R. (1999 [1989]). *The Emperor's New Mind: Concerning Computers, Minds and the Laws of Physics*. Oxford: Oxford University Press.

Peters, M. A., P. Murphy & S. Marginson. (2009). *Creativity and the Global Knowledge Economy*. New York: Peter Lang.

Plotinus. (1991). *The Enneads*. London: Penguin.

Vidal-Naquet, P. (1995). The Place of Greece in the Imaginary Representations of the Men of the Revolution. *Politics Ancient and Modern*. Cambridge: Polity Press.

Wagner, A. (2009). *Paradoxical Life: Meaning, Matter, and the Power of Human Choice*. New Haven: Yale University Press, 2009.

2. Creation

PETER MURPHY

Romanticism and Platonism

One of the continuing challenges for any theory of creativity is to define its relation to the Romantic view of creation. There is no doubting the power, attraction, and the success of the Romantic concept of creation, just as there is no denying its deep flaws. Early Romantic theories of spontaneous creation spawned an array of related concepts—ranging from national self-determination to moral autonomy to self-organizing societies to the autopoiesis of nature. In each case, whether it was applied to events in nature or to deeds in society, creation meant self-formation. The Romantic idea of immanent determination assumed that agency of any kind, conscious or not, was the cause of its own consequences. External determination was a sign of a lesser or in many cases a morally unpalatable form of determination. A cluster of popular nineteenth-century ideas, from the liberal concept of the self to the Darwinian conception of social and biological evolution, supposed that everything from human choice to social development to natural history was the result of agents acting on themselves, becoming something different in the process. The media of such change might be conscious choice, intent or will. It might be unconscious mutation, adaptation and development. But, conscious or unconscious, in each case the outcome of change was an 'organism' with a higher level of complexity, internal differentiation or maturity.

The clearest objection to this notion of Romantic autopoiesis—or immanent self-determination—is that *nothing arises by itself*.[1] This anti-romantic view is one side of a great cultural schism that has divided western intellectual life for almost three centuries. At its heart are two contrary ways of looking at the world: one Romantic, the other Platonic. The first eulogizes contingency, the

second delights in constancy. The Romantic soul longs for fluidity and transformation. Its being is becoming. It exists to transform itself into something
else. The emphasis in the case of the Platonic soul, in contrast, is on form rather
than transformation. Platonism, in whatever guise it happens to assume, pays
attention to the a-temporal, and not just the temporal, dimension of creation.
Creation is first and foremost a function of what is permanent. Permanence
is prior to and precedes change. Beginnings and ends pre-suppose something
that does not begin and does not end. All chance and change, all mutability
and contingency, are conditioned by certainty and permanence. Accident is
inconceivable without its opposite necessity, and the durable in human experience unites what is timeless and a-temporal with what is time bound and born
in time.

It may well be that time is simply a dimension of space. Consider the ultra-
tiny state of the universe at the big bang, containing numerous spatial dimensions at the ultra-small scale. When expansion occurs and the scale of the
universe changes, so the time dimension of space appears. This is the routine
paradox of all creation. One thing [suddenly/imperceptibly] appears as another thing. Thus space [appears as] time, matter [as] meaning, inside [as] outside, start [as] end, the boundless [as] the boundary.[2] Accordingly, Dante
'begins' his journey 'in the middle of things,' just as Hal switches to become
Henry V.[3] In a sense, the universe and all it contains is a wonderful oxymoron,
a very good joke, an excellent metaphor—go ahead and pick your metaphor.
If certain theologians of the early Christian church were right to assert that creation is *ex nihilo*, then that is so only because in fact nothing *is* something.[4]
That is true in the same paradoxical sense that Marshall McLuhan remarks of
the Columbia University media studies professor in *Annie Hall*—'you mean
my fallacy is wrong?' Nothing in the modern experience is more fallacious than
the primacy of permanence, but that does not mean that permanence is not
primary.

To live in modernity, a person must bow down to one or other of the warring culture gods. A choice must be made—either Romanticism or Classicism.[5]
But like most choices, this is not a choice at all. One does not choose if one
bows down. Like everything else interesting in creation, contingency readily
pirouettes to become its opposite—necessity—and those who are most animated by dramatic necessity are those most able to act—when it matters—with
spontaneity. Yet, even if the 'choice' of romantic or classic is not really a
choice, nonetheless it is still a grave alternation. For the one of the pair that
has the upper hand determines the tone and tenor of the times. Every soul and
each society is what they are because of the tacit 'choice' that they make
between (the primacy of) Romantic contingency or Platonic durability.

Romanticism rests on a simple proposition: the world as we know it is filled with contingency. It is characterized by difference, diversity, variety, and novelty. This is a world in which things and events can always be other than they are. The one and only constant of the world is that there is no constancy. Things change in time and alter across space. The highest value claimed by the romantic is richness. Richness is an effect of pluralism, and pluralism is generated by the play of contingency. Recognition of contingency is not peculiar to 'modern times.' It is true that, since the late eighteenth century, there has been an enormous fascination with the power and effect of variation. But classical antiquity was also keenly aware of the multiplicity of manners, mores, customs, laws and societies. Late antiquity thought of richness as a bounteous overflow from God. The Renaissance mixed this Neo-Platonism with a worldly sense of dynamism. The age of seventeenth and eighteenth-century Enlightenment spoke approvingly of innovation and exploration.

In all of its modes, contingency indicates the potential for things to be 'different' from what they are and perhaps 'other' than what they are. It is difficult to believe that there was ever a society that did not have some idea of contingent variation. After all, the human imagination allows us to envisage what does not exist. If only for survival purposes, this mental ability is highly functional. Yet it is also true that certain societies have a heightened sense of contingency. They experience more of it, and they experience it more deeply. The classical Greeks and Romans certainly did in comparison with the tribes and kingdoms that surrounded them. Their philosophers, historians and geographers often commented on the differences between societies. Yet, despite this, those same philosophers, historians and geographers usually concluded that an immutable nature existed alongside the contingent variability that they observed in society.

Plato was not the first to observe the paradox of permanent nature and contingent society. He was, though, perhaps the most influential thinker to do so. He did much to entrench the distinction between things that are in flux, like the opinion (*doxa*) of city dwellers and their laws (*nomoi*), and things that endure—most especially *phusis* or nature. Nature shapes society. Nature in this sense means something above the obligatory legislation of the state or the venerable law of custom. While laws change in time and customs change in space, nature is constant in both space and time. As the Roman statesman Cicero put it: 'True law is right reason in agreement with Nature; it is of universal application, unchanging and everlasting . . . It is valid for all nations and all times.'[6]

To appeal to nature in this way was commonplace in Europe until the end of the eighteenth century. Classical nature was known by different names. Sometimes it was just called 'nature,' other times 'natural law' or the 'law of nature.' In the seventeenth century it acquired the tag 'natural rights.' Anyone who invoked such terms understood that they implied something valid for all times and places. There were always schools of thought that rejected the idea of universal validity. Yet the challenge to classical nature was considerably more muted in the age between Cicero and Montesquieu than it was in the period after that. The nineteenth century began with the Romantic assault on the idea of invariant nature. This escalated in the twentieth century into a war on 'metaphysics' (Martin Heidegger's word for Platonic nature).[7]

War is not too strong a term. The political implications of the struggle over the question of 'the nature of nature' were never far from the surface. When Romantic ideas swept Europe, gathering pace from the end of the eighteenth century, they brought with them a new notion of nature. Romantic nature was unlike Platonic nature. It was distinguished by change rather than by durability. It was a nature that always in transition—a contradiction in terms from a Platonic standpoint. It was moody, ever-changing, and short-lasting. It was epitomized by the moment of transition of something into something else. This was the moment of birth of the new out of the old by its own doing, through an act or event of immaculate conception. Romantics deeply admired the historical past insofar as history was the study of nations-in-formation that were defined by purity of language or custom anchored in the spontaneous unalloyed origins of an authentic gothic past that was to be resurrected in national revolutions and rebellions to come—events that would emancipate the nation from the burden of external determination which seemed to carry all of the hallmarks of damnation.

The social implication of this was clear. Whatever this chameleon nature created—or legitimated—could only be valid for a particular nation or a particular period of time. Romantic nature would always supersede itself by acting of its own accord on its own self. Nothing was valid for all nations and all times. Nature's works were particular, not universal. From this arose the notion that truth was relative. Or as Johann Gottfried von Herder put it: all cultures are equally close to God. Ironically, though, the equality of cultures was unsustainable without natural law. Once the idea of a universal nature was struck out, so (implicitly) was the idea of God. When this happened, romantic nationalists quickly drew the conclusion that their nation or culture was better than the rest. The moral principle of the equality of cultures led unerringly to the practical conclusion of a hierarchy of nations. Historicists matched Romanticism's cultural particularity with their own conceptions of legal particularity. They argued that law was valid only for particular historical periods. The idea that a modern society could still learn things from, say, Roman law was rejected. 'Not learning from the past' of another society or epoch became a sign of desired purity. The greater a nation, culture, or legal system, the more pure or auto-poietic it is.

Purity is a function of the romantic desire to be free of determination. History stops and starts in eventful moments when normal causality, or determination 'from the outside,' is suspended. This desire for freedom from external determination has implications for the self as well as for society. A chameleon self emerged from the vat of Romanticism. The message pinned to its body was that 'he who is not busy being born is busy dying.' Romantics, aesthetes, and bohemians—and a very long list of their successors and admirers—desired to be authentic selves. Authenticity meant self-invention through uncaused causality—in other words, freedom from determination via the act of self-determination.[8] The shortest path to self-invention was defiance of social convention. Classical nature (*phusis*), it should be noted, also set itself apart from social convention (*nomos*). It was common, after all, for the universals of nature to trump local social norms. Romantic nature, though, legitimated a perpetual revolt against social norms. It did this not in the name of universals but in the name of change. Shock, newness, and difference were the sinews of an authentic condition that rejected the power of determination in human affairs.

Romantic 'nature' therefore was the antithesis of social determination. It promised indetermination, negation, and negativity—on an unheard of scale. Determination was properly answered with the act of negation. Romanticism despised positive models of self or society. Later on, in the same spirit, existentialists held that human beings could make their own selves by choosing themselves. Freedom from determination and freedom to choose one's own self had no durable content to speak of. In the end, indetermination was not far removed from nihilism. Nihilists concluded that new selves and new societies were groundless entities. These entities were born out of nothing and subject to the rule of nothing.

Pragmatism

Just as Romanticism and its multitude of successor philosophies posed a radical challenge to the concept of classical nature in Europe, Pragmatism did the same in the United States. In America the great critic of the idea of Platonic nature was John Dewey. In 1919, in *Reconstruction in Philosophy*, he outlined a commanding, and in many respects a brilliant, case against Platonism. He was ceaseless and persuasive in his criticism. He argued for the shift of philosophical attention from the eternal and the universal to the changing and the specific (47). Everything, he remarked, must present its birth certificate (48). What is important to self and society is not their durability but their possibility. We therefore need to pay attention to what is possible, which is to say, to what is contingent—and not to what is constant. Specifically, we cannot put our trust in a limited number of fixed forms—the alleged heart of Platonic nature (54). Platonism is the outlook of a closed world with fixed boundaries, Dewey argued. An open world—which is one of the defining characteristics of modernity—does not have immutable limits. It is always in transition even across boundaries.

Anyone living in 'modern' times is acutely aware that their world is a world that is fascinated by ideologies of transformation and change. Such ideologies assume that truth is temporal, truth judgments are temporary, and nature is transitory. What is true today is not necessarily true tomorrow. Truth is a conjecture waiting to be refuted. It will be refuted by the 'changing nature' of the world, and not least by the changing nature of nature. 'Circumstances have changed,' as politicians like to say. Likewise truth is mobile. Whatever is legitimate or right is legitimate or right 'here,' in 'our' country, but not necessarily 'there,' somewhere else, in someone else's country. Time affects judgment differently from space. Someone 'here' cannot judge someone 'there.' Usually, this applies in reverse as well. The 'hope' for something 'tomorrow,' on the other hand, makes it right, while the 'memory' of something 'yesterday' is often a 'bad' memory. Both the truth that looks forward in time and the truth that looks backward in time is subjective psychological truth. It is the truth of ever-changing moods.

Transitions both in time and space alter what is true. Thus we cannot 'impose' our values on another nation or culture. So runs an argument that has persisted through endless reinventions from early Romanticism to Postmodernism, Existentialism to Nihilism and beyond. Of course, the terms of this argument are tautological. For only in a world where values are 'local' is an 'imposition' of this kind conceivable. Yet, and here is a cruel irony, a contingent world of ceaseless transformation is indeed by definition open. It is not 'limited' as (allegedly) the Platonic world is. Yet this also means that 'local' truth judgments, as well as being local, can be projected across borders and generations. They invariably seep into the distance of space and the future of time. Romantics and their inheritors feel discomfort about the implicit universality of this, at the same time as they gain comfort from the fact that there are societies and selves that are open and not closed to change. This results in a vicious circle: We 'ought not' impose on others because we think our culture is contingent because we think that modern society is open because it does not respect limits which means that we do impose on others because we cannot do otherwise because we cannot abide limits. The only way of not being torn apart by the viciousness of this logical circle is to suppose that there is (one) enduring truth and that enduring truth is change. Change is the one constant and the only universal. Everyone must bow down before the strange self-refuting God of mutability. In a world of change, forever can only mean one thing: forever restless, forever contingent. The self that is born in time must remain trapped there. There is no contemplative timelessness outside of time. There are no spatial limits at which we can come to rest, at which time passes into paradox—and ends. There is no a-temporal realm.[9]

John Dewey was no caricaturist. He put the case of his Platonic opponents as well as any critic can. Mere flux, the Platonist observed, starts at no definite point, arrives at nothing, and amounts to nothing (57). Dewey replied that a form leads only to a defined, fixed or repetitious outcome—like an acorn that grows into an oak tree. Form, he insisted, was the emblem of a hierarchical universe where everything has a place and keeps its place. The Pragmatist—like the Romantic, the Existentialist and the Nihilist—believes that there are no limits (60–61). Accordingly, the Pragmatist cannot and does not try to define or delimit something that remains constant *in* change, but rather describes a constant order *of* change. The evisceration of limits means that the world, or at least the 'modern' world, is infinite. This means that there is no conceivable end to things. Nothing can be finished, let alone can be perfect or perfectible in this world. Ends are only 'ends in view.' Once they are achieved they are immediately superseded. The products of Platonic nature, in contrast, are stereotyped (68). The artisan—or in contemporary terms the designer—who copies forms makes essentially the same thing time and time again. Repetition rules the artisan's or the designer's behavior. Where Platonic nature is dominant, there is no progress, no development, and no experimentation—for perfection is perfect. To break free of Platonic nature means to gain the freedom to conceive new ends and aims that are not fixed in advance by immutable forms (68–72). The Greeks, with whom Dewey did battle, observed that such a world without form or limits is incipiently anarchic. Being everything (potentially), it is nothing (in reality). Being unformed, it is chaotic. On this has turned modernity's great culture war. Pragmatists and romantics, existentialists and nihilists agree on one thing: limits are to be defied. Limits are suffocating, as Dewey put it (66).

For the Pragmatist, change, becoming, and perishing rate higher than stability, permanence, and constancy. In the Platonic view, constancy is a defense against the erosion of meaning by what is momentary, fleeting, and transient. The Platonist and the Pragmatist have a different theory of the source of social and existential meaning. In one case, meaning derives from constancy in change; in the other case meaning derives from change. For the Pragmatist, constancy is a stodgy value. In contrast, the Platonist advises us to pay less attention to flux and alteration, and concentrate on discovering the permanent or durable forms that limit and shape the processes that alter in time. Platonism is based on the idea of pure knowing. Against such 'theoretical' knowledge, Dewey countered with the idea of 'practical' knowledge. Practical knowledge is the kind of knowing that depends on changes in things or that induces change in them (108–109). Practical knowledge, Dewey quipped, is the power to transform the world (112).

Modern detractors claim that pure knowing is old hat. Modern science, Dewey insisted, no longer tries to find some form behind each process of change (113). More sympathetically, though, Dewey observed that pure knowing was an idea that was fundamentally connected with aesthetic enjoyment and appreciation (115–116). It arose in a world—that of Greek antiquity—where the environment was beautiful and life was serene. Thus, the really fruitful application of pure knowing, or contemplative knowledge, is not in science but in the field of aesthetics.[10] Indeed, Dewey remarked, it is hard to imagine any high development of the arts except where there is a curious and loving interest in forms (126). There is an irony in this. Amongst the best, most vivid, passages in Dewey's body of work are those where he writes about art. The clear thrust of the corpus of his writing is to reject the Platonic Greeks. Yet he does respect them, and wherever he writes about art he betrays a desire for them as well. This is evident in Dewey's best book, *Art as Experience* (1934), where the importance of form in art is described consummately. While Dewey pointedly resists the Platonic conclusion that form persists through change, he nonetheless paints a metaphysical picture of art as a union of opposites.[11]

In *Art as Experience*, Dewey depicts art as the function of organized relations—pushes and pulls, contractions and expansions, lightness and weight, rising and falling (134). 'Polarity, or opposition of energies, is everywhere necessary to the definition, the delimitation, that resolves an otherwise uniform mass and expanse into individual forms.' The art of painting, for instance, is characterized by relations between complementary colors, foreground and background, central and peripheral objects, light and dark, up and down, forwards and backwards (157). Form organizes these polar energies such that they are balanced, and can be grasped as a perceptual whole (134). Dewey also observes that the rhythms of nature—alternating dawn and sunset, day and night, rain and sunshine—set the tone for art. Yet, for all of that, Dewey still insists that such patterns, whether of nature or art, are a type of order realized in change (150, 154). Pattern, form and shape are the 'ordered variation of change' (154). He firmly rejects the idea that 'the general is constituted by the existence of fixed kinds of things' or that there is something metaphysically anterior to all experience (286). The metaphysician, in contrast, supposes that the most important kinds of variation and change, as for example the alteration of light and dark, are a function of metaphysical universals such as rhythm and contrast. These universals are constant and they serve to organize relations. In doing so, they create meaning out of the material mass of the universe. They order change, rather than create an order 'of' change.

Dewey's follower, Richard Rorty, talked admiringly about how art, in the period from the Romantics through Nietzsche to Heidegger, was turned into the empire of anti-metaphysical poets hostile to Platonic presuppositions.[12] In the second coming of Dewey, Dewey's part-concessions to the world of forms disappear. Art in the anti-metaphysical mode is a medium of contingency. Anti-metaphysical artists use language to register 'difference.' They do this by the act of 're-describing' things—intimating a sense of Being that is forever un-homely, perpetually on the road to nowhere, caught in the ironic 'state' of 'flux.' Art introduces inventive 'metaphors' and new 'vocabularies' whose job is to mediate existential and social transitions. This is the art of a 'trans-formational world.' In contrast to this, Dewey's feeling for art, which is Greek in spirit, is not at all Romantic. One cannot see Dewey placing much faith in expanding the repertoire of 'alternative descriptions.' Yet, about all other essentials, Dewey and Rorty were in agreement. They equated freedom and contingency. They rejected the idea that there is a trans-historical, meta-social nature. On that rejection, everything turns. Rorty put it thus: there is nothing which stands to my community as my community stands to me.[13] There is no larger community that has a universal nature. Community is a contingent human artifact. It grows up according to the vicissitudes of time and chance. The argument of the Pragmatist thus begins and ends with the supposition that there is no permanent a-historical context of human life, no universal conditions of human existence, and no stamp impressed on us all.[14]

The Commons

The Platonist, of course, begs to differ. There is no doubt that the world, especially in 'modern times,' has much about it that is contingent. Those who have lived during the period since the end of the eighteenth century, with its accelerating pace of change, are acutely aware of the power of contingency. On the surface of things, little appears to be stable or fixed. Yet, underneath the surface of intensive change, there are some things that do not change. Even more importantly, the things that do not change make possible many of the things that do change, especially the most important things that are produced by the most modern—vertiginous and explosive—processes of change. The things and events that we value most, the greatest riches amongst the enormous wealth that we produce, are anchored in something deeper than mere change, variety or novelty. The Platonist supposes that change is always premised on the existence of permanent or durable forms. We anchor ourselves in the middle of the flux of life by observing and interpolating these forms. We create things and events of lasting significance by adapting and following these forms.

Form, shape and pattern are what endow things and events in the world with meaning or significance. Patterns repeat themselves. Thus, by their very nature, patterns are durable. But we also see patterns emerge in time. Natural history, social history, and individual biographies are all repositories of new patterns. But this is newness with a twist. For the patterns that emerge in time also resist time. This is because their emergence into the world is mediated by more basic forms. These elementary forms, or form-generating media, create shape and pattern in a primary sense. There are forms that emerge and disappear in time—and forms that are unchanging. The forms that appear and disappear in time have durability but not the kind of durability that distinguishes the elemental forms that are the building blocks of all other forms.[15]

As the biophysicist Alfred Locker put it, each temporal fragment of the world has a super-temporal aspect.[16] If this was not so, then time itself would be inconceivable. Time can only 'begin' because it already exists.[17] This is the paradox of the 'big bang.' Time can only exist prior to the beginning of time because it exists both in time and out of time. Time exists out of time as a Platonic form, as the super-sensible idea of time. Genesis, ontogenesis, phylogenesis, time series, progress, change, development, and evolution—all of these owe something to the super-temporal concept of time. Conversely, a-temporality is deeply implicated in the sphere of time. Every act or event in time has a super-temporal aspect. Platonic nature, contra Dewey, is not a matter of 'fixed' form. It does not endlessly repeat the same cycles of nature—like the growth of the acorn into the oak tree. This image of growth from seed to tree comes from Aristotle—or else from Goethe. At any rate, it is not Platonic.

It is true that super-temporal forms—be they the forms of goodness and justice or the idea of the carpenter's bed or the dog—are invariant. This proposition makes moderns skittish. Of all of the objections to the notion of forms, the most persistent one is the belief that invariance cannot account for creativity. Since the age of Romanticism, creativity has been the rock upon which the idea of Platonic nature has been regularly crushed. For Plato, and for most theories of art until the advent of Romanticism, creativity was a kind of copying. It was a mimesis. Artists copied nature's forms. Scientists discovered things in nature. Romanticism spurned these notions. Copying, imitation or mimesis could not, it was claimed, account for new and original works or for the evolution of natural history. Yet for all of its presumption, the anti-Platonic account in practice tells us little about where the new, the original, the evolutionary leap, the revolutionary event, or even the memorable reform comes from. The idea that they emerge out of nothingness, that they are an effect of indeterminate freedom, is literally an empty answer to the question. Chance (as, for example, in the chance mutations of evolution) is hardly a more satisfactory answer.

So can we then say in contradistinction that social actors, like artists or citizens, who compose things, do so by imitating the eternal forms of goodness and justice? The reasonable objection to this is that a just act or a good person in Plato's time and society is not necessarily the same as a just act or a good person today in our time or society. The counter to this objection is that the idea of justice or goodness is permanent but the way we 'copy' it, our mimetic relationship to it, varies. This reconciles what is permanent and what is contingent. One additional point, though, is worth making. If you look closely at Plato you find that whenever he talks about the forms of justice or goodness he routinely describes them in terms of more elementary forms or form-generating media—most commonly proportion, rhythm and harmony. Thus, the good soul is proportionate and balanced—the just state likewise. The Greeks already knew that justice and goodness varied between societies and times. What they also grasped was that there were some things that were still common to all societies, and that could be appealed to across all times.

We can see this by looking at the Pragmatists' own country, America. It is obvious that the United States is much more than a self-referential community preoccupied with its own contingency. At its core is a written constitution that was designed to persist through time and whose purpose is to institute a 'balance' of powers. For all of its flexibility and variability, this arrangement was built on deep continuities across time and space. These were inherited from the past, and it was assumed by the American Founders, correctly, that these continuities would persist far into the future. For all of its specific features, America's constitutional balance echoes a long history of schemes devoted to constitutional balance. These include England's unwritten constitution, the Venetian Republic, the Roman Republic, and fifth-century Athens. The idea of 'balance' is continuous. How the idea is used varies.

The Pattern of Nature

Commonplace examples illustrate the elegant dialectic of constancy and change. Take the case of the Platonic dog—or the Platonic bed. Each contingent bed or dog approximates these invariant forms. But what puts invariance into an invariant form? It is the same thing that makes a form, a form. The invariant bed has qualities that are realized, imperfectly, in reality. It has 'the fit' that we expect of a made object. It fits the horizontal human body, the room it is located in, the build, age and health of the person who sleeps on it, and so on. As with all forms it scales to fit the world. The artisan or manufacturer who makes it intuits, in better or worse ways, the ratios that make things fit. Sometimes we end up with beautiful beds, sometimes with ugly ones. The same is true of societies and souls.

But what then are we to make of the case of the dog? There is no artisan or legislator that makes a dog, though breeders do have a significant hand in shaping the characteristics of dogs including their temperament and build. Sometimes this work is beautiful and sometimes it is ugly. But forget domestication—on a more basic level animals have form, and they scale as well. It was the great zoological morphologist D'Arcy Thompson (1961/1917) who observed the regularities underlying the proliferation of animal species. He noted how all species, in fact all things that are living or lifeless in nature, solve a common problem. In nature, energy acts on matter to move it. Form is what results when these forces reach some kind of balance or equilibrium. When that happens, living and lifeless things take on a shape or pattern (10–11). Many of the same forms are seen in many different species. These are forms like cells, webs, skeletons, shells, membranes, crystals, and spirals. Even more abstract forms, like surfaces and flows, symmetries and hierarchies, equilibriums and rhythms play a crucial role in the emergence of the elegant and powerful forms of animated nature. A relatively small number of forms and form-generating media recur across the vast panorama of species.

Whatever role contingency, in the guise of chance mutation, plays in the natural history of these species, Platonic qualities like ratio and proportion—scaling in other words—also play a major role. D'Arcy Thompson cites many examples of the way species undergo transformation from one to another through the re-scaling of their dimensions (268–325). He projected the figures of species onto a two-dimensional Cartesian planar grid, and showed how, by changing the length and breadth coordinates of the grid, similarities between species become startling apparent. *Oithona nana* (a crustacean) morphs into *Sapphirina*, the *Polyprion* (a fish) into *Pseudopriacanthus altus*, and so on. The same kind of topological similitude is evident when he compares the skull of the chimpanzee and the skull of the baboon, the metacarpal bone of the ox, sheep and giraffe, and the pelvis of the *Stegosauras* and the *Camptosaurus*—and so forth. As Thompson changes the ratio of two-dimensional length and breadth, we can see the shape of one species visibly morph into the shape of another species. The key to species being is not difference but similitude.

Ludwig von Bertalanffy made a point similar to that of Thomson's precept that, in nature, energy acts on matter to move it—and that form is what results when these forces reach some kind of balance or equilibrium. There are two ways that any systemic arrangement forms. It can do so through rules and directive hierarchies—or alternatively through self-organizing order.[19] Rules and directive hierarchies require permissions and authorities in order to function, and the systems that they organize suffer entropy eventually. Self-organizing order in contrast is abstract and intuitive. It relies not on permissions and authorities but on aesthetic-mathematical-geometric principles such as balance, homology, oscillation, proportion, and symmetry.[18] Alfred Locker, who was one of Bertalanffy's first students, and who went a step further, questioned the attribute of 'self' in self-organization. It is not that systems cannot, or do not, attain automaticity or self-regulation. In a way, automaticity is the stand out characteristic of sophisticated systems. They arrange themselves—beautifully. Self-organization is a useful concept from that point of view. But the residually Romantic notion that systems are autarchic is much more questionable, and indeed something removed from Bertalanffy's own understanding of systems. Bertalanffy always emphasized the interchange between system and environment. Locker made more explicit the objections to the idea that systems are self-referential. Where Niklas Luhmann smuggled into system theory the Romantic preoccupation with self-reference, Locker did the opposite.[20] He understood the narcissistic propensity of Romantic theories, and took issue with the notion that either systems in general or species in particular are self-generating. He hypothesized that nothing arises by itself. He was critical of Romantic models of self-referential or immanent causality. He also pointed out the paradoxes that surround the notion of origin.[21]

Theorists in the Romantic slipstream are fascinated by the concept of origins, yet they also treat the concept naively and ignore its profound ambiguities. Whenever we try to speak of an origin, Locker noted, we find that the concept is fraught with paradox.[22] Take the case of Rousseau's 'origin of language.' Locker observed that language always seems to fail whenever we seize upon the theme of the origin of language itself. This is because language as a means for expressing something always presupposes itself as that which is to be expressed. The Romantic equation of producer (language) and product (language) substitutes an explanation of creation with a sleight-of-hand. Locker noted in effect that autopoiesis could not be obtained by circular or self-referential relations alone. He suggested that similar paradoxes and problems also surrounded the notion of evolution. Take as an example Darwin's theory of the 'origin of the species.' Darwin's deterministic explanations of evolution are curiously weak. The idea of the random mutation of species has to carry much more explanatory weight than it can ever really bear. The same applies to evolutionary explanations that rely on notions of uncaused causality, notably the adaptation of species to their environment. The human being who adapts does so via reflexive teleological causality, anticipating that if an adaptation is not made, then bad things will happen. Knowing that the animal is not a planning creature, animal adaptation is often treated simply as being spontaneous, that is to say, uncaused. One might even say, 'miraculously' the animal species that adapts saves itself from extinction. Morphological explanations in contrast suppose that organisms continually shape themselves, because nature is a shaping process, and, as conditions change, that constant morphological causality yields adaptations, and sometimes radical ones. The half-hearted compromise between deterministic and non-deterministic schemas of explanation—represented by the theory of natural selection—is no better. Darwinian evolutionary mutation and adaptation are true on some level, but they also beg more questions than they answer. They are not so much wrong as unsatisfying. They are a portrait quarter drawn.

It may well be that the creatures who are most adapted to an environment (those who are most fitted to it) are the ones that will survive. It may also be true that mutation produces traits that enhance a species adaptation or fit to the environment. But that begs the question: what is fit? Even if we suppose that the fittest survive, what does it mean to fit an environment? The morphologist explains fit in terms of metamorphosis, the scaling of forms.[23] Contemporary defenders of Darwin always assume that every critic of evolutionary epistemologies believes that there is a 'designer' (aka 'artisan') of creation, working out new product designs on a celestial whiteboard. David Hume long ago dismissed this notion in one sentence. He wondered aloud whether anyone had recently looked at the work of artisans and noticed how awful and botched much of their work is. Do we really suppose that nature is like this?

A theory that is critical of the concept of 'origins' does not necessarily imply either that nature in general or species in particular are 'designed' in the anthropomorphic ('shaping by humankind,' 'shaping by the divine artisan') sense of that word. Yet, on the other hand, to say that anthropomorphic accounts of creation are facile does not lend credence to any particular non-anthropomorphic theory of biological creation, for example Darwinism. To say that X is wrong does not mean that Y is correct. Morphological and morphogenetic accounts of biology arguably may explain more about 'fit' than does the theory of natural selection. Fit, after all, is a morphological concept. It is a reasonable supposition that random mutations play a part in morphogenetic processes, but it is also a very restrictive hypothesis to say that they play the only or the principal part. Nature, *phusis*, is shaping. There is no compelling reason to suppose that shaping that is both a mutation and that occurs randomly is the only kind of shaping that generates advantageous and inheritable traits in organisms. This is not credible. The theory of natural selection may preclude theories of divine artisanship but at the theoretical cost of excluding multiple kinds of theoretical hypotheses and research programs that focus on regular, non-random morphological processes of creation. When so many dazzling minds—from Plato through Aristotle and da Vinci to Goethe—were drawn to observe the workings of order, pattern and form in nature, it is not evident that chance causation, no matter how fashionable it became in restricted twentieth-century avant-garde artistic circles, is really more than an incidental explanatory principle for nature. As Einstein quipped, God does not play dice with the universe.[24]

Let us call the morphologist a Platonist. That's a metaphor. We need not take it literally. All that it says is that nature, *phusis*, is shaping. Shaping is a paradox. When bees all of a sudden 'swarm' (cluster), we observe a minute regular act of creation. Sometimes acts of creation are contingent, irregular and without precedent, yet, paradoxically, there is a precedent for all of them—for the shapes that creation takes (e.g. clustering) precede the act of creation, and all forms that emerge in time draw on patterns that exist outside of time. All that the Platonic critique of origins in effect says is that all non-paradoxical propositions about origins are fatal.[25] The mistake of the Romantics and their successors was to talk in a straight-faced way about origins as if it was a concept free of ambiguity. It is not. Origin is a paradox. It is the point of intersection between the a-temporal and the temporal. In creation both are in play simultaneously. Viewed in this way, it is difficult to be certain whether 'the act of discovery' is a matter of finding something that 'already exists' or whether it is a bringing into the world of something that otherwise 'does not exist.' If something is 'original' does it mean that it is 'new' or does it mean that it represents a 'return' to something pre-existing and more fundamental? In the act of creation, originality seems to mean both of these things at the same time, and this is reflected in the way all social actors (even Darwinians in their everyday life) use words like 'discovery' or 'originality.' These words encapsulate the tensions and ambivalences of the process of creation. The greatest ambivalence of all is the compounding of time and timelessness in the act of creation.

One of the corollaries of this line of thinking is that we very easily put too much emphasis on the role of intention and deliberation in creation. It is evident that creation in the physical and biological domain is not conscious in the way that existential and social creation is. Yet, even in respect of the strictly human domain, we can and do too easily overstress the deliberative, intentional, and judgmental aspect of creation. As Locker (1981) observed: self-reference simply cannot explain or found autopoiesis. Creative action is not the act of sitting down and 'planning' to produce something 'new' or something 'different' or something 'novel' with an 'end in view.' Likewise, the act of creation should not be confused with either judgment or criticism. Deliberation, judgment and criticism are all 'analytical' categories. They draw distinctions and mark out differences in order to make selections. They all discriminate. The act of creation, in contrast, is 'synthetic.' It composes and forms through acts of combination, mixing, blending, amalgamation, and the like. This includes the union of what is durable in time and what exists outside of time. Such synthesis relies on non-deliberative faculties. The most important of these is the faculty of intuition. Intuition is the apprehension of similitude and other kinds of synthetic qualities that draw together things (agents, events, forces) that otherwise would be set apart.

One of the peculiarities of human beings is that they are conscious of what they do. Their intentionality and reflexivity stands in contrast to the species represented in D'Arcy Thompson's zoological domain. The other notable peculiarity of human beings is that they inhabit a second, artificial nature. This is a constructed nature—a product of human making. Yet, not withstanding either human intention or reflection or the construction of human artifice, the push to create in the human domain still relies on many of the forms that are already familiar in first nature. Forms common to first and second nature include symmetry, proportionality, contrast, rhythm, balance, skeletons and backbones, nets and webs, clusters, flocks and clumps, tiling, tripartite structures, and hierarchies.

Whether nature is human nature or inhuman nature, that is to say whether nature is reflective and conscious or not, elemental pattern forms are not created by acts of deliberation or will. They are not designed purposively or teleologically. Both individuals and societies make many conscious choices and do so in response to contingencies. They judge and argue, criticize and defend the choices that they make. They do this on a larger and smaller scale. But contingencies and choices, large and small, are framed by patterns that are both transcendent in relation to human beings and immanent in nature. These patterns, in themselves, are not created by intent or deliberation. They are not contingent, and human beings are not always even conscious of the role they play in human action. Many of these pattern forms or pattern media are adapted from first nature. The selections involved in such adaptations may be conscious and purposeful up to a point. But, beyond that point, the selections are intuitive, and intuitions are carried on below the threshold of consciousness.

This is not to deny that human beings are reflective, intentional and discursive beings. They are that. Human beings give reasons for choosing one course of action as opposed to another. However reasoning and discourse, like judgment and criticism, have a limited capacity to 'fit' action into larger meaning-generating patterns—that is, to fit behavior into metaphysical frames. What is being drawn here is a strong distinction between intuition and discursive reasoning. Discourse is explicit and reflexive; intuition is tacit and difficult to articulate. Both are 'conscious,' but conscious in different ways. Intuition or *nous* is not conscious in the way that speech or *logos* is. Often we *feel* what we intuit, more than we *articulate* it, and when we articulate it, we do so by appositional conjunctions rather than discursive elaborations. This is the basis of mystical or post-rational forms of understanding.[26] The mystical mode of knowing is a way of accessing the super-temporal.[27] Intuition recognizes and deploys patterns. At its highest level, it produces patterns out of (deeper) patterns. Discursive reason relies on intuition for its starting point. Our discourse and our descriptions, our arguments and narrations 'give voice' to what is essentially the non-linguistic nature of patterns. The gap between intuition and articulation is never easily bridged.

The bridging problem is compounded because patterns do not have a particular sensory expression. They are not in the first instance visual or auditory or tactile. They are the invisible behind the visible, the silent dimension of sound, and the implied choreography of kinetic movement. The closest to a sensory metaphor used to describe intuitive patterns is 'figurative.' A figure is something like a kind of sketch. But a figure, while it hints at something sensuous, is primarily order and arrangement. The key thing about such order and arrangement is that it is not deliberate or calculated. This is so in the sense that nobody sits down and invents a shell or a spiral, a web or backbone, a hierarchy or symmetry. We do, though, endlessly and tacitly, and sometimes explicitly, draw on these forms to solve problems. Take one simple example: the great developments in communication technology in the late twentieth century that saw the emergence of the Internet. These developments were built on structural principles of webs, backbones, hierarchies, and the like. Nobody invented these forms. They were applied, and it was their application that led to the discovery of a new technology.

Similitude

What exactly is meant by 'applying' a form? Let us say that an engineer begins with a puzzle: 'what kind of communication system would most resist a nuclear attack?' The puzzle is solved with an intuition: 'one that is organized *like a web*.' How so? If part of the web is destroyed in an attack, messages can be re-routed through other parts of the web and will still reach their destination. A web has multiple connecting parts. '*Like a web*' is the kind of similitude typical of pattern thinking or intuition—or intelligence for short. In other words, creation is much more a function of similitude than of difference. A recurrent and key aspect of new things that come into the world is that they have a similitude with things, or rather with a pattern of things, already in the world. Similitude does not mean that they are identical with what exists. A spider web and a communication web are not the same. But they are analogous. Analogy turns things that are unlike into things that are alike. The most powerful analogies are paradoxes while patterns or forms are commonplace bases for making analogies.

The highest kinds of human intelligence show a remarkable capacity to identify similitude when others do not see it. This is most likely because pattern recognition lies at the center of human intelligence. The most interesting recent informed speculation in neuroscience, a notoriously difficult area, suggests that patterns are the fundamental media of intelligence.[28] Sense organs provide aural, visual and tactile inputs. But all that the brain knows is patterns. Describing this is difficult because the higher reaches of the neo cortex, the domain of intuition, resists linguistic description. Ludwig Wittgenstein talked about it as the domain of a paradoxical picture language—and about throwing away the ladder of language altogether. Others, like Castoriadis, have called it the domain of 'figuration.' Castoriadis was at pains to separate 'figure' from any sensory analogy, though.[29] Figures of the imagination are not visual or auditory, he insisted. The technologist Jeff Hawkins, likewise, dislikes the use of sensory analogies in explaining intelligence. He argues that there are no pictures in the visual areas of the human brain for there is no light inside your head, just brain activity firing in patterns. Whatever the senses input, this material is turned into shapes.[30]

The terminology of shape, patterns, pictures, and figures varies—but all point in the same general direction. Our knowledge of the world rests on configurations. It will probably be a long time before we can be confident about how this process really works. It is enough for the moment to simply say that we model the world. This allows us, amongst other things, to anticipate, plan and predict. But one should not assume that 'planning' is a good analogy for understanding how high-level cognitive modeling works. Planning and prediction are responses to the contingency of the world. The irony, though, is that we respond well to this variability when we have ample stocks of invariant representations of the world.

Our 'figures' of dogs and beds, monarchies and revolutions are generally stable. While there is a high degree of neuronal change in the lower reaches of the human neo cortex associated with sensory input, in the upper reaches, where patterns are stored in memory, there is relative stability.[31] The brain replicates the dialectic between constancy and change. Our senses register endless transitions. Our neo cortex, though, provides patterned or invariant representations of this variable world, so that order emerges out of the flux of experience. The store of patterns in human memory allows us to recognize things that are alike. Thus we recognize each contingent instance of a dog or a bed, a monarchy or a revolution as particular examples of an invariant form.

The Pattern of Patterns

How do these patterns come into existence? The Romantic view is that they come out of nothing. But, as we have seen, nothing arises by itself. The contrary view is that some patterns are built into the fabric of the universe. When we ask the question—'where do that patterns come from?'—one answer is that they constitute the a-temporal realm of creation. That is to say, they 'exist,' rather than that they 'come into existence.' They are 'being' rather than 'becoming.' They possess no birth certificate. They are what the ancient Greeks called *phusis* or the Christian Platonists called *God*.

Contemporary science suggests that the cosmos is built on a foundational super-symmetry of tube-like strings.[32] At the 'beginning' of the universe, as it is currently understood, these strings vibrated in ten and twenty-six dimensional space. They stretched and deformed but retained a perfect symmetry until tension finally broke their super-symmetrical pattern. It is this 'symmetry break' that led to the creation of the 'familiar' cosmos. Until the early twentieth century, the familiar universe was thought of in the same terms as Plato's three-dimensional universe. Then modern geometry, parting company with the flat-surface geometry of Plato and Euclid, began to 'envisage' an n-dimensional universe, beginning with Einstein's four-dimensions of space-time. When we look (say) at the case of the birth of modern art, we find artists copying four and higher dimensional space even when they retailed art ideologies that said that artists did not copy anything. Mimesis it turns out is just as powerful in the post-Euclidean age as it was in the Euclidean age.

Human beings, in a limited sense, are designers. They plan, intend, and reflect in time on their creations. One of the reasons for this is that the neurological structure of the human being is open. It is open in a very specific sense. Many of the invariant patterns that the human mind recognizes are not stored in the neo cortex but in the external environment—including in the artificial environment that human beings in society create for themselves. The most important of such environments from a cognitive point of view is the city.[33] The city, like the neo cortex, is a pattern machine. It is like the mind's prosthetic extension. Human beings thus copy nature in two senses. They copy the patterns of cosmic nature and artificial nature. Doubtless the latter owes much to the former but it is pointless to pursue the question of cosmos vs. artifice very far. What is important is simply that there are patterns in both cosmological and artificial nature. Creative, intelligent, curious human beings do interesting things with the patterns that they discover or encounter in both first and second nature. For example, Pythagoras' investigations of vibrating strings—the earliest string theory we know of—led to the discovery of harmonic ratios around which much of subsequent Western architecture was structured.

Patterns themselves have an interesting structure. They are composed of antitheses. Patterns unite light and shade, large and small, soft and hard, flow and obstacle, and so on. They unite what is unlike, indeed what is opposite. They do this because of the deeper substratum of form-generating media. While there is a significant range of such media, they are also remarkably recurrent across physical, biological and social nature, whether we are talking of the clustering of galaxies and industries, or the osculating patterns of lattice, hierarchy, and branching systems. As the genetist Sean B. Carroll notes, 'modularity, symmetry and polarity are nearly universal features of animal design.' [34] The same is also true of human architecture. The peculiar power of these media is to act as cement—the kiss or osculation—that binds unlike things. They create similitude where similitude did not exist or was not recognized. Creation is best described not as the generation of differences but rather in terms of the classical idea of *discordia concors*—unity in diversity. The act of creation (in the sense of the act of pattern formation) makes opposites agree and turns contradictions into antinomies. Pattern is a matter of agreement in things that are unlike—such as life and death. 'Courage is almost a contradiction in terms. It means a strong desire to live taking the form of a readiness to die.' Chesterton's paradox is powerful not because it is true, although it is that, but rather because the concepts of life and death are transformed in it from opposition to apposition. This is typical of creative thought—or as Neils Bohr put it: 'The opposite of a correct statement is a false statement. But the opposite of a profound truth may well be another profound truth.' When Bohr recognized patterns in nature, he recognized not just a wave and not just a particle pattern, but the paradoxical quantum wave-particle pattern. Similarly, Einstein's breakthrough came with his unification of space-time and matter-energy. Metaphor, irony, paradox, pun, and antithesis are ways in which intuition's conciliation of warring opposites finds expression in language. This expression is not discursive. It is not a demonstration of a correct statement. It is not an argument. Metaphor, irony, paradox, pun, and antithesis convey not truth but the architectonic symmetry and union of competing truths. They turn linguistic war into conceptual alliance.

Society and Nature

The balancing of contradictory concepts and truths is not a static condition. There is an inherent dynamism in making what is unlike into a likeness or similitude. This kind of wit—or whatever in physical and biological nature is the equivalent of this force of connection—is productive. Wit and paradox are propulsive. The classical notion of *discordia concors*, which has its roots in the pre-Socratic and Pythagorean-Platonic union of opposites, is an indicator that there is nothing static about Platonic nature. Platonism is not the world view of a closed world or a fixed society. The Platonic idea of nature respects limits. Limits, after all, are inherent in the notions of form, pattern and shape. But we should not infer from the notion of limits the absence of dynamism or even necessarily the presence of finality. There are many kinds of porous boundaries. Membranes—like strings—are one of the forms of nature. The most dynamic systems we know have boundaries but these are permeable. These boundaries are both limits and passages. Thus limits do not necessarily mean closure—just as the idea of classical nature is not necessarily a warrant for the social status quo either. Nature, even if conditioned by the a-temporal, does not imply a static condition. Greece and Rome were neither closed nor static societies. Indeed for centuries, nature, the law of nature, and the beauty of nature were equally appealed to in the defense of and in opposition to the laws of society and the commands of rulers.

Nature in the classical sense—conditioned by the a-temporal—was never ever just 'for' society or 'against' society. Rather, the inquiry into nature in a Platonic sense is a way of asking the question of what is durable in society and what is disposable? What is assumed is that durability, the paradoxical meeting point of the temporal and the a-temporal, matters. There is no doubt that breathlessly changeable opinion in politics, information in economics, and innovation in technology dazzles. Yet, as captivating as these things are, we need to remind ourselves that the most important acts of politics, economics or technology are built on deep structures that stretch over decades, centuries, even millennia—and that hint at what is imperishable and forever lasting and outside of time. *These transcendent structures do not proceed from deliberate will. Yet they are most evident in the freest of human societies.*[35] This is perhaps a reminder to us that human will and deliberation are frequently sources of tyranny and arbitrariness whereas the most satisfying of human experiences, not least of all the aesthetic experience, comes with the human being's intuitive recognition of—and adaptation—to patterned order.

Take for example the case of contemporary information technology. It is a protean medium for the instant delivery of opinion and information. Nothing would seem to be more of a vehicle for disposable punditry than interactive digital media such as weblogs. Nothing better signals the human hunger for information than 'real time' database-driven web pages. 'As soon as possible' is the ethos of the users of this technology. Yet information technology also has deep structures that are as important in defining it as the contingent flux of the daily posting of data or opinion to the web. We need to understand not only how a society generates contingent representations of itself in its news and data flows, but also how it creates invariant representations in the midst of these torrential run offs.

It is folly to take too much notice of flux. Human beings are all too readily seduced by comment and news. Scandal and crisis are absorbing, even addictive. But these are also usually overblown, full of distortion, and frequently hysterical. The soundness of opinion is rarely commensurate with either its immediacy or its volume. The sheer quantities of information and opinion should tell us something. For the most distinguishing thing about human intelligence is that it is economical. It is 'sketchy'—and, because of this, it is powerful. Intuitions are simple. They may sometimes be radical but they are also always terse. Accumulating data or broadcasting opinions has much less consequence than we often think. Unless data and opinion are accompanied by the kind of curt conceits, paradoxes, and metaphors that pattern recognition generates, they behave like noise on a telephone line. They are a distraction and a waste of time.

Doubtless information and opinion are accompanied by implicit claims to truth or rightness that can be tested in argument. Up to a point claims to truth or rightness can be discursively grounded in rational argument. But the brusque conceit that marries two seemingly incongruous representations (be it of sensations, beliefs or trends) is much more important than any 'logical' attempts to argue the truth or rightness of statements. We do sometimes learn things in arguments but it is not arguments that resolve debates or move self and society forward. It is acts of analogical and paradoxical intuition that do this. The universal pragmatic model of 'unlimited communication' is a mirage.[36] We can talk about and we can debate a decision, and even do this under the most 'ideal' of conditions—and still not produce a good decision. Often decision makers who are sequestered away from each other make much better decisions than those who meet each other (whether it be in the same physical room or in virtual forums) and debate issues. It is the gruff, one-line, shattering 'proof by analogy' that produces the most enlightening decisions, not interminable discussion through endless justification.

Analogies are most powerful when they bring together things that are most unlike each other. The sensations of cold and heat may seem far apart until we start to talk about 'the look of cold fire.' Such analogies are not only forged in words. They can be visual, aural, tactile, and so on. Indeed, word or textual analogies and paradoxes often work only because of underlying rhythmic structures such as iambic pentameter. Strong/weak rhythm is pure contrast. The paradox of it is that *contrast unifies*. Form is the union of contrast.

One way of understanding form, shape or pattern is to think of it as a set of aesthetic qualities—each of which has the capacity of drawing together things that are radically unlike each other. These qualities tempt us to think of things as being alike when we would not otherwise think of them as being even related to one another. Form forges the relation between dissimilar entities. Thus, for example, in modern parliamentary politics, there is an endless stream of views about better laws or more just administration. But great polities at their core have some simple forms that anchor the flow of opinion. 'Balance' is a classic example of such a political form. Often the most astute decisions are made by inspired balancing of competing considerations. Likewise, modern market economies function because of the equilibria of markets. These are constantly made, unmade and remade by untold billions of buyers and sellers. Buyers and sellers establish patterns. They have a strong intuition of equilibrium. The price of fuel may go up, because sellers are temporarily in a commanding position. Buyers will then support schemes to produce cars that are more fuel efficient—thus making a gallon of gasoline go further and re-establishing price equilibrium. Firms that invent a more efficient product will be the most successful in the market place.

Soul and Form

Efficiency is a paradox—the producing of more with less. To explain a paradox is often difficult. Yet human beings intuit such things with ease. This is why many of the most important decisions we make are not prefaced by discussion at all—and why what we say about a thing and what we do about it are often very different.

Human beings talk a lot about what they do, but they also do much silently. This is true of markets, for example. Advertisers bombard consumers with claims about the merits of products. But customers who buy goods from firms are often unmoved by the discursive claims directed at them. Rather they look for intelligible patterns in good design. They like objects that move in elegant ways, things that are good to hold, touch or to look at, or that are efficient to use. The things that inspire a product engineer who designs the goods are no different from what charges a consumer's preference. Economy and elegance, like mathematics and beauty, are closely correlated. Such non-discursive motives are pervasive in human affairs. They are pervasive because they echo something that lies deep in the constitution of the human self. We can think of this deep part of the human self in scientific terms as the deep structure of cognition or in humanistic terms as the movement of the soul.

The inquiry into nature is a way of asking what it is that is durable in the human soul and what is disposable? We can think of the soul as energy-matter animated by form. Form is what gives this energy-matter its significance or meaning. The soul craves meaning. It needs to make sense of itself and its relations with other selves. It does this through forms. Whenever we see a pattern in our own lives or in other lives, we attribute meaning.

Mostly this meaning is pretty trite. We are content that the world is fairly ordered, but we usually don't take much notice of it until something like a traffic accident disrupts the patterns of everyday life. Mostly we are unconscious of it. It is also true that in large part what souls (especially what modern souls) do and encounter is forgettable. In a world of high contingency, this is necessarily so. Most of our relations with others are of necessity thin. But some relations are exceptional. They are exceptional because they are informed by forms. The soul connects with other souls through those forms.[37]

No society can be completely contingent without destroying itself. The same applies to the human self. Contingency supposes negation. 'To be other' requires the negation or cessation or superseding of what is. But negation without some supervening constancy is nihilistic. Human beings need to be able to identify order and coherence in the midst of transition and change. Indeed, that is what human identity is. Order and coherence are closely related to permanence and stability. Human beings build their sense of peer trust, love and friendship on the basis of such qualities. In contrast, a self that is suspicious, wary, and fearful of intimacy lacks a sense of congenial order. The interesting question is how is order created in personal relationships? These may be peer relationships at work—or they may be those closer, deeper, and more intimate relationships of love and friendship. It is well know that everyone has multiple contingent relationships—from transient connections with people we pass in the street to vague acquaintances and neighbors who we are on nodding terms with to colleagues we pass in the corridors of office buildings. The bonds of peer relations, love and friendship are different from these. For they involve obligations and commitments that last. They also create things of significance.

Like great political acts or successful economies or powerful technologies, deep relationships are not contingent. Something that is resistant to flux anchors them. This something is form, shape and pattern. Take the case of love. Two people fall in love. Yet love exists independently of those two people. Their particular love is contingent. But love precedes them and goes on after they are dead or they have parted company. The lovers have their time and it passes. Love however continues unabated. Love, at least as our own contemporaries understand it, has not always existed as a human bond. There are many kinds of sympathy and affection and care that are not love as such but which have long served the human species. Love is a form that emerged in time. But like all forms born in time, it was built out of more elementary and universal forms like harmony and rhythm. A commonplace, in both antiquity and modernity, is the relationship of dance to lovers. The beat of the dance is the constant that stands in contrast to the contingency of lovers—that is to say, in contrast to their chance meetings and their chance lives. Dance manifests the rhythm and harmony of Platonic nature.

The most important, certainly the most long-lasting, and often the freest social institutions that we invent replicate some of the basic forms of nature. This may take the form of the balance of a constitution, the equilibrium of a market economy, the elegant fit of a technological device, the rhythm of the lovers' dance, or the symmetry of friends chatting in a café. These institutions operate in very distinctive ways—and sometimes in very paradoxical ways. One of the most paradoxical aspects of these institutions is that they are shaped by a transcendent nature, and yet they turn out to be the freest of human institutions. This is so because the beauty of pattern media frees human beings from reliance on commands and rules. Such emancipation from instructions and norms is never more than partial, but when and where it occurs human beings find it very satisfying.

The term 'paradox' means parallel opinions. Essentially this is what free institutions do. They function, via the medium of patterns, to take 'opinions' (*doxa*)—human preference, will, intent, desire, ambition and all of the other expressions of human contingency—and turn their rich but often arbitrary diversity into a pleasing unity. 'Out of many, one' was the way that the American Founders described this enterprise. This also describes an act of metaphysics.

This is the same type of act as that which was so beautifully described by John Donne when he wrote about love as the paradoxical 'we in us':

> Call us what you will, we are made such by love;
> Call her one, me another fly,
> We'are tapers too, and at our own cost die,
> And we in us find the'eagle and the dove.
> The phoenix riddle hath more wit
> By us; we two being one, are it.
> So, to one neutral thing both sexes fit,
> We die and rise the same, and prove
> Mysterious by this love.
>   (*The Canonization*)

Part of the function of social institutions is to mark out spaces where paradoxical relationships like love can flourish. Not all societies, and certainly not all institutions, encourage this. Yet some do. So out of them emerge those special spaces and places where the paradoxes and conceits of deep strange enigmatic relations like love are allowed to breath.

Conclusion

In the end, despite attempts to insist that only Romantics can be poets, it turns out that in fact the Platonist is also a poet. We should give up the presumptuous equation of Romanticism with poetry, and the equally dubious assumption that Romanticism trumps metaphysics. Romantic poets have for too long traded on contempt for society dressed up as the worship of contingency. The metaphysical poet has no contempt for society, and yet does not think society is necessarily or always right. Indeed, the metaphysician is aware that the most interesting types of societies are conundrums. They have aspects about them that meld the social and the meta-social together in paradoxical ways. They are based on enigmatic antinomies.

It is unsurprising, then, that John Donne was skeptical of the idea that ordinary social rites, like funerals and burials, can fully or properly accommodate the tensile force of love. Instead, he proposed that it is the 'pretty rooms' of hymns and sonnets that do this work:

> We can die by it, if not live by love,
> And if unfit for tombs and hearse
> Our legend be, it will be fit for verse;
> And if no piece of chronicle we prove,
> We'll build in sonnets pretty rooms;
> As well a well-wrought urn becomes
> The greatest ashes, as half-acre tombs,
> And by these hymns all shall approve
> Us canoniz'd for love;

Another way of thinking about this is the 'odd couplings' of nature. Nature produces unlikely pairs that nonetheless make sense. It unites fast and slow, high and low, black and white, large and small.

If it is indeed true, as Einstein and the Neo-Platonists agreed, that light is the universal constant—then nature is what unites the light absorbent and non-absorbent surface, the transparent glazed tone with the opaque one, high and low saturated colors along with warm and cool ones, and of course darkness and light itself.[38] This is the way that patterns are built up. Fast and slow, high and low, and the rest can be fitted together because of aesthetic principles like proportion, economy, and symmetry.

When we recognize these principles, which we do intuitively, we recognize a pattern. Such patterns 'exist' in physical and biological nature. Human beings, though, not only exhibit such patterns in their behavior, institutions, physical and biological characteristics—they also recognize and create patterns. They have a reflective and intentional relationship to pattern-forms—and also a productive relationship to them. Human beings mimic, adapt, apply, and produce patterns. We are who we are because we think in patterns. We are also who we are because nothing arises by itself. We are who we are because we produce, make, manufacture and create a world to live in whose meanings arise out of a crucible of pattern-forms that we cannot produce, make, manufacture or create.

Notes

1. This statement, a blunt rejection of Romanticism, comes from the theoretical biologist Alfred Locker (1981).
2. The term self-determination, used by Simon Marginson in the second model of imagination, represents one such imperceptible shift—in this case, between freedom and necessity, spontaneity and determination.
3. On the role of switching in the Shakespearean imagination, see P. Murphy (2009).
4. Niklas Luhmann (2000: 265) reminds us that the age of Donne, Cervantes and Shakespeare made extensive use of the art of paradox in order to undermine the distinction between being and non-being, being and appearance. This, Luhmann remarks, was something that science could never dream of. Yet the brilliant physics of the twentieth century—from relativistic to quantum to string theory—suggests the very converse. On the role of paradox in the age in Shakespeare and company, see Colie, 1966.
5. On the dialectic of romanticism and classicism in the modern age, see P. Murphy and D. Roberts (2004) and P. Murphy (2001).
6. Cicero, *De Republica*, III, xxii, 33.
7. See, for example, Heidegger (1991).
8. Words mean many and sometimes contradictory things. Self-determination is a case in point. It is perfectly possible to give a non-romantic account of self-determination, one that conjugates liberty and determination, freedom and necessity. Luther's notable gesture—'Here I stand, and I cannot do otherwise'—does exactly that.
9. In the second model of imagination, Simon Marginson presents a structural model of punctuated equilibrium in which long periods of stasis and equilibrium is punctuated by shorter periods of sharp change.
10. It should be noted that in fact great scientists frequently attest to the role of aesthetic form in science. Both art and science have roots in the beauty of mathematics.
11. Dewey (1934), 48, 134, 147, 155, 157, 180, 267, 277, 281, 288.
12. Rorty's counter-positioning of poets to Platonists—though it is clever, and though it owes something to Plato's dismissal of poets from the polis—is misleading in the sense that some of the most important, and certainly among the most compelling, poets are metaphysical poets like John Donne and the English Metaphysical school (Gardner, 1972) or like T.S. Eliot (1932) owes much to the imaginary of the metaphysical poets.

13. Rorty (1989), 59.
14. Rorty (1989), 26.
15. See the case of Oliver Selfridge's methodology for software development discussed in Stephen Johnson (2002), 52–57.
16. As described by Van der Meer (2005), 42.
17. Augustine put it this way: creation 'begins' not 'in' time but 'with' time.
18. Bertalanffy thought that one of Oswald Spengler's great insights was that social orders have a mathematical foundation (1975), 82.
19. On autopoietic order, see Bertalanffy (1968, 1975).
20. See, for example, Luhmann (1995).
21. See also Murphy and Roberts (2004).
22. Locker (1981).
23. Whereas the first model of the imagination outlined here presumes a morphological idea of biological nature (and of nature in general), in the case of the second model of the imagination, Simon Marginson postulates a 'neo-Lamarkian' conception of biological nature, with analogical inferences applied to social nature. The emphasis in the second model is on species adapting to their own conditions of possibility and to the possible trajectories open to them. A key concept utilized in this model is the idea of punctuated evolution, or punctuated equilibrium, influenced by the evolutionary biology of Stephen Jay Gould, Niles Eldredge, and Ernst Mayr.
24. Of course it is God that many followers of Darwin wanted to expel from science. But, in so doing, they had an awful habit of expelling meaning from the universe. They made the very reasonable point that anthropomorphic theories of nature dressed up in theistic or deistic garb were naive. Yet equally naive have been the various anthropomorphic and Promethean theories that vastly over-estimate the human determination of nature and that consciously and unconsciously have followed in the wake of Darwinian science. At times it seems that earlier projections of humankind onto God have been reversed through the attribution of a pseudo-divine capacity of human beings to impact, control and destroy nature. Neither view, both of which are tendentiously anthropomorphic, are convincing in the slightest.
25. This is elaborated in Murphy and Roberts (2004).
26. On the nature of such modes, see the discussion of the rationality of intellect in Agnes Heller (1985) and the union of contraries in Simone Weil (1987).
27. As noted by Van der Meer (2005), 16.
28. This is proposed by Hawkins (2004).
29. See for example 'The Discovery of the Imagination' (1997a), 213-245.
30. This proposition of Hawkins (2004), 56–63, closely resembles Einstein's report of his own thinking as the play of physical entities.
31. This is noted by Hawkins (2004), 75–83.
32. M. Kaku (1995); B. Greene (1999).
33. The centrality of the city is proposed by Barry Allen (2004), especially part 3.
34. Carroll (2006), 34.
35. This is the paradox that Jean-Pierre Dupuy points to with his concept of auto-transcendence. See the discussion of this in Bouchet (2007).
36. A classic work in the tradition is Habermas (1979).
37. As beautifully rendered by Lukács (1991).
38. Simon Marginson below notes the crucial evolution of the trilobites from soft bodied proto-trilobites 543 million years ago. The trilobites possessed a characteristic that

gave them a crucial advantage in relation to all other living things. When they evolved from proto-trilobites, 'the light sensitive patches on the sides of the heads of proto-trilobites turned into complex organs: holochroal compound eyes that produced visual images. They could see. They were the first animals to do so.

References

Allen, B. (2004). *Knowledge and Civilization*. Boulder, CO: Westview.

Bertalanffy, L. (1968). *General System Theory,* Revised Edition. New York: George Braziller.

Bertalanffy, L. (1975). *Perspectives on General System Theory*. New York: George Braziller.

Bouchet, D. (2007). The ambiguity of the modern conception of autonomy and the paradox of culture. In Anders Michelsen and Peter Murphy (eds). Special Issue on Autopoiesis, *Thesis Eleven: Critical Theory and Historical So*ciology No. 88, 31–54.

Carroll, S. B. (2006). *Endless Forms Most Beautiful: The New Science of Evo Devo and the Making of the Animal Kingdom*. London: Orion.

Castoriadis, C. (1997a). *World in Fragments*. Stanford, CA: Stanford University Press.

Castoriadis, C. (1997b). *The Castoriadis Reader*. Oxford: Blackwell.

Castoriadis, C. (1991). *Philosophy, Politics, Autonomy*. New York: Oxford University Press.

Castoriadis, C. (1987 [1975]). *The Imaginary Institution of Society*. Cambridge: Polity Press,

Colie, R. (1966). *Paradoxia Epidemica*. Princeton: Princeton University Press.

Csikszentmihalyi, M. (1996). *Creativity: Flow and the Psychology of Discovery and Invention*. New York: HarperCollins.

Dewey, J. (1948 [1919]). *Reconstruction in Philosophy*. Boston: Beacon Press.

Dewey, J. (1980/1934). *Art as Experience*. New York: Penguin Putnam.

Eliot, T.S. (1932). *Selected Essays 1917–1932*. New York: Harcourt, Brace and Co.

Gardner, H. (ed.) (1972). *The Metaphysical Poets*. Second revised edition. London: Penguin.

Greene, B. (1999). *The Elegant Universe*. New York: Vintage.

Habermas, J. (1979). *Communication and the Evolution of Society*. Boston: Beacon Press.

Hawkins, J. (2004). *On Intelligence*. New York: Henry Holt.

Heidegger, M. (1991). *The Will to Power as Art*, Volume One of *Nietzsche*. San Francisco: HarperCollins.

Heller, A. (1985). *The Power of Shame*. London: Routledge.

Johnson, S. (2002). *Emergence*. London: Penguin.

Kaku, M. (1995). *Hyperspace*. New York: Doubleday.

Locker, A. (1981). Meta-theoretical Presuppositions for Autopoiesis—Self-reference and "Autopoiesis." *Autopoiesis—A Theory of Living Organization*, Milan Zeleny (ed.), The North Holland Series in General Systems Research. North Holland, NY: Elsevier, 209–233.

Luhmann, N. (1995). *Social Systems*. Stanford, CA: Stanford University Press.

Luhmann, N. (2000). *Art as a Social System*. Stanford, CA: Stanford University Press.

Lukács, G. (1991). *Soul and Form*. London: Merlin Press.

Murphy, P. (2009). The power and the imagination: the enigmatic state in Shakespeare's English history plays. *Revue Internationale de Philosophie* 63:1. Brussells: Presses Universitaires de France.

Murphy, P. (2005). Cornelius Castoriadis. In George Ritzer (ed.) *Encyclopedia of Social Theory*, Volume 1. Thousand Oaks, CA: Sage, 82–83.

Murphy, P. (2005). Communication and Self-Organization. *Southern Review* 37: 3.

Murphy, P. & D. Roberts (2004)., *Dialectic of Romanticism: A Critique of Modernism*. London: Continuum.

Murphy, P. (2001). *Civic Justice: From Ancient Greece to the Modern World*. Amherst, NY: Prometheus/Humanity Books.

Murray, C. (2003). *Human Accomplishment: The Pursuit of Excellence in the Arts and Sciences, 800 B.C. to 1950*. New York: HarperCollins.

Penrose, R. (1999 [1989]). *The Emperor's New Mind: Concerning Computers, Minds and the Laws of Physics*. Oxford: Oxford University Press.

Rorty, R. (1989). *Contingency, Irony and Solidarity*. Cambridge: Cambridge University Press.

Thompson, D. (1961/1917). *On Growth and Form*, foreword by Stephen Jay Gould. Cambridge: Cambridge University Press.

Van der Meer, J. (2005). Alfred Locker's Critique of Evolutionary Thought: the engagement of evolutionary thought and Christian mysticism mediated by systems philosophy.

Weil, S. (1987). *Intimations of Christianity Among The Ancient Greeks*. London: Routledge.

3. Discovery

Peter Murphy

Discovery and Innovation

Creative acts deploy patterns. Conversely, the act of creation has its own patterns. It is explicable and understandable because it exhibits certain recurring features. Paradoxically that which is most fresh and unpredictable has characteristic repeating traits. Its acts of revolution both cycle back to an old refrain and explode in time confounding expectation. One of the characteristic patterns of creation is that it clumps and clusters—it does not distribute evenly across time and space. One of the primary expressions of this is the periodic golden ages of creativity. In less poetic terms, all that means is that creativity concentrates in specific times and places. This is true both of acts of creation and of the institutions that serve to mid-wife invention and to disseminate inventive creations to the wider society. At various times, academies, churches, colleges, guilds, patrons, councils and associations have performed this supplemental role, as hand-maiden to creation. In the twentieth century, both business firms and universities emerged as key institutions for creative dissemination and diffusion, and both have also acted as social crucibles for creation.[1] In these roles, both have played a central role in the arts- and science-based economies that emerged in the industrial age and transformed the economic and social landscape beyond recognition.

Everything comes with a price tag. As societies have become more self-aware of the role of invention in social life, the appetite has exploded for institutions that are associated with the dissemination and origination of the powerful ideas that undergird successful modern economies and societies. The appetite for higher education today is extraordinary and seemingly insatiable. More than thirteen thousand universities and colleges exist worldwide, and these numbers are multiplying. With appetite comes illusion. Most of these establishments are barely more than high schools, and quite a few of them are eccentric and marginal institutions. But, like airlines, there seems no discouraging entrepreneurs and governments from establishing them. Several countries count higher education amongst their most lucrative export industries.[2] Escalating percentages of 18–25 year olds attend university. Policy makers want to expand those percentages. All this would suggest that the university is in a golden age. But it is not. No one who works in a university anywhere would contend that today is a good time for higher learning. Managerially it ploughs ahead. But for all of its spectacular outward growth, and bureaucratic brio, the university is inwardly uncertain, intellectually dilapidated, culturally brittle, and spiritually numb. The point of the current work is not to state the obvious, but rather to indicate that the condition of the university is an expression of a larger systemic cultural problem—which is the running down of creative energy that has been going on in all advanced societies since the middle part of the nineteenth century. At the end of the twentieth century, after 140 years of this entropy, many of the most powerful states in the world declared themselves to be 'creative economies' and 'knowledge societies.' Universities jumped on this self-congratulatory bandwagon. But as compelling empirical data and wry philosophical observation confirms, societies today are massively less creative in real terms than their forbears of the High Modern era from 1900 to 1930. Indeed many of the creative peaks from the Renaissance to the Enlightenment put even the late nineteenth century and early twentieth century to shame. This is true of both the arts and the sciences.

Creative processes have two phases: discovery and innovation. Discovery is the most important, and the most difficult to understand, of the two aspects. Innovation is a derivative of discovery. Without the latter, the former does not exist. Innovation is also an ironic phenomenon. For innovation creates nothing new, but rather introduces discoveries to new audiences through interpretation, commentary, citation, augmentation, adaptation, modification, and application. Much, or most, of the institutional apparatus of the arts and sciences is concerned with innovation not with discovery, even though discovery is a condition of the possibility of all scientific and artistic value. Both the rate of discovery and the rate of innovation have generally trended downward in the last 140 years with only occasional upward spikes. The *rate of discovery* is a measure of the number of significant works created per head of population. The *rate of innovation* is a measure of the number of copyrights and patents produced per capita. The rate of discovery is an indicator of high-level creative activity represented by major figures, works and events in the arts and sciences. The rate of innovation, in contrast, charts a wider pool of intellectual activity. Most copyrights and patents do not represent major intellectual achievements. Nonetheless they are a good indicator of the impact of creative ideas as they are picked up, extrapolated and expanded on in the wider social innovation process. Innovation is the act of dissemination of discovery.

With the passage of a generation or two, a social and intellectual consensus forms about major intellectual accomplishments. It takes around 50 years for the consensus to form. After that it changes only incrementally over time. There may be late-arriving additions to the pantheon, like Jan Vermeer, but these are rare. The status of Bach, Mozart, and Beethoven is chiseled in stone. The ultimate judge of things, Time, is unforgiving. The pointless plaudits given to second-rate works invariably come to nothing. Fifty years on, the acclaimed plays of the angry young men and the kitchen sink realists barely rate a mention. It is very difficult for contemporaries to know what works and movements will have lasting significance. Critics rarely have good judgment. Note the number of excoriating first reviews of great novels. Our own time clouds our judgment. This is true for creators and audiences alike. So we can only make inferential judgments about rates of discovery in our time. Measures of innovation are useful in this respect. We can read backwards from the process of dissemination something about the underlying rate of discovery, while being uncertain about the canonical works produced by our own time.

What we can see from the data on discovery and what we can infer from the data on innovation is that during the last 70 years in particular, and in a more nuanced sense during the last 140 years, the intensity of production of great works has declined. This does not mean that no important or canonical works have been produced. Of course such works have been created. But the rate of new ideas production, the number of significant original works per capita per year, has overall declined. There have been periods of upswing since 1870, but these periods have not been sustained. We are less creative than we were 140 years ago. But we tell ourselves the obverse of this. The rhetoric of the creative society has become a consolation for a decline of creative intensity. Ever-more sophisticated means of mechanical and digital distribution, remediation, and recycling of ideas have masked the fact that creative copyright and patent industries and institutions, not least of all the universities, produce fewer and fewer serious works per capita at greater and greater cost per unit. On one side of a complex equation, we have seen prodigious wealth generated by a distributive leviathan that includes everything from the sale of movie seats to undergraduate university places to television broadcasting to the Internet. On the other side of the equation, the core driver of creation continues to lose energy and decelerate. Eventually there will come an axial point, and perhaps today we have arrived at that point, when the creative decline will begin to dissipate the masking agent, the distribution side of things. In the case of the university it is now eating the entrails of its own living corpse. It is not alone in this. Hollywood today is a vacuous parody of its glorious golden age, as is contemporary recorded pop music compared with its glory days of the late sixties and early seventies. For brief periods both bucked the longer underlying trend of creative unwinding.

The Logic of Discovery

One view is that the contemporary university has so many missions it has no mission. The contemporary university is torn between teaching, research, scholarship and public service. It does none of these things convincingly. It can justify each one of them, yet each attempt at justification sounds hollow. However this is not just a result of the university having several roles to fulfill. Rather, at the deepest level, the rational enterprise of justification is a source, perhaps even *the* source, of the problem state of the university. One of the heroes of the twentieth-century university, Sir Karl Popper, began his illustrious intellectual career with a work called the logic of scientific discovery.[3] But, really, this was a study of the rational process of the after-the-fact justification of discovery. It answered the question of how we validate what we have found out, or think we have found out. Mainly what Popper discovered was that paradoxically we cannot validate what we discover, but rather all we can do is falsify discoveries or find out their fallibilities and weaknesses. Curiously, though, this logic of scientific discovery evades the question of how the act of discovery or creation occurs. In a figurative sense this evasion is also what has happened to the university. It is very good at posterior justification, or at insistent falsification, but seemingly less good, certainly less systematically good, at incubating the act of creation.

In a lecture at Cornell University, in 1983, Jacques Derrida wittily remarked that 'as far as I know, nobody has ever founded a university *against* reason.'[4] I am going to suggest, here, that—really—that is what is required. In fact cultural conservatives going back to Edmund Burke have a long and distinguished history of voicing skepticism about reason, whether of the critical-falliblistic or the affirmative self-certain kind. I am going to suggest that we indeed ought to found a university against reason. Now, I take it that Derrida thought so as well—mainly because he observed the infinite regress that applies to reason. The idea of reason implies that there are grounds or principles for what we believe and what we do. Up to a point, there are.[5] Part of what university teachers do is to inculcate ways of reasoning and arguing from principles, evidence or authorities. But the scandal of reason is well known: what grounds are there to ground the grounds we have? What principles support our principles, what reasons do we have for our rationales? When I disagree with your reasons, and your rationales for those reasons, and the principles upon which those rationales rest, you will look at me with menace. I will tell you that I have heard all of those grounds, principles, and foundational maxims enunciated before, and respectfully I say unto you, you are still wrong. To which you will respond with either fight or flight knowing that obviously I am not a reasonable person because any reasonable person would not hold the views that I hold. You will declare me an enemy of your personal state, and beyond the pale of your office or your committee. You will then proceed to settle the matter that divides us by the exercise of power—the last resort of the government of reason, as Thomas Hobbes observed a long time ago. All proponents of reason turn into Hobbesian sovereigns in the end. Universities are filled with such sovereigns, some appointed, some not, all of whom wear the mask of reason.

Karl Popper was clever enough to try and avoid the infinite regress of reason and its inevitable resolution by power by allotting to reason the role of proving only that we are wrong, rather than demonstrating that we are right. The next step, taken by the post-modern generation, was to say that there are no foundations of reasoning—it is just a deep dark abyss. Look into its depths, and you will find nothing to support what you believe. Therefore, you can believe, and perhaps also do, whatever you want, or else, like Heidegger you may simply be enchanted by the nihilism of the abyss, and surrender yourself to its lethal embrace.[6] Of course, this is either silly or dangerous or both. So here we have an impasse. The cultural conservatives say that reason is often far from reasonable. Meanwhile reason, when called upon to justify itself, ends in an absurd state of infinite regress. So the conservative then points out that to plunge into the abyss, where every belief is permitted, is a horror show. Thus the skeptics of reason are forced to defend reason, while their enemies, the rationalists, turn into nihilists. Everyone, in the end, confronts a terrible truth. As in the case of Hamlet, the freedom of exploring and weighing every possibility of acting produces paradoxically an awful squalid passivity, the door through which the furies of chaos and destruction then proceed. So if we wish to found a university against reason, we should proceed very carefully, and if we wish to ground a university on reason, we should be just as careful.

We are in dangerous and difficult territory. What places us on this awkward terrain is the fact that reason is inadequate to its own self. Cornelius Castoriadis put it well: all rationalities depend on imaginary meanings. There is a bottom to the deep well of reason, and this bottom is constituted by these imaginary significations. We will explore later on what these meanings are, and how they come to be. To understand how they are formed, is to understand the act of creation and the logic of discovery. But for now it is sufficient to note that these meanings on which reason rests are social-historical creations. They are the artifacts of the process of collective imagining. In a lecture that Castoriadis gave at the University of Minnesota in 1986, he observed how variable the work of the collective imagination is—and how great cultures thereby rise and fall.[7] He noted that when a culture is on the rise we see an amazing number of geniuses and great works, as well as the genius of the entire community. This can be seen in the age of Pindar, Aeschylus and Sophocles. The same thing can be seen from Dante and Giotto through Shakespeare and Bach to Proust, Kafka, Joyce and Picasso. Yet, he observed, in the very same places, with the same geography, under the same sun, and with proximately the same people, proximately the same society produces little of interest or worth, and can spend centuries imitating rather poorly what has been done before. Castoriadis was indelicate enough to point out that this is *our* problem. We live in an Alexandrine age.[8] We live like the Hellenistic Greeks did, in the shadow of the infinitely more creative classical and pre-Socratic Greeks.

Trending Downward

While I would like to report that we are not Alexandrines, in fact the empirical and historico-metrical evidence strongly supports Castoriadis. So far as the rate of peak creation is concerned, we are not doing very well at all. I do not mean that there has not been some great works created in the last century. Of course there has been. There have been some very great works produced. But, collectively, the rate of creation has slowed—and our time does not compare well when we turn to the larger social history of creation. As Charles Murray's meticulous historico-metrical analysis in *Human Accomplishment* from 2003 illustrates, the incomparable golden age of the visual arts was between the mid-1400s and mid-1500s with a second peak in the mid-1600s.[9] Music creation peaks in the early 1700s and sustains a moderate high through to the middle of the 1800s. Western literature peaks in the early 1600s and again in the middle of the 1800s. Scientific creativity peaks in the later 1600s and then again for an astonishing period from the mid 1700s to the late 1800s.[10] Huebner calculates that high-level technology discovery peaked in 1873.[11] Similarly after 1870, the rate of major achievement—that is, the number of outstanding figures, works and events per capita, in the United States and Europe—in mathematics, visual arts, and literature also declines.[12] There were two countervailing trends: an upswing in the number of significant figures (though *not* works and events) in literature, science, and visual art from 1900 to 1920 and an upswing in technology advances in the period 1920 to 1950.[13] Nonetheless, what Nietzsche prophesized, did eventuate. In 1872, in *The Birth of Tragedy* Nietzsche predicted exactly what was coming: creative decadence.

This was an amazing observation given that it was made with foresight, not hindsight. It was a prediction based on acute sensitivity to and understanding of the enigmatic and difficult nature of imaginative breakthrough. Nietzsche proved to be the exception to the rule of creative decline, and there would be other important exceptions. But in the end the exceptions only proved the rule.

What is true of creative discovery is true also of the broader process of aesthetic and scientific innovation. America was the most creative economy and society in the twentieth century—by a vast margin. So it can be used as a convincing measuring stick of discovery and innovation in the period. Patents and copyrights are a proxy for creativity. Thus while most inventive acts have no formal legal status, those that do are a salient sample of the larger corpus of such acts. In spite of its comparative global creative power in all areas of the arts and sciences in the last one hundred years, the peak year for patents registered per capita in the United States was 1916.[14] The rate trended downward till 1985 where it stood at 50% of the 1916 peak. It rose again, as would be expected, in step with the information technology boom from 1985 to the present day. But even at its renewed highest in 2005 it was still only 95% of the 1916 per capita figure, which is extraordinary considering the incessant contemporary social chatter about innovation. Notably most patents today are registered by companies as opposed to individuals a century ago. It is not clear then that institutionalization has necessarily benefited technology innovation. What about the broader arts and sciences?

Registrations of copyrights per capita slightly increased between 1900 and today, though only because the number of categories of copyrightable objects increased markedly in the same period—meaning that copyright registration per capita in real terms actually fell. The 1890s appears to be the peak time for copyright creation in the United States once we take into account the increase in copyrightable objects during the period. Copyright registrations today cover a remarkable spectrum of creative works including non-dramatic literary works, works of the performing arts, musical works, dramatic works, choreography and pantomimes, motion pictures and filmstrips, works of the visual arts, including two-dimensional works of fine and graphic art, sculptural works, technical drawings and models, photographs, cartographic works, commercial prints and labels, works of applied arts, and sound recordings. In 1871, 12,688 copyrights were registered in the United States which had a population of 50 million.[15] That is the equivalent of 0.03 registrations per 100 Americans. In 1900 that figure had risen to 0.13. In 1925, it was 0.15, 1950, 0.14, 1978, 0.15. After this plateau, it rises in 1988 to 0.23, and then falls away again to 0.20 in 1994, then 0.18 in 2000 and 2007. Not only had the nominal figure per capita risen only marginally in a hundred years, but in the period since 1900 many new categories had been added to the schedule of protected works (Table 1). In spite of all the additional copyrightable works that this represents, copyright productivity per capita expanded negligibly in a century. In real terms, in effect copyright activity shrank. As with patents, the peak of copyright registrations in nominal real terms (i.e. not adjusting for later additional copyrightable objects) occurred at the turn of the century, in 1907, with 0.14 registrations per one hundred Americans.[16]

In contrast to the effective long-term downward trend, the turn-of-the-century, the late 1920s and the late 1980s were relative high spots. The presidential eras of Theodore Roosevelt (1901–1909), Calvin Coolidge (1923–1929), and Ronald Reagan (1981–1988) were the most creative in the American twentieth century.[17] The period between 1900 and 1909 coincided with a notable efflorescence of the American mind. The university in the American Progressive Age was epitomized by the work of John Dewey, William James, Frederick Jackson Turner, and Thorstein Veblen. The 1920s saw a second surge of American intellectual energies. In the universities, this was exemplified by the work of Robert Park and the Chicago School of Sociology and the iridescent Harvard pairing of Talcott Parsons and Joseph Schumpeter.[18] With the passage of time, it is becoming clearer that the 1980s was the other interesting intellectual decade of the twentieth century. Notably the 1980s in the U.S. saw a jump in R&D spending as a share of GDP from 2.1 % in 1979 to 2.7 % in 1984. It has remained around that level ever since.[19] Some of what makes the 1980s intellectually interesting is the ironic phenomenon of an inspired critique of a certain kind of cultural impasse.

The decade of the 1980s produced a lot of reflection on the state of university. That was true both in Europe and America. The decade was bookended by Jean-Francois Lyotard's *The Post Modern Condition* in 1979 and by Allan Bloom's *The Closing of the American Mind* in 1987 and Jacques Derrida's *The Right to Philosophy* in 1990.[20] This impressive gaggle of works on the social condition of knowledge and the university in retrospect also looks like the product of a 'bad conscience.' Collectively, these works betray a nagging sense that 'something is wrong' with the university and the larger culture it is embedded in. This was also the time that produced Saul Bellow's *Dean's December* (1982) and David Lodge's *Small World* (1984)—comic novels underpinned by well-formed critiques of the university. Perhaps the spiritual ailment of higher learning is best captured by two works of the period, both by Pierre Bourdieu—his *Distinction* (1979) and *Homo Academicus* (1984). These books had interesting things to say about the arts and sciences as social systems of status and prestige, and their power to create borders and adjudicate boundaries, but they had little to say about the vocation or the capacity of either art or science to produce cultural meaning. Unquestionably, in the

1980s there were shooting stars like Bourdieu and Derrida, Bloom and Bellow. Yet the larger intellectual firmament was less and less capable of producing imaginary meanings. That was Castoriadis' essential point.

The grey tones of this metaphysical picture are reflected empirically in the general level of innovation in the twentieth century—measured by the proxy of copyright and patent registrations. As noted, these either trended down, flat-lined, or else peaked briefly only to drop away again—while the rate of first-class creative discovery proved to be no better. As the available systemic historico-metrical data on major figures, works and events through to 1950 shows clearly, across both Europe and the United States there was no history-trumping peak of creative discovery in the twentieth century for any of the established arts and sciences.[21] About the period after 1950, it is more diffi-cult to draw definitive conclusions. Nevertheless, all suggestive evidence is that the larger lackluster condition was only reinforced in the latter half of the twen-tieth century.[22] If in the case of the visual arts, modernist art could not approach the rate of creative output of the visual arts of the 1400s–1600s, then the desultory era of post-modernism was certainly not going to make any impression at all. As far as the new arts and sciences in the twentieth century are concerned, they do not seem to have fared any better. If we take the cases of film and recorded music, both great American arts, their technology orig-inated in the nineteenth century in the inventions of Thomas Edison and oth-ers. The genesis of their industries occurred in the era of Teddy Roosevelt and Herbert Hoover. Their creative peak is the 1950s (film) and the late 1960s-early 1970s (recorded music). For film, a breakdown by decade of the Internet Movie Database (IMDB) list of Top 250 films, predominately Hollywood films, measured as a percentage of the total output of films for each decade in the last 100 years shows, in a graphic manner in Table 2, the story of the evolv-ing ratio of quality-to-quantity as film creativity peaks in the 1940s and begins to steadily and persistently decline after that. Bad cinema has increasingly sub-sumed good cinema.[23]

There is no golden age of creativity for the arts and sciences in the twen-tieth century anywhere that compares with Europe in the mid-1400s and the mid-1800s, and no signs of the onset of one in the twenty-first century. Arguably, the genius of the social imagination is fraying at the edges. In the last twenty-five years we have produced a long list of consoling ideologies granting ourselves august titles like the knowledge society, the creative econ-omy, the clever country, and so on. These labels though belie the underlying declining rate of discovery and creation that has dogged the most advanced societies. Even if this decline has been punctuated with rallies, the cumulative effect of this long-term trend is serious.[24]

Let us consider for a moment the social impact of the creative leviathan when it falters. The story I am about to tell begins in 2008, the year when the world banking system fell into crisis. This happened because banks had too many bad loans on their books. It happened in the first instance to American banks but their predicament only exemplified a larger global story. In the decade preceding 2008, American banks had a huge inflow of funds from abroad. At the same time they made imprudent loans to borrowers who either had poor credit histories or who wished to finance speculative housing investments. In the United States, both regulated and unregulated financial institutions behaved in the same way. So did banks across the world—who lent money to finance unproductive consumer debt and the like. All of this suggests that banks and other lenders had little commercial option but to lend to un-financial borrowers or for unproductive purposes because there was ultimately no better market for their funds. This, in turn, suggests that the banking system was in a state analogous to a mature or sunset industry. The market for money, even at low prices, had shrunk. Without new productive and financial classes of borrowers—in effect without new industries—there was little to salve the problem.

New industries and their socio-cultural forms are generated by acts of discovery and are financed by innovational investment.[25] The underlying problem of early twenty-first century capitalism is the declining rate of creation. A classic symptom of this is the booster-talk about the environment-friendly green automobile. If this had taken place in 1908—when the mass-market automobile was still revolutionary and there was real inventive competition between the electric and internal combustion engine—rather than in 2008, it might have yielded something of interest.[26] If an electric car could offer any energy or carbon economy, rather than simply transferring energy loss or carbon output from the car itself to the plants generating electricity and its transmission down the power lines all the way to the socket used to charge the electric car, then it might have some significance. As it is, applying belated heart massage to an arrested industry with technology that externalizes inefficiencies is not innovation in any meaningful sense.

The Manchester cotton industry in 1780s, the railroads in the 1830s, Pittsburgh steel in the 1870s, the Detroit car industry in the 1910s, and the Silicon Valley information industries in the 1980s created new leading industrial and commercial sectors. The American economy was severely recessed, during the Carter administration in the 1970s. The economy returned to prosperity because of the onset of a new wave of industrialization that took off in the 1980s. The primary driver of that was the rise of the then new information and communications technology (ICT) industries. The American economy climbed out of Carter-era gloom because the rate of innovation rose significantly in the 1980s during the Reagan years. Yet it did not stay at that elevated level. It fell away again during the Clinton years. The communications and information technology sector saved the American economy in the 1980s but it had run out of innovative power by the year 2000.[27]

By the time new media became a mass phenomenon it was old media. Its key elements had been in place since the 1980s (Table 6). The industry was innovative—meaning that between 1980 and 2000 it diffused key discoveries. It did not make those discoveries itself—they principally came from a handful of leading research universities. But the industry adapted, augmented, refined, combined, assembled, and re-assembled them. It did so for a time spectacularly, and then with diminishing returns—both cognitive and financial. 2008 was a re-run, in exacerbated form, of the problems of 1978. The ultimate problem was not the lack of aggregate demand in the economy, which could be fixed by neo-Keynesian techniques of budget spending and fiscal deficits, but rather a lack of sector innovation.[28] This is a recurring episode in the story of capitalism since the Industrial Revolution.[29] In 1820, the richest country was twice as wealthy as the poorest country in the world measured in GDP per capita. Today, the richest country is sixty times as wealthy as the poorest country.[30] The principal reason for this disparity is innovation. This is the capacity not just to produce but to produce new industries—and export old industries abroad.[31] Capitalism industrializes everything: art, sociability, publishing, eating, beauty, information, waiting tables, and so on. To industrialize, it must innovate. To innovate, it must industrialize. When the rate of innovation declines, capitalist economies find themselves in trouble. It should be stressed that this is not simply a function of science and technology. The rate of government spending in the USA in the 1930s was 3% of GDP. When, today, anywhere between 20% and 50% of the GDP of countries goes to government spending, it follows that social policy and ultimately social thought have just as an important influence on economic innovation as physics or chemistry do.

Quantity and Quality

Universities figure prominently in this story insofar as innovation is a derivative of discovery. Innovation is the process of ingenious imitation, adaption, augmentation, and dissemination of discovery. Universities are one of the institutions capable of producing high-level discoveries in the arts and sciences—though they are by no means the only such institution nor are they necessarily the most effective at eliciting peak creation. Writing in 1973, Daniel Bell, who is a very astute observer, thought that the university was on its way to becoming the primary institution of 'post-industrial' society.[32] This, arguably, turned out to be true. Yet 'post-industrialization' in the long run also turned out to be much less impressive in a larger historical sense than a number of its prophets predicted. Thus it can be concluded that the universities were the prime signifying institution of a less than prime historical period—or that they were much less able to lead innovation and stimulate creation than appeared initially to be the case at a time when they had assumed a great social weight. Three things are true. Like the larger culture in which they are embedded, universities have been running out of steam for a long time.[33] As universities also have been growing in size for a long time, their entropy has been partially disguised. Finally, all such processes are relative not absolute. There is no point at which the 'good era' switched to become the 'bad era.'

So then, do universities matter or not to the dual process of discovery and innovation? The short answer to this question is that universities do matter, but that only a very tiny handful of them matter. And still more brutally, only a small portion of staff in that tiny number of institutions contributes to creative discovery. This is the 5% principle. In OECD countries 5% of the faculty members in 5% of universities engage in significant levels of discovery. The numbers that contribute to the broader process of innovation are larger but only modestly so. Yet, in spite of the very small number of significant research institutions and actors, university research remains an important medium of discovery and innovation. Mostly it is a medium for innovation, even when it adopts the guise, or disguise, of discovery. Innovation though functions as the ecology for discovery. It is doubtful if the latter could occur without the former.

One of the most fundamental social facts about research is that it is highly concentrated. In the 1970s, there were 2,500 accredited colleges and universities in the United States, including public and private universities and liberal arts colleges. As Daniel Bell noted in 1973, 100—or 4% of them—carried out more than 93% of research generated by the sector.[34] And of that tiny group, 1% of them—21 universities—carried out 54% of total American higher education research, and 10 universities were responsible for 38% of the sector's research output. Today there are 2,618 accredited four-year colleges and universities in the United States.[35] In 2009, The Carnegie Foundation for the Advancement of Teaching classified 96 universities as 'research universities with very high research activity,' essentially the same as Bell's 1973 figure.[36] After thirty years of the 'knowledge economy,' the landscape remains essentially unchanged. Table 5 lists the top twenty American research universities (also coincidentally the top twenty research universities in the world). The 2008 Leiden University global index of research universities, from which this data is drawn, treats discrete University of California campuses as separate universities. To compare with Bell's data from the 1970s, this has been adjusted, and the University of California is listed once rather than multiple times in the top twenty.[37] The concentration of American university research is replicated elsewhere. Australia, for example, has 44 universities and 71 state-accredited degree granting institutions—115 universities and colleges in total. 14 are research universities—or 12% of the total.[38] Eight institutions, or 7% of the total, produce most of the sector's research.[39]

The technological science that was central to the emergence of the new media, communications and information industries in the years between 1970 and 2000 demonstrates very clearly the manner in which a very small group of research universities do matter in the contemporary process of social creation. The key building blocks of the digital communications and media industry are short to list. These are set out in Table 6. The key actors who created contemporary communications technology came from nine research universities, IBM, BBN, the RAND Corporation, and the Defense Department's Advanced Research Projects Agency. The list of universities is virtually identical to Daniel Bell's 1970 top-ten list with a couple of exceptions. They were the University of California, MIT, Harvard, Brown, Stanford, Illinois, Duke, Washington, and Oxford. A small number of leading research universities, capable of a very high level of flexible, open and porous interaction with one another, played an indispensable role in the creative phase of digital communication development.[40]

The question remains: why does research concentrate in a handful of institutions? The answer to the question is that discovery and innovation are rare human capacities. Very few people are capable of serious research, and the few who are capable of it like to associate together. This applies as much to the creative arts as to the creative sciences. Likewise, flocking behavior is just as powerful in the social sciences as in the humanities. Those who flock concentrate in small circles. Even in the limited sense of innovation, creativity is the preserve of a tiny number of people. Those who are capable of creative discovery in the arts and the sciences are exceptionally few in number. This has nothing to do with access to the means of creative production. A cursory look at any of the millions of blogs or any of the collective authoring sites or youtube video uploads of non-pirated materials will confirm that. Works of Beethoven, Bach, and Mozart make up 20% of the classical music performance repertoire today. This is not because listeners or programmers are conservative, but because in any field you can name, from the sciences to the performing arts, peak creation is exceptionally rare and innovation is uncommon. Out of the total population of scientists and engineers, a very small cohort of inventors is responsible for most technological patents. This is true in both industry and the university.[41] The majority of PhDs will produce little or no research after they receive their doctorate.[42] Though a doctorate is notionally a preparation for a research career, in practice it principally serves as a gate-keeper for undergraduate teaching. Correspondingly, only a very small portion of the potential researcher population will carry out research or systemic creation across their life span. The converse of this is that life-span researchers or creators are highly productive.

Serious researchers produce large quantities of research. This was first demonstrated empirically by Alfred Lotka in 1926.[43] Around 10% of creators produce 50% of the works in any field.[44] This applies to publications, creative art works, and patents equally. Lotka first observed the skewed distribution of creative output in his study of the publication record of nineteenth-century physicists and chemists. His data showed that 60% of researchers in print published only one article in a career. What Lotka observed in the sciences proved to be equally true of the social sciences, the creative arts, and technology. The distribution of creative output is massively skewed toward a few producers in any field. The same kind of skew also applies to the reception and performance of works. Abraham Moles calculated that all of the works that make up the standard performance repertoire in classical music are the work of 250 composers.[45] Dean Simonton notes that the bottom 150 of this cohort of 250 is each represented by one work only.[46] Collectively the contribution of the bottom 150 is 6% of the total performed repertoire. Mozart, Bach and Beethoven each in their own right contribute about 6%. Collectively their works make up 18% of the total standard performed repertoire. The top 10 composers contribute 40% of performed works.

It might be thought vulgar to talk about quantity in respect of the creative domain. This is a domain traditionally governed by criteria of quality and excellence. Atrocious creators with an insatiable mania to produce are not unknown. Yet more often the price of a lack of imagination is the eventual drying up of output once prosaic ambition has been fulfilled. On the other hand, in the case of those who are highly creative, there is not only a positive but also a very strong correlation between quantity and quality in research. So strong in fact to suggest that all of the well-meaning attempts to measure quality via peer panels, the ranking of journals and ultimately even citations are a waste of time and money. It turns out that the old rule-of-thumb of quickly reading someone's curriculum vitae and calculating the number of outputs per year is more reliable than anything. Simonton's numerous studies of high-level creators are very revealing in this respect.[47] As Simonton notes, the number of collegial citations that a scientist receives is strongly associated with the total output of publications. In fact, the total number of publications predicts the amount of citations received by a scientist's three most acclaimed works. Moreover, Simonton adds,

[t]his correspondence between quantity and quality holds over the long haul. For instance, the total length of the bibliography of a nineteenth-century scientist predicts how famous he or she is today. Thus, a scientist who was then in the top 10% of the most productive elite has a 50–50 chance of earning an entry in a recent edition of *Encyclopædia Britannica*. In contrast, their less prolific colleagues have only three chances out of a hundred of earning that distinction. Mendel could make a lasting impact on science with only half a dozen publications, but cases like his are not frequent enough to undermine the correspondence.[48]

The implications of this reach well beyond the matter of citations, or the quantifiable impact of specific items of research. They bear upon the very important question of what constitutes the animating medium of creative behavior.

The tradition that extends from Friedrich Schiller via Johan Huizinga to Herbert Marcuse was wrong.[49] It is work not play that animates creative action. R.J. Simon's study showed that eminent researchers work exceptionally hard, typically 60–70 hours a week for most of the year.[50] This is work in a consecrated sense. The Coles observed the intense devotion that eminent scientists have to their labors. They called the source of this, rightly, a sacred spark.[51] There is a very strong correlation between creativity and productivity. They are two sides of the same hallowed drive. The 1954 study by Dennis found that the average lifetime output of American scientists elected to the National Academy of Sciences was 203 publications, the median number was 145.[52] Zuckerman's 1977 study reported that American Nobel Prize winners published an average of 3.24 papers a year compared with the 1.48 papers published by peers with national eminence in science.[53] Albert's 1975 study calculated that psychologists who were recipients of the American Psychological Association's Distinguished Scientific Contribution Award averaged 2.9 publications a year.[54] Simonton calculated that Darwin averaged over two publications a year, Einstein almost four, and Freud over seven.[55] Joseph Schumpeter, the greatest economist of the twentieth century alongside Friedrich Hayek and John Maynard Keynes, wrote 5 million words in his lifetime, the equivalent of 50 books.[56] John Ford made 94 films before his first classic *Stagecoach* in 1939, and then made another 45 films after that.[57]

Mona Lisa's Smile

Having observed the strong empirical correlation between quantity and quality of research output, the question still remains as to what accounts for this? For good and great researchers, quantity of output is an expression of breadth—and breadth is a sign of curiosity about a large range of phenomena. Discovery requires the ability—intellectually—to make a union of disparate concepts. This is what Einstein and Nietzsche did. Einstein's theory of relativity connected the seemingly unrelated fields of Newtonian mechanics and electromagnetism. Nietzsche's marriage of the Apollonian and the Dionysian was equally dramatic. In larger social terms, what the physicist and the philosopher did is akin to what Schumpeter observed that entrepreneurs do when they conceive new technical, financial or organizational combinations. The periodic and unpredictable emergence of those miraculous combinations is the driving force of modern capitalist economies. The imaginative conjuring of such protean combinations should not be confused with the over-inclusive thought processes typical of those who, unfortunately, are mad. Imagination is the antithesis of cognitive pandemonium. It is synthetic, not inclusive. It integrates unlikely elements. It makes surprising connections. And it does this animated by a drive for coherence, form and meaning. Meaning is constituted by the emphatic integration of radically disparate elements of experience. This conjuration constitutes the core of the act of creation. This is why the most interesting research crosses the boundaries of fields and occurs at the intersection of disciplines.[58] It is a meeting and matching of incongruent essentials. Reputedly, the great twentieth-century sociologist Max Weber was once criticized by some academic hack for writing outside his field. When asked why he did this, Weber retorted: 'I'm not a donkey, and I don't have a field.' Weber was also massively productive, and he was productive because he wrote on an astonishing range of human concerns—from religion and ethics to economics and the city—all of which he integrated beautifully into an overarching study of human rationality. Tellingly, Weber's time as a professor was of very short duration.[59]

A very good second-rank scientist like Henri Poincaré (1854–1912), a winner of all the major science awards of his time bar the Nobel Prize, published some 500 papers and 30 books in his life time.[60] While perspiration without inspiration does not of itself produce interesting work, perspiration is nevertheless closely correlated to inspiration. Whether in the arts or the sciences, high-level creation requires familiarity with a number of fields. Often one of the characteristics of high productivity is fluid movement between fields and domains. As Poincaré, who was very reflective about these kinds of questions, noted, invention is related to combination. 'Among the combinations we choose, the most fruitful are often those which are formed of elements that are borrowed from widely separated domains.' [61] A classic example of inventive combination is the case of the creation of the Google search engine which came out of the coalescence of Sergey Brin's research on data mining systems with Larry Page's study of research citations.

Many philosophers insist that knowledge produced for its own sake is superior to useful knowledge. What the Page-Brin story indicates is that utilitarian devices depend on the imagination as much as sublimely and gorgeously useless things do. From the standpoint of the imagination, there is no cognitive peaking order. Samuel Coleridge gave an immortal definition of the imagination. The imagination is a synthetic power that reveals itself in the balance of opposite or discordant qualities.[62] Poets and inventors do not stand so far apart in this matter. This underscores Poincaré's observation that creative acts are formed of elements which are borrowed from widely separated domains. That is why disciplinary drudges, even highly published ones, who plough the same field continuously, produce little or nothing of interest. The imagination borrows things from the most unlikely sources and compounds them.

Collaborations like that of Page and Brin interpolate psychological as well as intellectual oppositions. When they first met, they disagreed on almost everything, and yet ended up as intellectual soul-mates and close friends. This is an incarnation, in the flesh so to speak, of the imagination. As Coleridge put it, the imagination reconciles the sense of freshness with familiarity, the usual and the unusual, steadiness and enthusiasm. This uncanny union of opposites is part of all creation. The mind of God is double-coded. If one had an equation for creation, it would be that one equals zero where the sign 'equals' is not a sign of 'sameness' but rather the sign of 'sameness and difference' at the same time. The mind of God is analogical. It is a synthetic medium, the ultimate medium of communication, out of which everything, all creation, arises. There are greater and lesser creations, but greater and lesser are simply different aspects of the same thing, creation.

Creation is an enigma. At the core of what is today widely regarded as the greatest work of visual art, Leonardo da Vinci's *Mona Lisa*, is a mystery—an enigmatic smile. What the smile communicates is un-decidable. Therein lays the heart of creation. Many of the most interesting bits of the world are un-decidable.[63] Partly this is because that which is un-decidable is the kernel of thought and the core of the human imagination. All thinking has its source in what is un-decidable. Take for example Immanuel Kant's idea that moral freedom resolves itself into the antinomy of freedom and necessity. This is because freedom occurs in accordance with nature, and yet free will is incompatible with nature's necessity.[64] Freedom thus interpolates both freedom and its opposite necessity. When such perplexing acts of interpolation happen, it is a sign that we are on the glorious but nonetheless precipitous terrain of thought. Thought is what animates art, philosophy, science and religion in their most potent aspects. Aristotle's unmoved mover is un-decidable, so also is Cubism's three- and four-dimensional allusions in two-dimensional pictorial space, Calvin's believer who is both free and predestined, and Adam Smith's economist who knows that sometimes the best way of intervening in human affairs is to do nothing at all. The Taoist demiurge, the carver who does not carve, Hegel's definition of place as a union of 'the here' and 'the now' and his idea of freedom as both 'subjective' and 'objective,' or Burke the Whig politician who became the great Conservative avatar—all of these examples point to the way in which serious culture, culture that produces enduring meaning, functions.

From such enigmatic acts of synthesis comes collective meaning—what Castoriadis called imaginary significations.[65] These are the cultural enigmas that lie at the bottom of the well of reason, and that animate reason. They are the gift of art, science, philosophy, and religion. They make sense of our world by perplexing us. The crucial point, though, is that they perplex us in interesting ways. As a result, they provide meanings that are inexhaustible. Castoriadis, the former Trotskyist, admired rational debate and the capacity of society to give itself its own laws. He was suspicious of the claims of authority, especially religious authority, to take the place of reason. Yet like many former Trotskyists, Castoriadis also ended up as a kind of a cultural conservative, who realized that reason had to be encased in imaginary significations, otherwise it becomes a vehicle of madness, as in the French and Russian Revolutions. Some thinkers, like the cultural sociologist John Carroll, compare imaginary significations to myths.[66] Castoriadis' own favorite explanatory analogy for them was Greek tragic drama. Another favorite illustration that Castoriadis often used was Bach's polyphony. Myth, polyphony and tragedy all contain a core of antinomy and enigma. The tragic figure for example spends a life knowingly avoiding what is foretold only for what is foretold to happen because of those knowing acts. The heart of human creation is mysterious, ambidextrous and double-edged. It is structured like a drama and it thrills like a whodunit. It is not boring. Even if we know what fate awaits the main character, we are still surprised by the twist of fate. We are caught unawares as the mask that fate wears is suddenly tossed aside. We never fail in some way to be surprised by this, or at least to marvel at fate's ingenuity, even if we see the production of the play many times. That is culture. That is how culture functions. That is how creation unfolds. It does so, like Bach's music, through antithesis. It interpolates its own opposite.

The act of creativity is not production according to rules. Immanuel Kant said as much, and he was right.[67] Laws, policies, methods and rules are by-products of a deeper process of creative action. They are epi-phenomena. What is this underlying process? In answering this question, we answer the question of what creativity is, and by inference we can better say what model of the university is likely to most contribute to the advancement of knowledge in the arts and sciences. The process of creative action is a process of bi-sociation. Bi-sociation was Arthur Koestler's term for the way in which contrary concepts (life and death, seeing and blindness, hope and despair) are merged in the act of creation.[68] The explanation of how this happens is irreducible to rules or norms, methods or laws. No policy or indicative direction can be invoked to explain creation. Creation may be mysterious, intuitive and enigmatic, but this does not mean that it is inexplicable. It just means that it is not explicable in the terms that we explain a rule-governed decision or juridical act. Methodical or rule-governed decisions are communicated by using analytic discriminations. In them, we distinguish clearly between life and death, seeing and blindness. In creative action, we do not so discriminate. Creative acts rely on strange looping between concepts, wherein the blind person sees. The creative mind is analogical and paradoxical.

The Schlegel brothers, writing in *The Atheneum*, declared that 'the course of all poetry is to suspend the course and the laws of rationally thinking reason, and transport us again in the lovely vagaries of fancy and the primitive chaos of human nature.' [69] This is exactly what a university should not do. It should not be an institution governed by fantasy or chaos. Yet I also said at the outset that we should not found a university on reason. Let me explain why these two propositions do not contradict each other. At stake in this antinomy is the definition of the imagination. There is a school of thought that would like to define the imagination in terms of chaos and fantasy. This is fatally misleading. Genuine acts of imagination are both securely tied to reality and impressively coherent in nature. The philosopher Roger Scruton has made a compelling case that the imagination and its works are not the product of fantasy but are anchored firmly in reality.[70] Or, to put it more bluntly, nothing has infantilized the art of film more than special effects. Those rare individuals who do transform meanings radically more often than not are very practical. Shakespeare, the master of the imagination, was a successful businessman. That, at least, we know about him. Highly imaginative persons are frequently great institution builders and organizers. They may be at times a bit strange, because their minds make unusual connections. But that does not mean they are impractical—quite the contrary.

Castoriadis often reiterated the point that imaginary significations are coherent. Human beings have an impulse to create meaning, and meaning makes sense. Yet creative acts are surprising and stimulating. They tease and confound expectations. If not, they are not creations, but simply dull plodding. The essence of great art and science is that it stimulates. Berlyne observed that the arousal of the mind comes from the collative properties of novelty-familiarity, complexity-simplicity, surprise-predictability, ambiguity-clarity, and stability-variability.[71] If we are not stimulated, we become bored and morose. But being stimulated should not be confused with the irrational attempt to elicit surprise without predictability or variability without stability. The excessive, boundless, chaotic and fantastic are not imaginative, except when they are deliberately deployed in small doses. The imagination draws together. It is collative. It is synthetic. In the first phase of creation, *divergent thinking* opens onto a near-infinite range of materials, possibilities, representations and ideas. In the second phase of creation, *convergent thinking* unites and integrates.[72] The imagination binds together the shards of experience using dazzling analogies, comic incongruities, brilliant metaphors, teasing paradoxes, and the rest. If the imagination is arrested in its first phase, all it produces is fantasy and chaos, the fruits of unbounded fragmentary experience—unreason in other words.

Universities are rule-governed institutions. They are founded on reason. Yet an institution of higher learning that is founded on reason alone will end in desiccation. It will be governed, as it so often is, by specialists without spirit. The problem is that reason, and the hunt for knowledge, is a kind of asceticism.[73] The rational ascetic types make endless calls for austere professionalism and pseudo-severe rigor. They delight perversely in intellectual and social abstemiousness. As wielded by the ascetics, reason's power is analytic. It demarcates. It draws distinctions. It discriminates. It creates discipline boundaries and knowledge fields. That is how analytic knowledge advances. In drawing boundaries and in establishing fields and disciplines, the reason of the university is a function of power. Disciplines are established and maintained by rules and resources. Reason, so enacted, is proficient—up to a point. Some things are achieved by the analytic circumscription of inquiry. Once fields of knowledge are defined, gaps in understanding can be identified and filled up in a careful, cautious manner. Yet, in time, these gaps become smaller and smaller, and the knowledge enterprise more bland and less interesting. One response to this arid outlook is irrationalism. Irrationalism's impulse is to defy borders with a swirling chaos. It venerates the remains of the day of a world that has been pulverized into fragments. A second, altogether different response is to re-invigorate the imagination. The imagination's domain is not power. Yet neither is it power's ludicrous alter-ego, mayhem. The imagination instead generates and venerates meaning. It integrates what has been torn asunder. It marries the fragments of experience. A university founded on the imagination looks upon the whole of creation and draws a breath of wonder.

Power and Meaning

The imagination is synthetic, not analytic. The question in perpetuity for the university is how synthetic imagination can be reconciled with analytic reason? In answering this question, let us first redouble our insistence that the imagination is not irrational. It is not an invitation to nihilism. It is not anti-institutional, even if it is resistant to institutional aridity. So then what kind of university—given that the university is an institution of power—is capable of generating meaning, the fruit of the imagination?[74] This question is also a way of re-stating the question that we began with: why is the university today so poorly? It *is* inwardly uncertain, intellectually dilapidated, culturally brittle, and spiritually numb. Why? It certainly suffers from the larger downward impetus of creation. But it also contributes to this as well. So what is its special contribution? One way of understanding the problem of the university is to think of it as a function of the relation between power and meaning. Neither is dispensable, so their relation is crucial. One can re-phrase this in terms of the vexed relationship between teaching and research. The idea of the teaching discipline, as the very phrase indicates, is a translation of the fruits of the imagination into the analytic power of the university. It refines imaginative constructs into consumable curricula, apportions time to study, examines the performance of students, and it legislates the standards of understanding. Frank Leavis's language of rigor echoes through the windy halls of this gilded bastion of normative chastisement.

The function of teaching is not to create knowledge but to transmit it to undergraduate students. As a consequence of this, both Galileo and Einstein did poorly in their days as undergraduate students. Their lecturers were conspicuously hostile to their intuitions. Darwin painfully remembered that 'during my second year at Edinburgh I attended Jameson's lectures on Geology and Zoology, but they were incredibly dull. The sole effect that they produced on me was the determination as long as I lived never to read a book on Geology, or in any way to study the science.' [75] The irony, as Dean Simonton noted, was that Lyell's *Principles of Geology* which Darwin took with him on the *Beagle* was crucial in his formulation of the theory of the origin of the species.[76] Conversely, as the Lucasian Chair of Mathematics at Cambridge University, Newton lectured to empty classrooms. The mathematics of the Newtonian universe was incomprehensible to students. Newton's mathematics had not been reduced to a teaching formula. Newton was not the only one to have experienced this—Nietzsche, Veblen, all experienced the same.

The nineteenth century saw a solution to this problem: the invention of the research university. The pioneer was Wilhelm von Humboldt who, as the Prussian Minister of Education, established the University of Berlin in 1809.[77] The university was focused on research and graduate instruction, and it had a dual structure of departments and institutes.[78] Its early faculty included Schelling, Fichte, Schleiermacher, Hegel, Savigny, and Schopenhauer. Johann Fichte, Friedrich Schleiermacher, together with Humboldt, provided the conceptual architecture of the university.[79] The intellectual premise of the research university called the very idea of the university into question. Its premise was self-education. The idea of self-education had been made possible by

Gutenberg's printing press. It had become a tacit assumption of Protestantism in its revolt against clerical authority, and later was taken over by the secular Enlightenment.[80] Self-education, the ideal of the creative mind, appeared to make the institution of the university redundant.[81] Why bother with such an institution when voracious readers can educate themselves with books and intellectual media? The Fichte-Schleiermacher-Humboldt idea of the university provided one reason to think otherwise. Fichte put it beautifully. It is not 'the contents of the book' that are important but the 'the principle of improving the contents.'[82] Schleiermacher drew the crucial distinction between the transmission of knowledge and the production of knowledge. Accordingly, the lecturers in a university should not recount what is known but rather reproduce their own realizations so that the listener may constantly not simply collect knowledge but rather directly observe the activity of 'reason' as it creates knowledge, and imitate it in this 'act of creation.'[83]

This is a compelling precept. The professor's primary function thus is not to transmit knowledge but to provide an observable and imitable model of how to produce knowledge.[84] An excellent example of this kind of creative modeling is provided by the great American composer, Elliot Carter, who recounts how he began serious composition because of the influence of Charles Ives, who was one of the towering creative masters of the American Progressive age. Carter subsequently went to Harvard University but ended up avoiding the department of music there altogether. 'Ives encouraged me to be a composer very early on in my life. I wrote some little things before I studied music that were settings of James Joyce and other things, and he thought they were quite interesting and I should be encouraged. And it was partly due to that factor that I finally decided to be a composer. Then I realized when I went to Harvard that the music department disliked contemporary music and I was very unhappy. I finally studied English Literature and didn't study with the music department at all.' [85]

The Berlin archetype was taken up in 1876 by Daniel Coit Gilman, the first President of Johns Hopkins University. Johns Hopkins was founded as a graduate school focused on research. The first American PhD had been granted in 1870. As Louis Menand notes, by 1880, four years after it opened, Hopkins had more than a hundred graduate students compared to Harvard's forty one, and its faculty had published almost as much research as had been published in the previous twenty years by all the faculty of all other American universities combined.[86] In the 1880s Charles Sanders Peirce taught at Hopkins at the same time John Dewey, Frederick Jackson Turner, and Thorstein Veblen were doing graduate studies there.[87] The Progressive Era mind was born there. Dewey was recruited along with his friend George Herbert Mead to the University of Chicago in 1894, soon after the university's foundation in 1891 on the same model as Johns Hopkins. It was at Chicago that many of the most enduring forms of American thought would reach maturity.[88] The fly in the ointment of the graduate university, though, was Harvard University. Harvard had been founded as a teaching college. Under Charles W. Eliot it followed Johns Hopkins lead into graduate research. However, Harvard's next president, A. Lawrence Lowell (1909–1934), shifted the focus away from graduates and back to undergraduates and course work.[89] A tiger's spots are difficult to change. The witty and urbane Clark Kerr noted that in the 1930s, 40s and 50s, residence halls, student unions, playing fields, undergraduate libraries, and counseling centers proliferated in American universities.[90] Universities were on the way to becoming student welfare states. The age of therapeutic pedagogy and the pastoral university was dawning. All in all, the Americans moved in an ambiguous manner. They developed the useful distinction between the undergraduate teaching college and the research university with a mission centered on graduate schools. That distinction then to a significant extent was undermined by the turning of the research university into what Clark Kerr called the multiversity devoted to graduate research, undergraduate teaching, and public service. In 1963, in *The Uses of the University*, Kerr catalogued brilliantly the problems created by the multiversity.[91] Fifty years later the problems are exactly the same, and will never be solved. They are inherent in the idea of the multiversity.

These problems are principally the result of an insoluble tension between teaching and research in the multiversity. If you doubt that teaching and research have such an uneasy relationship, then consider that all of the summa cum laude and honors achievement awards from an undergraduate university are very poor predictors of creative accomplishment in either the arts or the sciences.[92] The Goertzel study's data on the educational attainment of eminent figures, including eminent creators in the arts and humanities, showed that high creative performance in later life most strongly correlates with the part-completion of a tertiary degree. Formal undergraduate study contributes little to the formation of the creative mind, and often induces sheer boredom on the part of those who later on will demonstrate remarkable intellectual capacities. The discipline and field structure of the teaching university—its departmentalization and specialization—is a clear culprit.[93] Conversely the strongest predictor of later creative achievement is voracious reading.[94] Such reading—or the viewing of films and the like—are the mark of a wide-ranging mind that is driven to connect elements that seem otherwise to be unrelated to or unlike each other. In difference, similarities are observed. The best undergraduate program in a research university for a creative mind would be a series of independent reading units that encouraged vast reading and synthetic composition.[95] But instead the regular undergraduate program has to satisfy the normal student need for minimal reading and analytic specificity, and the appetite for the procedural, methodical and sequential organization of knowledge.[96] In other words, everything the theoretical mind is impatient with.

So why, in light of this, has the idea of the small standalone research university struggled to survive? In a practical sense, there is always the problem of money, but that is not really a satisfactory explanation—for money follows culture. The ultimate problem is a deeper social anxiety about research. Research is prestigious, yet it triggers latent social fears. Given the querulous and forbidding nature of much great research, and the silly nature of much that pretends to be great research, this is understandable. One way that social anxiety presents itself is the question often asked: is it worth spending money on? Legislators and university administrators are wary of its cost and unsure of exactly how to calculate its social benefit or economic value. Following the example of Robert Solow, economists have calculated the benefit of technological research on workforce productivity. This however overlooks Joseph Schumpeter's much more fundamental observation that innovation drives the long-term business cycle via the intermittent creation of new industries.[97] Given the assumption of the incalculability of research, legislators and administrators have found that the simplest thing to do is to amalgamate research with undergraduate teaching. Teaching, in their eyes, has a more self-evidently calculable value represented by market fees or state subsidies. The consequence of doing this, as Clark Kerr wryly noted 50 years ago, is that permanent staff in the multiversity either off load their teaching onto contract or sessional staff—or else seek out federal research grants in order to bid down teaching duties and evade the demands of the teaching university. The external grants system creates the illusion of a research paradise for professors ducking teaching, but in fact it delivers them up to a research prison—as the grant system interpolates so many geriatric discipline and field assumptions at the same time as it drives up the university's unfunded administrative liabilities and inflates its bureaucracy.

The Americans at least avoided what was done in Australia. One of the worst decisions in the history of the university was taken in Australia in the late 1980s by the Labor Government of the day.[98] This was to abolish the distinction between the tertiary teaching college (the College of Advanced Education) and the research university. Given the wave of popularity of F. A. Hayek's economic philosophy at the time, it is probably not uncommon for him to carry the blame for this. The irony, and it is not inconsiderable, is that Hayek's view was completely the opposite. In his major work from 1960, *The Constitution of Liberty*, Hayek offers an eloquent restatement of the Fichte-Schleiermacher-Humboldt view of the university.[99] He proposes that the state should subsidize forms of learning that have a general social benefit. This did not apply to vocational training such as law, medicine and engineering where greater proficiency acquired would be reflected in greater earning power. It did apply to scientists and scholars because the benefit a community earned from these groups could not be measured at the price at which they could sell their services because that benefit depended on much of their contribution being freely available to the community (382–383). Hayek was very clear about where governments should allocate the limited money they can spend. This was on select research universities whose research had a benefit for the community as a whole. He was also very clear about the character of such universities. In them, instruction is inseparable from the advance of knowledge by research. 'The introduction to those problems which are on the boundaries of knowledge can be given by men whose main occupation is research. During the nineteenth century the universities, particularly those on the Continent, in fact developed into institutions which, at their best, provided education as a by-product of research and the student acquired knowledge by working as an apprentice to the creative scientist or scholar' (388). It is hard to think of a better, more concise definition of the research university. As Hayek ruefully observed, by 1960 the great part of university work had become a continuation of school instruction. 'Only the "graduate" or "postgraduate" schools—in fact, only the best of these—are still mainly devoted to the kind of work that characterized the Continental universities of the last century' (388–389). Hayek, doubtless with intention, invokes the distinction that Schleiermacher and Humboldt made in the design of their university between school 'instruction,' the 'university,' and the French-style research 'institute.' School instruction was directed and sequential, the university was free and wide-ranging, and the institute was analytic and narrowly-focused. As demand to give larger and larger portions of the population a university education grew, so university learning turned into school instruction. The apprenticeship of the student to the creative scientist or scholar fell into disuse. If this was seen, as it probably was, as conferring a benefit on all to enjoy higher education, the paradox was that it also decreased another benefit for all which is the public good that research provides a society. If contemporary societies think they still get the benefits of research to the degree that their nineteenth-century predecessors got them, they are mistaken. If contemporary citizens think that the teaching universities will deliver such benefits now or in the future, they are equally mistaken.

Whatever form it takes, the mismatch between the research university where teaching is a by-product of research and the teaching university where teaching is not a by-product of research is a serious one. Teaching is a function of cultural reproduction. This is an indispensable social function. Yet it is one that has an uneasy relation with cultural creation. It is possible to teach undergraduate students about irony and paradox but it is not possible to teach them ironically and paradoxically. A successful undergraduate program can be based on great creative works or periods. But these are the works and periods of the past. Allan Bloom in *The Closing of the American Mind* (1987) made an eloquent case for teaching the great books. Frank Leavis's advice in *Education and the University* (1943) was to build a curriculum around the works and events of a great creative period. He chose the seventeenth century. No one and no society achieves creative breakthroughs without such benchmark measures. They are as important as every congealing sub-sub-field of knowledge represented by the multitude of electives on offer to undergraduates in the contemporary university. While the latter are often touted as new knowledge, electives are really the long tail of discoveries made years before. Each is an incremental institutional innovation, a form of analytic specialization and field power. Make no mistake though—if you teach a new mathematics or a new philosophy, you will end up like Newton or Nietzsche, alone in the classroom. No one will speak to you, because you are incomprehensible. Where the learning orientation of graduate researchers is overwhelmingly intuitive and theoretical, that of the undergraduate student is the obverse. It is predominately non-conceptual. As Robert Hutchins once quipped: 'When young people are asked, "What are you interested in?" they answer that they are interested in justice: they want justice for the Negro, they want justice for the Third World. If you say, "Well, what is justice?" they haven't any idea.' [100] If you happen to be the exception to that rule, a preternaturally theoretical student like Einstein or Galileo, the chances are your lecturers will ignore you. You are an irritating anomaly. You will be bored.

So what is to be done? There are two answers to this question. One is to go back to the model of Humboldt's Berlin and Gilman's Hopkins. This is to create specialized, dedicated graduate universities or autonomous faculties with an explicit commitment to high-level creation in the arts and sciences. Alvin Johnson at the New School for Social Research in New York achieved a version of this with the founding of its semi-autonomous Graduate Faculty in 1933.[101] Leo Strauss, Max Wertheimer, Hannah Arendt, Hans Jonas, Alfred Schütz, and more latterly Agnes Heller were faculty members there. France's École des hautes études en sciences sociales is another example. Castoriadis was a Director of Studies there, after a career as an economist and psychoanalyst. Bourdieu, also one of its faculty members, gave a precise description of its distinctiveness.[102] In *Homo Academicus* (1984) he described an institution that was inclined to academic innovation, open to the international environment, and encouraging of academic visitors. It recruited graduate researchers on the basis of dossiers.[103] Its members were vigorous defenders of the value of original research in contrast to the dominant university preoccupation with the reproduction of culture and the teaching imperatives of syllabi, examinations, large student audiences, and the production of text books and survey materials. The École des hautes études' faculty included Alain Touraine, Pierre Manent, Claude Lefort, François Furet, Louis Dumont, Jacques Derrida, Fernand Braudel, Roland Barthes—and both Bourdieu and Castoriadis. In such a world, seemingly small matters make a big difference. Take the use of dossiers to recruit PhDs. This reflects the fact that it is not possible to predict performance at a post-graduate level based on under-graduate scores, just as it is not possible to predict undergraduate performance based on high school results. Schleiermacher observed this long ago, noting also that 'the selection and admission of students is more art than science.' [104] Yet this art is not an arbitrary one. For the two real predictors of long-term creative performance are voracious reading and early output. The latter reflects the fact that distinguished creators typically begin composition and publication in their early twenties.[105]

A second alternative to the traditional matrix of the teaching university is the model, one of several, introduced by Robert Maynard Hutchins during his remarkable tenure as President and later Chancellor of the University of Chicago from 1929 to 1951. Hutchins developed a dual structure still extant of departments based on teaching disciplines and committees that were interdisciplinary in nature and that crossed institutional boundaries without transgressing them. The departments teach undergraduates and provide discipline-based doctoral supervision. The committees attract highly motivated, independently minded graduate students, and offer doctoral supervision to graduate researchers who have wide-ranging curiosities that cannot be contained by the analytic borders of the University of Reason. The most famous of the committees, the Committee on Social Thought, was founded by Hutchins along with the historian John U. Nef, the economist Frank Knight, the anthropologist Robert Redfield, and the classicist David Grene.[106] Over the years the committee was home to Leo Strauss, Hannah Arendt, Friedrich Hayek, Allan Bloom, Edward Shils, Saul Bellow, Stephen Toulmin, Charles Rosen, Paul Ricoeur and John Coetzee.

The relationship between power and meaning is not straightforward. There are many prestigious teaching departments, research institutes and universities. Yet the instances of works that leave a lasting impression, and outlive their progenitors, are very few in number. There is a strong correlation between such works and milieus of collective creation. Lonely genius is a myth, and as such intellectual congregations are very important. It is clear that these congregations cannot be wished into existence by rules and resources. Yet equally it is true that milieu need and exhibit institutional form. Neither 'institutional anarchism' nor 'institutional drivers' explain transcendent thought. Institutions can aid the imagination. They can impede the imagination. They can also stay out of the way of the imagination. Possibly this latter rubric best explains the interesting case in Australia from the 1980s, that of La Trobe University's social sciences. The latter was not comparable in institutional scale or power to the universities of Chicago or Paris, though it was comparable in scale to the New School, for example. It illustrates that institutional size and power is not the sole factor in cultural creation. Indeed the curious fact about the nuclei of cultural creation is that they are small even when they are located, as they will often be, in large influential institutions. Even if that is so, it is invariably a tiny handful of creative actors who make the crucial difference.

La Trobe Social Sciences is a case where there was no obvious institutional design at work.[107] It is an example, if anything, of Adam Smith's hidden hand, though it did have a very interesting bi-polarity at work. One important initial spark in the 1980s was the monumental presence there of Agnes Heller, the exiled former student of the great Marxist intellectual Georg Lukács. An exceptionally talented ensemble of academic associates, graduate researchers, interested by-standers, and inspired skeptics formed itself around her. They coalesced into an enduring Social Theory cohort that is still active today and which still continues to grow. The group reached across a number of Melbourne universities, and included a wide spectrum of intellectual views. Many of the members of the cohort became contributors to or editors of the journal *Thesis Eleven* (1980-). The work of the Social Theory group hatched at La Trobe was matched in range, depth and resonance by the work of the La Trobe Seminar on the Sociology of Culture organized by Claudio Veliz and John Carroll. This seminar was the seeding ground for a series of major works including Veliz's *The New World of the Gothic Fox* (1994) and Carroll's *Humanism: The Wreck of Western Culture* (1995) and *The Western Dreaming* (2001). The distinguished La Trobe historian John Hirst—author of works such as *The Strange Birth of Colonial Democracy* (1988) and *The Sentimental Nation* (2000)—was a regular participant in the Seminar, as was the historian Geoffrey Blainey, then at the University of Melbourne, and the most widely read writer on Australia of his generation.

It is not evident that La Trobe University as an institution contributed that much directly to what in retrospect was a very important intellectual confluence. But it did not impede it either. There was a significant degree of informal intellectual commerce between departments at La Trobe in the 1980s, which is a key condition for intellectual efflorescence.[108] The Social Theory group and the Sociologists of Culture were like twin suns in orbit around each other. They were notionally political opposites, one social democratic and post-Marxist, the other conservative, but both were deeply interested in the nexus of culture and society. Implicit in much of their work was the intuition that culture and society were a 'union of opposites.' Looked at for long enough, each one turned into its contrary. Political oppositions were similarly capable of sly interpolation. This was a powerful form of intellectual bi-sociation and a propellant of a distinctive form of inquiry that teasingly crossed boundaries between art and society, left and right, and the humanities and social sciences. Both cohorts also had a strong instinctive sense of what earlier research milieus had achieved elsewhere, and noted how they did it, and applied it. Veliz and Carroll were drawn to English models. The Social Theory cohort adopted practices from the French, German and American models. During the first fifteen years, the latter showed a lot of interest in figures connected to the École des hautes études such as Castoriadis, Touraine, Braudel and Lefort. Later they would turn their attention to Anglo-American examples. Both cohorts displayed a distinct epicurean streak as well, which was partly an Australian trait, and partly a symptom of their aversion to the rational asceticism of the over-professionalized university.

The bi-polar milieu at La Trobe was very productive.[109] Works were created en masse in situ and later in absentia as the chief actors and their protégés dispersed to other institutions and other countries.[110] A recurring thread in much of this work was the idea that aesthetics is a powerful way of understanding society—a notion that the Social Theorists shared with the Sociologists of Culture. The peak moment of this dual milieu was 1979–1985 but its influence was felt well beyond its original time and place. Heller's *A Theory of History* (1982), *The Power of Shame* (1985), *Beyond Justice* (1987) and *General Ethics* (1989) were written or re-written in her Australian exile from 1977 to 1986.[111] Carroll's *Guilt: the grey eminence behind character, history, and culture* (1985) appeared in the same period. While that volume was a transitional work, its sub-title pointed to the something about the immanent power of La Trobe's double milieu and its collective cross-cutting interest in 'character, history, and culture.' Heller would later create an existential moral philosophy in *An Ethics of Personality* (1996), and Carroll would go on to produce a decade later an existential theory of culture in *The Existential Jesus* (2007). In both, the ghost of Kierkegaard appeared. In both also, as in so many of the works that ultimately came out of La Trobe's fertile double milieu, the twin deities of society and culture were interrogated as if they were inseparable, perhaps even on some level identical.

Here we see at work what is often missing in various worthy efforts to engineer great intellectual enterprises. They simply lack what Castoriadis called the imagination's power of unification. No rules or resources can compensate for that. The imagination's power of unification does not come easily. It is not institutional power per se, but rather it is the power to create meanings, or to imagine how meanings are created. All that a great research university is, all that it can be, is an institution that recognizes and encourages milieu of this kind, even if what these milieu do sometimes seem to be perplexing or even irritating. Bourdieu's term for this irritation was heresy. A great research university is one that places its rules and resources, and the material of reason, in the service of the various heterodox enterprises of the imagination. For if it does not, there can be no creation in the true sense, and no peak creation. We can only know in retrospect, with the distance of at least fifty years, which of these enterprises worked and which did not. Most will not work, or will only partially work. There is nothing we can do to overcome that. All we can do, all we must do, is seed enough of these uncanny circles of knowledge such that we repeat in kind what happened in London in the 1940s when those brilliant exiles from the old disappeared world of the Austro-Hungarian empire, Karl Popper, Ernst Gombrich, and Friedrich Hayek, all found themselves in the same seminar at the London School of Economics.[112] When that happens, you know you have a university founded on the imagination.

Tables

Time line	Categories Added to the US Schedule of Copyright Protected Works
1912	Motion pictures (previously registered as photographs)
1953	Recording and performance of non-dramatic literary works
1972	Sound recordings*
1980	Computer programs
1984	Semi-conductor chips
1990	Architectural works
1998	Vessel hulls
TABLE 1	* (Congress extended federal copyright law to sound recordings superseding various state protections including antipiracy and unfair trade practice laws)

Decade	First Class Films as a Percentage of Total Film Output
1920s	0.025%
1930s	0.046%
1940s	0.126%
1950s	0.122%
1960s	0.057%
1970s	0.054%
1980s	0.041%
1990s	0.033%
2000s	0.025%
TABLE 2	Figures are based on the sample of all films produced in 1927, 1937, 1947, 1957, 1967, 1977, 1987, 1997, and 2007

Top Ten US Research Universities 1970 (in descending order)
University of California system
MIT
Columbia
University of Michigan
Harvard
University of Illinois
Stanford
University of Chicago
Minnesota
Cornell
TABLE 3 Based on Daniel Bell, *The Coming of Post-Industrial Society* (New York: Basic Books, 1999 [1973]), p. 245.

Top 11–21 US Research Universities 1970 (not in rank order)
Yale
Princeton
Pennsylvania
North Carolina
Wisconsin
Michigan State
Ohio State
New York University
California Institute of Technology
Rochester
Washington

TABLE 4 Based on Daniel Bell, *The Coming of Post-Industrial Society* (New York: Basic Books, 1999 [1973]), p. 245.

Top 20 US Research Universities 2008 (in rank order)
MIT
California
Stanford
Harvard
California Institute of Technology
Chicago
Washington
Yale
Johns Hopkins
Columbia
Duke
Michigan
North Carolina
Northwestern
New York University
Boston
University of Pennsylvania
Washington University St. Louis
Emory
Vanderbilt

TABLE 5 Based on data from the 2008 Leiden University index of world research universities

TIME LINE	DISCOVERY	CREATOR	AFFILIATION
1961–1964	Model of distributed packet-switched communication	Paul Baran	UCLA Masters in Engineering graduate & RAND corporation employee
1962–1968	Advocacy of networked commuting	J.C.R. Licklider	MIT Professor & (1962–1968) head of the Information Processing Techniques Office at ARPA, the U.S. Department of Defense Advanced Research Projects Agency.
1959–1967	Stanford lab created bit-mapped screens, precursors of graphical user interfaces, multiple windows, and the computer mouse	Douglas Engelbart	University of California PhD graduate, Stanford University
1965	Coined the concept of hypertext	Theodore (Ted) Nelson	Masters in Sociology, Harvard University
1967	The first working hypertext system	Andries van Dam & Ted Nelson	Brown University; van Dam second ever recipient of a PhD in computer science (from University of Pennsylvania)
1969	Model of Interface Message Processors (IMP) computing for routing messages between machines, aka routers	Wes Clark & Larry Roberts	MIT PhD in Electrical Engineering (Clark & Roberts); chief scientist in the ARPA Information Processing Techniques Office (Clark)
1969	Adoption of the first IMP	UCLA	UCLA
1969	Issuance of notes ("protocols") governing exchanges between machines	Networking Working Group	Research students from various graduate programs
1969	The first backbone of ARPANET	UCLA & Engelbart's Stanford lab	UCLA/Stanford University
1972	Email (between users of different machines)	Ray Tomlinson	MIT Masters of Science graduate & employee of the technology company of Bolt Beranek and Newman
1974	Transport Control Protocol (TCP) for inter-networking packet-switched computer networks	Vinton Cerf & Robert Kahn	Stanford University mathematics graduate (Cerf) & ARPANET administrator and MIT graduate (Kahn)
1974	Manufacturers began to offer personal computers for sale, and a new phrase entered the language	Various	

TIME LINE	DISCOVERY	CREATOR	AFFILIATION
1975	Microsoft's first program for the Altair	Bill Gates & Paul Allen	Harvard University (drop outs)
1977	Modem	Randy Suess & Ward Christensen	Chicago computer hobbyists; Christensen IBM employee
1978	Online Bulletin Board System (BBS)	Ward Christensen	IBM employee
1979	USENET news groups system	Tom Truscott & Jim Ellis	Duke University graduate students
1980	ENQUIRE institutional hypertext system	Tim Berners-Lee	Oxford University graduate and CERN, Switzerland, employee
1989–1991	World Wide Web	Tim Berners-Lee	Oxford University graduate and CERN, Switzerland, employee
1991	Mosaic graphical interface browser for the WWW	Marc Andreessen & Eric Bina.	University of Illinois undergraduate (Andreessen) & programmer (Bina)
1994	Webcrawler, first full text web search engine	Brian Pinkerton	University of Washington graduate student, later PhD in Computer Science
1997	Google search algorithm	Larry Page & Sergey Brin	Stanford University MSc (Page) and PhD (Brin)
TABLE 6			

Notes

1. Firms and universities share some common characteristics and have many distinctive traits. That they both function in the twentieth century as incubators of various kinds of innovation and discovery does not obviate marked differences in their operating purpose, style and assumptions.

2. 'In little over two decades in Australia, the UK and New Zealand, education export has grown from nothing into a service industry providing a significant chunk of tertiary education costs: about 15 per cent in Australia and 10 per cent in the UK. In Australia the education of international students is the third largest of all export sectors, behind coal and iron ore but ahead of tourism, gold and the agricultural products that sustained the settler state for most of its history: wool, wheat and beef. In certain Australian institutions, including universities with a global role in research that are prestige providers to local students, a large minority of all students are fee-paying internationals. Australia has 14 designated research universities each with over 7000 full fee paying students. In many smaller private colleges specializing in business studies or English language teaching, foreign education is the core business…In Europe foreign education of other European nationals is encouraged by the

Europeanization process and provided on the same basis as domestic education. The education of non-Europeans is often subsidized and in some cases such as parts of Germany is free of tuition charges. Outside Europe and Japan the commercial mode is more dominant. In total 12 per cent of all international students are educated in the UK, 10 per cent in Australia, 2 per cent in New Zealand, 3 per cent in Singapore and 2 per cent in Malaysia. China educates 6 per cent of all international students, many on a commercial basis. The worldwide value of the industry was $28 billion USD in 2005 and is now estimated at $40 billion dollars USD…Most of this money flows as transfers from the emerging economies to the Anglophone zone.' Simon Marginson, 'Space Making Strategies' in Simon Marginson, Peter Murphy and Michael Peters (2009).

3. *Logik der Forschung* (1934), which first appeared in English as *The Logic of Scientific Discovery* in 1959.

4. Derrida (2004), 135.

5. As Gilbert Chesterton observed: 'The real trouble with this world of ours is not that it is an unreasonable world, nor even that it is a reasonable one. The commonest kind of trouble is that it is nearly reasonable, but not quite. Life is not an illogicality, yet it is a trap for logicians. It looks just a little more mathematical and regular than it is; its exactitude is obvious, but its inexactitude is hidden; its wildness lies in wait.' G. K. Chesterton (2004 [1908]), 74.

6. Murphy (2008), 65–78.

7. Published as 'The Crisis of Culture and the State' in Castoriadis (1991).

8. 'The Crisis of Culture and the State,' Castoriadis (1991), 219–242; 'Culture in a Democratic Society,' Castoriadis (1997), 338–348. 'Imaginary and Imagination at the Crossroads,' Castoriadis (2007), 71–90.

9. Charles Murray, *Human Accomplishment* (2003), chapter 14.

10. The cultural geography of these moments is also highly concentrated. The geographical core of peak creation in the visual arts is the Italian Renaissance cities from the mid-1400s to the mid-1500s and the Low Countries in the 1600s. The geography of peak music creation is centered on North Italian cities and Central European cities between Vienna, Munich and Prague. The geography of peak literary creation is centered on Elizabethan London in the early 1600s—and on nineteenth-century London, Paris, the north-western corridor that runs from Paris to Berlin, St Petersburg, Moscow, the Chicago-Boston-New York triangle and California. The geography of peak science creation is the most dispersed in multiple points of concentration across the United Kingdom, Central and Northern Europe, the Chicago-Boston-New York triangle and California. These geometrics extend through to 1950 only. See the maps in Murray (2003), 301–304.

11. Huebner (2005), 980–986. Silverberg and Verspagen (2003), 671–693, offer a somewhat different medium-term picture but the same long-term conclusion. Their quadratic analysis shows a higher level of innovation during 1850–1900 that levels off around 1930, or in the case of patents, 1920. Silverberg and Verspagen's general assessment is that the rate of basic innovation slowed down in the twentieth century after a period of relatively rapid increase in the later half of the nineteenth century. The authors' caution about this analysis stemmed from the fact that the data they analyzed extended only to the end of the 1970s.

12. Murray (2003), 312–320.

13. The mid-century upswing in technology discovery noted by Murray (2003: 315) has

also been observed by economists. See Field (2003).

14. The figures cited are drawn from Huebner (2005: 984–985) and Smart (2005). http://www.accelerating.org/articles/huebnerinnovation.html.

15. The figures cited are from the United States Copyright Office, U.S. Census Bureau, Current Population Reports, and from Boldrin and Levine (2008), chapter 5.

16. Boldrin and Levine (2008), chapter 5.

17. The history of U.S. copyright registration is graphically represented in the statistical chart in Boldrin and Levine (2008), 100. For U.S. patent registration, see Figure 3 in Huebner (2005), 985. For graphic depictions of comparable trends across both the United States and Europe, as it affects major works and inventions, see the charts in Murray (2003), 428, 437, 441.

18. After a series of visiting appointments, in 1927–28 and 1930, Schumpeter joined Harvard's Economics department on a regular basis in 1932. On that, and his relationship with Parsons, see McCraw (2007).

19. Carlsson, et al. (2009).

20. Lyotard's work was originally a report on knowledge for the Conseil des universités du Québec.

21. Murray (2003) analyses data on peak creation through to the cut-off point of 1950. Murray's methodologically-cautious findings are consistent with Huebner (2005: 980–986) who shows that the peak of major science and technology discoveries across the globe measured per capita occurred in 1873.

22. As this decline increased, the obverse effect of the decline was the intensification of national research management schemes by national governments that suffered from both a bad conscience that this was happening and a desire to ignore that it was happening by devising consoling proofs that profound research was going on. An early pioneer of this double code was the Thatcher government in the United Kingdom, and it was followed by similar models in Australia under the Hawke-Keating government and in New Zealand, and elsewhere. One of the self-deluding consequences of this was the equating of innovation with discovery. Other delusions followed. Quality or excellence in research, it was thought, could be measured by ratings made by panels of peers or else by the national ranking of departments on the basis of quantitative outputs such as numbers of PhD completions, or the amount of grant dollars received by researchers (principally from national research councils) or the number of articles published by researchers. The Engels-like attempt to convert quantity into quality was only marginally less silly than the mute inability of any expert panel or group to explain how or why or on what basis it reached any ranking of persons, groups, works or fields. Pinning a tail on the donkey would have been just as effective, and certainly more plausible. Institutional measures of research 'impact' scaled the depths of the modern researcher's tabloid-like instinct for sensation, and were quite reminiscent of the discreditable appetite for 'shock' of the third-rate, third-generation, mid-twentieth century institutional Modernists. All of these ludicrous 'measures' occluded historical comparisons of performance for the very good reason that such comparisons show that contemporary research per capita is—on average—not that good and sometimes pitiable in contrast with centuries past. The global indexes and comparisons that Simon Marginson dissects in chapter five—while they are more informative than national comparative data—similarly hide contemporary research from unflattering historical comparisons, allowing the global research university to continue to complacently confuse the trivial with the significant, and dis-

semination with discovery.

23. The data is drawn from the large-scale Internet Movie Database, and uses that database's comprehensive listing of film titles produced compared with the same database's listing of the Top 250 films voted by its regular users. The Top 250 films are ranked according to user ranking of them as anything between a 0-star and 10-star film. All the films in this rank order attract tens of thousands and many of them hundreds of thousands of user scores.

24. Its corrosive effect on science is seen in the behaviour of the influential climate science circle connected to the Climatic Research Unit (CRU) at East Anglia University, who were among the principal proponents of the global warming climate hypothesis that emerged in the late twentieth century and became centre-stage in world science policy at the dawn of the new millennium. The chief actors in the Unit's milieu violated many of the key norms of public science. They cherry-picked and massaged data, refused to publish raw data so that evidence for scientific claims could be independently reviewed, resisted Freedom of Information requests to release data, denied the possibility of counter-hypotheses, denigrated their critics, opposed the right of anyone to criticise them, hid private doubts behind public assertions of certainty, and sought to obstruct the publication of critics research. The integrity of the data in the CRU's databases and the assumptions inscribed in the computer modelling of global paleo climate left much to be desired. In contravention of standard scientific methods, failed predictions of global warming were viewed by the group, and many others, as irrelevant to the standing of its scientific claims. In part this was poor science badly done. In part it was the mutation of science into ideology, and an eroding of the long-standing sceptical foundations of science that go back to the ancient Greek world. When the word 'sceptic' becomes a dirty word in the vocabulary of the scientist, as it did in the middle of the global warming debate, then science has a real problem. When a science is judged to be 'settled' or 'consensual,' a similar problem exists. The idea of a settled science, virtually a contradiction in terms, became the dogma of many climate scientists in spite of warnings about the unreliability of climate models that in the view of the physicist Freeman Dyson 'use fudge-factors rather than physics.' As Galileo put it in 1612, writing to Mark Wesler, 'in the sciences the authority of thousands of opinions is not worth as much as one tiny spark of reason in an individual man.' Naturally, there are many things that any science takes for granted. It would be a waste of everyone's time to do otherwise. But that does not mean that those things cannot be called into question if by doing so interesting counter-hypotheses, ideas, and explanations can be explored. When scepticism is outlawed by the pseudo-consensus of the bossy and the loud-mouthed, science turns from the work of trialling, contesting and refuting truth-claims to one of gathering support for millennial ideologies and moral panics. When science begins to think that the world is 'coming to an end,' we ought to be able to recognize that there is something absurd in the air.

25. Innovational investment is investment in new industries, not in old industries. The economist Robert Solow (n.d.), commenting on Joseph Schumpeter, remarked that Schumpeter 'seemed not to understand what Keynesian economics was about, or why it won over the younger generation. For example, he described Keynes as the apostle of consumer spending (in contrast to his own emphasis on innovational investment). But in fact consumer spending is passive in Keynes's General Theory. The driving force of the aggregate economy is actually investment spending...' But this

misses the point of innovational investment—it is not ordinary investment, but extraordinary investment in industry sectors that have not previously existed. Schumpeter argued that a static capitalist system does not increase wealth, but at most maintains it. Capitalism only increases wealth by innovation, by the discovery or invention of new production processes, products, technologies, and organizational methods that lower costs and create new markets.

26. The first design of a small electric car was by Professor Sibrandus Stratingh, Professor of Chemistry and Technology at the University of Groningen in the Netherlands. The car was built by his assistant Christopher Becker in 1835.

27. Robert Solow (n.d.) makes an observation about Joseph Schumpeter's *Capitalism, Socialism and Democracy*: 'The book reiterates the standard Schumpeterian vision of capitalist turmoil and transformation, with the entrepreneurs as the indispensable heroes. This time he suggests a mechanism within capitalist society that (inevitably?) causes it to undermine itself. The children and grandchildren of successful entrepreneurs, precisely the people with the right DNA, are seduced by inherited wealth into intellectual pursuits, the arts, aristocratic habits, perhaps even into left-wing or at least anti-capitalist ideologies. It is not the proletariat that blows up the capitalist edifice, which is in fact good for the proletariat. It is the second generation of successful entrepreneurs that lets the ground floor decay.' A curious variation of this happened with the ICT industry, arguably not to the second generation but the first generation that gravitated to social causes to spend their money on rather than continuous invention and innovation. It made them intellectual heroes but it rather foreshortened the duration of their technological and organizational zeitgeist.

28. Peter Drucker made a similar point in the early 1980s, a previous time of serious recession and one equally enchanted by monetary solutions to productive problems. An advocate of Schumpeter's economics, Drucker was equally skeptical of Keynesian fiscal policies and Friedman's monetarism. See Peter Drucker (1983).

29. Writing at the tail end of America's great depression, Schumpeter observed: 'We are just now in the downgrade of a wave of enterprise that created the electrical power plant, the electrical industry, the electrified farm and home and the motorcar. We find all that very marvellous, [yet]…we cannot for our lives see where opportunities of comparable importance are to come from….Technological possibilities are an uncharted sea. We may survey a geographical region and appraise…that the best plots are first taken into cultivation, after them the next best ones and so on. At any given time during this process it is only relatively inferior plots that remain to be exploited in the future. But we cannot reason in this fashion about the future possibilities of technological advance. From the fact that some of them have been exploited before others, it cannot be inferred that the former were more productive than the latter. And those that are still in the lap of the gods may be more or less productive than any that have thus far come within our range of observation….There is no reason to expect slackening of the rate of output through exhaustion of technological possibilities.' Joseph Schumpeter (2006 [1942]), 117–18).

30. Angus Maddison (2001, 1995). See also the Historical Statistics data at http://www.ggdc.net/maddison/.

31. 'These revolutions periodically reshape the existing structure of industry by introducing new methods of production—the mechanized factory, the electrified factory, chemical synthesis and the like; new commodities, such as railroad service, motorcars, electrical appliances; new forms of organization.' Schumpeter (2006

[1942]), 68. 'Those revolutions are not strictly incessant; they occur in discrete rushes which are separated from each other by spans of comparative quiet. The process as a whole works incessantly, however, in the sense that there always is either revolution or absorption of the results of revolution, both together forming what are known as business cycles.' Schumpeter (2006 [1942]), 83, footnote 2.

32. Bell (1999 [1973]), 245–246.

33. John Carroll in his essay on the university in *Ego and Soul* (2008: 155) is right when he says simply: 'The humanist university has run down.' This is confirmed by the story of the foundation of American universities. Their prime period of foundation was from after the Civil War through the 1890s. 'The greatest rate of increase in the number of colleges and universities operating in the United States occurred during the last four decades of the 19th century. The Morrill Act of 1862 established the land-grant state colleges. A large number of public institutions of higher education were already in existence at the time of the Morrill Act. But this legislation, together with the Hatch Act of 1887, was important in creating state institutions that would not only educate large numbers of Americans but would play an influential role in the development of research and technology programs with practical applications to industry. Almost five times as many private institutions as public institutions were founded over the period 1860–1899. It was in the late 19th century that wealthy American industrialists endowed many of the great private research universities. The creation of these private universities was aided by the fact that the U.S. government made donations to institutional endowments deductible under the federal income tax. Relatively few institutions of higher education were founded after the turn of the century, and those that were have not tended to be as prestigious. Among the 35 private institutions in the top 50 universities in the 1999 rankings of U.S. News and World Report, only one was founded after 1900. Of the top 35 liberal arts colleges, only two were founded in the 20th century.' Kent Hill http://www.ausicom.com/filelib/PDF/ResearchLibrary/US%20research%20data.pdf, accessed 12 May, 2009.

34. Bell (1999 [1973]), 245.

35. The Association of American Colleges and Universities.

36. http://www.carnegiefoundation.org. The difference between an American research university with very high research activity (A) and a regular doctoral-granting university that carries out research (B) is indicated by the following 2009 Carnegie figures based on 2002–2004 data. The mean number of humanities doctorates for A is 45, the mean number of social science doctorates is 38. In comparison, the mean number of humanities doctorates for B is 9, the mean number of social science doctorates is 10.

37. The Leiden ranking separates out each of the University of California campuses, while I have compounded them. The ranking is available at http://www.cwts.nl/ranking/world_100_green.html, accessed April 27, 2009. The index is a measure of publications and citations per capita adjusted for field biases. The top non-US university, the University of Cambridge, ranks 26 on the index while the top continental European university, Zurich, ranks, 29; Oxford University, ranks 30.

38. Adelaide, Australian National University, Melbourne, Monash, New South Wales, Queensland, Sydney, Western Australia, Flinders, Macquarie, Murdoch, New England, Newcastle, Tasmania. Valadkhani & Worthington (2006) add University of Wollongong to the list.

39. Gallagher (2009) notes that the Group of Eight undertake 72% of higher education

basic research and 41% of Australia's total basic research.

40. Because this was a technological science, in which invention is skewed toward youth, graduate students were notably key players in this story. Youth is significantly correlated with creativity in some fields such as performing arts or poetry, but the obverse applies in other fields.

41. 'Ernst et al. (2000) examine the patent activity of inventors working in 43 German companies in the chemical, electrical, and mechanical engineering industry. They, too, find that a small group of key inventors is responsible for the major part of the company's technological performance. Agrawal and Henderson (2002) find a highly skewed distribution of patents for the MIT engineers in their study: 44% were never an inventor on a patent during the 15-year period; less than 15% had been granted more than five patents; and less than 6% had been granted more than 10. Azoulay et al. (2005) find that 19% of their sample of publishing university researchers working in areas related to biotechnology had one or more patent between the date of their degree and 1999.' Stephan et al. 2007, 71–99.

42. In the United States, in the sciences, five years after graduating, 14% of PhDs will have produced no articles at all, and 40% will have produced only between 1 and 5 articles in the period. The data is from the 1995 National Science Foundation Survey of Doctorate Recipients, and is reported in Stephan, et al. 2007, 71–99.

43. Lotka (1926), 317–324.

44. Lotka's original study said that 6% of producers create 50% of the output of a field. Later research showed that Lotka's calculation of the output of the most productive was too generous. Dean Simonton's summation of sixty years of further research of the topic concluded that typically 10% of creators produce half the output of a creative field. Dennis (1955), 277–278, Simonton (1999), 149 and (1984), 78–79. Kyvik (1989), 205–214, concluded that 20% of *tenured* faculty (i.e. excluding contract and casual staff) at Norwegian universities produces 50% of the sector's output. Half of the researchers produce 85% of the output. Dennis (1955) examined the distribution of productivity in seven domains. Across all of the domains, 10 percent of creators contributed 50% of output, while 61% of creators made only one contribution each. The most prolific creator in a given domain tends to be 57 times as productive as the least productive creators.

45. Moles (1966 [1958]).

46. Simonton (1999), 150.

47. Simonton (1999), 154–197 and (1984), 78–92.

48. Simonton (1999), 154.

49. Schiller (2004 [1795]), Huizinga (1995 [1938]), Marcuse (1955).

50. Simon (1974), 327–335 and Simonton (1984), 139.

51. S. Cole and J. R. Cole (1967), 377–390.

52. Dennis (1954), 180–183. '…when a member of the National Academy dies, a biographical sketch and a bibliography appear in the Biographical Memoirs of the Academy. A bibliographic count was made for each man whose bibliography appeared in the Biographical Memoirs between 1943 and 1952, inclusive, and who reached age 70 before his death…According to the bibliographies as published, these 41 men were responsible for a total of 8332 works. This means an average of 203 per person. The highest record was 768 items, the lowest 27. Eleven had 300 or more publications each. Only 15 had fewer than 100 publications each. The median number was 145' (180). See also the comments on this by Simonton (1999), 154–157 and

(1984), 78–80.

53. Zuckerman (1977). See also Simonton (1999), 154 and (1984), 84–85.

54. Albert (1975), 148.

55. Simonton (1984), 84.

56. Schumpeter's biographer, Thomas K. McCraw, Isidor Straus Professor of Business History, Emeritus, at the Harvard Business School notes that 'He published about five million words—two million in English and three million in German, much of which has now been translated into English and many other languages. I'm including in this total his books, articles, book reviews, and published lectures. I don't include his thousands of letters and copious diary entries. To put the five million words into perspective: a book of 300 pages contains about 100,000 words. So by this measure Schumpeter wrote the equivalent of about 50 books. And he did it without co-authors and with minimal research assistance. He was an obsessive and indefatigable scholar: a very unusual combination of a grind who was also a great showman, a ladies' man, and an altogether electrifying personality.' Nick Schultz, n.d.

57. Alfred Hitchcock (b. 1899) made 58 films as a director. He had made twenty-two films before his first semi-classic, the 1935 film, *The 39 Steps*, aged 36. He created a string of marvellous films through his forties, fifties and sixties.

58. 'The very act of creation in science involves the combination and recombination of previously unrelated ideas to form original and unconventional assemblages...While it is possible for novel assemblages to emerge from the permutation of ideas within a single discipline, it is increasingly believed that the creation of new scientific knowledge—creativity—is enabled and accelerated by fusing ideas from multiple disciplines:' Rhoten, et. al. (2009), 84.

59. In 1894, Weber was appointed professor of economics at Freiburg University, and then to the same post at the University of Heidelberg in 1896. He had a nervous breakdown in 1899, and he did not return to teaching. He resigned his position in 1903, and took on the role of associate editor of the *Archives for Social Science and Social Welfare* in 1904 and continued thereafter effectively as an independent scholar until 1918 when he took a teaching professorship at the University of Vienna, and the same at the University of Munich in 1919. He died in 1920, a casualty of the Spanish flu epidemic, aged 56.

60. Miller (2000 [1996]), 344. Robert Merton notes that 'The total number of scientific papers published by scientists differs enormously, ranging from the large proportion of Ph.D.'s who publish one paper or none at all to the rare likes of William Thomson, Lord Kelvin, with his six hundred plus papers, or the mathematician Arthur Cayley, publishing a paper every few weeks throughout his work life for a total of almost a thousand.' Merton (1988), 606–623.

61. Miller (2000 [1996]), 354–355.

62. Samuel Coleridge, *Biographia Literaria*, II.

63. By un-decidable I do not mean the inability to decide, the disease of relativism. A good society requires people who are decisive and who have strong wills. A faithless condition in which no one believes in anything, or who use the inability to decide as a rationalization of a weak character is unimaginative. As John Carroll (*Ego and Soul*, 149) observes in an important essay on the failures of the modern university, relativism is one of the key things that accounts for the abating energy of the university and its loss of purpose. Un-decidability is different from indecision. It refers to those polarities that cannot be decided between but must be thought together.

Such thinking together requires massive strength of character and at the same is a potent stimulus to the imagination.

64. Kant (1964). See the concluding section, 'The Extreme Limit of Practical Philosophy.'
65. Castoriadis, 'Individual, Society, Rationality, History' (1991), 47–80.
66. Carroll (2001), 9, 13, 14 and (2008), 4–8, 150.
67. Kant (1952), 180, 181.
68. Koestler (1964).
69. August Wilhelm von Schlegel and Karl Wilhelm von Schlegel cited in M. Nordau (1900), 73.
70. Scruton (2005), 55–67.
71. Berlyne (1971).
72. Castoriadis talks about the imagination's power of unification and power of organization. See Castoriadis (1997), 230, 259.
73. This was one of Nietzsche's complaints. It is echoed persuasively by John Carroll. See especially *Ego and Soul*, 156.
74. Agnes Heller drew the helpful distinction between 'objectivation for itself' (knowledge that creates meaning) and the 'objectivation for and in itself'(institutionalized knowledge). The latter in part is a function of a power that has an ambiguous relation with meaning. An example of the difference between the two is the science of cosmology with its capacity to stimulate wonder, and laboratory science that does on occasion divulge wonderful things and at other times borders on tedious routine. See Heller (1985).
75. Darwin (1993), 52.
76. Simonton (1999), 119.
77. Humboldt's creation was first named Friedrich Wilhelm University.
78. Humboldt's view was that 'Just as primary instruction makes the teacher possible, so he renders himself dispensable through schooling at the secondary level. The university teacher is thus no longer a teacher and the student is no longer a pupil. Instead the student conducts research on his own behalf and the professor supervises his research and supports him in it. Because learning at university level places the student in a position to apprehend the unity of scholarly enquiry and thereby lays claim to his creative powers.' Humboldt (1903–1936), vol 13, 295–283 (here 260–261).
79. Crouter (2006), 140–168; Röhrs (1987). Key works included Fichte's 'On the Duties of the Scholar' (1794), 'On the Destiny of the Scholar' (1794), 'Deduction of a Plan for a Higher Institution of Learning to be established in Berlin' (1807), Schleiermacher's 'Lectures on the Method of Academic Study' (1803), 'Occasional Thoughts Concerning Universities' (1809).
80. Lambropoulos (1993).
81. The love of self-education by very high-achieving and creative personalities is a visible theme in Goertzel, et al. (1978). '…in 90 percent of the homes in which the eminent persons were reared, there was a love of learning' (13), 'Children who become eminent love learning but dislike school and schoolteachers who try to confine them to a curriculum not designed for individual needs.' (p. 337) 'The family often has a large library.' (343) 'Sixty percent of the three hundred disliked school…' (345)
82. Röhrs (1987), 20.
83. Röhrs (1987), 20.
84. This does not preclude lecturing, rather it goes to the spirit that the lecture is does

in and the relation with those who audit the lecture. After all, Hegel gave immortal lectures. As Hegel's colleague, Schleiermacher, put it, 'Few understand the significance of using lectures, but, oddly enough, this practice has always persevered despite its constantly being very poorly done by the majority of teachers. This continuance is clear proof of how very much lecturing belongs to the essence of the university and of how greatly it is worth the trouble to reserve this form of instruction always for those few who, from time to time, know how to handle it correctly. Indeed one could say that the true and peculiar benefit a university teacher confers is always in exact relation to the person's proficiency in this art.' (Crouter, 159)

85. Tusa (2004), 93–94.
86. Menand (2001), 257.
87. Other professors of the time included Granville Stanley Hall and Herbert Baxter Adams. Hall was the first president of the American Psychological Association and organized visits by Sigmund Freud and Carl Jung to give lectures in 1909. Adams, who was an historian, coined the term 'political science.'
88. Murphy (2006), 64–92.
89. Kerr (1963), 16–17.
90. Kerr (1963), 17.
91. Kerr (1963). On Clark Kerr, see Simon Marginson (2008).
92. Simonton (1984), 74.
93. One of the most interesting of the alternatives to the discipline-based university is the collegiate university. Its most successful examples are the English universities of Oxford and Cambridge. An admirer of the collegiate model, Roger Scruton (2006: 167) observes that: 'In modern universities, academic posts are available only to those who are working in some recognized subject, with a faculty and curriculum of its own. In the Cambridge that I knew many of the fellows were attached to no university faculty, and pursued researches that no university bureaucracy would endorse with a grant or stipend.' Scruton relates that his tutor (Dr Laurence Picken) was a scholar in the fields of biochemistry, cytology, musicology, Chinese, Slavonic studies and ethnomusicology, and was a world expert on Turkish musical instruments, Bach cantatas, ancient Chinese science and the reproduction of cells. Scruton was a student of Jesus College, Cambridge. He was later to become Professor of Aesthetics at Birkbeck College, part of the University of London, also a federative college system, though one in which each constitutive college is really a semi-autonomous discipline-based university in its own right. It is notable nonetheless that all of the leading research universities in the United Kingdom—the G5 composed of the London School of Economics, Imperial College London, University College London, University of Oxford and University of Cambridge—have a collegiate history. The London School of Economics and University College London are colleges of the University of London while Imperial College became independent of the University of London in 2007. As the previous volume in this series, *Global Creation*, pointed out, creativity and structures of dual power are often aligned. The collegiate university (not to be confused with collegial fraternities)—by seperating college and university, and giving them different functions—induces a state of dual academic power, with evident consequences.
94. Goertzel, et al. (1978), and the commentary on this by Simonton (1984), 74.
95. One model of such undergraduate education is the English collegiate universities of Oxford and Cambridge. Roger Scruton (2006: 166) relates his own experience of

Cambridge in the 1960s. 'Nothing else was required of the student in the humanities apart from the weekly (or sometimes twice weekly) essay. Lectures, which were arranged by the university and not by the college, were optional. It was up to the lecturer to interest the students; should he fail to do so, then he would find himself talking to an empty hall. The advice often given to the new undergraduate was to attend the best lectures, in whatever subject they happened to be. Although reading philosophy at Cambridge, many of the lectures I attended were given by the departments of English, Modern Greek and German. It was not unknown for an undergraduate to be awarded a first-class degree without ever having attended a lecture. The important thing was to read, to write and to defend what you had written during that crucial hour of advocacy and interrogation.'

96. This is the kind of knowledge that Schleiermacher thought inappropriate for a university. University inquiry is a type of global inquiry. '...the totality of knowledge is to be presented, accounted for, and in this manner the principles and, as it were, the fundament of all knowing are brought into perspective so that each person gains what it takes to become acquainted with every area of learning.' (Crouter, 156). The capacity to carry inquiry in every direction distinguishes the university from schools and from research institutes. The university is concerned with the overall unity of knowledge.

97. Solow (1956), 65–94. The idea that the economic value of research is its impact on workforce productivity dominates justifications of research activity. See for example the KPMG report. Solow won the Nobel Prize in 1987, and was in a minor way a student of Schumpeter's at Harvard. Other students of Schumpeter included Robert Heilbroner, Nicholas Georgescu-Roegen, Alan Greenspan, and Paul Samuelson.

98. The Minister responsible was John Dawkins, who from 1987 to 1991 was the Australian federal government Minister for Employment, Education and Training.

99. Hayek (1960), 388–389.

100. Berwick (1970).

101. Rutkoff and Scott (1986).

102. Bourdieu (1988), 102, 105, 107, 111.

103. It is not possible to predict how a student will perform at a post-graduate level based on under-graduate performance, as it is not possible to predict undergraduate performance based on high school results. Or as Schleiermacher observed, 'the selection and admission of students is more art than science.' Crouter (2006), 158.

104. Crouter (2006), 158.

105. Simonton (1984 : 84), Zuckerman (1977), Dennis (1956), Goertzel, et al. (1978).

106. David Grene's part in the founding of the Committee in many ways sums up its animating spirit. As his obituary observed, Grene was a brilliant classicist and a colourful character. 'His own quirks could provoke colleagues, including the chairmen of the classics and English departments at Chicago, who fired him the same day. He marched straight to the brilliant and autocratic university president, Robert Maynard Hutchins, who had clearly anticipated such events. He pulled a note from his file. "This man is not to be fired without my permission," it said. Mr. Hutchins decided the safest course was to steer Mr. Grene clear of formal departments altogether. He made him one of the five founding members of the Committee on Social Thought, an interdisciplinary group that Mr. Grene himself called "an odd nest of birds."' Martin (2002).

107. Excepting possibly, the ghost of a design—La Trobe University was established in

1967 on the basis of a collegiate model of university. Within a few years of foundation, the model had fallen into abeyance, but a little of its spirit may have lived on for a time.

108. The Seminar on the Sociology of Culture had good relations for instance with David Tacey in the English department, author of *Patrick White: Fiction and the Unconscious* (1988) and the historian Inga Clendingen, author of *Aztecs* (1991) and *Reading the Holocaust* (1998).

109. On the Social Theory side of the ledger, the range of works produced by the milieu includes Ferenc Feher's *The Frozen Revolution* (1987) and *The French Revolution and the Birth of Modernity* (1990), John Rundell's *Origins of Modernity* (1987), Heller and Feher's *The Postmodern Political Condition* (1989) and *The Grandeur and Twilight of Radical Universalism* (1991), David Roberts' *Art and Enlightenment* (1991), Johann Arnason's *The Future That Failed* (1993), *The Peripheral Centre* (2002) and *Civilizations in Dispute* (2003), Peter Beilharz's *Labour's Utopias* (1991), *Transforming Labor* (1994), *Imagining the Antipodes* (1997), and *Zygmunt Bauman: Dialectic of Modernity* (2000), Peter Murphy's *Civic Justice* (2001), Murphy and Roberts' *Dialectic of Romanticism* (2004), Arnason and Roberts' *Elias Canetti's Counter-Image of Society* (2004), Simon Marginson, Michael Peters and Murphy's *Creativity and the Global Knowledge Economy* (2009), and Eduardo de la Fuente's *Twentieth Century Music and the Question of Modernity* (2010).

110. Agnes Heller is Hannah Arendt Chair of Philosophy in the Graduate Faculty at the New School for Social Research. Claudio Veliz was Professor of Sociology and Dean of the School of Social Sciences, La Trobe University, Melbourne, Australia (1972–1989) and Professor of History and Director of the University Professors at Boston University (1990–2002). Johann Arnason held a personal chair in Sociology at La Trobe University from 1994 to 2003. John Carroll is Professor of Sociology at La Trobe, as is Peter Beilharz. Simon Marginson is Professor of Higher Education at the University of Melbourne. Peter Murphy is Associate Professor of Communications at Monash University. Eduardo de la Fuente is Lecturer in Communications at Monash University. David Roberts is Emeritus Professor of German at Monash University. John Rundell is Associate Professor of Social Theory at the University of Melbourne. Ferenc Feher was Senior Lecturer at the New School at the time of his death in 1994.

111. Following her relocation to the Graduate Faculty of the New School for Social Research in New York, Agnes Heller completed her trilogy of work on ethics, *General Ethics* (1989), *A Philosophy of Morals* (1990), and *An Ethics of Personality* (1996) followed by a shift into the terrain of aesthetics, with *The Concept of the Beautiful* (1999), *The Time Is Out of Joint* (2000), her study of Shakespeare as a philosopher of history, and *The Immortal Comedy* (2005), where she reflects on the comic phenomenon in art, literature and life.

112. Gombrich remarked 'You may remember that I contributed to the Schilpp volume ["The Logic of Vanity Fair" in *The Philosophy of Karl Popper*, ed. P. A. Schilpp (LaSalle, Ill.: Open Court, 1974), pp. 925–957], and I mention there that I attended Hayek's seminar [at the London School of Economics] when Karl Popper read his paper on the poverty of historicism, which naturally interested me very much because I had been very skeptical of the sort of Hegelian approach to the history of art. And we talked a good deal about that too, but we talked of many other things as well. You mentioned, incidentally, that Popper is mainly known as a philosopher

of science, which is true, but after all, his book The Open Society [The Open Society and Its Enemies (London: Routledge & Kegan Paul, 1945)], is largely also a work of scholarship about the ancient world, so he is also a historian.' Levinson (n.d.).

References

Albert, R. S. (1975). Toward a behavioral definition of genius. *American Psychologist*, 30, 140–151.

Bell, D. (1999 [1973]). *The Coming of Post-Industrial Society*. New York: Basic Books.

Berlyne, D. E. (1971). *Aesthetics and Psychobiology*. New York: Appleton-Century-Croft.

Berwick, K. (1970). Interview with Robert M. Hutchins, *Don't Just Do Something*. Santa Barbara, California: Center for the Study of Democratic Institutions, 1970. http://www.cooperativeindividualism.org/hutchins_on_center_democratic_institutions.html accessed April 25, 2009.

Boldrin, M & D. K. Levine. (2008). *Against Intellectual Monopoly*. Cambridge: Cambridge University Press.

Bourdieu, P. (1988). *Homo Academicus*. Stanford, CA: Stanford University Press.

Carlsson, B., Z. J. Acs, D. B. Audretsch & P. Braunerhjelm. (2007). The Knowledge Filter, Entrepreneurship, and Economic Growth. *CESIS Electronic Working Paper Series*, Paper 104, October. http://www.infra.kth.se/cesis/documents/WP104.pdf accessed 27 June 2009.

Carroll, J. (2001). *The Western Dreaming*. Sydney: HarperColllins.

Carroll, J. (2008). *Ego and Soul: The Modern West in Search of Meaning*. Melbourne: Scribe.

Castoriadis, C. (1991). *Philosophy, Politics, Autonomy*. Oxford: Oxford University Press.

Castoriadis, C. (1997a). *The Castoriadis Reader*. Oxford: Blackwell.

Castoriadis, C. (1997b). *World in Fragments*. Stanford, CA: Stanford University Press.

Castoriadis, C. (2007). *Figures of the Thinkable*. Stanford, CA: Stanford University Press.

Chesterton, G. K. (2004 [1908]). *Orthodoxy*. Mineola, NY: Dover.

Cole, S. & J. R. Cole. (1967). Scientific output and recognition: A study in the operation of the reward system in science. *American Sociological Review* 32, 377–390.

Crouter, R. (2006). *Friedrich Schleiermacher: Between Enlightenment and Romanticism*. Oxford: Oxford University Press.

Darwin, C. (1993). *The Autobiography of Charles Darwin: 1809–1882*, Nora Barlow (ed.). New York: Norton.

Dennis, W. (1954). Bibliographies of eminent scientists. *Scientific Monthly* 79 (3), 180–183.

Dennis, W. (1955). Variations in productivity among creative workers. *Scientific Monthly* 80, 277–278.

Dennis, W. (1956). Age and productivity among scientists. *Science* 123, 724–725.

Derrida, J. (2004). *The Eyes of the University, Right to Philosophy 2*. Stanford, CA: Stanford University Press.

Drucker, P. (1983). Modern Prophets: Schumpeter and Keynes? http://www.peter-drucker.at/en/texts/proph_01.html accessed 14 May, 2009.

Field, A. J. (2003). The most technologically progressive decade of the century. *The American Economic Review*, September.

Gallagher, M. (2009). Australia's research universities and their position in the world. http://www.go8.edu.au/storage/go8statements/2009/AFR_HE_Conference_2009.pdf accessed March 17, 2010.

Goertzel, M. G., V. Goertzel, & T. G. Goertzel. (1978). *Three Hundred Eminent Personalities*. San Francisco: Jossey-Bass.

Hayek, F. A. (1960). *The Constitution of Liberty*. London: Routledge.

Heller, A. (1985). *The Power of Shame: A Rational Perspective*. London: Routledge.

Hill, K. (n.d.). Universities in the U.S. National Innovation System. Center for Business Research, L. William Seidman Research Institute, W. P. Carey School of Business, Arizona State University.

http://www.ausicom.com/filelib/PDF/ResearchLibrary/US%20research%20data.pdf, accessed 12 May, 2009.

Huebner, J. (2005). A possible declining trend for worldwide innovation. *Technological Forecasting & Social Change* 72, 980–986.

Huizinga, J. (1995 [1938]). *Homo Ludens: a study of the play element in culture*. Boston: Beacon Press.

Humboldt, W. (1903–1936). Der Konigsberger und der Litauishe Schulplan. In A. Leitzmann (ed.) *Gesammelte Schriften*. 17 vols, Berlin, volume 13.

Kant, I. (1964). *Groundwork of the Metaphysic of Morals*. New York: Harper and Row.

Kant, I. (1952). *The Critique of Judgement*. Oxford: Clarendon.

Kerr, C. (1963). *The Uses of the University*. New York: Harper and Row.

Koestler, A. (1964). *The Act of Creation*. New York: Dell.

KPMG. (2009). *Economic Modelling of Improved Funding and Reform Arrangements for Universities*, 31 March.

Kyvik, S. (1989). Productivity Differences, Fields of Learning, and Lotka's Law. *Scientometrics*, 15:3–4, 205–214.

Lambropoulos, V. (1993). *The Rise of Eurocentrism: Anatomy of Interpretation*. Princeton, NY: Princeton University Press.

Levinson, P. (n.d.). What I Learned from Karl Popper: An Interview with E. H. Gombrich. The Gombrich Archive. http://www.gombrich.co.uk/showdoc.php?id=92 accessed 3 May, 2009.

Lotka, A. J. (1926). The frequency distribution of scientific productivity. *Journal of the Washington Academy of Sciences* 16 (12), 317–324.

Maddison, A. (2001). *The World Economy: A Millennial Perspective*. Paris: OECD.

Maddison, A. (1995). *Monitoring the World Economy 1820–1995*. Paris: OECD.

Marcuse, H. (1955). *Eros and Civilization*. Boston: Beacon Press.

Marginson, S. (2008).Clark Kerr and the Uses of the University. CSHE Ideas and Issues in Higher Education Seminar, Centre for the Study of Higher Education, University of Melbourne. http://www.cshe.unimelb.edu.au/research/seminarpapers/Clark Kerr15Dec08.pdf accessed 2 May, 2009.

Marginson, S., P. Murphy & M. Peters. (2009). *Global Creation: Space, Mobility and Synchrony in the Age of the Knowledge Economy*. New York: Peter Lang.

Martin, D. (2002). David Grene, Colorful Expert On the Classics, Is Dead at 89. *New York Times*, September 17.

McCraw, Thomas K. (2007). *Prophet of Innovation: Joseph Schumpeter and Creative Destruction*. Belknap Press.

Menand, L. (2001). *The Metaphysical Club*. New York: Farrar, Strauss & Giroux.

Merton, R. K. (1988). The Matthew Effect in Science, II: Cumulative Advantage and the Symbolism of Intellectual Property. *Isis*, 79:4, 606–623.

Miller, A. I. (2000 [1996]). *Insights of Genius: Imagery and Creativity in Science and Art*. Cambridge, MA: MIT Press.

Moles, A. (1966 [1958]). *Information Theory and Esthetic Perception*. Translated by Joel F. Cohen. Urbana: University of Illinois Press.

Murphy, P. (2008). The Pitch Black Night of Human Creation: Calling Heidegger's Philosophy of Terror to Account. V. Karalis (ed.) *Heidegger and the Aesthetics of Living*. Newcastle: Cambridge Scholars Publishing.

Murphy, P. (2006). American Civilization. *Thesis Eleven: Critical Theory and Historical Sociology* 81, 64–92.

Murray, C. (2003). *Human Accomplishment*. New York: HarperCollins.

Nordau, N. (1900). *Degeneration*. New York: Appleton-Century-Crofts.

Popper. K. (1959 [1934]). *The Logic of Scientific Discovery*. London: Routledge.

Rhoten, D., E. O'Connor & E. J. Hackett. (2009). The act of collaborative creation and the art of integrative creativity: originality, disciplinarity and interdisciplinarity. *Thesis Eleven: Critical Theory and Historical Sociology* 96, 83-108.

Röhrs, H. (1987). The Classical Idea of the University, its Origin and Significance as conceived by Humboldt. *Tradition and reform of the university under an international perspective: an interdisciplinary approach*. Edited by Hermann Röhrs in cooperation with Gerhard Hess. New York: Peter Lang.

Rutkoff, P. M. & W. B. Scott. (1986). *New School: A History of the New School for Social Research*. New York: Free Press.

Schiller, F. (2004 [1795]). *On the Aesthetic Education of Man*. Mineola, NY: Dover.

Schultz, N. (n.d.) Interview with Thomas McCraw, *Creative Destruction: The Words of the Prophet*. http://www.tcsdaily.com/article.aspx?id=060107C accessed 4 May, 2009.

Schumpeter, J. (2006 [1942]). *Capitalism, Socialism and Democracy*. London: Routledge.

Scruton, R. (2005). *Modern Culture*. London: Continuum.

Scruton, R. (2006 [2000]) *England: An Elegy*. London: Continuum.

Silverberg, G. & B. Verspagen. (2003). Breaking the waves: a Poisson regression approach to Schumpeterian clustering of basic innovations. *Cambridge Journal of Economics* Vol. 27(5), 671–693.

Simon, R. J. (1974). The work habits of eminent scientists. *Sociology of Work Occupation*, 1, 327–335.

Simonton, D. K. (1999). *Origins of Genius*. New York: Oxford University Press.

Simonton, D. K. (1984). *Genius, Creativity, and Leadership*. Cambridge, MA: Harvard University Press.

Smart, J. (2005). Measuring Innovation in an Accelerating World: Review of "A Possible Declining Trend for Worldwide Innovation." Acceleration Studies Foundation.

http://www.accelerating.org/articles/huebnerinnovation.html

Solow, R. M. (1956). A Contribution to the Theory of Economic Growth. *Quarterly Journal of Economics.* 70, 65–94.

Solow, R. (n.d.) Robert Solow reviews *Prophet of Innovation: Joseph Schumpeter and Creative Destruction*, by Thomas K. McCraw. http://economistsview.typepad.com/economistsview/2007/05/robert_solow_on.html accessed June 27, 2009.

Stephan, P., S. Gurmu, A. J. Sumell & G. Black. (2007). Who's Patenting in the University? *Economics of Innovation and New Technology.* 16(2), 71–99.

Tusa, J. (2004). *On Creativity.* London: Methuen.

Valadkhani, A. & A. Worthington, Ranking and Clustering Australian University Research Performance, 1998-2002. *Journal of Higher Education Policy and Management.* 28: 2, 189-210.

Zuckerman, H. (1977). *Scientific elite.* New York: Free Press.

MODEL TWO:

Global Imagination

4. *World*

SIMON MARGINSON

> 'When I first looked back at the earth, standing on the moon, I cried.'
> —ALAN SHEPARD, COMMANDER APOLLO 14 US MISSION, IN AN INTERVIEW
> OCTOBER 1988

I. History

Vision: The Trilobites

The Earth and the other planets formed about 4.6 billion years ago. For at least the first one hundred million years the frequent impact of large asteroids generated too much heat to allow life to form. It is not known when life first appeared, a subject of endless theorization and simulation. But by 3.5 billion years ago there were several types of bacteria and archaea. Oxygen-generating photosynthesis was occurring on sea floors.[1]

By two billion years ago, atmospheric oxygen reached a moderate level. It is likely that animal life appeared in the sea only in the last billion years, initially in single cell form. Multicellular animals require larger levels of oxygen to ensure the diffusion of the gas throughout their bodies. Fossils of multicellular animals date from less than 600 million years ago.[2] These animals grew in size. The fossil record shows that soft-bodied animals began to diversify spectacularly less than twenty million years before end of the Proterozoic era at about 560 million years ago, probably following a further increase in the level of oxygen generated by plants.[3] By then some members of the Ediacaran fauna[4] were able to move about on the sea floor.[5] Simple shallow horizontal burrows have been traced, with no signs of branching or complex movements. These animals were almost certainly segmented earthworms. The first hard skeletal forms appear at the end of the Proterozoic. Sponges, one of the first and the simplest animal forms, contain some hard matter. There were also small animals living in cylindrical shells whose genus has not been identified. Some of their shells display tiny bore holes indicating that active predators had emerged.[6]

The ages of the earth, its global ecological history, are defined in terms of geological strata. The titles of those ages often indicate the place where the relevant rocks were first sighted. This has resulted in some arbitrariness, in that the categories have been shaped by geological locations as well as ecological events, but for the most part the divisions between ages reflect important moments such as mass extinctions. The Cambrian era, which began about 542 million years ago, was named in 1852 by the Cambridge geologist Adam Sedgwick, teacher of Charles Darwin, using the Latin term for Wales, *Cambria*. In the case of the Cambrian, the boundary indicates not biological extinction but fluorescence.

According to the fossil record, between 544 and 538 million years ago there was an extraordinary growth and diversification of animal species. This event, the most important in the history of complex organisms, is termed the 'Cambrian Explosion.' Though only a small number of animal phyla (kingdoms) have been detected as living before 544 million years, by 538 million years there were 38 phyla, the same number as today. These included the early chordates, ancestors of fish and all other vertebrates including humans. Equally remarkably, by 538 million years ago, all phyla had developed distinct hard external parts, armaments and defences. Shells, armour, teeth, spikes and claws had appeared. And many animals could move freely. The benign soft-bodied pre-Cambrian world had vanished.

The Cambrian Explosion is a particularly clear-cut example of the manner in which transformations in living nature proceed not in linear fashion but in fits and starts. The paleo-biologist Stephen J. Gould famously christened this 'punctuated evolution.'[7] A major innovation occurs or there is a catastrophic change in the environment. All species are affected. New opportunities open up and there is a burst of developments. Eventually the niches are filled and everything settles down again, changing at a much slower pace. The question is *why* did the Cambrian Explosion happen? Clearly, if all phyla developed hard external parts simultaneously, without much change in their internal design, some kind of environmental factor was involved. So what was it? Darwin registered the puzzle but had no solution. The abrupt appearance of the Cambrian fossils 'must remain inexplicable,' he found. This 'may be truly urged as a valid argument' against the views advanced in *On the Origins of Species*, he noted in the sixth and final edition of that book in 1872.[8]

In 2003 evolutionary scientist Andrew Parker published *In the Blink of an Eye*. This provided a plausible answer to the question about the Cambrian explosion that had puzzled Darwin. Among the new animals at the beginning of the Cambrian were a group of arthropods that were to become highly abundant. They became the dominant animals of their time, like humans are today. They survived in the sea in much the same form though in many different species for 300 million years. They were also ancestors of the insects, who colonized the land before the amphibians, the reptiles and the mammals. These animals were the trilobites. They are familiar to fossils collectors because there were so many of them. Trilobites evolved from soft bodied proto-trilobites 543 million years ago.[9] These first trilobites possessed a characteristic that gave them a crucial advantage in relation to all other living things. When trilobites evolved from proto-trilobites the light-sensitive patches on the sides of the heads of proto-trilobites turned into complex organs: holochroal compound eyes that produced visual images. They could see. They were the first animals to do so. 'Suddenly, and for the first time, an animal could detect everything in its environment. And it could detect it with pinpoint accuracy.'[10] And the trilobites could comprehend their immediate setting, as far as their eyes could see, as one relational space.

Once the first trilobites had eyes, everything followed from that. Sight is the most powerful sense because it cannot be evaded. Unlike sound or smell or taste or touch, light and sight are always there. As Parker notes, 'light is the most important stimulus to animal behaviour in the vast majority of today's environments'; that is, those environments in which light is present.[11] The trigger of the Cambrian Explosion was vision.

Vision changed what animals did and governed the kind of animal that emerged. In the late pre-Cambrian, the soft-bodied proto-trilobites were among the first animals that could swim rapidly and maneuver mid-water.[12] This capacity to move around freely helped them to obtain their food, which consisted of debris floating in the sea or falling to the ocean floor. But being the first animals to see in three dimensions transformed the agenda of the trilobites. Their eyes took in the tempting soft-bodied morsels of protein that were floating past all around them. They quickly acquired aggressive limbs and began to take chunks out of their fellow creatures. 'The majority of early trilobites were active predators. They moved rapidly to hunt their prey.'[13] Soon they terrorized the seas; first in a long line of alpha carnivores that would later include the formidable mammal-like reptiles of the Permian era, the gorgonopsids; the mighty *Tyrannosaurus Rex* in the late Cretaceous; the sabre-toothed cats that menaced our hominid ancestors during the Pleistocene; and us. Also the trilobites might have started to take pieces out of each other.

Some animals did, because almost as soon as trilobites had acquired the means of killing, they also grew hard outer shells. Later they evolved the trick of rolling up into a ball like an Australian echidna to protect their vulnerable parts.[14] They could also see predators coming and evade them.

By then the ocean had become a much livelier place. The wonderful asset of vision gave the trilobites a vital first mover advantage but it did not remain a trilobite monopoly. Once eyes became the primary source of competitive advantage, they were developed independently by five more phyla, including many of the chordates. (The last was to prove instrumental in many ways. For example, it enabled some latter day chordates to develop the visual arts, art historians, and critiques of the cinema's fascination with special effects: see chapter three). The emergence of eyes stimulated brain development, augmenting complexity, and vision became joined to limbs that controlled bodily movement and the control and manipulation of objects in the environment, including plants and animals. Meanwhile the behavioural changes associated with vision made hard body parts essential for even those creatures that remained without eyes. Weapons became ferocious. Vision soon became associated with visual signaling, display as a means of aggression, and strategies of disguise. There were many innovations and adaptations. A few species developed multiple eyes, or eyes on stalks that could be moved into cracks and corners or popped up from behind a rock. One early Cambrian animal, the remarkable looking *Opabinia*, possessed five eyes that guided a long flexible nozzle which had food gathering pincers located at its end. These pincers carried teeth used for grasping food which was brought back into the creature's mouth. A large arthropod from the same period, the predator *Anomalocaris*, wielded two long appendages like arms with sharp spines for capturing prey. Some paleontologists estimate that *Anomalocaris* was up to two metres long, adult human size.[15] Many trilobite shells are found with holes exactly matching the spines of *Anomalocaris*. The giant predator could move freely through the water, propelled by flaps along both sides of its body, and not all the trilobites were able to get away.

Vision and Mobility

Thus vision also generated a new age of mobility. 'Eyes are most useful if one is also highly mobile' (Parker).[16] The capacity of animals to move under their own direction had preceded eyes. But by enabling them to instantly take in a whole environment, vision in three dimensions allowed them to become more strategic about searching and eating food, attack, defence or finding a mate. Vision enhanced choices and choice-making and heightened the capacity to anticipate. For example, it enabled an animal to judge the distance and speed of other animals in relation to the self and hence the potentials for collision and avoidance. Mobility in turn enabled vision to be more fully exploited. It multiplied what eyes could do. Animals could go somewhere in order to see, and to make use of what they saw. The visible environment became a field of individual passage. This created the potential for cycles of migration and other deliberate changing of habitat. (And later, the emergence of the housing market. The trilobites have a lot to answer for).

The coupling of vision and mobility, and the supervision of relational spaces within the field of vision that is enabled by vision, are central factors in human existence today. Through vision coupled with free movement across space and the direction of bodily appendages and behaviours within and across space, we replicate the experience of the first trilobites in the Cambrian sea in both real and imagined forms. Movement is guided by vision. The processes of picture formation and the accumulation of visual data are facilitated by movement. For example using visual triangulation, observing a spatial setting from different vantage points over time; and through sequential observations, as when successive conjoint landscapes pass before us from a railway carriage; we broaden and deepen our inner pictures of the world. As Peter Murphy argues in chapter one, when people imagine and create they do so above all in pictures, drawing on the lifetime of data that has been accumulated by the dominant sense. Visual images populate our thoughts and memories. We dream primarily in images and not in sounds or smells or tastes or textures. The process begins very early. Children can see at birth, and vision, facial expression and non-verbal gesture mediate early sociability. It is a year before children learn to walk. Even so, once the child can stand upright, she/he immediately begins to use vision more actively and in greater depth. At much the same time that the child achieves the vision/mobility coupling, which is the crucial step from infancy to childhood, she/he develops relational speech. It is no coincidence that the child often learns to walk and to speak in the same month. If pictures are more fundamental than words, they are also conditions of words.

After childhood the vision/mobility coupling continue to vector human life. Despite the high private cost of automobiles, and despite the strong collective logic in favour of public transport on both economic and environmental grounds, during the twentieth century the use of automobiles diffused rapidly and on a worldwide basis and attached itself to all human activity. When driving, vision and mobility work closely together. Free unimpeded driving on the open road is especially attractive to many people and brings with it a sense of power and freedom, as is often noted. Flying helicopters and small planes can be even more compelling, with its exhilarations of speed and maneuverabili-

ty and the wide vistas of the Earth below. It seems that the larger the relational
environment that can be surveyed, the greater is the pleasure. It is true that
some people suffer from agoraphobia, the fear of open spaces where there is
nowhere to hide, but this is much less common than claustrophobia. 'Don't
fence me in,' the song says. It might well also say, 'Don't stop me looking,'
but while confinement behind locked doors is a possibility remembered from
childhood, the possession of vision is something that the sighted mostly take
for granted. Of the heroics of the disabled, we admire those of the blind the
most. To those with vision the struggle of the unsighted is utterly brave, a life
conducted against overwhelming odds.

The vision/mobility domain is the zone of significance in which shelter
is found and the next meal will come, in which potential mates and friends will
show, in which enemies to be avoided will appear and can be evaded. We feel
alive when we are in this zone. Certainly, we have been programmed to enjoy
being there. The sight/mobility coupling motors many human pleasures. It
seems that once people have secured food, shelter and resolved their relations
with each other, additional desire to exercise the vision/mobility function kicks
in. Speed guided by vision is a central principle in many sports. Forms of virtual mobility that depend on the visual sense have become a central pastime
of daily life. People use vision to move around vicariously. They multiply
their points of view via television, film, screen-based computing, movement-
oriented video games with their virtual universes, and geo-navigation. The last
technology allows the relational space of choice to be defined, apprehended
and explored in a self-guided manner. The joining of video technology to
telecommunications networks allows the world to be conceived as a set of
instantly reachable familiar faces. As in desktop computing, the video component of mobile phone networks, and even instantly transmitted still photographs, begin to compensate for the thinness of the network mode. The lack
of visual definition and depth in electronic networking renders it less attractive than face-to-face encounters in the same place but visual contact enables
a more compelling synchrony to form. Weak ties get stronger—or deeper.
Tellingly, all the sight/mobility technologies (cars, TV, video games, phones)
have revealed themselves as *highly* addictive. Each technology has diffused universally through the modern world at an extraordinary speed and is now
among the first facilities that are acquired by people in developing countries.
Freedoms first discovered by the trilobites have never been forgotten.

Imagining the Global

Oceans are ubiquitous and connected. Animal species can move across the
world without barriers, subject only to changes in currents and water tem-

peratures. Trilobite fossils show up in the fossil record at the same time all over the Earth. The trilobites achieved a borderless visual/mobile global power, as the dinosaurs, the mammals and then certain mammalian primates were to do in later times. Nevertheless, though universal domination was their lot in life, the trilobites did not know the whole world or understand their place in it. Though their eyes were sophisticated, better than those of many later species, all they could see was the immediate surroundings. They did not possess an apparatus for memory and therefore were unable to accumulate and process data that would have enabled them to recreate space and time in the imagination. There were no trilobite big pictures or trilobite long views. Their striking effects on the global eco-system were played out without them being aware of those effects and without the exercise of any reflexive intent. Even so, in this their unreflexive globalism, the trilobites were no different to all of the species that followed, including those that acquired the capacity for memory and imagination. Few if any humans had a notion of the global until the sixth century B.C.E. It was not widespread until 500 years ago. It did not become central to human imagining until the last fifty years.

Yet by several methods, in which the vision-mobility coupling is central, people have acquired the capacity to visualize and move within a relational space that is planetary or global in scale. This global dimension is far larger than neighbourhood and nation, and more bounded and singular than were the empires of the sixteenth to nineteenth centuries, composed of non-proximate pieces of land seized in military forays. The early modern trade and bible empires that grew out of the barrel of the European gun reached audaciously across face of the world but were nevertheless semi-fragmented and partial in their geographic coverage. In form 'the global' is more holistic and integrated. It is more like the contiguous classical empires of Rome or China than the Spanish or British domains. But in contrast with Rome and China, which drew much of their self-definition from the hinterlands of Eurasia that lay outside their borders, in the 'global' setting there is no longer a barbarian perimeter and an unknown or untamed darkness beyond. 'The global' is a bounded interdependent sphere, a world unto itself, an inside without an outside. All is visible and within touching distance, give or take a day or two in flight and a week of jetlag. In this global dimension, which is both the day-to-day world of screens and airports, and a mental landscape that we inhabit, people are mobile self-determining subjects: trilobites on a planetary scale. For those with the means to move across global space, or the material and mental freedom to enter the global as a virtual space (and at this stage perhaps a third of humans can do one or both), the global aspect has become understood as a worldwide relational dimension that is also a sphere of fluctuating change, variety, opportunity, movement, passage and action.

But this is getting ahead of the argument. How did humans do it? Let us trace the evolution of the global imagination, which is also the imagining of the global, step by step.

Material Ecology

The global has a materiality that is prior to human memory or reflexivity. 'One generation passeth away, and another generation cometh: but the earth abideth for ever' was the way it was put in the sonorous phrasing in the King James Version of the Christian Bible.[17] It was wrong--the Earth does not 'abideth forever', it is almost certain that the planet will still be there after humans have gone, and probably after all biological life has gone. But the point is that the rhythms of physical nature are larger than life and its cycle of photosynthesis—not to mention society, art and the intellect. This is not to say that nature is fixed or outside change, only that nature is prior and posterior to our perception of it. In turn, this irreducible natural materiality of the global is an essential condition of human imagining of the global. This is not only because human imagining itself is a process of nature, and not just because 'the abstract externality of nature is space' (Hegel).[18] It is also because the roots of global imagining—and the present book suggests that this is true of human imagining most of the time—lie in phenomena that the eyes can see and that are appropriated and recast in the mind. We can see the Earth as a single sphere, so we can imagine it as a bounded and interdependent system. The image of the world in space is now so commonplace that it is easy to forget how recently it entered human history.

For nearly the whole of history humans had no means whereby to observe the world as a single integrated globe. Like other animals, we understood some manifestations of the global without the complete sense of world, the sense of a whole. The turning Earth and its material global ecology were beyond our grasp.

The continuous engine of that material global ecology is the interplay of atmosphere and ocean across the top layer of the geology of the planet. These elements together drive the climate. The surface geology takes in rock formations, the slow tectonic movements of Earth's plates that shift the forms and locations of continents and mountain ranges, and occasional eruptions from the molten interior: volcanic eruptions can have marked and sometimes catastrophic effects on the climate. At the same time the global ecological system is also affected by factors external to it such as fluctuations in the light and heat of the sun, changes in the orbit of the earth and in its rotation, and the episodic arrival of comets and asteroids from elsewhere in the solar system. In addition one more element internal to the global eco-system also affects it in an eclectic manner. That is life forms themselves. They draw their conditions of existence from the global eco-system and from time to time they recipro-cate, feeding back transformative effects. The effects of life forms on global ecology long predate the industrial revolution, forest destruction and the burning of fossil fuels. The first trees took root on land in the Devonian era about 380 million years ago. At first they were located next to seas, lakes and rivers and grew in swamps and marshes. Proximate water was essential. Then the emergence of the seed liberated land plants from dependence on proximate water and allowed forests to spread all over the earth for the first time. This triggered further changes. Tree roots release chemicals that weather rocky soil rapidly. Weathering consumes carbon dioxide in the atmosphere. The spread of trees in the Devonian intensified weathering, reducing the concentration of carbon dioxide, and this weakened the greenhouse effect and cooled glob-al climates. This triggered an ice age that became associated with one of the most devastating mass extinctions in the fossil record. This destroyed most of the trees.[19] (The trees were unaware of what they were doing and negotiation of 'slow grow' protocols and 'no grow' zones was beyond them). An inevitable assertion of balance? Perhaps not. There was nothing inevitable about the evo-lution of seeds.[20] But it was some time before the forests returned. When they did it was at a higher rate of oxygen concentration and carbon dioxide absorp-tion in the warmer, moister world of the Carboniferous, in which trees were huge and great coal deposits were created.

For life on land the awareness of planetary ecology is insistent. Though fluctuations in heat, sunlight and storms affect life in the oceans, the seasons are more important on land because of the crucial role played by precipitation. As they spread on land the plants became closely attuned to the seasons and the animals that followed them out of the sea did likewise. In the sea chordates in the form of fishes had developed memory, and their successors on land, the amphibians, could grasp the rhythm of the seasons and thereby synchronize with the natural world. Perhaps this synchrony with the seasons brought them as close as they could come to global imagining. The seasons continued to regulate the lives of every one of the later chordate species, humans along with the rest. Seasonal markers registered the changes in plants and animals, and triggered the migratory movements of big game and the nomadic cycles of human societies. Seasonal patterns regulated fertility in the human world as in every animal kingdom. These cyclical patterns ran through every human culture and religion, many of which developed circular notions of time and fate. The capacity to manage the seasons became even more basic to human sur-vival during the Ice Ages when weather contrasts were extreme and there were inexplicable climatic variations. This taught humans crucial lessons in contingency and adaptability alongside the older lessons of seasonal pattern, repetition and order.[21]

The climate settled into a milder and less variable state in the Holocene, after the end of the last gasp of the Ice Ages, the thousand year freeze called the Younger Dryas which finished about 11,600 years ago.[22] More regular weather patterns allowed agriculture to generate predictable yields and made it possible for fixed Neolithic settlements to form. The seasons and their association with climate were reaffirmed, and a new infrastructure of concepts and rituals was built around their observance in order to maximize crop yields. Later Neolithic and post-Neolithic civilizations in the Middle East, Egypt, the Americas and East Asia lifted seasonal observation to a highly sophisticated level, creating complex astronomy, long count dating and early forms of climatology. Awareness was moving incrementally closer to a sense of the global. But the vision was still pre-Copernican. It seemed the eco-system revolved around the human observer. Some humans credited themselves with shaman powers so as to order the eco-sphere, but they were unable to imagine it as a space to be explored and formed by activity of their own devising, which might have enabled genuine global creation. Nor was there a clear notion of a singular interdependent world, rounded and bounded, within a larger universe. Humanity was yet to achieve detachment, yet to shift the location of the subject, taking the vital step away from the Earth in order to see it.

Science of the Global

In the pioneering civilization of Sumer the Earth was imagined as a flat plate floating in the outer ocean. This design later entered the first Greek maps. From Pythagoras onwards, a succession of Greek philosophers used inferences—from observation and from abstraction—to conceive the Earth as a sphere. When a ship moved across the horizon, its lower portion fell out of view first. Momentarily its masts could be seen alone. This suggested the Earth had a curved surface. Plato taught that from the air the world would appear round. Aristotle noted that when a traveler moved south through Egypt and beyond, the constellations changed and the most northerly stars were less accessible to sight. This could only happen if the Earth was a sphere. Further, during a lunar eclipse the Earth cast a spherical shadow on the moon. In these arguments it is apparent that it was the use of vision, joined to forms of movement, that enabled the conception of space to be reconceived. The vision/mobility coupling allowed the early Greek notion of the global to emerge. In his *Meteorologica* Aristotle divided the world into five climatic zones: two temperate areas separated by a hot equator and two inhospitable polar regions girdled with ice. The notion that the world was round became a commonplace in the educated circles of the Hellenic world, though for the most part it was still assumed that the Earth was the centre of the universe. In the fifth century C.E. the Indian astronomer and mathematician Aryabhata is said to have estimated the circumference of the Earth at 0.15 per cent less than its actual value. In the eleventh century the great Persian scientist Abu Rayhan Biruni came almost as close. However, these measures were secured by complex technical calculations. The visual evidence was indirect. The notion of a single, bounded interdependent global sphere did not assume a central place even in the intellectual world, and it failed to take root in popular awareness, in which a flat Earth prevailed.

A larger global imagining did not happen until the sixteenth century in Europe. The fundamental change that occurred was a major advance in mobility. As was discussed in chapter 5 of *Global Creation,* seaborne exploration driven by early modern empire building and religious fervour in Spain and Portugal took ships around the whole of the Earth for the first time. Magellan's expedition completed the first voyage in 1522, leaving behind Magellan who was killed in the Philippines after the hardest part of the job was done. Later they were followed by the Dutch and the English whose interests were more specifically limited to trade and plunder. At the same time advances in European astronomy, underpinned by the new optics, replicated and then moved beyond the earlier theorizations of Greece, India and the Middle East and the Muslim world. The Polish savant Copernicus formulated the notion of a round Earth within a heliocentric solar system, although potential opposition from the Catholic Church inhibited publication until 1543 just before his death. The Danish astronomer Tycho Brahe and his assistant and successor Johannes Kepler took the scientific picture further. The crucial difference between Brahe's time and Aristotle's time was that the movement of ships around the world had made its planetary character a matter of everyday observation and explanation, pitching the developing science into the fount of popular reason while raising its value. It was apparent to all, regardless of what the Church had once taught, that if sailors moved westward for long enough they eventually returned to Europe. Now the 'global' as a physical form could be imagined as an instantly recognizable icon. The sphere was one of the small number of universal shapes: it was the form taken by the sun and the moon, which were crucial to the rhythms of the seasons and the management of agriculture and were often at the heart of religion. Correspondingly, the global could readily be imagined as a single relational space, whether as a space of empires and terrors, or a diversity of peoples and trading opportunities. 'The globe' entered the lexicon. Model globes, with most of their surfaces filled in with known continents and a few mythical bits for the unknown, entered the studies of gentlemen-scholars. As in the Cambrian, a change in mobility was prior to vision, but the two fostered each other.

Even then, a full visual sense of the global was yet to energize the imagination. Neither the survivors of Magellan's expedition nor Copernicus could actually see the Earth turning. Through the age of early modern imperialism, and in the growing convergence of societies, economies and state systems that followed in the eighteenth and nineteenth centuries—a time and space in which global flows and relationships were ever more influential in human affairs[23]— 'the global' remained confined to the level of an idea realized as a model. It was impossible for vision to directly apprehend the whole of the living globe at once. It was a ball in the study or on the navigator's bench and just that: the popularization of the model had been a great step forward but there it stayed. No doubt this contributed to the curiously marginal status of global affairs in conceptions of human society in Europe and the Americas. The border zones of trade and passage remained separated from the felt heartlands of nations, even nations whose capitals were located in seaports that were closely dependent on global travel, and open (as all urban civilizations long had been) to the global flow of ideas.

The Idea Made Whole

In the nineteenth century ballooning—and then in the twentieth century flying—enhanced the sense of the world. As the plane climbed and everything could be seen at a glance, the curvature of the earth became more apparent, in the manner of the view through a camera lens as focal length becomes progressively reduced. A larger relational space was laid out to view than the highest mountain range could provide. The manner in which the pilot could surmount the landscape and move across it with perfect freedom offered a heady superiority in choice making and control. Flying also conferred military advantages and a first mover presence in cross-Atlantic commerce, and it strongly attracted the business and propertied elite. Air travel absorbed an increasing volume of military and civilian investments as the century unfolded. After world war two it moved decisively into mass transport, first in the continental United States and later elsewhere. Airports began to resemble the railway stations of the nineteenth century. Sea passage fell away. Imaginings of wind and sail and swell had punctuated early modern music, literature and painting. These imaginings moved between the fierce and fearsome beauty of the elements, and lighter Adriatic moments in which sails were caressed by wistful Vivaldian zephyrs and foam rose to the prow. J. M. W. Turner was fascinated by both sides of the alternation with his storms at sea and his skies in

Italian harbors. Sea travel with its interlock between self and weather, its tacking to the wind, spoke to ideas of human agency in which craft and fate were finely balanced. But flying promised a more certain domination of nature: a conquest of distance and time that was more predictable and complete.

Flying evolved from faster and faster land hugging movements to the eventual negation of terrestrial gravity and the leap into space. The vast space programs of the United States and the Soviet Union had no immediate benefits for the civilian populations. There were payoffs in industrial innovations but these normally emerged well downstream. Nevertheless, these programs drew almost unquestioned support, due to the logic of the Cold War. That logic was binary. If the 'other side' gained superiority in space, then, as night follows the day, the outcome would be the eclipse of the sacred nation and the end of 'our way of life.' The Soviets put up the first artificial satellite (in 1957), sent the first dog into space and were the first to bring a man safely from orbit (Yuri Gagarin in 1961). Gagarin was the first human to see the Earth from beyond it. The next year the young Bob Dylan released a self-titled album, his first. In the second last track, in which he gestured to Woody Guthrie, one of the influences that had shaped him, Dylan sang of an old world with a new familiarity that many were to come to share:

> Hey, hey, Woody Guthrie, I wrote you a song
> 'bout a funny old world that's a-comin' along
> Seems sick an' it's hungry, it's tired an' it's torn
> It looks like it's a-dyin' an' it's hardly been born.
>
> ~ Bob Dylan, 'Song to Woody,' *Bob Dylan*,
> released by Columbia on 19 March 1962

To its great relief the American government was the first to reach the moon in 1969, in front of a world television audience, justifying the vast scientific investment. At the climactic moment of payoff, astronaut Neil Armstrong fluffed the scripted lines. He was meant to say 'that's one small step for a man, one giant leap for mankind,' but with half the world watching he left out the indefinite article ('a'). Contradicting himself, contrasting a small step for 'man' with a giant step for 'mankind,' Armstrong hit the lunar surface. The mistake did not matter. More than ever, this was a case where the image was more important than the text. The astronaut's wooden speech scarcely registered. But, in hindsight, we can say that it was the choice of significant occasion that was the error, and not Armstrong's faulty recall. The part of the space program that was transformative was not the small number of visits to the moon. Since the 1970s, there has been no popular pressure to revive the expensive moon landings. The crucial moment was the visual moment that the new mobility had made possible. It was the sight of the Earth from space. Gagarin's successor astronauts and cosmonauts photographed it and filmed it—and transmitted the pictures back to Earth. The great and singular image of the blue-green planet with its bands of white cloud, floating against the black void of the universe, was burned everywhere into the popular mind. In that moment the idea of 'world' was made whole.

Once again we find that nothing is as strong in our brain as sight. The most potent visual memories are hypnotic in their intensity. They condition all our behaviours. (Likewise, when the video recording of the planes crashing into the Twin Towers in New York in September 2001 was sent around the world, it was rendered utterly unforgettable, enabling the US military interventions in Iraq and Afghanistan and helping to shape the global politics of the next half decade). That first sight of the Earth from space instantly created an iconic visual form: The Planet. Immediately the world-in-space began to grow in centrality in every culture. The poster mushroomed in teenage bedrooms. References to the world turning in space bobbed up unexpectedly in the lyrics of several popular songs of the late 1960s, seemingly unrelated to the rest of the narrative, such as 'While my guitar gently weeps' (the Beatles) and 'In the ghetto' (Elvis Presley). The image soon gathered a massive political and spiritual baggage. It was no coincidence that the ecological movement, with its twin roots in science and spirituality, and its fecund naturalism, dates from this time. For the world-in-space immediately appeared as totally normal, rendered authentic by the rhythms of season and daylight. The image could be viewed more than one way and each reinforced its emotional power. Closer up the Earth in space was huge and sufficient in itself. Yet from the moon the Earth rising on the horizon was small and to be pitied, as Dylan knew. Several moon astronauts described it as 'fragile' and 'precious.' It evoked an intense feeling of owning and belonging. It was altogether part of the self.

The world made whole spoke to a new universal of the human condition. In the moment the Earth was seen from space, everyone found a home that they knew but had never known, a planetary home they shared with everyone else. The idea was novel, thrilling, challenging, uncomfortable and attractive. This was a community beyond 'my community' (chapter two). Everything— kin, neighbourhood, town, city, nation and empire—was relativized by it.

One morning I woke up and decided to look out the window to see where we were. We were flying over America and suddenly I saw snow, the first snow we ever saw from orbit. Light and powdery, it blended with the contours of the land with the veins of the rivers. I thought autumn, snow...people are busy getting ready for winter. A few minutes later we were flying over the Atlantic, then Europe, and then Russia. I have never visited America, but I imagined that the arrival of autumn and winter is the same there as in other places, and the process of getting ready for them is the same. And then it struck me that we are all children of our Earth. It does not matter what country you look at. We are all Earth's children, and we should treat her as our mother.

(attributed to Soviet cosmonaut Aleksandr Aleksandrov,
Soyuz T-9 mission, 1983).

The one-world idea was not a new concept. It had long been part of world religions, and imperial dreams, and some of the claims of science and philosophy. But the sight of the Earth in space popularized it everywhere in a visual form of extraordinary aesthetic power. It was this moment, even more than the birth of the Internet two decades later, that launched the era of communicative global convergence, cyber capitalism and synchronous dependence. In this moment was created a global dimension that would shape its myriad human agents, while at the same time it would be interrogated by them, explored by them, populated by them, arranged by them, claimed by them and exploited by them in the manner of all visible spaces. In this one moment of sight global systems trumped all others.

Both the romantic and the classicist might draw differing comforts from that moment. The step towards the world in space was a step back into naturalism, into a larger setting whose roots lay deeper than human society. Yet when taken holistically it was apparent that this world was fragile, seething with human ecological change and with an uncertain future. There was also the prospect that 'it' could reflexively recreate itself. Regardless, beyond the romantic/classical antinomy, the old vision/mobility coupling was at work. Advances in mobility put the astronauts beyond the Earth and so opened the global relational space in full perspective, like the first sight of the Cambrian sea in all its three-dimensional splendour. In turn, this heightened sense of the global no doubt played its part in the rapid take up of cheaper and faster air travel in the 1980s, and of virtual mobility, networked communications in the 1990s and after, in which people began to move within the global dimension as if it was their own locality. And no doubt this made conceptions of the global knowledge economy and the global strategies of universities, notions that would have been grandiose or meaningless at an earlier time, seem like extensions of common sense. That sight of the blue-green Earth turning in space changed what could be taken for granted. It changed the human mentality forever. It made possible the global dimension of action. At that moment, 'the global' connected with the full resources of the imagination.

From Global Imagining to Global Space

The world turning in space was the iconic visual imagining. Worldwide air transport, followed by synchronous worldwide communications, laid out the forms of the networked global landscape and provided the means of global mobility. In the 1980s the cheapening of prices and deregulation of airlines sustained a great expansion in volumes. The new confidence in global passage enabled by the speed, ease and accessibility of air travel meant that migrants, whether temporary or permanent, began to conceive their transfer less as a one-way passage and more as an open return journey. They factored regular trips back to their original homes into their planning, living in more than one zone at the same time and so triangulating their observations of the world. They kept in touch with all their locations using media and communications technologies cheaper in price and richer in the complexity than the telegraph or the telephone available to their predecessors. The resulting evolution of global, multiple and hybrid mentalities is captured in one of the most influential of all papers on cultural globalization, that by Arjun Appadurai.[24]

As the medium of mass communication and image and data flow the Internet took shape in the first half of the 1990s. By 1995 it was no longer optional for businesses and universities in the industrialized nations. By 2000 universities in the emerging nations had also connected. The reach of the network expanded at an amazing rate. The number of Internet users grew from 0 to 26 percent of humans in only twenty years. Rapid growth was inevitable during the period of early adoption but it continued through the second decade. Between 31 December 2000 and 30 September 2009 the members of the one-World communicative community expanded from 361 to 1734 million, reaching 74 per cent of the population of North America and 52 per cent of those in Europe, though still only 19 per cent in Asia and 7 per cent in Africa.[25] As in the Cambrian sea, as vision and mobility became quickened, the expansion of mental capabilities followed—this time it was not via biological evolution and the development of new body parts but through networked technologies. Humans could now immerse themselves in multiple messaging systems, and search engines and deep data banks. They shared common operating systems and engaged in the transfer and sharing of complex data, text and images. The means of communication in turn enabled a great range of new kinds of collective and individual production. The e-world became blended with observations collected during travel and face-to-face meetings. Virtual exploration preceded geographical moves and instant messaging managed personal encounters. Like the Cambrian sea the World had become a space that could be seen and imagined at the same time; a space for mobility, exploration and action. Like the Cambrian sea it was bounded by geography and the reach of vision, and open in the imagination. But the geographical reach and the scope for imagining were far greater than in the Cambrian.

So the global dimension of action was born, at the end of the Holocene, amid the crisis of climate change that spoke so readily to the one-World consciousness that ecology had helped to foster. Accompanying the ever-expanding communication system and its ever-intensifying uses was a force-fed ideology of globalism, which was seen as the decisive form of modernism. 'Global' and 'globalization' were everywhere, buzz words in the marketing lexicon, pivot of the explanations of governments, economists and social theorists alike. Increasingly the global space was the site where desires for products, novelties, new selves and freedoms were located. And that brings us into the present tense.

II. Global Space

Recent arguments are less likely to imagine global convergence as an unstoppable external force. More often they emphasize the subjective and constructive aspects of how the global is imagined and produced. No doubt when global climate change starts to bite in the form of rising sea levels, the emphasis could swing back. The oscillation between objective and subjective, between material limits and the scope for imagining and agency, is endemic to the global. Space has both materiality and a subjective element. Heidegger distinguished the spatial universe of the human subject, 'being-in-the world,' from the 'reality' of the world.[26] Space is plastic. We shrink and elongate it at will. In many respects the spatial forms that we inhabit are brought into being by human activities: by our imaginings and productions, by the ways we organize and govern ourselves. But we can only make space our project because, as in the Cambrian sea, when the perceiving agent sees space, space in its irreducible materiality is already 'there.' The factor that changes when we manipulate space is us: our perceptions, imaginings, motions and strategies. Here the green-and-turning Earth reveals the double material/symbolic role of all iconic images, which at one and the same time become located in the world and lodged in our heads. On one hand the World is a three-dimensional descriptor of place and places. It is a set of factual coordinates that enable the navigation and control of space. On the other hand, the World is both potter's wheel and potter's model. It is the starting point of a thousand projects for rethinking the globe as a network of productive agents, or a space of flows, or a map of power, or money. All these projects are dimensional, spatial. All involve the forming and bulking out of global space itself.

What are the characteristics of global space and space making? Four stand out. One is the de-severing of distance, which is the signature of the more global era. The second is the desire for synchrony with other persons across global space that is associated with de-severing. The third is the changed but continuing role of locality or place within the global dimension. The fourth is the above-mentioned plasticity of global space, which is made and remade and utilized for many different and often creative strategic projects.[27]

De-severing

'De-severing' is the mental process whereby people bring remote locations close to them and vanish physical distance in their minds.[28] Here space and closeness are not simple functions of physical distance or the speed of messaging. The implications of de-severing for subjectivity are crucial in understanding global space-time. In *Being and Time* Martin Heidegger notes the logic of de-severing extends progressively outwards across the Earth. No place is now beyond imagined proximity. There are places we may not wish to go, such as the glacial ice of the central Antarctic plateau, 2.8 kilometers above sea level, where the average temperature is a windswept minus 48 degrees centigrade. But it is within our reach, we can imagine being there and know what it looks like. Heidegger also notes that technologies enable de-severing. His example is the radio. There are many more.

Yet like the radio and Internet and the other technologies that facilitate it, de-severing has its limits. We can imagine the abolition of distance by seeing in our minds the extent of space and the end of the journey. In that respect space is highly plastic to our perceptions of it. Nevertheless our bodies must move in space, and in its materiality, space remains irreducibly there. De-severing is often discussed in terms of 'space-time compression,' meaning that the passage across space whether real or virtual occupies a shorter period of time-as-duration, or becomes simultaneous as in synchronous communication. The apparent compression of space is measured by an actual reduction of time. Here it might seems that de-severing is driving that fetish for ever-shorter duration that is a constituent elements of modernity. Heidegger suggests this. But the notion of space-time compression can be misleading. In de-severing and space-time compression the perception of time-as-duration *as such* remains unchanged. Particular time is shortened but not the understanding of time-as-duration itself. In the global dimension time is not remade in the manner that space is remade. Rather, space making and the conquest of distance enabled a truncated experience of time. Short-termism has older roots than contemporary communicative globalization and the de-severing associated with it. The imagined de-severing of the world does not conflict with a long-term imagining of the trajectory of the world. Paradoxically de-severing can bring the long term, the history of the world, closer to the observer.[29]

Synchrony

More strange than de-severing itself, because less accessible to technological explanation, is that, with de-severing, comes the expansion and intensification of synchrony between humans across distance. Synchrony is another aspect of the subjective experience of time, different to that of time-as-duration. 'Synchrony' (or synchronism) refers to concurrence at the same point in time. This concurrence is deeper than accidental coincidence. Synchrony is the sharing of the same time in a common rhythm. It is driven by sociability, and by the desire for a sustainable connection with others. To live in the same rhythm, we must synchronize our times with each other's. At first we work at synchrony. But it becomes familiar. We learn to slip into it. Sometimes synchrony is largely established through a process of one-way adjustment whereby one person follows another. Sometimes it is created through the mutual evolution of a shared practice. All going well, as we familiarize ourselves with each other, the desire to relate that powered the original drive towards synchrony is reproduced and enhanced. In some societies the requirements for synchrony, the layers of customary politeness, are complex. Japan (chapter six) is one example. Other societies are simpler and more accessible. But all have been altered by contemporary globalization, which is associated with a great change in the conditions of synchrony.

Global synchrony is more than simply establishing a communicative link across borders. It consists in living in a common time, for part of our lives, with people anywhere in the world. Along with the shortening of time-as-duration it is one of the temporal partners of the spatial practice of global de-severing, which is the process of imagining ourselves close to those in distant locations. It is also the inter-subjective aspect of de-severing. Faster global mobility and the 'thicker' global traffic in people and ideas have better enabled both global de-severing and global synchrony while also rendering them more attractive. The desire for global synchrony helps to explain the imagining of de-severing, and vice versa. For the trilobites, the chief benefit of vision and mobility lay in the search for food. Some humans cross borders for plunder. Most have friendlier intentions than the trilobites had and they are much more interested in creating synchrony.

The desire to extend the field of vision and opportunity and with it to synchronize with human others is the reason that global mobility and de-severing have become more easy and attractive than they were. Once achieved, de-severing—especially in the form of electronically-mediated communication—enables human association in the low risk form of loose and disposal ties. In this setting, people become highly adept at managing a large number of partial encounters, opening many new opportunities for synchrony. Global synchrony does not presuppose an emotional engagement. Unlike local relationships, global synchrony may work best when the affective dimension is absent. The hallmarks of the universal communicator are openness, fluency and certainty of judgement, and a capacity for disinterested friendships. Mozart is said to have possessed these qualities in abundance.[30] Fast, loose and disposable non affective ties based on apparent transparency—temporary forms of synchrony with few obligations and no hidden dangers—are also ideal for business. The absence of ongoing obligations leaves all future options open. These factors help to explain why many explore the Internet in solely economic terms. But the practices of enhanced synchrony extend well beyond economic life. In knowledge flows and scholarly work, the effects of global synchrony have been akin to those of a supernova. Most creative people, not to mention the many others who disseminate text and image, readily adapt to electronically-mediated synchrony with its flat relations and its ease and speed of access, distribution and exit. We do not know how much open-source knowledge flows have grown, but data on Internet usage[31] suggest that they have almost certainly expanded faster than commercial intellectual property, and much faster than either formal academic publishing or the size of global trade and the GDP production economy.

These changes have far-reaching implications for human identity, and for human agency which is the active self-determining component of identity. Identity is bordered. It draws stability from the distinction between 'Us' and 'Others.' This dualism survives in the global era but in an Internet world it breaks down more readily than in the past. The rigid stability of identity falters. More than before, the sense of self must be deliberately, consciously made from the ever-growing range of choices. At the same time the capacity of humans to make themselves as they will has been enhanced. Synchronous relations at a distance are primary devices of self-making. Meanwhile a much larger 'Us' is in the process of formation, at the edges of awareness. This is the incipient world society. This 'Us' is less compelling but is also less confining than kin, neighborhood and nation. 'Otherness' is weakened by these developments.

In one respect it is a less secure world. Freedom always brings with it a glimpse of the void. Synchronous friends can come from anywhere. We are less sure of who we are. On the other hand the basis for the old kind of Cold War, vectored by fear of the Other, has gone. With the emergence of the Internet and the beginnings of the global communicative community the Wall against the Other began to come down, at the same time as the fall of the Berlin Wall brought the official USA/USSR Cold War, the one that drove the space program, to an end (1989). Old habits die hard. The Wall against the Other still stands in the imaginations of many. It still underwrites military forays and brings down governments. It still fosters fear and visits violence on Others. 'Fear, she's the mother of violence' as the Peter Gabriel song says.[32] But the foundations of the Wall against the Other are gone, and over time the Wall must break up. There are still many fears and dangers but they are no longer those of a Manichean universe. We can finally lay that beast to rest. And so we move slowly forward.

Place and Positioning

In a world in which people are no longer conclusively defined by their enemies, location is more important. This is a paradox of globalization. Space is de-severed yet place is the starting point for everything else. The world's spaces are all visible to us, all close at hand, so that geography matters more than it did.[33] When the old forms of Otherness—the old separations of gender, religion and ethnicity ('race')—are dissolved via communicative inclusion then place and the history of place become the platform on which human agency is erected. Place is space and time concentrated together. 'The Here is at the same time a Now, or it is the point of duration. This unity of Here and Now is Place' (Hegel).[34]

Yet in the global setting place is less constant than it was. In some locations mobility itself is uppermost, as in hot desking in business, or in the world of the globally mobile scientists who spends three years in Toronto, two in Singapore, another in Shanghai and a few shorter stints in Berne. Many people, and many institutions, now live in more than one place. Some claim for themselves a strategic advantage in having no place at all and a license to roam free across the globe. Or their place lies in global passage itself, like living in the airlines. It is too easy to identify with the Tom Hanks character in *Terminal* who is locked into the bowels of the airport with nowhere else to go, confined to that unsettling post-arrival limbo prior to administrative processing based on citizen identity. This mobility and the multiplicity of the 'here and now' is a primary feature of the spatial strategies of global businesses, and also of the strategies of contemporary research universities, as chapter five will discuss. By changing location within the global field organizations and individuals grasp differing potentials. For example by centring some of their activities offshore, or by referencing their performance against global comparators rather than those within the nation, these universities secure a partial independence from national governments. The importance of place in the global dimension lies not just in fixidity but in alterity. Yet each is necessary to the other.

Global Strategy

Global subjects create a strategic landscape for themselves in which they move and act. Like the first trilobites, contemplating their soft-bodied dinners as the latter slowly swam around in front of them, once humans envision the global landscape they can locate all of the different entities—human, natural, technical—within it. Then they position themselves both within and above that landscape. This dual vision, in which the observer-participant moves readily between short view and long view, is key to the capacity for strategic action. It creates a highly flexible vantage point, one both grounded and mobile, and capable of rapid action while remaining aware of the larger relational space and its possibilities. The ease of oscillation—between observer of the world from space and the participant within that world, between imagining the big picture and shaping the near at hand—also enables a ready reflexivity, whereby one's own global effects (and the absence of effects) are monitored. Global space making does not mean the 'discovery' of natural relations, borders or territories that have been put in place by globalization or are necessary to it. Even if globalization was so predictable (and it is not) spatiality is constructed by human agents. To repeat, the difference between now and the Cambrian is that humans have the scope to create the global dimension as well as work with what they find there. This process of creation brings together at one time material space, the imagining of space and mobility, and movement through space. Global subjects are the product of a vast accumulation of actions to which they continuously contribute. Globalization, which is the processes of global integration and convergence and system building, is re-making space. It also enables and compels human agents, governments, businesses and universities to re-make space for themselves.

At any time, global space-making, like all kinds of creation, occurs within limits set by global systems and actions created in the past. Within these limits are many possibilities. From time to time innovative actions break out and create new forms (and limits). Being early and a work in progress the communicative global dimension is more open than is national or local life. It is also rife with unexpected consequences. For example the Shanghai Jiao Tong University researchers who published the first world ranking of universities in 2003 had no idea that their data would grip the world imagination and usher in a new era in which a global university system was visible for the first time. All the individual global forays, whether through the Internet or real-time world systems, add up to something more than any one agent intends. The global dimension is the visible consequence of formative human actions. It is also unknown, a dark forest of possibility where the future is hidden, more than are most futures. We now know an imagined world community, based on a neurological network, can be made real, and we also know that it changes everything. Three decades ago we did not know this. What is next?

Despite the addictive shock of the new, and the volatile pleasures humans seem to derive in jumping at every electric charge that is transmitted into them from the external settings, those same human subjects also want certainty under their own control. They like to choose between comfort and the pleasures of danger, fear and flight, and like their forerunners in vision, the trilobites, they want predictable benefits from the energy absorbed by mobility. The global dimension is cluttered with projects designed to secure imagined outcomes for their creators. Many such projects set out to exploit the openness of the global dimension. In the process they often enlarge the space of open relations. At the same time, and often initiated by the same agents, there are also projects designed to close off parts of global space for the benefit of particular interests—for example by defining the global dimension as an asymmetric trading space, or as a militarized space subject to command and control. In the university sector, companies and universities might try to seize first mover advantage by working the status systems long central to university life, for example by shaping a system of global university rankings. Or they might use global action to secure market values, for example by monopolizing the intellectual property created in the pharmaceutical exploitation of a rainforest. Or they might lobby governments to secure new openings for enterprise, for example when foreign providers gain privileged access to a national education system. Once they secure the intended valuation system, or market share, or regulatory niche, these agents then move to create an enclosure that blocks the competition and turns first-mover advantage into something more permanent. This is not creation for its own sake, like the artist who cannot help but paint. No doubt certain global innovations are for the joy of it and certain agents want to build the architecture of the global common good. Some open-source web-building is devoted to both objectives. Still, many global innovations are the work of businesses or governments or universities that want presumptive power or money or status. In those cases, any general good created is of the invisible hand variety, spillovers from the dining table of private interest. But it all helps to construct the global dimension of action.

Of course in the global setting by no means all individuals and organizations use creative strategies. Taken as a whole agents exhibit a mix of mimetic behaviour and innovation and there is always more of the former than the latter. But in the first stages of the contemporary global era, all are more or less striking out into the unknown. Global activities necessarily are less defined and less regulated than other fields of endeavour. It also seems that the risks are higher. Yet just as the new possibilities of life with vision were profoundly motivating for the trilobites, it is apparent that contemporary global possibilities fixate and excite humans in a special way. Though the dot.com crash of 1999–2000 stopped much of the commercial e-learning it scarcely hurt the globalization of education and research in other spheres. From 2008 onwards, through the global financial crisis and world-wide downturn that followed, and despite the fact that most cross-border activity does not pay for itself and has to be subsidized from scarce local funds, globalization in higher education and other sectors has continued to roll out. The formation of the global dimension of action seems to be largely independent of the global business cycle.

Knowledge

Yet in the early imaginings of the communicative global space in the 1990s, it was mostly framed as a worldwide economic market. This was not only because corporate interests and national competition helped to drive the partial global integration, or because Internet systems were shaped by global companies and constituted a vast new industry in their own right, or because neo-liberal norms and visions were ascendant in policy circles. The world market was also an older imagining. It was a product of the era of early modern imperial globalization with its division of labour between colonies and metropolis. The ever-growing world market was brought to imaginative form above all in Karl Marx's notebooks of 1851, the *Grundrisse*, with their prescient feel for borderless global trends.[35]

Nonetheless world markets have not synthesized into a single world economy. While Internet marketing had opened a new era of instant commerce and this too helped to bring everyone closer, and though capital, labour and sites of production are more mobile across borders, the borders remain intact. Those borders are political economic in character. Politically, nation states remain almost as potent as in Marx's day. National financial systems are more closely intermeshed and mutually affective but have not and cannot dissolve into a single world money system. Political economy and the creation of economic value are a zone contested between national and global modes of organization. In the absence of a global democratic polity and global citizenship, the neo-liberal claim that globalization had created a single global trading market simply constitutes another round of the old nineteenth-century free trade imperialism. As in the nineteenth century it is again the Anglo-America nations, the incubators of neo-liberal ideology and policy, that look to be the winners in an imagined singular 'world market' led by New York and London.

Globalization has not transformed the world or even 'the economy' into a single market. But notwithstanding the obvious variety of cultural forms, the cultural face of globalization is more facile than its economic face. It is above all in the cultural domain that one-world imagining is nurtured and its fruits have become manifest. In the global setting elements of cultural globalization such as images and ideas and knowledge move more freely and are less read-ily controlled than are economic goods and financial values.

In hindsight it can be seen that the surprisingly rapid take-up of global-ization in research universities has been conditioned not only by an advanced capacity for synchronous relations and a spirit of executive enterprise that many did not realize that universities *qua* universities possessed, but also by the exceptional global fluidity of knowledge, which is the operational currency of the university sector. Knowledge is like music in that *la grande lingue*, the long line of flow, is predominant. While it is being heard each good piece of music sustains a sense of endless continuity.[36] Likewise ideas and knowledge have lin-eage. They are always connected in time to what came before and what will come after. We can never finally know where new knowledge begins. In con-trast the commodity form is bounded, truncated in space and time so that the economic value of each commodity can be defined, limited and possessed. In a market economy, each act of production and each transaction are actions that are born again and constitute defined and limited acts of time. Hence the easy rapport between capitalism and modernity and the bonfire of traditions that seems to attend capitalism in its most dynamic moments. But knowledge, like music, sits easy with its traditions and it cannot be confined or possessed.[37] Its instruments and tonal forms may be specialized, but once it is created then knowledge like music fills the air. It flows anywhere and everywhere even to the ends of the earth (or the linguistic zone). Knowledge flows not in straight lines or sheets like water but in a sudden unpredictable manner, like quicksil-ver on a metal table. Fast and contingent, antecedent and adaptable: knowl-edge and cultural globalization never finish.

And so the global university is open. This brings us to chapter five, *University*.

Notes

1. Stanley, 2009, p. 256.
2. Claims of earlier dates have not been conclusively confirmed.
3. *ibid*, p. 275.
4. Animals from this period are named after the Ediacara hills in the Flinders Ranges in South Australia where the first fossils were found.
5. *ibid*, p. 273. Some evidence from China suggests there may have been mobile life forms as early as 580 million years ago—*ibid*, p. 273.
6. *ibid*, p. 275.
7. Gould, 2002, Ch. 9.
8. Parker, 2003, p. xv.
9. *ibid*, p. 221.
10. *ibid*, p. 272.

11. *ibid*, p. 45.

12. *ibid*, p. 259.

13. *ibid*, p. 248

14. Trilobites also had the ability to quickly seal any body sections exposed by predatory attack by forming calluses, another innovation of the remarkable Early Cambrian— *ibid*, p. 249.

15. Stanley, 2009, pp. 294–297.

16. Parker, 2003, p. 276.

17. Ecclesiastes, 1(4).

18. Hegel, 2008, p. 34.

19. Stanley, 2009, pp 325–327 7 p. 334.

20. It is hard to deny contingency when contemplating biological evolution just as its presence is rife in human history. Mozart might have died of rheumatic fever when he was young instead of at 34 years and the world would not have had his music. Someone else might have made the music of Neil Diamond or the Bay City Rollers or the Style Council, they occupied niches waiting to be filled, but no one else would have made Mozart or Bach. Likewise the trilobites did not have to develop eyes, and if they had not, it might have been many more million years before vision emerged, if it happened at all. Not all evolutionary niches have always existed. Some innovations change the rules and there is no going back.

21. Burroughs, 2005.

22. Recent evidence suggests that the extended reversion to Ice Age conditions in the Younger Dryas was triggered by a comet colliding with Earth. Note that the abrupt warming at the end of the Younger Dryas shows how dramatic climate change can be. 'Amazingly, oxygen isotope measurements in ice cores reveal that the climatic warming that ended this event took place within just three years, *most of it during a single year*. Isotope studies suggest that the climate of Greenland warmed *by about 7 degrees Centigrade*'—Stanley, 2009, pp. 501 & 504–506 (emphasis added).

23. This argument is put by Bayly, 2004.

24. Appaduri, 1996.

25. Internet World Statistics, 2009.

26. Heidegger, 1962, 146.

27. These matters were explored in Chapter 5 of the book *Global Creation: Space, mobility and synchrony in the age of the knowledge economy*. They are reviewed more briefly here.

28. Heidegger, 1962, 139.

29. Nevertheless perceptions of time-as-duration are capable of many variations. Globalization can be understood in different ways depending on the notion of time-as-duration that we imagine. In our minds we can speed up time-as-duration or we can slow it down and almost stop it. We can be short-term in our thinking and living, locked in hyper-modernist fashion to matters of near immediate duration, or we can take the longer view. We might consider the particular long-term rhythms of *la longue durée* as urged by Fernand Braudel (1985). Or temporal rupture and discontinuity as highlighted by Michel Foucault (1972) or Stephen J. Gould's (2002) punctuated evolution. By changing the imaginings of duration we highlight one or another element in history and/or shift the horizon of what is important to us.

30. Blom, 1974, 127 & 265–266.

31. webometrics, 2009; Internet World Statistics, 2009.

32. Gabriel & Gabriel, 1978.
33. Harvey, 1990, 294.
34. Hegel, 2004, 40.
35. Marx,1973/1857–58.
36. Copland, 2009/1939, 26–27.
37. Compare with Eric Blom, 1974, in *Mozart*: 'That is the worst of music—and the best: it will not be possessed' (p. 285).

References

Appadurai, Arjun (1996). *Modernity at Large: Cultural dimensions of globalisation.* Minneapolis: University of Minnesota Press.

Bayly, Christopher A. (2004). *The Birth of the Modern World 1780–1914. Global connections and comparisons.* Oxford: Blackwell.

Blom, Erich (1974). *Mozart.* Revised edition. London: J.M. Dent and Sons.

Braudel, Fernand (1985). *The Perspective of the World.* Volume 3 of *Civilisation and Capitalism 15th–18th Century.* S. Reynolds (trans.). New York: Fontana Press.

Burroughs, William J. (2005). *Climate Change in Prehistory: The end of the reign of chaos.* Cambridge: Cambridge University Press.

Copland, Aaron (2009 [1939]). *What to Listen for in Music.* New York: New American Library.

Dylan, Bob (1962). Song for Woody. Bob Dylan. New York: Columbia.

Foucault, Michel (1972). *The Archaelogy of Knowledge.* A.M. Sheridan Smith, (trans.). London: Tavistock Publications.

Gabriel, Peter & Gabriel, Jill (1978). Mother of violence. *Peter Gabriel II: Scratch.* Relight Studios, Hilvarenbeek, Amsterdam: Charisma & Atlantic.

Gould, Stephen, J. (2002). *The Structure of Evolutionary Theory.* Cambridge: Harvard University Press.

Hegel, G. W. F. (2004/1830). *Philosophy of Nature. Part II of the Encyclopaedia of the Philosophical Sciences.* Oxford: Oxford University Press.

Hegel, G. W. F. (2008/1820). *Outlines of the Philosophy of Right.* T. Knox, (trans.). Oxford: Oxford University Press.

Heidegger, Martin (1962). *Being and Time.* J. Macquarie & E. Robinson, (trans.). New York: Harper and Row.

Internet World Statistics (2009). Accessed 29 November, 2009 at: http://www.internetworldstats.com/stats.htm.

Marx, Karl (1973). *Grundrisse: Introduction to the critique of political economy.* Written in 1857–58. Martin Nicolaus, (trans.). Harmondsworth: Penguin.

Parker, Andrew (2003). *In the Blink of an Eye.* Cambridge: Perseus Publishing.

Stanley, Steven M. (2009). *Earth System History*, 3rd edition. New York: W.H. Freeman and Company.

Webometrics (2009). Webometrics ranking of world universities. Accessed 28 June 2009 at: www.webometrics.info/

5. *University*

SIMON MARGINSON

'The 20th century scheme of the university is more or less deeply rooted in
each nation and the national culture.'
—TAKESHI SASAKI, PRESIDENT, UNIVERSITY OF TOKYO, INTERVIEWED
JUNE 2004

I. Global University Space

In the last two decades there has been a growing potential for specific
domains of global action, global systems that evolve within the larger global relational space. It has happened in business, trade and finance, where
instantaneous communication enables screen-based world markets operating
in real time. It has happened in image, fashion and entertainment, where
Americanized commodity sectors have rolled out to all corners of the world
and begun to pluralize around diverse themes, centres and modes: design in
Milan, filmmaking in Bollywood. And it has happened in universities and
research, the focus of this chapter.

Since the early 1990s, research universities have embraced the global
dimension. The last fifteen years have seen an extraordinary fecundity in university strategies, and the emergence of novel cross-border forms of higher education and research. In grasping important changes, we begin with the
language of the past. Yet while global convergence in higher education and
knowledge was (and sometimes still is) imagined in the terms of the commercial globalism of the World Trade Organization, or in terms of an older
multilateralism, and both of these are part of the mix, it is specific to contemporary globalization and specific to research universities. Suddenly the
global dimension of knowledge and information has become a new and powerful relational domain, alongside and sometimes over the national and local

dimensions of action that long vectored the university. The sudden potency of the global dimension is demonstrated in the popular excitement about global university rankings, which began in 2003 and 2004 and quickly became front-page news in countries across the world. In many research-intensive universities, cross-border activity has moved to the very centre of strategic affairs. Issues related to globally measured performance, globally recognized research and avenues for the growth of cross-border activity often preoccupy university leaders.

The exception to all this is the universities of the United States, which are fixated on the national status competition that is termed the higher education 'market' that the *US News and World Report* rankings are seen to encapsulate.[1] Likewise citation patterns show that overall, American university personnel are much more interested in the research and scholarship produced by fellow Americans than work from elsewhere. For the US universities, the global dimension is primarily a source of graduate research students for the American knowledge economy: students from China and India now play an indispensable role in US engineering and applied sciences. This inward-looking stance frustrates university personnel from other parts of the world, who, despite patrician American university politeness, are rarely treated with equal respect. This insularity, in which competition in America is seen as the 'world series' in the universities just as it is in baseball, is the corollary of United States domination in the global knowledge economy. Over half the leading research universities are American, including 17 of the top 20 as measured in terms of research performance, led by Harvard. The sheer weight of American higher education in the world means that despite American inwardness, and despite the fact that international activity is often marginal to their heartland, US universities tend to lead the way in the creation of global activity. For American universities, such activity is a spill-over from the core domestic mission of teaching, research and service. Nevertheless, talent matters—and the tapping of other countries creates national competitive advantage. The global dimension is a source of imported value, and American universities do what they need to do to keep that value flowing in. But in the universities of some other nations, such as Singapore, the global dimension plays a very different role. It is the main arena of reference. More than that, it is the heartland itself.

The point that needs repetition is that unlike the Cambrian sea that was first revealed when trilobites grew vision on their heads (chapter 4), the global relational environment in higher education and research is not just explored and exploited by research universities and government managers of education systems, it is also *created* by them. And the global knowledge economy is the product of not just spatially framed vision, the sight of world from space, but also of the inner vision of the imagination. In the process of working with the freedoms and opportunities opened up by global convergence in communications and transport, global agents recreate not just the field of possibility but themselves and their mentalities.

In other words, university making and space making have become creative activities in their own right, practiced by multi-performing university leaders who draw on a portfolio of qualities and roles, from business entrepreneur to scientific boffin to patron of the arts. Sometimes they are artists themselves of a kind. Most are timid. Some are bold. A few make changes that reverberate through the university world. These university leaders are supported by teams with an assemblage of specialized skills. Yet much rests on their own 'animal spirits' and visioning.

Strategies

The rise of university strategy as a field of inquiry and a zone of construction raises the question of the locus of creativity. Has it shifted from the academic disciplines to the institutional agency of the university, and from the research professoriate to the university executives? Are very bright people increasingly drawn to quasi-entrepreneurial roles at the head of these organizations? We will come back to this.

Before then, the chapter will review the global moves being made in the university sector. As discussed in the preceding volumes in this series,[2] the relational space of global higher education and research is constituted on one hand by old methods of capacity building and relationship building, such as national public investment in the concentration of research activity, and cross-border partnerships between universities, and on the other hand by new forms of activity that work with the augmented technologies and sensibilities of a more global era. Table 1 (see end of chapter) summarizes the strategies in higher education and research that constitute the global knowledge economy, or at least the university part of it.[3]

Older kinds of strategy are often starting points for the new ones. It was a short step from the conventions of one-to-one university partnerships to the world-spanning multiple partnership. In the university alliance or consortium, groups of like-minded universities from different countries exchange students; collaborate in research; and benchmark their educational quality, services and organizational systems against those of each other. The framing of these consortia is often consciously spatial, in that they include universities from all of the continents of the world, or reach across a specific geographic region such as the Pacific Rim. Many universities are members of more than one such group. Levels of commitment vary. Often the memberships of consortia are more dead than alive. But when they do wake and move partner relations can be transformative. This is a theme with many variations. The partnership and the consortium have an ever-growing list of functions. Some institutions have moved away from the standard consortium of 20–30 partners, creating tighter and busier relations with three or four other institutions grounded in a detailed portfolio of shared activities. One form of cooperation is the jointly badged international degree awarded by two or more universities, involving a period of study in all participating institutions. Collaborative forms extend further in research. Cross-country groups and other networked forms are becoming dominant mode in some scientific work. There is joint and sometimes multi-lateral financing of large-scale facilities such as particle accelerators. Data on international research collaboration show that in most nations there has been a marked increase in the last two decades.[4] Cross-border doctoral education and short-term academic visits have also grown. Trends in long-term academic migration are less clear.[5]

The commercial export of educational services has developed rapidly. Full fee-paying international education has grown at more than twice the rate of tertiary enrolments as a whole. About half of the world's three million cross-border students are engaged in it. The global market value is estimated at $40–50 billion USD per annum. In Australia educational services have become the third largest export sector in terms of annual values.[6] Commercial international education is focused especially on globally portable qualifications in business and technologies, and English language learning. The production of degrees for foreign students as a capitalist business, most of which takes place in public research universities, was first developed via government policy and regulation in the UK, Australia and New Zealand. The capitalist mode has also taken root in Malaysia, Singapore and China, and is likely to spread further.

Another, more explicit, and broadly global strategy is national invest-ment in the infrastructure of cities and sites that aim to be 'global hubs' in the k-economy. In the 'hub' model, first initiated by Singapore, the city or site are imagined as a concentration of education and research activities that attracts worldwide research talent, fee-paying students, foreign universities as providers, and development capital. The model is expensive and difficult to make hap-pen, especially if the location concerned has had little prior global role. Nevertheless, the idea of becoming a global hub, a primary node in the glob-al network, has captured the attention of developmental strategists in many nation-states. The strategy seems more likely to be viable in cities already locat-ed within the primary zones of global economic, demographic and cultural pas-sage, such as Paris or Shanghai or Los Angeles. Perhaps it is not surprising that the first hub strategies were launched in nations that lack that status but want to have it. It seems that the education hub is the cart that will drive the horse of global economic power. Following Singapore, which at least was halfway to global status, Malaysia has talked of being a global educational hub, though its claim is grounded more in investment in marketing than investment in infrastructure. There is a limit to the extent to which a hub can be sustained by image-making alone. Then there are the Gulf States. On the edge of the desert, the dazzling buildings of 'global education villages' are open for business (or so they hope). The island of Mauritius in the Indian Ocean, where educational modernization has been effective, is yet another would-be global hub. In future stronger world centres may build more plausible education and research hubs. First innovators are not always the most stellar creators. It was primarily the composer C. P .E. Bach, not his father Johann Sebastian, who fashioned the sonata form and led the musical transition from the baroque to the classical, in which the sonata was brought to its formal climax in the pristine work of Haydn and Mozart.

A more modest cross-border strategy than the hubs, but perhaps more effective and equally transformative, is the formation of branch campuses on the soil of foreign countries. Such campuses have appeared in East and Southeast Asia, Africa, India, Latin America and also Western Europe. They are mostly established by universities from English-speaking countries. In this strategy, institutions cross borders rather than students. The parent universities partly set aside their long dependence on connectedness to particular localities. The branch campuses maintain identity ties back to the parent university. Nevertheless, being grounded in two national-cultural locations at once, some such institutions have begun to develop multiple and hybrid forms of teaching and learning. Another form of the cross-border movement of institutions is that of e-universities and other virtual institutions offering teaching programs online. While there have been significant investments in such institutions, especially by universities and consortia in the United States, to this point only one, the University of Phoenix, has proven sufficiently attractive to enroll large numbers of students. In part this is because virtual education has never the prestige of face-to-face programs, and also because the e-university prototypes developed so far have been mostly characterized by low-cost business models, and therefore low teaching intensity, and curricula that are not varied for particular national or linguistic contexts. Both factors render e-learning relatively unattractive to students. In the exceptional case of Phoenix the model is relatively expensive, teaching intensive and closely tailored to specific markets in vocational tertiary education.

In addition to these partial forays in making the global, there have been two kinds of moves designed to configure the global dimension of higher education at the level of the world as a whole. The first was the attempt of the World Trading Organization (WTO-GATS) through the negotiation of protocols and laws governing trade in services, including educational services. This was designed to rework worldwide education as a single trading environment. It depended on the willingness of nations to treat foreign educational providers as equivalent to local providers in terms of subsidy, market entry and operating conditions. The WTO-GATS initiative foundered when few nations were prepared to set aside favoured national treatment of their educational institutions, underlining the point that for most nation-states, schools and universities constitute more than trading units. They are part of the core economic, social and cultural infrastructure.

The second kind of move designed to shape the world as a whole in education and research is that of global comparison and ranking. In contrast with the WTO-GATS agenda these initiatives have gained widespread traction in a short space of time. In school education the results of the OECD's comparative survey of student achievement in reading, mathematics and science are watched closely by policy makers and have become entrenched in public debates about schooling. The OECD comparisons have highlighted the position of high performing countries such as Finland and Korea, not just in relation to educational performance but as economic and social models. In higher education the main form of comparison relates to research performance. The first and still the most prominent data collection is that by Shanghai Jiao Tong University Graduate School of Education. Innovation policy makers focus on publication and citation counts, which are improving rapidly and may soon take in non-English language work. The public is more moved by omnibus rankings that purport to summarize the global standing of universities by combining performance in heterogeneous areas into a single number. This enables ordinal league tables, such as those issued by the *Times Higher Education Supplement* in relation to all aspects of a university (or so the *Times Higher* claims), and Jiao Tong in relation to research. By these means the global knowledge economy, in all its diverse complexity, is reduced to a single hierarchy based on a uniform model of the idealized Anglo-American university.[7] It seems that this reduction, far from detracting from the authority of rankings, enhances their cultural reach. Global university comparisons in this form have relativized and suborned all national university systems except that of the United States.

In the next phase the evolution of a broader range of rankings, and the potential for specialized rankings based on different types of institution, promises to make room for diversity of purpose. For example webometrics ranks universities according to their presence in online publishing.[8] European nations are developing a comprehensive classification and multi-purpose rankings of higher education institutions that will enable a range of comparisons, specific to institutional mission, in place of one single league table.[9]

The chapter now continues the discussion of global space making in universities by drawing on empirical observation of global university imaginings.

II. Imaginings of University Presidents

University leaders are among the larger trilobites swimming in the global knowledge economy sea. Part II draws on their own accounts of global imagining and strategy. The quotations are extracted from a program of case studies of the global strategies of national research universities, mostly located in Asia-Pacific countries.[10] The study included one national (public sector) research university per country. In all but two cases they were among the nation's top two research universities in measured performance.

The global dimension of higher education is formed by three kinds of action: acts of imagination, acts of production and acts of regulation. In acts of imagining, university leaders envision the global dimension as a field, and imagine the global activities of the institution prior to the attempt (not always successful) to create those activities. The global dimension also involves acts of production: global outputs such as the dissemination of research knowledge, messages, open courseware and other web postings, and global teaching as in commercial degrees and e-Us. In working in the global space, universities and systems build or augment the capacity of institutions and their personnel to operate globally, especially in research. They also develop global connectivity, not just electronically but through partnerships, networks and staff and student exchange. For some university executives connectivity and capacity seem to function as ends in themselves, but they are also conditions of global production. In acts of regulation, national governments and meta-national agencies such as the European Commission shape global activity with partial effect by funding specified activities and conducting bilateral negotiations such as those designed to facilitate mutual recognition of institutions and degrees. More rarely there is multilateral action by nation-states in concert such as the Bologna process in Europe, the WTO-GATS negotiations on trade in education, and the creation of AHELO, international comparisons of learning outcomes, by an OECD conference of education ministers in 2007 (OECD, 2008). In addition bodies such as OECD and the World Bank not only provide forums for multilateral negotiations between separated nations but intervene on their own behalf as global agencies with distinct agendas.

Daniel Drache makes the point that one feature of the global setting is a 'decline in deference' whereby individual agents and self-determining organizations communicate and operate more openly on their own behalf.[11] In part this derives from the inability of nation-states to patrol the domains lying between them and across them. In part it is because in the global space, local actions and voices can achieve a larger resonance than they did before. University leaders, who are often lambs at home but lions abroad, exemplify this decline in deference. All else being equal global agents have more freedom from constraint, and greater agency. Some global agents such as research universities also have superior resources and hence more effective freedom than others. But what an individual university does with its freedom is part controlled by itself.

Vision

Drache also remarks that 'in previous times the technology of communication was highly centralized along with the mechanism of governance and public authority.' In contrast, today 'the technology of communication and structures of public authority are highly decentralized, networked and driven by a model of social relations rooted in a complex culture of consumption.'[12] This has created a new kind of shared public space consisting of networked private nodes in which the system architecture is outside direct state control.[13] In other words global communicative systems are not only an enlarged cauldron of imagining, they foster free agency itself. For the university presidents, rectors and vice-chancellors (hereafter 'presidents' used only) interviewed for this study, communicative technologies were key to their imagining of the global and of their place as active agents within it.

> I've got a computer full of e-mails from around the world from colleagues with whom I once would not have communicated because it would have taken two weeks for the letter to arrive, and two weeks for the response, and they would have waited another two weeks, so by this time you've forgotten what the issue was about. It doesn't happen like that now. There would be very few staff and probably very few students on this campus who do not interact with another country on a daily, certainly on a weekly basis. (*Ian Chubb, Vice-Chancellor, Australian National University*)

Often the research universities, or individual academic units within them, had been early adopters of the Internet within the nation.

> I became dean of the business school about twenty years ago. We were the first in the country that introduced the Internet. We were the first point of contact. We wanted it because around here [the University] they didn't let us connect with Singapore, Hong Kong…And it grew…it was 1991. I wired my whole faculty, so faculty members could use the Internet from their desks. *(Khunying Suchada, President, Chulalongkorn University, Thailand)*

All the presidents said they were regular and active users of email. Most used the Internet frequently to trap media and other sources. At the same time managing information flow was a major issue for most of them. Some mentioned that data overload was creating serious difficulties.

Constant travel is also a feature of every president's life, and a vital source of data.

> Now it is the era of information. We get lots of information from personal networking, and university organizations overseas, which always conduct workshops about the development of universities in the era of globalization. We also get information from the Internet, and journals of higher education, which can give us perspective. Next week I go to England for a meeting of Indonesian rectors on university management. We have been invited by the British Council. *(Usman Chatib Warsa, Rector, Universitas Indonesia)*

> It's absolutely astonishing how much one now draws information from all over the world in making any decision, about any aspect of the university. You no longer have to rely on colleagues who have actually travelled abroad. It's certainly changed. I'm old enough to remember when travel was quite exotic, when colleagues would come back with slides from some remote place. In the small town where I grew up, you would have the high school auditorium filled with travelogue presentations where some individual would present a speech and show slides. This was remarkable and highly entertaining, and would keep an audience spellbound. And now of course airplane travel is not a romantic or glamorous luxury, it's a nuisance, a necessary nuisance. Electronic communication occurs instantly, and you have information and embedded slideshows on every imaginable structure and institution. You can do a virtual tour of half the universities of the US. *(David Naylor, President, University of Toronto, Canada)*

Nearly all of these presidents emphasized networking with university presidents in parallel institutions in other nations, and in their own nations also. Their participation in consortia and other international meetings provided crucial sources of data and perspective. Talking to people in like positions is not only mutually reinforcing of the agency of university presidents, it also directly facilitates their observation and imagining of the global space. There is a tendency to synchronize with other presidents and trust them as observers. The eyes of the other presidents become extensions of their own. Joint meeting and discussion enable them to build a unified multi-location picture of the global space, identifying both what is common to all universities in that space and what varies on the basis of nation and locality.

Beyond the Internet and meetings, these individual leaders used diverse techniques of information gathering and imagination making. Many but not all were regularly briefed by specialist personnel who collected data on international matters. Others tended to form their views alone. Only a few were extensive readers. The constraint was always time:

Presidents and Vice Chancellors are in extraordinarily transactional jobs where the contemplative moments are few and far between. When you have them you have to decide whether you're going to put your feet up and think for a change, and try be strategic, or whether you will go on information acquisition mode. My few quiet moments are carefully parceled out between the two activities. The information acquisition is often internationally directed. *(David Naylor, President, University of Toronto, Canada)*

WORLD

When imagining the global, the presidents talked about convergence, integration and worldwide inter-dependence. Globalization was primarily understood by them in terms of the ubiquity of connections. Two presidents in interview made almost identical comments to the effect that it was no longer possible anywhere for communities or enterprises to function on a solely local basis, in isolation not only from proximate neighbours but a much broader map of agents. 'It is impossible to isolate the university. That would be a mistake,' stated the rector of the national university of Mexico (UNAM). He also noted that the compulsion to connect, and the new openness to global and market forces, meant it was all the more essential to nurture academic freedom.

Several presidents analyzed globalization in terms of tendencies towards the formation of a single world. In both Mexico and Japan globalization was explained in terms of global ecology. The president of Vietnam National University, a climate scientist in his own work, talked in terms of Heidegger's notion of de-severing: 'making the distance less.' Globalization cannot be objectively measured, he stated. 'It is not scientific, not exact.' It is a 'feeling.'

Globalization makes the world more connected, more collaborative, more flat. That's my feeling about globalization. Reducing geographical boundaries. No geographical boundaries. Making the distance less. And you cannot live and work alone. Before you could. Now you cannot. You cannot do everything your own way. *(Mai Trong Nhuan, President, Vietnam National University Hanoi)*

The world will become one. It's not that countries disappear or that the barriers between them will go away, no. But the system of the world will be more of a unified system. People can reach each other. *(Khunying Suchada, President, Chulalongkorn University, Thailand)*

The term 'globalization' connotes an array of outcomes going far beyond the conventional view of closely linked world markets. In tandem, leaps of technology and the Internet have shrunk time and space as well as leveled the global playing field. We live in a shrinking, flattening world. *(Shih Choon Fong, President, National University of Singapore)*

Most of the presidents also saw globalization as creating a more competitive, open and opportunistic environment for universities and their graduates—though apart from the President of NUS in Singapore, only one other interviewee used the Thomas Friedman terminology of the world as flat with its implication of a level playing field.[14] Among these presidents there was little faith in imaginings of equality. Half the presidents in the study stressed that global competition made local universities and national systems vulnerable to enhanced competition.

> I don't actually see globalization as a universal good. It has created more problems than it has given value in many instances. For us it means potentially hugely increased competition and a level of uncertainty that adds an unnecessarily difficult dimension to managing complex institutions....I do see benefits from freeing markets from unnecessary constraints but you can't make them totally free. For a university like this, I'm confident that we could survive in a much freer more competitive environment. But if it's totally deregulated no Australian university would survive. *(Ian Chubb, Vice-Chancellor, Australian National University)*

However, few of the interviewees modeled the global explicitly and primarily in terms of world markets. (The economic notion of globalization showed more in the the first interviews conducted in 2004–2005 than those conducted in the 2006–2009 period, suggesting that once dominant economic readings of globalization were being progressively displaced by notions of the global as communicative integration). Notions of higher education as an economic competition, and teaching as a commodity, were explicitly critiqued in Mexico and Thailand. In each of these nations the university president explicitly attacked the WTO-GATS agenda and expressed concern about the potential entry of for-profit foreign providers in vocational education or e-learning. The commercial approach was seen as likely to empty out the quality of programs, reduce open collaboration in research, and expand the gap between technology-rich and technology-poor nations.

Only the NUS president was clearly comfortable about discussing the globalization of research universities in terms of economic markets. Significantly, at the time the interviews were conducted, Singapore was the one nation where public funding was rising sharply and the neo-liberal ideology based on markets, competition and scarcity was not associated with the degree of scarcity of resources for higher education that was apparent elsewhere.

THE FIELD OF GLOBAL HIGHER EDUCATION

Networked global activity is multidirectional and always changing. It seems that no president has information systems that allow her or him to map and track the field of global higher education on an ongoing basis. Informal faculty contact and exchange elude executive surveillance. Some presidents in the study referred to a weak fit between their official global activities and priorities, and the patterns of discipline level work. NUS seemed to be more on top of the detail of its global activity than the other universities. But most of the presidents were at ease in talking of the global dimension of higher education. They seemed to grasp its patterns almost instinctively. Those patterns were seen as open but vectored by the global hierarchy of universities in terms of resources, status and research power. All of the presidents emphasized the standing and effects of US universities, which are the strongest nodes in the global setting in terms of both research and institution building. US institutions embody concentrated connectivity. Vera and Schupp define 'connectivity' as follows:

> Connectivity, that is to say the capacity of large networks to combine a high degree of local clustering with a relatively low average path distance between nodes, helps understand the rapid expansion of knowledge, institutions or organizational patterns throughout the world without implying that the world should be considered as a unity. Worldwide scale-free networks are actually constituted by a few highly connected clusters which facilitate the flow of information, but this does not mean that information affects the whole of the network at the same time or in the same way. This is an idea that combines globalization with diversity, and which enriches the notion of the complexity of social systems.[15]

American universities wield both 'networking power,' which is power to affect others inside and outside the university networks, and 'network power' which is the power to set templates and standards and eliminate alternative models.[16] Thus, when asked to name the institutions that most impressed them as possible models for imitation, the presidents focused on Harvard, Stanford, MIT, Caltech, Berkeley and/or the University of California system as a whole, even though the conditions of possibility of these US institutions could not be replicated in their own countries. Some mentioned large public research universities such as Wisconsin, and Cambridge in the UK. The major European universities were rarely acknowledged by name, except by the Rector at Leiden in the Netherlands. However, in the non-English speaking countries in Asia there was a strong desire, albeit expressed in general terms, to source models of universities from Europe (especially Germany) as an alternative to the USA/UK. In the USA itself the Provost at the University of Illinois in the United States, Linda Katehi, was wary of the dominance of US models. She defined 'globalization' in imperial terms as 'assimilating others to what we do rather than changing ourselves.' To Katehi, the preferred approach was 'internationalization,' which means learning from other countries and cultures, changing one's own outlook, and acquiring a sense of living in 'a much larger world.'

In relation to Asia there was universal agreement among the presidents about two factors. First, the recent development of research universities in China was impressive and China was becoming a great higher education power. Second, NUS Singapore was very impressive, not just in its global work but in all respects. All of the university presidents in the study but one had active partnerships with NUS. Of the universities in the interviewee group, the second most connected was Illinois in the USA. At the time of the interviews Illinois had just negotiated a major agreement with NUS and the senior officers at the American university sang the praises of the Singapore university.

The potential of regional factors was obvious. Most presidents acknowledged the significance of proximate neighbours in their geographical region. Europe was centrally important for the Dutch universities. Leiden had initiated the League of European universities, a consortium consisting of almost all the strongest research-intensive institutions. At both Toronto in Canada, and UNAM in Mexico, higher education in the USA exerted the main outside influence on faculty work. At UNAM, where there was a choice in regionalization strategy between looking north and looking south, the rector noted that Latin America had been neglected. Very few UNAM students went to Spanish-speaking countries, aside from Spain. He was hopeful that a small scale regional scholarship scheme might start to shift the field of vision. All of the Southeast Asian presidents maintained active networks with universities from other countries in the Association of South East Asia Nations (ASEAN). At the University of Tokyo links in East Asia had recently received strategic emphasis, and likewise Vietnam National University had begun to meet regularly with the counterpart leading East Asian universities in Japan, China and Korea. At the Australian National University (ANU) in Australia, the building of relationships in the Asia-Pacific region was entrenched in the original design of the university. One of the ANU's four founding research and graduate schools was the Research School of Pacific and Asian Studies.

As most of the presidents saw it, the greatest single influence in shaping the global sector was university rankings. The exceptions were Illinois in the USA where the preoccupation was with national rankings, and Mexico where the UNAM rector expressed himself largely indifferent to global comparisons. The problem for most presidents is that they are judged—by national government and public media—according to their global rankings performance, regardless of technical flaws or national-cultural bias in the rankings. In one case, the University of Malaya, a decline in the *Times Higher Education Supplement* ranking had recently triggered the non-renewal of the president's contract. Ironically the frustration for Chulalongkorn in Thailand was that a *Times* ranking of 121, a strong showing for an emerging nation, secured little recognition by the government. This may even have contributed to continued funding problems.

> That's what they said. Even though we don't give Chula lots of money they can still do well, they can survive. Don't worry about them. *(Khunying Suchada, President, Chulalongkorn University, Thailand)*

To be able to operate effectively in the global setting, each university knows it has to be strong in research—to be a 'World Class University'[17] or 'Global Research University.'[18]

> Our ambition is to meet international standards. To be in the top 200 universities in the world. Of course, this is the long-term vision. Not in one day...Our mission is to become a research university that meets international standards. We focus all our efforts to achieve that. *(Mai Trong Nhuan, President, Vietnam National University Hanoi)*

> We are now putting a lot of effort, money and resources and manpower into the research field...promotion to professor and associate professor now depends largely on publication. *(Hashim Yaacob, Vice-Chancellor, University of Malaya, Malaysia)*

In this study the aspiration was felt with some anguish in those universities that are most marginal to the global metropolis in the Atlantic countries, such as Universitas Indonesia, Vietnam National University and the University of Malaya in Malaysia. They knew the gap was very large. The aspiration was less of a concern in Thailand. A sense of coming from behind in research also troubled Auckland in New Zealand and UNAM in Mexico, two institutions that were in the Jiao Tong top 300. In all the non-English-speaking countries there were pressures on faculty to publish more in global journals.

STRATEGY MAKING

Like composers of classical music, university presidents create 'for the circumstances of the moment, not for prosperity.'[19] Unlike composers, their creations remain bounded in time. The forward visions of universities are defined in terms of 2020 or 2030 but their strategies rarely look further than five years ahead, which is the rhythm of presidential contracts. From time to time the universities recast the map of their global activity. But much of this is just marketing; the new phase is usually in continuity with the old. Global connections and activity are mostly built as a series of incremental improvizations.

But there was a strong sense of imperative in many of the interviews. For some presidents leading the university into global engagement was almost a call to arms. They saw it as essential to do more than respond to global signals. It was necessary to be proactive. All but the presidents in Malaysia and Indonesia were upbeat about the potentials of global strategy:

> We feel that the global environment as a whole is a very rich environment. There are lots of benefits, if we think the right way and do it fairly, [without] taking away benefits from other people...We can enjoy the way that everything is so open. *(Khunying Suchada, President, Chulalongkorn University, Thailand)*

Strategy always must be nested. Decisions on capacity building and connectivity are closely affected by the particular university's conditions, resources and location; including not just its global position and the region but also the positioning strategies of the nation-state. In this study the university that stood out for the close unity between university strategy and national strategy was NUS. That university was also unique in its degree of emphasis on global factors in strategy. This was a function of the nation's strategic position:

> Singapore is a tiny island with some big neighbours, e.g. Australia, China, India, Indonesia and Japan. With no retreat or hinterland, globalization is not an option but a necessity for Singapore. We have no choice but to think 'global,' breathe 'global' and to be 'global.' We constantly have to ask ourselves: 'How can we build mutual respect?' 'How can we be useful and relevant to the world?'...Singapore was global before the term 'globalization' became fashionable....In a global economy characterized by intense competition for talent, ideas and capital, Singapore's universities have also had to re-make themselves to stay relevant and thrive...NUS has undergone a dramatic transformation from a predominantly teaching institution training competent manpower for Singapore to a research-intensive university respected in the global arena, and from a governance and management system closely aligned to the civil service to one based on performance and global best practice. *(Shih Choon Fong, President, National University of Singapore)*

Singapore's size creates constraints. 'We're a small country. You can bring tremendous intellectual power to Singapore...[but] there's a Chinese saying ...you cannot put too many lions on a hill. There's only a few hills in Singapore' (NUS's Shih). Offshore activities can be used to grow the number of 'hills.' At the same time the offshore centres and partnerships had to be constantly worked into the overall priorities of the University. Singapore had established a sophisticated national-global strategy, but New Zealand was still in the throes of developing both, and the relationship between them:

> Thirty years ago New Zealand universities were clones of Britain. It wasn't until after the [second world] war that New Zealand universities stopped sending the final examinations of their students home—and I use the word deliberately—to England to have them marked. People still say to me why do you have a graduation in May? The answer of course is that if you sit an examination in October/November and you put it on a boat to England, you give it a month to be marked and you put it on a boat back to New Zealand, when does it arrive? Well, it arrives in time for you to graduate in May; that's why we have May graduations. Until 25 years ago everybody went to the UK for their PhD, most people for their postdocs in the UK. Lecturers mainly came from the UK. *(Stuart McCutcheon, Vice-Chancellor, University of Auckland, New Zealand)*

In the first phase of creation 'divergent thinking' opens a 'near infinite' range of potentials, noted Peter Murphy. 'In the second phase of creation, convergent thinking unites and integrates.' Several presidents emphasized that global imagining requires them to maintain an open outlook, alive to the hetero-geneous strategic options. The price of this openness was a constant problem of selection, not just in relation to partners and actions but also in relation to imagining and monitoring. As noted this was compounded by the lack of dis-cretionary time in which to imagine and explore the different strategic options. (Plane time was often essential for these presidents.) The difficult initial prob-lem was the scope of strategy. One logical response to globalization was to broaden cross-border ties to include most world regions. Indeed, most pres-idents would have liked to plant the flag in every continent. For example in the 1980s, the University of Auckland stretched its attention from the UK to North America; in the 1990s it discovered Asia and focused closely on China. But the spreading process had created a rolling series of priority dilemmas, because convergent thinking was lacking.

> Our fundamental problem is we try to do too much. We do too many things badly, and not enough things particularly well…We've got 300 MOUs, but which ones matter? We've got 5000 international students. Are they all of equal value to our strategy? We've tended to try to do a bit of everything. The trick is to sit down and think more carefully about what we're trying to achieve and who we can deal with properly. *(Stuart McCutcheon, Vice-Chancellor, University of Auckland, New Zealand)*

Of the universities in the study only NUS in Singapore, with its crafted glob-al strategy and active portfolios in each carefully chosen part of the world, seemed to have solved the problem of priority setting to its own satisfaction. Its global strategy was locked in by NPM management systems. 'A performance-driven framework for research funding has helped to ensure value-for-money in research activities as well as focus resources in niche areas where NUS is able to achieve global excellence,' stated the NUS president. But at NUS strategy had to be fine-tuned continually and was less pre-set that it appeared:

> Q. You said, 'we have a unique pathway.' We are doing our own model. But that raises an interesting question about the strategic thinking itself. If there's no model, no pathway already established, no parallels, no imitation to make—which is the way most people 'innovate,' they imitate something else that's suc-cessful—how do you imagine what the alternatives are? How do you imagine the options you then choose between? How do you think it all out?

> A. I used to sail when I was in North America…I can see that we have to be glob-al and national. I see that as the destiny. As to how we get that, that's what the sailor does. We've got to tack. Sometimes the undercurrents get strong, we give way a little bit, and then when the opportune moment comes we go back. So our strategy is evolving…More important is that we know the overall direction. We have a compass, but the exact roadmap will unfold as we go along. *(Shih Choon*

Fong, President, National University of Singapore)

The presidents focused their institutional efforts in domains where global activity was seen to be under-developed. Thus the University of Tokyo placed no official emphasis on forging relations with US universities. There was no need to do so, as many members of staff were already active there. The official strategic focus was on building stronger relations in Western Europe and in Asia.

Most presidents were confident in their capacity to implement a global strategy across the institution. But some mentioned the need for an enhanced capacity to steer academic behaviour and priorities. This was a primary concern for President Takeshi Sasaki at the University of Tokyo. At the time of the interview Tokyo was early in the process of 'corporatization,' a New Public Management (NPM) reform designed to establish a more entrepreneurial and business-like university. At the time of the interviews at Universitas Indonesia a similar change was taking place there, and this was also the case in Singapore, where NUS had been re-established as a not-for-profit company. At Chulalongkorn in Thailand reforms to enhance university autonomy had stalled. NPM organizational systems have long been entrenched at Auckland in New Zealand and the ANU in Australia.

The presidents of all of the non-English-speaking universities acknowledged the need to build facility in global English. This was a central element in their strategies. With less of a sense of imperative, the universities from the four English-speaking countries in the study acknowledged that their personnel and students were not sufficiently effective in non English-speaking contexts. They all felt that mono-lingualism prevented a more reciprocal pattern of people flows and retarded collaboration. The pious hope of these presidents was to treat facility in Chinese national language as a priority in their capacity building strategies. But no substantial scheme to achieve this was in place in Australia, New Zealand, the USA or Canada.

Mobility

If the presidents—as global agents—form university networks, then at the same time those networks foster global agency. It must be said that not every nominal network or partnership is important. On the opening night of *Die Entfuhrung* in Vienna in 1782, the Emperor Joseph II told Mozart that the score contained too many notes.[20] Likewise, most of the presidents thought their university had signed too many superfluous agreements, 'too many empty MOUs' as one put it—with foreign partners. No doubt there was more justification for this remark than for that of Joseph II.[21] In this group of universities it was again NUS in Singapore that seemed to extract the most value from its role in consortia. NUS then housed the secretariat of the Asia-

Pacific Rim Network. But in all the universities, one to one partnerships that were active could be highly generative. Some involved major commitments of time and money. Of the potential areas of global production, the presidents most often mentioned research collaboration, staff exchange, foreign student enrolment, and local student exchange abroad. Electronic communication provides a framework for acts of imagining, whereas travel is necessary to most of the acts of production. In research and publishing the Internet is a primary and sufficient site of production as well as communication.

> The fundamentals of collaboration are not always completely covered by the electronic age and communications...There are glimmerings of [video-conferencing] getting better. That may become more of an alternative, but right now we aren't there yet, and having participated in lots of video conferences, you can't substitute for in-person contact, shared beverages and proximity. (*David Naylor, President, University of Toronto, Canada*)

Across all the interviews there was more discussion of practical issues and problems in relation to people mobility than any other aspect of global relations. The presidents emphasized growth in cross-border people movement, including official university visits, ongoing faculty business at discipline level and student exchange. Presidents in the English-language universities emphasized the growing heterogeneity of their student populations, particularly the increased numbers of students from non-English and non-European backgrounds. NUS was again the most active in people movement. At the time of the interviews it had more than thirty joint degrees with 19 partner universities around the world, and 220 student exchange agreements in 38 countries with over 1600 student places per annum. Its goal was to send 20 per cent of undergraduates abroad for one semester each. There were summer programs or field trips in China, Indonesia, USA, Belgium and Australia, five joint research laboratories and numerous collaborations.

Among all the presidents a more nationally diverse student body was seen as a positive attribute of the university and an end in itself. Nearly all of them could name the number of countries from which their students came. Several emphasized that their graduates worked in many parts of the world, and that students needed to be prepared for this, though there was little discussion of the possible implications for teaching and learning. At Leiden the rector Douwe Breimer talked of creating 'a mini global environment' inside the university which would expose the student to 'different views and different opinions,' thereby becoming 'more of a global citizen.' Similar concepts were floated at NUS in Singapore and by Richard Herman, Chancellor of the Urbana-Champaign campus at Illinois. But sending local students abroad for part of their studies was difficult to achieve, everywhere, except for Leiden and

Twente in Europe, and for NUS. The barriers to outward mobility were cost, and in English-speaking nations, lack of student motivation.

Issues related to the global mobility of talent—how to become more effective in competition for researchers, how to stop local researchers from leaving after graduation with PhDs, how to draw good people from abroad, and how to keep them happy and hold them once they were inside the university—constantly preoccupied all presidents, regardless of how strongly the university was positioned in the global field.

> In today's knowledge-driven global economy, talent, ideas and intellectual capital have taken centre stage....NUS has to compete in the global arena against universities with access to broader and deeper talent and resource pools. We believe that the quality of faculty is the single most important determinant of the quality of education and research. (*Shih Choon Fong, President, National University of Singapore*)

There were many unresolved issues in relation to people movement that affected global capacity. In all of the case study universities it was said that there was inadequate funding for student scholarships, regardless of how much was already being spent in that area. It seems there can never be enough of such funding. Another issue was lack of accommodation for students, including foreign students, which was emphasized at Tokyo and Leiden in the Netherlands. At Illinois there was great concern about a recent slowdown in the supply of international graduate students from China. At a number of universities brain drain and unequal inward/outward flows were burning issues. In Mexico a large proportion of the best doctoral and post-doctoral personnel were lost to the USA every year. The rector at UNAM wanted the Mexican government to introduce a 'brain gain' program that would bring in new academic labour to compensate for outward movement. In New Zealand, Auckland was losing staff to locations where salary levels were higher, while the country's geographical isolation from the global metropolis was another factor that contributed to brain drain. Relative salaries tended to position the universities within the global hierarchy of attraction power. There was no clear solution to brain drain in Vietnam and Indonesia where rates of pay were 10 per cent of those applying in the USA. In Malaysia academic employment was attractive to staff from nations such as Indonesia, and to some extent India, but it had limited pulling power in the Middle East and none in Europe or the English-speaking world. Meanwhile neighbouring Singapore was paying US-level salaries, five times the level of Malaysia, and recruiting vigorously.

> We would very much like to bring foreign staff...but the salary at this university cannot attract them, unlike Singapore. Singapore have a lot of money and they can bring in many people. It is very, very competitive, their salary. (*Hashim Yaacob, Vice-Chancellor, University of Malaya, Malaysia*)

Another obstacle to inward academic mobility was national regulation and/or protectionism in the academic profession. Where pay rates were fixed centrally according to public service norms, university presidents had little discretion. In most of the countries under study it was difficult for foreigners to gain permanent employment and in some cases, any employment. For example at the University of Malaya, the best option available to staff entering from outside the country was a three-year contract. In the Netherlands there was political ambivalence about migration and visa delays were a case-by-case problem. In Japan, the national language inhibited potential recruits—a concern for the University of Tokyo which wanted to grow its foreign professoriate. Universities in the settler societies of Canada, the USA, Australia and New Zealand benefited from the habitual openness of their nations to migrants. At the University of Toronto there was a typically Canadian enthusiasm for cultural openness, mixing and cosmopolitan virtues. 'I think there is optimism about globalization in Canada that is probably greater than in any other nation' (David Naylor, President, University of Toronto). Within the case study group this attitude was shared, in more muted fashion, by ANU in Australia and Illinois in the USA, and also Leiden in the Netherlands where the university's own broad-based competence and longstanding enthusiasm in global work was in contrast with the unease about foreign immigration and 'non-traditional Dutch' citizens in parts of the Dutch polity.

Academic mobility is affected by more than salaries, national regulation of academic labour and immigration regimes. Professional cultures, national identity, vocation and personal affect also come into play. These aspects can work in favour of universities in less wealthy countries, partly countering tendencies to brain drain. For example some professors at Vietnam National University had employment options in North America or Europe but had stayed in Vietnam, or returned there from abroad, because of their commitment to the nation and its educational development. The prestige of national research universities, such as those included in this study, always makes them more attractive to researchers and lecturers, though it seems that in a more mobile global setting the pulling power of this factor has diminished. Other universities in the same countries, that do not benefit from national prestige factors, have rather weaker pulling power.

Some research universities in emerging national systems used foreign linkages in a systematic way to drive improvements in educational quality. For example Vietnam National University (VNU) sourced approaches to teaching, research and governance from across the higher education world, particularly the USA. It had signed collaborative agreement with Illinois (chemistry), Brown (physics), Wisconsin (mathematics) and the Haas business school (economics). Under these arrangements VNU adapted the American curricula and teaching technology and sent its staff to the US universities for training. The American institutions also sent personnel to Vietnam to conduct staff development, benchmarking and evaluation exercises. The VNU president reckoned these initiatives had been successful but noted that the payoffs were slow and mostly invisible. This was a problem. The national government was eager to see quick improvement in VNU's ranking.

National and Global

All the presidents interviewed for this study were closely aware of their local context and national regulation as one of the factors that framed it. This is the domain of realpolitik that every president wears as a second skin. In going global they combine a grounded local identity with loose and malleable forms of cross-border association. But to see their global visions as ephemeral would be wrong. Global comparison is inevitable, global activity motivates them and global synchrony is a pleasure. Though the global dimension connects to only part of the work of each university, and it is costly, for these presidents it was unquestionable that research universities were continually engaged in building global activity. This perspective was not always shared by their students or governments. Globalization embodies different modernist reflexivities to those of the nation-state. This is key to understanding the contemporary university.

The dividing line between the 'World Class Global Research University' and 'the not WCGRU' is not just a distinction within each national system. It also demarcates the global sector of higher education and research, which is those universities that participate effectively within the global dimension of action, from other higher education institutions. Additionally it determines a distinction within each research intensive university, between (1) research and doctoral education which are globally referenced, and (2) first degree teaching and graduate professional programs that service local communities and are nationally and locally referenced. In the global universities there is no automatic synergy between the national and global drivers of activity. In the interviews tensions in vision and strategy were apparent, except in Singapore. The relationship between nationally vectored activity and globally vectored activity is more positive sum than zero sum. On the whole global success strengthens a university's position at home. Perhaps UNAM in Mexico was an exception. The 200,000 student strong UNAM had a national role that was so broad and deep that it seemed to marginalize global linkages. It is almost as if UNAM functioned as a (largely autonomous) state instrumentality in the field of universities while foreign affairs and trade were left to other branches of state. Some other Mexican universities, less prestigious at home, put a greater emphasis on their global role and connections.

Unsurprisingly all of these presidents wanted more autonomy in relation to government, and better support from government. No doubt as the governments saw it, this was having it both ways, but no president questioned the tactics of this position. Most of the presidents emphasized that their own commitment to global activity was not matched by national funding and regulation. Governments expected the universities to perform well in global competition but provided insufficient support. However, university presidents value global activities partly because they conduct them beyond the reach of government. Here the capacity of the presidents to operate independently of government is greater when they are chosen by the university governing body or community, not appointed by the ministry. Universities controlled the appointment in Singapore, Tokyo, the Netherlands and the USA, Canada and Australia. In Thailand government routinely appointed the person recommended by the university. In Malaysia government control as exercised through appointment was direct and affected leader behaviour. There was provision for a second three-year term, but vice-chancellors regarded as too independent were not reappointed. In addition the vice-chancellor at the University of Malaya was required to secure specific government approval for each Memorandum of Understanding that was signed with a foreign partner. In Vietnam the president did not question the process of government appointment, but did want greater autonomy:

> When I met the president of Vietnam I said: 'I do not ask you for more money. Give me more autonomy.' More freedom. More responsibility. More transparency. More flexibility to meet the requirements of our society and globalization. More autonomy. We have full autonomy in teaching and research. But not in staffing and finance. *(Mai Trong Nhuan, President, Vietnam National University Hanoi)*

All presidents reported that private income had increased. Most also stated that their overall financial position had been weakened by constraints or reductions in government spending. Only NUS in Singapore was doing well. In Indonesia, Malaysia, Singapore and Japan corporatization reform had been coupled with a cut in the share of the budget covered by government, despite continued direct and indirect controls over much of the universities' activities. Cuts to state government funding were hurting in Illinois. Public funding was less of an issue in Toronto, but ANU in Australia and Auckland in New Zealand were sharply constrained financially. Unlike most other Australian universities, ANU is not strong in the commercial market in international education. It receives special research funding from government. Its extensive offshore activities are financed largely from research budgets.

All the presidents were partly or wholly constrained in their capacity to vary tuition charges to domestic students. This set limits on the capacity to be a quasi-private commercial university as imagined by the New Public Management (NPM). In most of the case study universities the overall financial position had deteriorated during the NPM era, as shown by symptoms such as increases in student-staff ratios and the part casualization of teaching. Global activity had to be financed from the same pool of resources used for teaching and administration. Notably, no president questioned the need to maintain and increase that global activity. Despite the constrained resource position there was no substantial debate within the institutions about the need to become more globally effective.

Global Power

Matthews and Sidhu remark that notions of global freedom centred on 'the free floating, fleet-footed' individual with 'boundless opportunities' are usually premised 'on the dispositions, aspirations and opportunities of the Euro-American, first world, elite masculine subject.'[22] This survey of university leaders underlines the point. Those who do not fit the 'Euro-American, first world, elite' descriptor have a lesser range of options. Global mobility is a near universal in the imagination but in practice it is limited by the national and institutional hierarchies of knowledge power that are stamped on the minds of every university president. Their imagined global trajectories and strategies are often out of reach, particularly in research. Here global equality/inequality are shaped by two vectors. One is linguistic and cultural. The other is measured by political economy.

In relation to culture, a principal strategic problem for presidents from non- English-speaking countries, as they saw it, was the dominance of the Anglo-American world in higher education, especially in relation to university rankings. It was emphasized that the rankings criteria favoured the USA. The university presidents from non-English-speaking countries were also troubled about the invasive potentials of Anglo-American models of the university. They wanted greater plurality of values.

Q. What do you understand by the term globalization?

A. The unification of culture by the United States. It's a very bad aspect of the present phenomenon of globalization. The idea of globalization should mean that all people can access the Internet equally. Japan is an advanced, developed country. We have a completely different culture from the Western world. I think this is quite special....United States' culture rushes into Japan as in all over the world, symbolized by Disneyland and Macintosh and Macdonalds. This is partly destroying Japanese traditional culture. *(Hiroshi Komiyama, Executive Vice-President, University of Tokyo, Japan)*

Globalization has brought Indonesia into a big arena where the countries become borderless...globalization comes into all countries. The problems are different from country to country. Other countries may be more prepared than Indonesia in facing globalization. If Indonesia is not prepared the country will become the consumer of developed countries...Western culture can now easily come into Indonesia. *(Usman Chatib Warsa, Rector, Universitas Indonesia)*

As noted, the provost of the University of Illinois had qualms about the outward projection of hegemonic American k-power. But for the non-hegemonic powers the global projection of national culture would be a positive outcome if it could be achieved, for example in Indonesia and Thailand.

I think the Thai people are special in the way they behave...we are considerate of other people's feelings. I think that is a unique Thai way. We smile a lot, we are courteous, and we work very hard. Those that work offshore, they are mostly smart, and they work hard, and at the same time they have these interpersonal skills that can work with other people. I would love to think that my students also have morals and good governance in their heads and the integrity of being a good citizen of the world. *(Khunying Suchada, President, Chulalongkorn University, Thailand)*

The bigger powers must understand that education is not universal. Education has got to be tailored to the culture. *(Hashim Yaacob, Vice-Chancellor, University of Malaya, Malaysia).*

Yet the enthusiasm for national culture that was felt by the non-Western presidents could not be be practiced without invoking dilemmas. The same vice-chancellor from Malaysia also talked about the need to engineer a shift in research activity from national language to English language journals. There was no choice but to participate in the global knowledge system, however it was arranged. The non English-language nations preserved elements of local intellectual tradition, but they could scarcely overturn the weight of American research and assert an alternate definition of knowledge, and in the sciences locally based knowledge had little standing anywhere. Here the tectonic fault line between cultural centre and cultural periphery coincided with a similar hierarchical structuring of the political economy. There were few resources to sustain non-global knowledge because on the whole it was practiced in the poorer universities in the group. Problems of political economic inequality were emphasized by the presidents from Malaysia, Thailand, Indonesia, Vietnam and Mexico. In Indonesia and Vietnam the university could not afford subscriptions to basic journals.

Globalization [ideally] would be a world without borders. But we must always be aware than in the globalized world the field has not developed this way. The players are not the same size. What will be good for the bigger power may not be good for the smaller power....What we are looking forward to in the globalized world is that things become freer and things become shared, but they must be shared...if it is rules of the jungle, best man wins, we are all dead. *(Hashim Yaacob, Vice-Chancellor, University of Malaya, Malaysia)*

Globalization affects differently each country and each group of countries. It has a completely different impact in the strongest economies such as the United States and many of the European countries, and the newly developed Asian economies, than it has in countries such as Mexico, and the effect it may have in the least developed countries. It has an impact that really increases inequities. That has made very difficult the dialogue at global and internal institutions, because the effects are perceived by government and society in one country as different from the effects that are perceived in another country. *(Juan Ramon de la Fuente, Rector, UNAM, the national university of Mexico)*

These patterns affected the character of the global alliances formed by the presidents. The politics of alliance building combines national and global referencing in a complex manner. First, there is a tendency of leading national research universities to network with universities in other countries with a national status similar to their own, regardless of the respective global position of the two institutions. A common national role facilitates mutual recognition and the building of trust relations. In this respect national referencing sets the frame and global alliances are multilateral in form and based on parallelism. Second, and contrariwise, the leading national research universities from emerging and middle-level nations find it an advantage to network upwards to universities from stronger nations (especially the USA) regardless of the status position of the developed country university, because of the potential transfers of resources and expertise. In this respect the framework and process of referencing are global. But third, leading national research universities in the emerging nations are wary of being exploited for the gain of foreign partners. For example, the president of Chulalongkorn in Thailand noted the university was regularly approached with offers of partnership from institutions wanting to use Chula's national status to open up Thailand. Here the point of reference for making decisions about alliances was again global, and the Chulalongkorn president emphasized the need to build trust on the basis of commonality of mission and values. She was prepared to work with institutions with middle-level status in their own countries, not just the national leaders, providing their 'heart' was right. It had to be 'something that will benefit the world. I don't want you to come here just marketing your education. It just turns me off.'

We can see that in the sum of the incremental decisions made from the vantage of single institutions and national systems, about how to manage university trajectories amid global inequality, and the associated presidential judgments (often made on the run) about forms of commonality underlying partnerships, a new university world order is emerging.

III. Interpretations

Global Niches

But more than a miscellany of separated incremental decisions is at work here. What open or hidden forces determine the emerging patterns of global university activity? What relations, systems and laws of motion (if such things exist) govern the emergence of new forms of knowledge and new modes of university organization in the communicative global knowledge economy? What has shaped the division of labour, or rather the different divisions of labour, between the national higher education systems—and between different types of institution, different university missions, the programs and strategies employed? What evolutionary dynamics are at work? As in chapter four, once again it is useful to look for clues in that valuable storehouse of potential insights into the human condition, the story of the Earth and biological evolution. In the literature on new environments, parallel questions are asked by evolutionists, such as how do new species consolidate a position within an emerging eco-system? What determines the available positions? What is the scope for innovations in form and behaviour, for new ways of doing things? How do these freedoms change over time?

Biological eco-systems are characterized by interdependence between species that occupy different niches; such as herbivores and carnivores, species using speed or disguise, species utilizing nimbleness or bulk, species that are material generators and those that are waste feeders, and so on. The various niches are interactive and synergistic. Interpretations differ on the extent to which biological equilibriums are stable. What is clear is that the occupants of the niches change over time more readily than do the niches themselves. The history of life suggests there are two kinds of pivotal moment in which there is large-scale creation of a whole eco-biological system, along with an enhanced rate of innovation in species and types of species. The first pivotal moment is the kind of major change in the conditions of life that triggers a new relational environment that is built from the ground up. One example is the augmentation of oxygen that permitted multi-cellular animals to develop. Another is the trilobites' development of vision. This might be called the 'green fields' form of eco-creation. The second such pivotal moment is a mass extinction that sweeps away most of the old species and old rules of interaction; an extinction in itself sufficient to constitute a new start.[23] When a mass extinction takes place, many of the old niches are emptied. This opens space for newcomers. A key role is played by survivors from the past era. These soon morph into new forms and change their functions in response to new strategic opportunities. As we shall see, not only do the new or remade species find themselves slotting into empty niches, in the wake of a profound extinction there is also scope for the remaking of the whole system of niches and interactions. There have been five great mass extinctions in the biological realm since the Cambrian explosion around 540 million years ago, and it may be that a sixth extinction on this scale is now taking place. The two kinds of eco-creation, green fields and mass extinction, have much in common. Each is fundamental in its scope for creation. A difference is that, in green fields creation, new forms coexist with old forms for some time into the future.

The arrival of the global knowledge economy as a new relational space more closely approximates the first kind of change, green fields creation, than that of mass extinction. In the global knowledge economy, the older forms of life have not been extinguished. The pre-1990 university was international in temper and had a global presence. It advanced a slower movement of knowledge, ideas and personnel from its border, in an 'early modern' form of globalization.[24] The global dynamics were less primary and less transformative. The green fields dimension has grown in, amongst and alongside this pre-1990 university. The emergent global dimension is fed and conditioned by the early modern university systems, even as it chafes against and breaks beyond the bounds of the nation-state that shaped those early modern systems. Here the Cambrian co-exists with the pre-Cambrian, and they are in some tension with each other. But it is easy to underestimate the novelty. It is too easy to understand the paradoxical knowledge economy in the terms of twentieth-century finance and manufacturing capital—though clearly the k-economy is something new, in the manner in which quick-silver flows of knowledge generate a host of new businesses, while also eluding the conventional form of economic commodities. Likewise, in evolutionary biology there has often been a tendency to underplay the extent of the novelty and creativity that is manifest in eco-creation at the major turning points.[25]

The greatest of all the mass extinctions occurred 250 million years ago at the end of the Permian when about 95 per cent of all living species died out. It is this mass extinction that comes closest in form to green fields creation like the Cambrian, or the knowledge economy today. In reviewing the Permian extinction, and the recovery phase that followed, in which very different biological systems emerged in the early Triassic, Douglas Erwin emphasizes that new systems and new niches within the relational order were entailed. 'Most models of mass extinction assume that extinction is a giant hand sweeping pieces off the board, but leaving the board and the rules of the game intact,' he notes. In these arguments, 'biotic recovery becomes a process of replacing the pieces on the chessboard and letting the game resume.' In this reasoning, specialization can only succeed 'when new species find an empty niche, symbolized as an empty space on the board. Once a niche is filled, the incumbent prevents a competitor from displacing it.' Once the niches are filled 'there is less room for new species and speciation slows.' The rate of innovation falls away.[26] However, Erwin argues, this conventional picture is overly determinist and static. 'During some mass extinctions, the board collapses entirely, and as the game resumes, it becomes half chess and half backgammon, with some rules drawn from poker. Moreover, the rules evolve during the recovery.'[27] The chessboard model assumes that niches exist 'independent of the species that construct them, instead of being constructed by them.'[28] For Erwin, 'niches are created by the organisms that occupy them through adaptations to the physical environment and to the other species with which they interact.'[29]

Likewise in analyzing the dynamics of higher education Pierre Bourdieu argues that within a relational field, position-taking agents respond to both the available opportunities and the competitive moves that are made by each other.[30] Despite his insights into the dynamics of positional competition in the university sector Bourdieu underestimates the potential for 'species' to create new niches, new positions within the field, let alone transformation of the field as a whole. He does not anticipate a creation as sweeping as that of the global university. However, as Erwin notes, there is broad potential for new niches and rules of interaction only at certain exceptional moments, such as Cambrian-style innovative radiation, or mass extinction. When Bourdieu wrote, the present global transformation of the university was just beginning and was scarcely discernable.

The global dimension of higher education and research is in a phase of emergence and species radiation in which there are few rules and the new ecosystem is only partly formed. When a genuinely new relational setting emerges, it is marked by the past but it does not necessarily replicate all of the rules of the old order. It entails new systems. The new ecology is characterized not just by new species of animal, which in the present case include all of the universities that have become more global in temper. It is also characterized by new kinds of species, for example, research universities in the UK and Australia that export programs to foreign students on a commercial basis alongside the subsidized teaching of locals. More radically, new forms of specialization have emerged, in new evolutionary niches in the green fields ecology, for example global hubs, e-U's, and transnational campuses on the shore of foreign providers. These moves have no precedent in national education systems or in cross-border university relations prior to 1990.

In a newly emerging eco-system, until the patterns become set, the rules are open to broad-ranging innovations. The field itself, which is the map of possibility, is a site of creation. Arguably, the global k-economy is in that phase. Some innovations may not survive (the first e-U's and the would-be hubs in the Gulf States, like theme parks in the desert, are two that spring to mind), but others will. Countries and institutions that moved early to develop and occupy newly created niches such as transnational education will enjoy strategic advantages. Various global system-building moves being made now, such as university classification, research metrics, the measurement of learning outcomes, omnibus university ranking, and the commercial delivery of foreign education to the four corners of the world, may pre-set later developments and retard the potential for alternate systems. But as long as new niches and novel systems remain possible, early victories can be by-passed or trumped by alternative approaches. Later things will start to settle. The scope for new niches will diminish and the rate of species creation will slow. Which mix of activities and relations will become dominant in the longer run is still an open question.

Global Commonality

Erwin also remarks about periods of evolutionary radiation that 'positive feedback allows the total number of possible species to expand as diversity grows.'[31] The long period since the Cambrian explosion has seen a significant growth in the number of families of animals. Temporary reductions in species diversity during periods of extinction have been more than made up during periods of recovery.[32] However, all else being equal, biological diversity tends to reduce when biologically independent regions are brought together, as when the worldwide super-continent of Pangaea formed during the Permian, or when North and South America became joined at Panama a few million years ago. 'The more biotic provinces, the greater the total global biodiversity.' For the same reason the spread of non-native species around the world, which is another form of biotic homogenization, tends to reduce biodiversity.[33]

Likewise, all else being equal, the formation of global or regional systems in higher education and research—for example disciplinary evolution in the sciences on a worldwide basis, the single global publishing system in English, university classifications and ranking using common templates, systems that facilitate people mobility by integrating institutional accreditation and the description of graduate qualifications, student exchange protocols, the partial convergence of national quality assurance systems—reduce aggregate diversity and narrow the range of variation. This reduction in diversity is both one of the advantages and one of the disadvantages of globalization. The paradox is that standard systems enable global relations to develop. And by definition, global systems entail a new scope for the expression of diversity and new dimension of creation. There can be no broad-based encounter with diversity unless homogenizing systems create the environment in which these encounters take place.

The discussion of diversity in universities and research usually stops at this point, at the level of the general. However, it is instructive to explore different modes of diversity in universities, for example in relation to the foundational idea of the university, in relation to the knowledge contents of its programs, in relation to its political economy, and in relation to its organizational culture and design.

The global knowledge economy in higher education and research consists of a complex network of institutions and national and regional systems. These different agents are unified by a common university imagining. This university imagining has overlapping origins in the scholarly cultures of the ancient West, ancient East and the Islamic world; the public cultures of Greece and Rome; mediaeval Europe; the building of modern nation-states; the Humboldt university in Germany; twentieth-century science and Clark Kerr's American research university. This common imagining is associated with common symbols, ceremonies and institutional values. Everywhere we find the pre-eminence of status and display in universities. The mode of meetings in academic units—in which words are often an end in themselves and the need for scholarly consensus often prevails over the need for decision—repeats itself from system to system. The sector is also drawn together by an approach to scholarship common throughout the world, a single system of knowledge in the mathematically based disciplines, and common modes of intellectual production and communication such as the book and the journal. On the other hand, there are differences within the common university imagining. For example, knowledges in the humanities and some of the social sciences and domains of professional vocational training can vary considerably between countries. The respective roles of place, seniority and merit in structuring the academic professions also varies considerably from country to country.

The political economy of higher education, including its policy missions, diverges a good deal from nation to nation. The economic systems of higher education vary by nation, and between public and private sectors, and between elite and mass universities. Some universities provide places on the basis of free tuition. Some charge high fees. Some are 90 per cent government funded or more; in some the 'taxpayer' is merely a junior partner. Some universities raise market revenues like independent corporations. For those scholars who see political economy as the core constituent of the field of power in higher education, the continued fragmentation in this respect would suggest a fundamental diversity of form. This would place a serious question mark over the notion of a global university dimension.

Yet the sociology and the organizational culture of universities are more homogenous than the political economy and policy framing of higher education would suggest. Across the world there is a fast-growing similarity between modes of university organization. Styles of leadership and the habits of management are converging. Everywhere something like the American university presidency is in vogue or being considered. As discussed in *Global Creation*, a long wave of NPM reform is running through the world university sector. A similar set of administrative techniques and performance pressures, albeit locally nuanced and subject to national policies and cultures, seems to flourish almost everywhere. In certain nations systemic reforms began two decades ago, for example in the UK and Australia. In many nations NPM reforms began to roll out of the mid 1990s or later. Systems such as that of Vietnam are undergoing 'corporatization' now, and in nations such as Thailand it is largely still to come. The growing resemblance of organizational forms is more than a case of convergent evolution in response to common stimuli, in the manner in which insects, reptilian pterosaurs, birds, and mammalian bats each developed wings of a kind different to the others. The element of similarity in university systems is greater than in such cases of convergent evolution. Outside Western Europe, the United States and Egypt—where earlier university foundations still survive—contemporary research universities everywhere are a product of the modernizing project of the nation-state. During the last two centuries the forms of the nation-state have spread across the world, a process still unfolding. Like all institutions of the high time of the nation-state, the university has long been subject to processes of global imitation.[34] However, the point is that global homogenization and scope have intensified. The profound similarity of codes, structures, systems and organizational behaviours is driven partly by converging state templates for reform; partly by direct university-to-university mimetics; partly by the manner in which all of the world's organizations (not just universities) seem to take more similar forms, as will be discussed below; and partly by the intangible spirit of the age.

LOST WORLDS

To grasp the weight of this new convergence in university forms, and its grounding in communicative globalization, it is useful to compare the global university sector with other fields in which there is a miscellany of individual sites or nodes within the zone of a common cultural imagining. The point is made more forcefully by going outside the modern period. One example is the hundreds of city-states that constituted the ancient Mayan civilization in Mexico, Belize, Guatemala, Honduras and El Salvador during what archaeologists define as the 'classical' and 'post-classical' eras of the first millennium C.E. For most of the period each individual city-state was independent of its fellows. Regional empires became a feature of the lowland Mayan states during the later classical periods but even then the individual cities ran their own affairs and implemented their own designs. At the same time the whole Mayan zone was remarkable for the degree of cultural commonality across the region. Though languages were diverse, in the highly developed adaptive agriculture, in religious motifs and practices, in the monumental architecture and the theatrical ceremonies led by monarchs and nobility, in the nature of the sacred objects, in the structures of family life, and in ceramics and painting, forms were common across the Mayan world. For example there were local variations in ceramic styles but Mayan types of ceramic object were the same and distinct from those of the other main pre-Columbian civilizations. Innovations and variations spread across the region in recognizable patterns, flowing from site to site via trade, travel, gifts and religious practices. The Maya had a long history in trade, which continued and probably extended in the postclassical period despite the collapse of many cities. Archaeologists note 'evidence for an extremely wide distribution of similar or identical material' and suggest that trade encouraged a common cosmopolitan imaginary across the Mayan zone.[35] Some Mayan traditions reproduced in the classic and postclassic proved to be so potent that they survived the decline of the civilization, and the almost three centuries of Spanish occupation and the Mexican state repression that followed. Some elements of the ancient Mayan imagining still persist, hybridized with Mexican Catholicism and modernity.

Interestingly, in political economy, governance and organizational life there was often a greater degree of diversity between the Mayan city-states, than in farming and art. As in ancient Greece, when confronting problems of social organization a range of solutions were devised. The degree of autonomy possessed by farmers and perhaps by artisans varied more from place to place than did their products. Arthur Demarest and colleagues emphasize that Mayan polities were 'highly variable.'[36] Sites 'did not differ culturally, only in political integration.'[37] For example, levels of centralization and decentralization differed from site to site. So did the supporting political ideologies. In some cities the rulers controlled the social surplus or shaped trade, or managed the common infrastructure. In other cities the production economy was largely decentralized to families or local communities, which enabled agriculture that was sensitive to micro-ecological variations, and the ruler might control little more than the pyramids and temples at the centre of the urban area,[38] though the ruler's role tended to expand in times of war. Mayan monarchy varied from absolute rule, to leadership shared with members of the aristocracy, to forms of constitutionalism with a council of elders, to a monarch presiding over a group of decentralized semi-autonomous polities, which appears to have been the chosen expedient in the final stages of the kingdoms of Copan and Tikal.[39] Later, in the postclassic period, in much of the Mayan world sacred kingship was phased out while the council of elders remained. The size of polities also varied freely between different zones and across time. Spheres of influence were sometimes closely demarcated and sometimes overlapped freely. Some Maya lived in unitary states, or states that were sometimes unitary and at other times not. In certain cases a group of polities was organized around a common centre of cultural practice without the exercise of control by that centre or by any one individual site.[40] Likewise, when one city achieved control over another through war or through the process of colonial foundation, the forms of domination and autonomy were liable to vary markedly. Control could be exerted through economic life, or shared warfare, or religious ritual rather than through governance.[41] All the above arrangements could alter, and they did. 'The sociopolitical processes that created limits between coexisting polities were complex, overlapping and changed frequently.'[42]

There are striking parallels in this respect with ancient Greece, with its variations between individual and collective forms of production; the variable positions of artisans and merchants; and the distinctions between tyranny, oligarchy and forms of democracy. In Greece, as among the Maya, the city-states were heterogeneous in their political economy and governance while conscious of their shared religion, culture and identity, including the distinction between themselves and people living with other traditions, that the Greeks called 'barbarians.'

The Mayan zone shared with the global knowledge economy a process of cultural homogenization via trade and the passage of sacred objects. The difference between the ancient Maya and the contemporary environment was that in the Mayan universe, not only was there no single polity as in the states of ancient Rome, China and central Mexico that coincided with the Maya, but the mechanisms of circulation, exchange and communication were not sufficiently inclusive and compelling to drive global standards and homogenization in social organization. Despite a heritage shared across the vast terrain of five modern nations, most of the short Mayan lives (no skeletons indicate an age greater than 35 years) were lived in walking distance from home. Traders were unusual people. Foot travel was slow. The Maya created paved highways encouraging movement between proximate settlements but these rarely extended for more than a few kilometres.[43] Most importantly there was no instant communication at a distance. While the desire to synchronize across sites was strong in matters seen as centrally important to identity such as farming and religion, the members of each Mayan city did not imaginatively absorb the organizational settings of other communities. Except for the case of migrations that took place when a city site collapsed; migrations that were one-way and assimilationist rather than reciprocal and regionally integrative in character; the Mayans experienced only one set of social norms, their own. There was no Mayan best practice in governance, or processes of cross-site benchmarking or quality assurance. As in Greece, social organization was free to be eclectic and local. Our world has lost that freedom.

It lost that freedom not so very long ago. Within recent memory sui generis modes of organization were still possible in the university sector. In the 1960s and 1970s several new public universities in the UK and Australia such as Sussex, Griffith, La Trobe and Murdoch embarked on contrasting experiments in distinctive forms of organization, including novel disciplinary identities, problem-based and area-based studies, multi-disciplinary schools, more open facilities, participatory governance and the collectivization of administrative roles. A feature of many of these experiments was the detonating of some of the status distinctions traditional to the university, and there was an implied critique of the role of higher education in reinforcing status distinctions in the economy and society ('credentialism'), in keeping with the egalitarian temper of the 1960s campus-based New Left. There was also a critique of the vocational mission ('instrumentalism'), and of the role of university science in warfare, often couched in terms of a universal refusal of all notions of the utility of universities. The contrast between these experimental forms and the mainstream organizational world was greater than that between the pre-NPM and post-NPM mainstreams. These experimental sites, funded almost entirely by governments of the day on the basis of institutional autonomy, exhibited site-specific variations in internal organizational cultures that were as great as those that characterized the Maya. The best of these experiments left a mark on the larger university environment. The emphases on cross-disciplinary units, research teams and transparency in governance, and the commitment to sustainable ecology, were decades ahead of their time. But to be ahead of the time in organizational culture is no longer a virtue in research universities. The contrary is the case. Rogue organization once presented itself as boldly creative. Now organization is referenced to the larger relational environment, not self-referenced, and, regardless of its merits, autarky appears awkward and risky. It is less than fully functional in a competitive political economy: penalized in status, difficult to market and a poor fit with standard modes of data collection, comparison and accountability. In a league table with only one institution, comparison is impossible.

GLOBAL ORGANIZATIONS

The counter-cultural experiments of the 1960s–1970s rejoined the mainstream in the 1980s–1990s. Universities now ground their claim to be innovators through the research role and the creation of global linkages and site-based infrastructures, not in changes to the 'idea of a university.' New epistemological structures can be tried as long as they function by common rules. Within the NPM template some universities are remarkable creators of global relations. But in organizational culture itself, all have been NPM-ed. They opt for brand distinctions rather than participatory decision systems, the abolition of status, or unique missions.

Perhaps the frame of collective identity formation has changed. As we have seen, the Maya were united by common cultural and religious patterns that proved highly resilient, while often sharply differing in social organization and governance. For us, design cultures often vary and this encounter with imaginative variety is one of the joys of the world. But organizational culture has become a common practice. This worldwide homogenization of organization is not just a university phenomenon. Something similar is happening in most domains.

In a study of *Globalization and Organization*, Gili Drori and colleagues note that complex organizations now evolve in environments 'global in scope' in which 'individuals are both empowered and disciplined on a global scale.'[44] In these environments 'universal notions of organization emphasizing broad new themes like governance and human resource management flow very widely…universalistic claims are particularly amenable to global diffusion.'[45] Local factors do not dissolve; national polities 'leave lasting imprints on local institutional structures and interact with the external influences to produce systematic variations'; and factors specific to particular kinds of organization (such as research universities) play a part. In the world of organizations 'the complex interaction between global scripts, on the one hand, and national, sectoral and organizational factors, on the other, produces a varied landscape in which isomorphism and decoupling are commonplace.'[46] Locality retains more shaping power than some globalist theorists admit, while globalized forms of organization foster individual agency. But the main message is about homogenization. The 'locals of the modern world become relatively standardized variants of locals everywhere else.' From this conformity individuals gain rights and standing.[47]

Drori and colleagues also remark that the scope for sameness across all organizational domains has been advanced by the spread of mass tertiary education. 'Education is no longer a cultural frill of some distinct status or occupational groups and has become the central component of social stratification for whole societies worldwide.'[48] In a parallel collection of papers one study is focused on universities themselves. Francisco Ramirez remarks that universities are undergoing a 'transnational' process of rationalization marked by the 'decline of tradition and charisma as legitimating sources of university identity.'[49] This move is not simply 'transforming the university into a business.' It is specific to the university form.[50] It involves the creation of a new kind of university that is enterprising and strategically nimble, and transparent and connected. The hallmarks of this rationalization of the university are social inclusion, social utility and organizational flexibility. As it has spread the common model has proven irresistible. Closing the reproductive circle, we find that globally standardized universities produce graduates who become the subjects of standardized organization systems and cultures in all other professional domains. Again, as in the sphere of knowledge, research and ideas, the university is central to globalization.

CREATIVE STANDARDIZATION

The global university world is much larger and more uniform than the Mayan and Greek city-states, and there is no longer a non-Mayan or non-Greek periphery outside the university. Though governance is often nuanced to local circumstances, it is no longer reducible to free local idiosyncracy. It is usually subject to national regulation, though it is not reducible to comprehensive rational prescription. On the whole the global university world is less diverse then its predecessor. But a 'world' in which the separated human groups are only episodically in contact is not a unified sphere. The formation of a single visible global dimension of action, which is the making of the world, has brought separated university traditions together (even if on unfair terms loaded in favour of Anglo-American science universities,[51] as other universities know, and as some of the presidents who were interviewed were at pains to point out). The downside is that certain nationally specific organizational forms of value are being boxed in or weakened, such as the socially inclusive nation building university in Latin America, which as in the case of UNAM in Mexico is a different beast with a larger role than the US university. So far global university design has been mono-cultural. The classification systems that will foster greater diversity within the common organizational templates have yet to be implemented, though they are beginning to emerge, particularly in Europe.[52] It is likely that in the outcome some forms of diversity in university mission and type will become factored in to the emergent global systems while other forms of diversity will become marginalized and disappear.

At the same time, three things must be emphasized. First, diversity is not the only good. Common systems enable many human benefits, enabling functioning economies, polities and systems of communication, and providing for individual rights. Second, people often pursue homogeneity. This is more than timid mimetics or sheltering. Commonness can also be a strong choice. We see this desire to follow and conform in fashion, where it alternates with the desire to be different, and also in all of the claims to status, in which tried and true symbols are the only ones worth having. More generally, the drive for homogeneity underpins human relations. People desire sameness in the practices of life in the same manner that they desire communicative synchrony. Third, the standardization of former diversities in science and the organizational cultures and designs of universities have made possible the global relational space and opened the way to its new kinds of creation and diversity. Standardized systems are the platform for innovation, as was the red regime of tooth and claw that was pioneered by the trilobites. This eliminated the larger part of the old soft bodied animal diversity amid a tsunami of invention taking wholly novel forms.

Again we find that destruction accompanies creation. Schumpeter's idea of creative destruction has a long antecedent in imaginings of Brahma the creator and Shiva the destroyer. But the evolutionary lesson of the mass extinctions is that each Brahman rebirth is more than simply another turn of the wheel: it is also a new era and propels life in unexpected directions. After the end Permian catastrophe the Triassic fauna was very different to the Permian, opening the way to the dominance of the dinosaurs. Likewise, once the Cambrian radiation happened the soft-bodied pre-Cambrian world never returned. And neither will the pre-1990 university.

In the world of the global-in-formation, diversity—that apparently universal good which is never universal (or else there could be no universal) and is not always good—is in the hands of Brahma and Shiva. The third great figure in the Hindu pantheon, Vishnu the preserver, is less helpful. Diversity in cultural forms is rarely preserved unless those forms are remade for the times. But the formation of the global space opens the way to a host of new diversities in form and voice. Here the creation of the global university dimension has implications that extend well beyond higher education. One is the formation of common organizational culture. Another is the convergence in university design fostered by that culture and by research cooperation, global comparison and competition. A third is the common systems of knowledge and of researcher mobility. All of these developments position research-intensive universities at the centre of an emergent global public space whose content is knowledge, information, discussion, criticism, sometimes agitation and above all, synchronous communication. In reflecting on globalization Daniel Drache notes that 'the theology of market fundamentalism rejects the concept of a public sphere...yet the return of the public domain is undoubtedly the watershed event of our times.' [53] Drache defines the global public domain as a sphere of agency. 'The public domain, above all else, is a forum in which to be heard.'[54] This global public space is a shared zone for private agents. It is not 'public' in the sense of the government-owned public sector of the nation-state. There is no global state, no interlocked infrastructure of state-owned institutions at world level. The global public space is more like a civil society. At the same time it reprises Hannah Arendt's notion of the public sphere in antiquity as 'a space of appearance and recognition, a space where individuals were recognized and actions could be judged.'[55] The open-source element[56] in higher education and knowledge also recalls the idea of the public sector as an open commons.

Research universities have one foot in a global civil society to be—and derive much of their agency from their global role and connections. The other foot continues to be held firmly by nation-state regulation which remains a potent force. This enfolds a tension in the global research university.

Glonacal

Drache remarks that 'just as printed text was instrumental to the modern forms of national identity, so hypertext has given birth to the powerful idea of the global citizen connected to other citizens through the networked public.'[57] All inclusive norms of 'global citizenship' have a power that is solely informal. When there is no global state there cannot be a 'global citizen' in any practical sense. It is like the persistence of the idea of 'Roman' identity long after the Western Empire had collapsed. Nevertheless, the case of the holy Roman Empire, and that of the Catholic Church, the other successor to Rome, show that fictional identities located in imagined spaces can carry substantial power. The idea of global community now finds itself at loggerheads with the formal authority of the nation-state. The more bounded citizenship of the nation-state is not so much territorial as exclusive. Wherever they reside in the world, national citizens are chosen people. Others are Others. For the research universities that (in their global moments) imagine no limits within the circle of the world, the resulting national/global tension is a fact of life. This tension might be worsening.

THE NATION-STATE

In his survey of *The Birth of the Modern World* Christopher Bayly demonstrates how the antinomy of national and global has passed through several stages.

Globalization has a long history. Bayly begins with 'archaic globalization.' This was constituted by 'the older networks and dominances created by the geographic expansion of ideas and social forces from the local and regional level to the inter-regional and inter-continental level.'[58] Archaic globalization had many centres, including Egypt, the Middle East, Europe, Iran, India, China, Southeast Asia, Mesoamerica, and South America between the Andes and the Pacific. It was fostered by a universalizing expansionary form of kingship, and expansive cosmic religions that spread more broadly than did the pre-modern empires. It also saw the dissemination of scriptural languages, knowledge, arts and shared understandings of bodily health and human society. Thus in its early stages the expansion of European civilization was one among the several varieties of archaic globalization 'rather than a world system in the making.'[59] But by the seventeenth century European world empires were sustaining an 'early modern globalization' alongside archaic globalization. Early modern globalization, nation-based and 'proto-capitalist' in temper, was built by worldwide maritime trade and accelerated commerce and especially the profits of New World silver and Atlantic slavery. This era saw the rise of quasi-governmental 'European chartered companies, arms of mercantilist state power, the royal trading entities created in the Asian world to handle and control these burgeoning trades.'[60] By the mid-eighteenth century a true global imperialism was emerging. The functions of the trading companies became divided between private capital on one hand, and state arms and administration on the other. Larger and more professional armies became central to state building, though at this stage 'neither race nor nationality, as understood at the end of the nineteenth century,' were dominant concepts.[61]

The ambitions and profits of imperialism, and especially the leap forward in military technology and organization during the imperialist wars between England and France and the revolutionary and Napoleonic period after 1780, triggered the evolution of a tighter, more instrumental and more controlling form of nation-state in England, France and Prussia.[62] At times 'the principle of power seems to have cut lose completely from its social moorings.'[63] This became the modern state of today. Compared to its predecessor forms of states it entailed closer supervision of the population and national economy which were seen as resources for the benefit of the state. State supervision was supported by metaphors of nation as family and the state as parent. The new nation-state made greater use of specialized knowledges and modes of micro-regulation. In contrast with the older world empires the modern state did not see cultural diversity as good in itself. Its systems encouraged uniformity. The more decisive border between nation and Other was (and in some cases still is) managed by using race, religion and other essentialist notions of identity.

'The meaning of the nation had become…narrower and less inclusive, the state more intrusive.'[64] For example notions of single religious identity were often mobilized in place of an earlier tolerance.[65] On the world scale the modern nation-state was characterized by strong notions of sovereignty, mutually exclusive territories and zero-sum notions of citizenship that could be modified only with difficulty. Increasing energies were channeled into fostering a national imaginary. This was a principal driver of the growth of mass schooling in the second half of the nineteenth century. The failure of the emerging universities to consistently reflect the 'national interest' (meaning the interest of the state) became a recurring concern of officials, for whom the problem was unsolvable without suborning the university so firmly as to compromise its role in relation to knowledge.

This more systematic kind of state spread to most of Europe, the United States and Japan in the nineteenth century, reaching the rest of the world in the twentieth century. Bayly calls it 'the internationalization of nationalism.'[66] The process of state formation, which continues today, is characterized by policy borrowing and a growing similarity across the world[67] between the modes of military power, state administration and regulatory institutions. This corresponds to the global sharing and partial convergence in most other realms of life, including science and knowledge, the arts, fashion, conversion agendas in religious practice, and the universities and research. The modern nation-state thinks globally, in the sense that it is aware of the pattern of worldwide relations and its position within them, but does so almost exclusively from a nationally particularist viewpoint.[68] Always, the agenda of emergent nation-states is to be more competitive in economy, military, technology and demography—and ultimately to become as strong as the leading states. Often national culture is also conceived as a theatre for self-assertion and competition. It is inevitable that from time to time states will over-reach themselves in the drive to be, if not great powers, then at least larger than their proximate neighbours: pre-empting each other's military, economic and scientific development, encroaching on each other and exhausting their own resources. Bayly notes in relation to post-Meiji Japan in the late nineteenth century, where the modern nation was being built at an extraordinary rate (see chapter six):

> One Japanese statesman opaquely put it, when urging the extension of Japanese power to mainland Asia, 'If the sun is not extending it is descending …If the country is not flourishing it is declining. Therefore to protect the country well is not merely [to prevent] it losing the position it holds, but to add to the position it does not hold.'[69]

The same idea of pre-emptive expansion for defensive purposes, the same aggregative imperial madness, had long driven strategy in Britain and France and was now doing so in Germany. Would be 'powers' have to keep expanding at their border. It is the game logic of the territorial nation, as old as the Persian Empire and the later Roman Republic.

For Bayly the story of the modern world is the rise of these more virulent and effective nation-states, beginning in the early nineteenth century. In contrast with accounts that see the political 'superstructure' of the nation as driven by the capitalist industrial economy at the base, Bayly argues that the modernization of nation-states preceded the main surge in industrial productivity and the rise of autonomous national capitals. Much of this modernization and the subsequent development of industry were driven by the imperatives of international competition and the fighting of actual wars. Nations had to best their rivals in coal and steel and later in oil. The experience of warfare locked national populations to the nation-state project. In this context economic exploitation was the handmaiden of imperial conquest, not its motor. The emergence of a stronger endogenous economic dynamic and accelerated productivity advance dates from about 1890 but the state stayed in the picture. The history of war and recession in the twentieth century shows that when push came to shove, weak nation-states could be railroaded by powerful capitalists but strong nation-states held the trump cards. In the twentieth century middle-class economic aspirations drove the creation of state instrumentalities that were designed to realize them, but significantly, those state apparatuses often went on to acquire a life of their own, surviving regardless of economic utilities and fluctuations. States also intervened more or less continuously to create or foster new kinds of economic production, and still do. The GDP economy itself was a state creation (albeit one that now sits awkwardly with cross-border flows). In the neo-liberal era, notwithstanding the convenient fiction that the state has evacuated the economy, and the endogenous dynamic of finance, state-led quasi-markets extend well beyond the terrain of markets proper. When global finance began to come apart in 2008 in the USA as in China the nation-state quickly filled the gaps. Modern states are never really out of the picture.

Yet while all this state-building was happening, partial convergence and integration on the global scale was also gathering pace via transport, trade, migration, the telegraph, mass media and the telephone. 'Ideas freely jumped borders.' As noted above in relation to global organization, this did not necessarily translate into uniformity. Life continued to be shaped by national and local factors. 'Global patterns could as much give rise to assertion of specificity and local variation, as sameness and emulation. The point is that everyone was conscious of global changes and patterns and of each other.'[70] Nation and world offered different horizons of possibility. The first horizon was a visible and radical reduction of the second. Bayly suggests that this reduction in itself is one of the drivers of global synchrony. 'The paradox of globalization reveals itself. The hardening of boundaries between nation-states and empires after 1860 led people to find ways of linking, communicating with and influencing each other across boundaries.'[71]

In the twentieth century national particularism achieved its highest expression in the two world wars, with their mind numbing human carnage, material destruction and concentrated ecological devastation. At the same time some of the conditions for the evolution of a borderless world society were being put in place. Now the emergence of telecommunications, the Internet and screen-based synchrony has heightened the potential for national/global tensions. These are now felt in every sector of society.

POLYPHONY

Thus the world is vectored by two distinct sets of cross-border relations. The first is the global dimension of action, which has been discussed in this chapter and its predecessor. The second is the international dimension of action, which is the world perceived from the vantage point of the nation-state. International is inter-national, meaning relations between distinct and separated nations. Internationalism, whereby those relationships between nations are enhanced, is a specific product of the period of the modern nation-state. It presupposes an approach to cross-border relations in which nations, their authority and identity remain essentially unchanged. Likewise multilateralism rests on the premise of national sovereignty and scarcely acknowledges global vistas except as spaces for inter-national bargaining. The United Nations, the ultimate expression of a benign multilateralism, is a forum for talk between zero sum nation-states, not an independent agent designing global relations to be. Hence the UN combines universal inclusion with irrelevance. It has been sidelined by globalization, which is another world, corrosive of all forms of Westphalian authority, that punches holes in sacred borders and creates systems that envelop them. Globalization is slowly detonating national sovereignty and internationalism. Imaginings of the nation-state remain potent in this era. It is sustained by massive inertia, interests and resources. It offers all the comforts of home. But sea-tides are not commanded by national monarchs or by propaganda. Globalization does not eliminate the nation any more than it eliminates region, locality and self. Rather it relativizes them.

Discussing national-global tensions in regulation, Roger King notes a study by Paradeise and colleagues of seven European higher education systems, which finds 'clear signs everywhere that universities are experiencing an organizational turn that pushes them from dependent administrative bodies or loosely-coupled professional bureaucracies towards autonomously managed organizations.'[72] As the agency of institutions strengthens it pushes against the boundaries. Whatever the nation, when university leaders imagine globally, they are at cross-purposes with their states. The interviews with the university presidents repeatedly demonstrate the national-global tensions in seeing and doing. Governments are almost always national and international in their reasoning. But the imagination of university professors in many disciplines tends to the global. And while university presidents must be adept in both ways of seeing, many are increasingly focused on the global dimension where most research is conducted and opportunities to build status and activity are more open than in the regulated national settings. For example, both state and university focus on the competitive position at the world level. But this can assume different meanings. For government the issue is the rewards that the nation can extract from international dealings, for example fee revenues from foreign students. The nation-state is concerned to augment the performance of its research universities only if they generate status for the nation and innovations that are captured by the national economy. Research universities care about their national and local standing. They secure prestige when they attract highquality students. Yet what matters most to them is their position within the global knowledge system, beyond the nation.

The balance of national and global imaginings varies from nation to nation, and also between different types of higher education institution. High research universities are the most global in temper. Even so, and generalizing freely, research university presidents in the United States and also Japan (of which more will be said in chapter six) tend to imagine their strategic agendas primarily in national terms. As noted, however, when US universities go global, they can act to great effect. This is not true of universities in Japan. In contrast research university leaders in the UK, much of Western Europe and Australia are less bound up in a national imaginary. This is not to say these presidents are ineffective in the national domain.

Of all the institutions of the modern nation-state, the research university is the most global in its imagining. This imagining connects to the emerging global public sphere. It places research universities, along with global agencies and information companies, in the forefront of the slow but discernable movement towards world society. Inevitably this agenda will take research universities further beyond the bounds of the nation-state that is their regulator.

The interviews with the presidents also underline the complexity of university strategy. The trilobites faced a mighty challenge but were required to operate in only one environment (though at least this meant they had less forms to fill in). University presidents, the trilobites of the global knowledge economy, must be simultaneously adept in all three environments, global, national and local. We can characterize their setting as a *glonacal* one which combines action in the three dimensions and synergizes between them. Glonacal = *glo*bal + *na*tional + lo*cal*. The complexity is that global, national and local are often heterogeneous in their agents, relationships, drivers, behaviours and resources. It is not enough for a university president to coin a melody, to sing it in tune and to sing it in harmony with partners. The skills required are larger. They are the skills of polyphony, which is the most complex of music. Polyphony requires the artist or listener to concentrate on two or more strands of music at once. Three strands are more difficult than two. It helps if the three lines of music are following a common rhythm. And it helps if the agency that funds the production of the music also shares the aesthetic. But these conditions are by no means always present in music and they are less often present in universities. This poly-flexibility is central to the creative capacity of research universities as institutions in this era. It is the capacity to work with fluency and sureness of judgment across and between local, national and global agendas.

The Locus of Creativity

The creativity of universities as institutions, the forming of the global dimension of action and the strategic acumen of their leaders, is only part of the story of universities and creativity. What then of research universities as concentrations of talent and 'innovation' in the global knowledge economy?

Common sense would suggest that the more the university form is manifest across the world and concentrated in intensive fashion in the leading cities and nations, the more creativity there must be. In form universities are 'stranger cities' as discussed by Peter Murphy in chapter one, thronged with aliens, travelers, exiles and migrants and the more globally engaged that universities become, the more their polyglot otherness is fed. But does every stranger city morph into a cauldron of creativity? Because the university houses research and scholarship and foregrounds discovery on the world scale it seems to epitomize creativity as a social and institutional project. But does it? Murphy remarks that while the university 'is very good at posterior justification' it is less good 'at incubating the act of creation.' Universities have assumed 'great social weight' but are 'much less able to lead innovation and stimulate creation' than first appears. Why? One possible explanation is that modern research universities never were very good at fostering path-breaking creativity. This is partly belied by the fecund work in American universities in 1890–1920, in which the basis was laid for the social science way of seeing, and the transformative science of the Manhattan project and of university genetics in the middle part of the twentieth century. A second explanation is that within universities the locus of creation, the main line of path-breaking innovation, has moved from the study and the laboratory to the more transparent (and better rewarded) achievements of the university executive office. Many of the best and brightest are drawn from the dry discipline of concentrated thought to the free-ranging generics of institution making, organizational creativity and global glamour. They opt for a life of incessant fund-raising, diplomacy and would-be problem solving, the perpetual modernization of university systems and facilities, and monument building.

That life has burdens but it also has attractions. The university president is more than the great *daimyo*, politician and entrepreneur. On the grounds of the institution he or she is Oval Office, doyen of the arts and civil society and the Secretary of State for Foreign Affairs in the *ancien regime* all rolled into one. And maybe the times compel Pharaohs and not da Vincis. If Pharaohs have a vanity other than power it is the vanity of pyramids, which is the status of display and the desire for immortality. Pyramids are an elite-driven social project common to every ancient civilization, as common as water management. After other geometries usurped the pyramid the desire to conquer death with stone or metal continued in temple building, Roman public architecture, mediaeval cathedrals, noble halls and the steel-glass skyscraper palaces of today. Likewise the modern university is prone to architectural forms of display. Pharoahs do not foster acts of disturbing novelty and creativity as ends in themselves; they employ tame artisan-creators to create orthodox displays for the purposes of the royal line. Certainly, it is easier for university leaders to hire someone else to be an architect with a conventional brief than to personally overturn the rules of design. (The one Pharaoh who clearly rewrote the rule book, Akhenaten, who founded the first monotheistic state religion in the fourteenth century B.C.E., suffered a Pharaoh's ultimate punishment: loss of immortality. The restored priesthood erased his name from the Egyptian records after his death, referring to him only as 'the Enemy').

But like all forms of status competition the fruits of pyramid building are only partly satisfying. Only one pyramid in each site can be the greatest, and only one can be the largest in the world. And new pyramids generally follow what came before. This does not inhibit the status culture in universities nor its conventional forms of expression. The number of Nobel Prize winners and 'HiCi' researchers drives university rankings. In universities, display is manifest in the buildings, facilities and equipment in which high-status researchers are housed (or would be housed if the university had them). It is remarkable how often research universities with growing class sizes and chronically unable to expand post-doc numbers can find $100 million for a new synchrotron or for classrooms for the foreign business students. Nevertheless, the issue at stake here is not the personal vanity of university leaders. Indeed, many presidents are not personally vain. Whether personally vain or not a good university president must display, because symbol making is intrinsic to the contemporary university form. Likewise global consortia and global hubs are expensive and rarely generate either GDP or stellar creativity, but they are created again and again. Not only must a global university and knowledge nation cut a global figure at home; in the global knowledge economy the display of visible evidence of modernity, especially research capacity, stands in place of substance. It is the closest universities can get to making the k-economy real, for the substance always remain undefined, but knowledge gathers authority in these visible hints of its potential. Of course pyramids are at best a means to an end. While Egypt created the pyramids of Giza, Sumer experimented with forms of writing and mathematics that proved much more important.

A third explanation is more pessimistic. There might be a zero-sum relationship between the creation of original works and the creation of new institutional forms. Putting it more bluntly, the systems of university organization may be hostile to the incubation of acts of creation. 'The act of creativity is not production according to rules' notes Murphy, suggesting that when notable creative work occurs inside universities, it is produced outside and perhaps against the rules of the university itself. The rules of modern institutions are harder to evade than those of their predecessors. The double life, the code switching between conformity and autonomy which was epitomized above all by science in the Soviet state, is wearisome. No doubt this is one factor that channels the creative imagination away from the disciplines and into organization building and the making of global space. There the creator obtains harmony with the research university, which has become the signature institution of the intellect—but by adopting forms of creation where the ultimate goal is not works, or knowledge, or a life lived differently or a new world to be, it is the self-making university systems as ends in themselves. Worse, in building the university *qua* university its managers create a simulacrum of innovation. The university is shaped by performance cultures and human resource management in which research is a quasi-economy driven by simulated outputs and dollar rewards, every teacher is a researcher, and each researcher focuses on short-term achievement and bloats the quantity of real and apparent outputs. This piles disposable 'new knowledge' on knowledge into a mountain of paper. In the middle, vital ideas are suffocated beneath the simulacrum. This is more insidious than deploying research buildings as symbols of research capacity. At best the flashy buildings based on yesterday's corporate designs house bona fide academic works within them. In contrast organizational systems that foster the production of pseudo-knowledge simply absorb creator time and thereby block out potential acts of creativity.

Yet the simulacrum resonates with many inside the university. Here we find one of the drivers of that universalizing strand in official government/university discourses of the knowledge economy, and the point where those discourse are decoupled from the creative process. As Murphy notes in chapter three long-term patterns show that a handful of university researchers and scholars carry out work of great importance. But in the simulacrum *every* research academic is a great creator (or could be one if their teaching loads were reduced). Here a talent for boosterism is more useful than invention. After all, research management systems cannot identify major works. Crucial ideas become apparent only in the longer term and via more indirect routes. In research management the quality of ideas is defined by the prestige of journals where they are published and the number of mimetic echoes in citation counts. When were intellectual turning points ever measurable by the hierarchical democracies of status markets? It is all nonsense and everybody knows it. The conclusion is inescapable: the simulacrum is the end in itself.

This is not to say that science and ideas and discovery do not matter to universities. On the contrary, managing real science and ideas and their dangerous potentials is the ultimate point of this strange parallel universe.

Human societies have been captured by science, which feeds the greed for continuous change and for rotating technological novelties, for high modernity. Those same societies in turn have captured science and used governments, markets and universities to do so. People are ambivalent about scientific discovery, chronically disturbed by old or new ideas in any field that undermine the verities and fearful of minds that may harbour ineffable and unpredictable secrets. The university is meant to hold in these imagined anarcho-chaotic potentials of creativity and the dangerous capacity of discoverers to set social agendas. Systems of research policy and management are not only designed to harness academic labour for institution-building, they render research and scholarship transparent and tether them to systems of administered status and economic reward, to predictable behaviours. It is the disciplining of the disciplines. Nation-states design the systems that research universities use to condition themselves. States secure this form of governmentality by bringing to bear the forces of legality and funding. The other collective sectors that organize society—media, professions, and business when it acts in concert— also expect research universities to discipline the disciplines. Universities have long formalized, codified, arranged and transmitted knowledge. For a long time much of the knowledge came from outside them, as in seventeenth- and eighteenth-century European science. But now universities are meant to contain the creation of knowledge as well. Thus the dark side of research universities is that they limit creativity. Their role is to tame creativity by turning it into more predictable 'innovation,' preferably innovations with demonstrable utilities.

In the best book on the modern American university, Clark Kerr remarked famously that research policy drives the contemporary university.[73] Why? If there is a turning point when we can say that the global research university was born it was 8.15 am on 6 August 1945 when the first atomic bomb was dropped by the US airforce *Enola Gay* from above the port city of Hiroshima in Japan. On the ground in Hiroshima more than 200,000 lives were taken. The same number were destroyed by another bomb at Nagasaki a few days later. The second world war, which was already at its last gasp, ended a few days later, enabling the military to justify the $2 billion USD invested in the Manhattan project. After that there was no longer meaningful debate about the dangers of new knowledge, or the national necessity of global technology. The task of the research university became to control ineffable scientific knowledge by turning it into visible technologies. The university had to be global in reach because powerful science could emerge from anywhere. Within two decades of Hiroshima Soviet Russia, the UK, France and China had the bomb and the Soviets were in space. The emergence of the global research university in turn accelerated the single global science system. Inevitably its language was English, less because it was the language of money than because it was the language of the bomb.[74] Subsequently, research policy and management was and is preoccupied by two matters. First, the absorption of scientific talent and the monopoly of discovery. Second, funding systems and behavioural incentives that transform science into commercial or military technologies. Research in the social sciences and scholarship in the humanities are marginal to this quasi-economy, but are nevertheless patterned by it. In the quasi-economy grants and publications are everything. Philosophical ideas are nothing. Meanwhile creativity itself is invisible. Periodically research projects using methods from business or organizational sociology try to define university creativity so as to administer it. It remains invisible.

TENSIONS

In the end, two kinds of tension are inherent in the research university in the contemporary global era. The first tension of the global research university is that it is a national project whose field of operation is global. The two dimensions, global and national, are heterogeneous in form and in purpose. The global dimension has no purpose. In the national dimension the main purpose is that of nations as an end in themselves. The second tension is that the research university is a creative global project immersed in the open possibilities of knowledge in the global dimension, a project that is designed explicitly to foster creativity, that builds an enclosure to capture, control and limit the creative process.

The problem of national and global will be explored further in chapter six with reference to that most nationally enclosed of all the creative civilizations, Japan. Given present tendencies it is unlikely that research universities will evolve into a stable system that combines these two heterogeneous dimensions of national and global. Globalization has become too compelling and transformative, over-determining the national space. With the possible exception of universities in the strongest nations—notably the United States whose universities have everything to be gained by channeling imperial American power, and have a facility for glonacal action—this global-national tension will push the research university beyond the bounds of its own conditions. Nation-states that regulate and partly fund the research university will become increasingly frustrated by this. For example governments in Western Europe and Australia-New Zealand will ask 'how do *we* benefit from funding basic research?' This is likely to drive a crisis in the university form. Yet at the same time its globalization may confer on the research university a special role in the formation of world society, grounding them in a larger public domain (and in some cases a larger economic market) than at any earlier time in the history of the university and also broadening their material base. Much will depend on the evolution of universities in China and the rest of East Asia, the third major zone of higher education after North America and Europe, particularly on the extent to which universities in Asia move freely outside their state regulatory systems in the manner of universities in Western Europe at present.

The second tension suggests that while in the medium term the social role of research universities will continue to strengthen, a growing part of creative intellectual work will occur elsewhere. If the locus of creativity in universities has partly shifted from intellectual communities to executive offices and the making of global relations, then we should look to the new Cambrian radiation itself, the global relational environment in which research universities are only one of the species. And if the formal systems of the global research university are designed to manage and limit the flows of knowledge and ideas then we can assume that in the open-source global environment they will be utterly inadequate to the task. Quicksilver global flows of images, ideas and knowledge spill quickly and freely, beyond codification. No system can script global flows or police global people association. Creators inside and outside universities will interact freely and circulate their work. It is not that the black economy which is the open-source environment is inherently more creative than the world of institutions. It is just that the open-source environment is large and open. The scope for imagining is limited at any one time but it is unlimited in time. In the end, it will be apparent to all that the research university's role in knowledge formation is more restricted than the role it claimed in 2010, when this book was published. Or else the university will morph into something looser in which the conditions of its interior creative activity move closer to those outside, and its already remarkable global infrastructure is fitted for larger human agendas than itself.

As long as there is human agency and imagining there is reason to be optimistic about creativity, despite the limitations built into contemporary university design. The present global Cambrian radiation provides the largest reason for optimism so far devised. We cannot envision the limits on what is possible in this vast new domain of imagining.

TABLE 1. Research universities as the trilobites of the global age: Developmental strategies that are creating the global dimension of higher education and knowledge

	Strategy	Description/examples	Global spatial meanings
Strategies largely driven by national governments	Capacity building in research	Investment in research universities and institutes designed to lift the volume and quantity of research activity, with a view to strengthening national R&D-led innovation and/or the position of national universities in global rankings. There is now a global 'arms race' in innovation spending in many countries. May be joined to policies of greater concentration of research in selected institutions, merger programs, etc. *e.g. China, Korea, Germany, France*	A long-standing policy option for 'national competition states' that has taken on a new urgency and greater importance in the more global era.
	Recreation of the nation/city as a 'global hub' for education and research activities	Building of the global role of local education and research institutions, together with investment in precinct, infrastructure and changes to policy and regulation designed to attract foreign education and research providers, students and investment capital. *e.g. Singapore, Qatar*	Designed to pull global flows of knowledge, people and capital towards a particular locality. May be joined to national capacity building in research, and educational export.
	Negotiation of a global system of free trade in educational services, through WTO-GATS	Nations deregulate their education systems sufficiently to permit entry of foreign providers on the same terms as local providers, including subsidies etc.	The recreation of worldwide higher education as a single space for business and trade. (This has had little support among either national governments or universities and has not happened).
Largely university-driven strategies	Partnerships between universities	Universities sign agreements with similar institutions in other countries and carry out cooperative joint activities in personnel and student exchange, curriculum, research, university organization, benchmarking, etc. *e.g. all research universities*	A longstanding strategy used much more in the last two decades. The effect is to create a lattice-like network around each university as the node. Some of these nodes are much thicker than others, indicating broader and more intensive global connectedness.
	University consortia	Formal networks consisting of a large number of university partners, typically 10–30. Sometimes more intensive micro-consortia are developed, with 3–5 part-ners. Activities are for university partnerships,. *e.g. Universitas 21, Association of Pacific Rim Universities*	Consortia are also positioning devices with universities drawing status benefits from the strongest of their partners. The level of activity conducted through these large networks varies, but some universities drive a significant proportion of global work this way. Others maintain a broad set of connections and options.
	Transnational campuses	Universities establish branch campuses in another country, either in their own right (providing the premises themselves) or in alliance with a local partner that manages the site. Branch campuses are specifically permitted to operate by the local authorities. *e.g. University of Nottingham (UK) in Malaysia and China, RMIT University (Australia) in Vietnam*	Such foreign campuses can influence local educational developments over time, and also encourage more multiple or hybrid approaches and reciprocal flows of influence, with potential to leak back into cultural change within the 'mother' insti-tution.

TABLE 1 *(continued)*

	Global 'e-Universities'	Virtual delivery of programs on the Internet, by either established universities or commercial providers created for the purpose. Curriculum, student assessment, credentialing and administration are provided from one central location. Teaching intensity varies. *e.g. Cardean University, U21 Global, University of Phoenix online*	Between the mid 1990s and the early 2000s there were significant investments in stand-alone e-U's but they were unsuccessful in recruiting students. E-learning provided alongside or joined to face-to-face programs has been more successful. *e.g. the University of Phoenix*
Strategies driven by both government and universities	Export of education on a fully commercial basis	Higher education in a national system deregulated as necessary to enable the provision of full fee places to international students, with provider institutions free to determine price and volume. *e.g. UK, Australia, University of Phoenix*	Now a large-scale trading industry and the one established form of global educational capitalism. It has accelerated cross-border student mobility and positioned universities and students as entrepreneurs/consumers, though both also engage in non commercial global activities, *e.g. in relation to research.*
	Knowledge city developments	Investment by universities, city authorities and governments in precinct and infrastructure, designed to attract foreign education and research providers, students and investment capital. A more modest version of the 'hub' strategy often centred on promoting a small number of universities in the city. *e.g. numerous cities*	Versions of this strategy are widely practiced among nations with advanced education and research systems. Some cities place much emphasis on this kind of mission in their development profiles. The balance between commercial international education and R&D varies.
	Regional developments in higher education and research	Agreed regional (pan-national) cooperation between national higher education systems including common research grant programs; measures to align degree structures, curriculum contents and professional requirements; common systems for the recognition of institutions and qualifications, and quality assurance systems; comparison, ranking and evaluation of institutions on a regional basis. *e.g. the formation of the European Higher Education and European Research Areas via the Bologna reforms*	Regional system building and partial convergence in higher education and research in Europe is creating a meso-level of activity between the national and global dimensions, and in the longer run positions Europe so as to be able to act as a unit on the global stage. It also encourages enhanced investments in higher education and research in Europe. There are embryonic regional developments in South America and Southeast Asia.
Strategies pursued by multi-actors (universities, governments, publishing companies, etc.)	Data-based global comparisons of universities, and of research and publication/citation outputs on a university-wide or field specific basis.	Comparisons of the number of leading researchers, publications and/or citations used to generate a vertical 'league table' of university performance. *e.g. Shanghai Jiao Tong University rankings, Leiden CWTS, Taiwan HEEACT* Comparisons of universities based on a range of elements combined into a single index and league table. *e.g. Times Higher Education Supplement*	Outside the USA global comparisons have been decisive in imposing on all universities overarching measures of performance and status, relativizing national performance measures, which are now constantly referenced in debate about higher education and in investment decisions by students, researchers, business and industry, and government. More than any other method global rankings create an imagining of the global dimension of higher education

Notes

1. USNWR, 2006.
2. In particular Marginson, 2009b; Marginson, 2010a & 2010b.
3. These strategies were explored in detail in chapter six of *Global Creation*. They are briefly reviewed again below.
4. NSB, 2008.
5. Marginson, 2009a.
6. For more discussion of the growth of the global business sector of international education, and the issues and problems of commercially vectored cross-border student mobility, see Marginson, et al., 2010.
7. SJTUGSE, 2009; Times Higher, 2009. For a full discussion see Marginson, 2009b.
8. webometrics, 2009.
9. Van Vught, 2009.
10. This research program is supported during 2008–2011 by the Australian Research Council. So far case studies have been conducted in 13 research-intensive universities (all but one are leading public sector or 'national' universities) in 12 nations, mostly in Asia-Pacific countries, including the Pacific Americas. A case study consists of interviews with the president (or university rector or vice-chancellor), vice-presidents with responsibilities in relation to international matters and research, other leaders or administrators who work in the international domain, and deans and research professors in engineering and social sciences. The interviews focus on imaginings of globalization and of the global strategic context, university activities in areas of cross-border practices, and relations between national policy and regulation, and the global agendas of the university.
11. Drache, 2008, 5 & 61.
12. *ibid*, 7
13. *ibid*, 93.
14. Friedman, 2005.
15. Vera & Schupp, 2006, 423. See also Knox et al., 2006.
16. King, 2009, 10–11.
17. SJTUIHE, 2009.
18. Ma, 2008; Marginson, 2008.
19. Blom, 1974 (1935), 98.
20. *ibid*, 115.
21. *ibid*, 115. Mozart politely but firmly replied that the score contained the right number of notes, neither too many nor too few.
22. Matthews & Sidhu, 2005, 53.
23. Erwin, 2006, 15.
24. Bayly, 2004.
25. This argument is made by Erwin, 2006.
26. Erwin, 2006, 219.
27. *ibid*, 220.
28. *ibid*, 239.
29. *ibid*, 243.
30. Bourdieu, 1984; 1988; 1993. See Marginson, 2010c.
31. Erwin, 2006, 244.
32. For example for marine animals see Erwin, 2006, 29.

33. Erwin, 2006, 44.
34. Bayly, 2004.
35. Chase & Chase, 2004, 23.
36. Demarest, et al., 2004, 546; Carmean, et al., 2004, 425.
37. Laporte, 2004 ,199.
38. Demarest, et al., 2004, 566.
39. Valdes & Fahsen, 2004, 151.
40. Laporte, 2004, 199.
41. For example in the Southeastern Peten region—see Laporte, 2004, 201.
42. *ibid*, 201.
43. An interesting exception was the causeway (*sacbe*) between Coba and its dependent city Yaxuna in the Yucatan in Mexico. This construction was 100 kilometres in length—Palma, 2004, 537.
44. Meyer, et al., 2006, 259.
45. *ibid*, 260.
46. *ibid*, 261.
47. *ibid*, 267.
48. *ibid*, 265.
49. Ramirez, 2006, 225.
50. *ibid*, 241.
51. Marginson & Ordorika, 2010.
52. van Vught, 2009.
53. Drache, 2008, 18.
54. *ibid*, 9.
55. *ibid*, 13.
56. Marginson, 2009b.
57. Drache, 2008, 15.
58. Bayly, 2004, 41–42.
59. *ibid*, 42.
60. *ibid*, 44.
61. *ibid*, 46.
62. *ibid*, 64ff.
63. *ibid*, 474.
64. *ibid*, 167.
65. The culmination of state strategies of divide and rule on the basis of colour and religion was achieved by British imperialism, which incorporated fixed notions of separate identities into constitution making and geographical boundaries. The British fostered stable political and legal systems, yet created partition in India, the racialization of the Malaysian polity, the division of Ireland into two conflicting territories, and the Balfour Declaration in Palestine which established a bounded Jewish state on the grounds of a cosmopolitan Palestine. Britain also for long tolerated apartheid in South Africa until it became impossible to do so. All of these divide and rule polities had disastrous downstream consequences, and after world war two partition in India and the apartheidization of Palestine became primary sources of global instability. There is no solution in sight to the problems created by either of these acts of state-structured identity.
66. Bayly, 2004, 41.
67. *ibid*, Chapter 1.

68. Typically the nation-state's moments of universal identification, when all the nations speak as one, are exceptional and occur under conditions of globally shared disaster, as at the end of the two world wars, and in the face of earthquakes, tsunamis and some medical epidemics. The Great Depression of the 1930s was not sufficient to burst the bounds of nationalism in this manner.

69. *ibid*, 232.

70. *ibid*, 4.

71. *ibid*, 199.

72. King, 2009, 13; Paradeise, et al., 2009, 229.

73. Kerr, 2001/1963; Marginson, 2009b.

74. The Peace Museum at Hiroshima records that American President Franklin Roosevelt sought British consent for the use of the A-bomb as early as 1942. Churchill and Roosevelt agreed that early to use it on Japan rather than Germany.

References

Bayly, Christopher A. (2004). *The Birth of the Modern World 1780–1914. Global connections and comparisons*. Oxford: Blackwell.

Blom, Erich (1974). *Mozart*. Revised edition. London: J.M. Dent and Sons.

Bourdieu, Pierre (1984). *Distinction: A social critique of the judgment of taste*. London: Routledge and Kegan Paul

Bourdieu, Pierre (1988) *Homo Academicus*. Cambridge: Polity.

Bourdieu, Pierre (1993). *The Field of Cultural Production*. New York: Columbia University Press.

Carmean, Kelli, Dunning, Nicholas & Kowalski, Jeff Karl (2004). The rise and fall of terminal classic Yaxuna, Yuchatan, Mexico. In Arthur A. Demarest, Prudence M. Rice & Don S. Rice (eds.), *The Terminal Classic in the Maya Lowlands: Collapse, transition and transformation*, pp. 424–449. Boulder: University Press of Colorado.

Centre for Science and Technology Studies, Leiden University, CWTS Leiden (2009). *The Leiden Ranking*. Accessed 31 August 2009 at: http://www.cwts.nl/cwts/LeidenRankingWebSite.html.

Chase, Diane Z. & Chase, Arlen F. (2004). Hermeneutics, transitions and transformations in classic to postclassic Maya society. In Arthur A. Demarest, Prudence M. Rice & Don S. Rice (eds.), *The Terminal Classic in the Maya Lowlands: Collapse, transition and transformation*, pp. 12–27. Boulder: University Press of Colorado.

Copland. Aaron (2009 [1939]). *What to Listen for in Music*. New York: New American Library.

Demarest, Arthur A., Rice, Prudence M. & Rice, Don S. (2004). The terminal classic in the Maya lowlands: Assessing collapses, terminations, and transformations. In Arthur A. Demarest, Prudence M. Rice & Don S. Rice (eds.), *The Terminal Classic in the Maya Lowlands: Collapse, transition and transformation*, pp. 545–572. Boulder: University Press of Colorado.

Drache, Daniel (2008). *Defiant Publics: The unprecedented reach of the global citizen*. Cambridge: Polity.

Erwin, Douglas H. (2006). *Extinction: How life on earth nearly ended 250 million years ago*. Princeton: Princeton University Press.

Friedman, Thomas (2005). *The World is Flat*. New York: Farrar, Straus and Giroux.

Gould, Stephen, J. (2002). *The Structure of Evolutionary Theory*. Cambridge: Harvard University Press.

Higher Education Evaluation and Accreditation Council of Taiwan, HEEACT Taiwan (2008). *2007 Performance Ranking of Scientific Papers for World Universities*. Accessed 28 June 2008 at: http://www.heeact.edu.tw/ranking/index.htm

Kerr, Clark (2001 [1963]). *The Uses of the University*, Fifth Edition. Cambridge: Harvard University Press. First published 1963.

King, Roger (2009). Policy internationalism, national variety and networks: Global models and power in higher education states. Draft paper.

Knox, Hannah, Savage, Mike & Harvey, Penny (2006). Social networks and the study of relations: networks as method, metaphor and form. *Economy and Society*, 35 (1), 113–140.

Laporte, Juan Pedro (2004). Terminal classic settlement and polity in the Mopan Valley, Peten. In Arthur A. Demarest, Prudence M. Rice & Don S. Rice (eds.), *The Terminal Classic in the Maya Lowlands: Collapse, transition and transformation*, pp. 195–230. Boulder: University Press of Colorado.

Ma, Wan Hua (2008). The University of California at Berkeley: An emerging global research university. *Higher Education Policy*, 21, 65–81.

Marginson, Simon (2008). *'Ideas of a University' for the Global Era*. Paper for seminar on 'Positioning University in the Globalized World: Changing Governance and Coping Strategies in Asia. Centre of Asian Studies, The University of Hong Kong; Central Policy Unit, HKSAR Government; and The Hong Kong Institute of Education. 10–11 December 2008, The University of Hong Kong. Accessed 5 December 2009 at: http://www.cshe.unimelb.edu.au/people/staff_pages/Marginson/Marginson .html.

Marginson, Simon (2009a). The academic professions in the global era. In Jurgen Enders and Egbert de Weert, *The Changing Face of Academic Life: Analytical and comparative perspectives*. Houndmills: Palgrave Macmillan, 96–113.

Marginson, Simon (2009b). University rankings and the knowledge economy. In Michael A. Peters, Peter Murphy & Simon Marginson, *Creativity and the Global Knowledge Economy*. New York: Peter Lang, 185–216.

Marginson, Simon (2010a). Space, mobility and synchrony in the knowledge economy. In Simon Marginson, Peter Murphy and Michael A. Peters (eds.), *Global Creation: Space, mobility and synchrony in the age of the knowledge economy*. New York: Peter Lang, 117–149.

Marginson, Simon (2010b). Making space in higher education. In Simon Marginson, Peter Murphy and Michael A. Peters (eds.), *Global Creation: Space, mobility and synchrony in the age of the knowledge economy*. New York: Peter Lang, 150–200.

Marginson, Simon (2010c). Higher education as a global field. In Simon Marginson, Peter Murphy and Michael A. Peters, *Global Creation: Space, mobility and synchrony in the age of the knowledge economy*. New York: Peter Lang, 201–228.

Marginson, Simon, Nyland, Chris, Sawir, Erlenawati and Forbes-Mewett, Helen (2010). *International Student Security*. Cambridge: Cambridge University Press.

Marginson, Simon & Ordorika, Imanol (2010). 'El central volumen de la fuerza' Global hegemony in higher education and research. In Craig Calhoun (ed.), [title and page numbers to be advised]. New York: Columbia University Press

Matthews, Julie & Sidhu, Ravinder (2005). Desperately seeking the global subject: International education, citizenship and cosmoplitanism. *Globalisation, Societies and*

Education, 3 (1), 49–66.

Meyer, John W., Drori, Gili S. & Hwang, Hokyu (2006). Conclusion. In Gili S. Drori, John W. Meyer & Hokyu Hwang (eds.), *Globalization and Organization: World Society and organizational change*, pp. 258–274. Oxford: Oxford University Press.

National Science Board, NSB (2009) *Science and Engineering Indicators*. Accessed on 9 April 2009 at: http://www.nsf.gov/statistics.

Palma, Rafael Cobos (2004). Chichen Itza: Settlement and hegemony during the terminal classic period. In Arthur A. Demarest, Prudence M. Rice & Don S. Rice (eds.), *The Terminal Classic in the Maya Lowlands: Collapse, transition and transformation*, pp. 517–544. Boulder: University Press of Colorado.

Paradeise, C., Reale, E., Goastellec, G. Blieklie, I. (2009). Universities steering between stories and history. In C. Paradeise et al. (eds.) *University Governance: Western European comparative perspectives*, pp. 227–246. Dordrecht: Springer.

Ramirez, Francisco O. (2006). The rationalization of universities. In Marie-Laure Djelic & Kerstin Sahlin-Andersson (eds.). *Transnational Governance: Institutional Dynamics of Regulation*, pp. 225–244. Cambridge: Cambridge University Press.

Shanghai Jiao Tong University Graduate School of Education (2009). *Academic Ranking of World Universities*. Accessed 1 November 2009 at: http://ed.sjtu.edu.cn /ranking.htm.

The Times Higher (2008). World university rankings. *The Times Higher Education Supplement*. Accessed on 30 March 2008 at: www.thes.co.uk [subscription required]

US News and World Report (2006). *America's Best Colleges, 2007 Edition*, pp. 77–79 & 81ff. Washington: USNWR.

Valdes, Juan Antonio & Fahsen, Frederico, (2004). Disaster in sight: The terminal classic at Tikal and Uaxactun. In Arthur A. Demarest, Prudence M. Rice & Don S. Rice (eds.), *The Terminal Classic in the Maya Lowlands: Collapse, transition and transformation*, pp. 140–161. Boulder: University Press of Colorado.

Vera, Eugenia Roldan & Schupp, Thomas (2006). Network analysis in comparative social sciences. *Comparative Education*, 42 (3), 405–429

van Vught, F. (ed.) (2009). *Mapping the Higher Education Landscape: Towards a European classification of higher education*. Heidelberg: Springer.

Webometrics (2009). Webometrics ranking of world universities. Accessed 28 June 2009 at: www.webometrics.info/.

6. *Nation*

SIMON MARGINSON

'All historians are world historians now, though many have
not yet realized it.'
—CHRISTOPHER A. BAYLY, *THE BIRTH OF THE MODERN WORLD 1780–1914*,
BLACKWELL, OXFORD, 2004, P. 469.

Nation-bound human agency is always combined with fraught engagement across the border. This tense coupling is inherent in the project of nation. Any bordering of space poses the issue of what happens beyond the border. No territorial space ever remains completely sui generis, though as we shall see, for a time Japan came close to this. Moreover, the centering of identity on the nation is secured by Othering the outside of the nation. In classical Rome and China those beyond the border were classified as 'barbarians.' It is always thus. The rise of the nation-state was accompanied by the intensification of early modern globalization in the era of worldwide shipping and imperial conquest, in which the Othering of non citizens conditioned their exploitation, enslavement, marginalization and extinction. In the era of the modern nation-state which began in the early nineteenth century, both national boundedness and cross-border engagement became practised with a new level of intensity. This sharpened the tension between them. To deal with that tension states more tightly policed their geographical borders and became equally fierce in controlling the boundaries of identity in the minds of citizens. As far as they could, they confined cross-border relations to inter-national relations between unchanging sovereign states--to control those relations and minimize the potential for transformative impacts at home.

But in the era of communicative globalization now about two decades old, cross-border activity between and across the nations is shaped not simply by relations between sovereign and self-protecting nations, but by global systems that exceed nations. These systems will always elude exhaustive regulation by political structures that cover only part of the Earth. There is a jagged disjunction between on one hand global imagining, systems and action; on the other hand the nation-state and national-particularist forms of human identity. But though the global can no longer be shut out, even for short periods of time, nations will continue into the foreseeable future. And societies can draw from a range of solutions to the problem of the jagged differences between national and global. In matters of identity and agency, societies are always path-dependent, but they also have options and can do new things. Human identities can be more or less bounded, and bounded in differing ways. There are many kinds of relation between self and Other. Some nations have designed themselves so as to minimize the danger of self-transformation though synchrony across borders: their processes of learning and reflexive judgments are referenced inwards. Japan is a highly developed example of this. Other nations are more open to the influence of the Other, but always in selective ways, and as far as possible on their own terms. America is particularly good at this.

In turn these approaches to relations between self and Other have differing meanings for the imagining of world society. At one extreme, mutually exclusive nations are seen as the sum of the world. There is nothing more to be had. Here the global domain is seen as merely an accidental by-product of collisions between nations, which generate problems of national security and inter-national and multilateral relations and conflict. At the other extreme, the nation is seen as not just parochial but ephemeral, doomed to dissolve into the one-world melting pot that is 'Spaceship Earth' populated by 'global citizens.' Commonality is all there is. Amid the growing weight of the global dimension in human affairs some theorists have declared that the nation-state is finished, even that national identity is obsolete. The first claim is premature, especially in the absence of a global state. The second claim is absurd, with its implication that location-based groupings joined by cultural inheritance will vanish from identity. But the point is that more than one approach to 'nation' is possible, and there is much at stake in the choice.

All nations maintain a core with hegemonic intent, whether that hegemony is exercised merely within the formal territory of the nation or has a wider ambition. Part of the raison d'etre of the machinery of the nation-state is the reproduction of the hegemonic core. Often national identity draws on histories and traditions that precede the nation-state, whether those of a people long settled in one place, or religion, or something else. It is important to distinguish 'nation' from 'state,' though the modern period has brought them closer together, and in some cases the nation-state is the main motor of national identity. Sometimes the state is the only force binding a disparate population and territory together and providing common cultural elements.[1] On the ground of the territorial nation enforced by the state, some nation-states manage the internal diversity of the population by inclusion, and others by exclusion. Most use a strategic mix of these approaches. Beyond the border, some nation-states advance the role of the nation in the world by shutting out the world and Othering it. Some are more open to outsiders, and readily absorb strangers into their own evolution, as do the settler states, such as America and Australia. Each such strategy has its own set of profits and costs. But globalization, which renders firm boundaries unsustainable, is changing the conditions in which these strategies are deployed.

As Part I will discuss, the most coherent and successful of all pre-modern European polities, that of ancient Rome, achieved an intriguing solution to these problems. At the end of the fecund but unstable late Republic, Augustus shaped an Empire whose Western half endured for the next four centuries. Building on the available cultural resources, including the pairing and contrast of Greece and Rome, the Augustan settlement was a flexible solution to problems of nation, identity and boundary. There was space for a range of self-determining identities and foreign influences, while Roman political and cultural dominance were strengthened and secured. The Augustan settlement contrasts with the more insular solution to the problems of nation, identity and boundary that was devised in the parallel settlement of the nation in Japan in the Tokugawa/Edo period after 1600 C.E., the legacy of which persists today. Japan is discussed in Part II. Part III considers universities in Japan, and summarizes the national/global problem.

I. Rome

After three generations of fluctuating government, military forays, civic violence and civil war in the Republic, Octavian, later known as the first emperor Augustus, took power from 31 B.C.E. to 14 C.E. and established a stable regime. The Augustan settlement re-engineered the city in architectural, administrative and aesthetic terms, remade relations with its dominions, and refashioned the governance of the Republic for world empire. It put in place values, systems and institutions that left such a strong mark that they are still clearly visible in Europe and North America. Well before communicative globalization, and without the de-severing of physical distance and multiple synchrony that have reworked the nation and rendered its boundaries more porous, a cosmopolitan world community was created. Rome was built on elite excess, gender subordination and slavery, and it was more socially hierarchical than the modern world, but Augustus remade it to become increasingly open in cultural terms. Augustan Rome imagined itself as universal. The premier national poet of the time was Virgil, who fixed the Augustan principate at the climax of his long narrative of the Roman story. In Book 1 of the *Aeneid* Jupiter forecast the future of the city:

> Then Romulus, proud in the tawny hide of the she-wolf, his nurse
> shall take up the line and found the walls of Mars
> and call the people Romans after his own name.
> On them I set no bounds in space or time;
> but have given empire without end.[2]

Rome was not the first empire to claim that. But as well as pushing forward on Rome's military fronts, Augustus formed a flexible, expanding polity. This created a universalizing dynamic within the Empire. Republican exclusion was replaced by a system that over the next two centuries became increasingly inclusive. Augustus began the process by fully involving the Italian cities in the Roman cultural and political world, while continuing to tolerate their civic autonomy and distinctive language and customs. After Augustus, successor emperors extended his system across the whole empire. In *Rome's Cultural Revolution* Andrew Wallace-Hadrill notes that 'the political transformation of the Roman world is integrally connected to its cultural transformation'[3] and that '"culture" serves 'to mark changing identities, to legitimate and reproduce systems of power.'[4] Here Augustus had much to work with. Within Romanness, a wide range of identity positions were accessible. The geographical spread of the Roman world and its trade, administration, military passages, religions and tourism opened a multiplicity of languages, cultural sets and local traditions:

> The Roman empire became a great 'middle ground,' not simply of the 'Roman' versus the 'other' (in various degrees assimilated to Rome), but an enormous multi-sided exchange across a vast territory, in which influences came from everywhere and flowed to everywhere.[5]

The Augustan settlement mobilized all this in support of the polity. We take inclusiveness for granted, in the vote-getting strategies of politicians and the marketing strategies of corporations, but only some nation-states use it, some of the time. The early imperial Roman cultural universe was characterized by a partially cosmopolitan spirit under Roman hegemony; a high degree of devolution to local cultures and administrations within central control; and a dual between Roman and Greek practices that provided fertile resources in almost every cultural domain, from public architecture to private life. There was much code switching between different cultural zones. Identity, the extent of openness and forms of belonging were all accessible to state manipulation. As Peter Murphy notes in chapter two, the Romans were intrigued by human diversity, while sustaining notions of a common human nature. They were also in no doubt about the superiority of Rome, which functioned as a norm that guided them and the collective end they sought. As they saw it, the roots of Roman superiority were not genetic endowments or even social organization, but timeless Roman values (*mores*). This argument was repeatedly made by Cicero[6] and others in the late Republic and drove successive attempts by the Senate and early emperors, including Augustus, to put back the clock on morals and return to the pristine standards of an imagined past. From time to time foreign influences were denounced as the source of national decline, only to be tolerated again. In the Roman encounters with diversity within a common system, the growing openness, the tensions between diverse currents and dominant norms, and the advanced human capacity for code-shifting and for reflexive referencing between the different cultural zones, there is something contemporary, even 'advanced global,' about the Roman world.

National Tradition

The Augustan settlement was a pre-industrial modernization of the type that occurred from time to time in the ancient and mediaeval worlds. Such moments of modernization could be the springboard for a protracted period of national or imperial dominance. It was done by the Tang in China, Justinian in the Eastern Empire in transition from Rome to Byzantium, Charlemagne in greater Gaul, Kublai Khan in China, and others. Pre-industrial modernizations were typically engineered from above by a potent state under charismatic leadership. They were acts of synthesis and hybridity in which received habits and resources were remobilized and combined with the recasting of systems and ideologies from the centre. Modernization shook up elite positions, provided for a temporary widening of upward mobility and created more transparent and effective infrastructures and armies. The temporality of these pre-industrial modernizations was different to that of industrial-capitalist modernizations. Capitalist modernization is characterized by a long process of continuous change driven by short cycles of innovation and obsolescence. It is less dependent on state charisma and the iconic historical moment, though from time to time the motor is overhauled by a Bismark, a Thatcher or a Chinese Communist Party. But the Augustan modernization drew its material not from destruction of the past but from a one-off renovation of the past. It did not kick-start a protracted process of change. The ultimate goal was not innovation without end, where the shock of the new conceals the path dependence and social and cultural reproduction beneath, as in the modern world. The goal was stasis. The object was to reset eternal Rome on a new basis which perfectly embodied its timeless nature, while using the moment of conservation to secure a profound transformation. The modern world disguises its reproduction behind ultra-change—the pre-modern world disguised change behind the eternal verities, like scholarship in mediaeval Europe or painting and calligraphy in China. Augustus systematically codified and reworked 'Romannness,' the national-cultural tradition central to Roman public discourse. Andrew Wallace-Hadrill notes that:

> ...tradition is peculiarly subject to invention...A shared history or myth of origin is a key ingredient in defining a sense of ethnic identity. Work on a wide variety of societies, from African tribes to modern nation-states, has shown both the vital role played by such shared histories, and the way in which tradition is constantly reinvented, above all in times of radical social and political change. To invoke the ancestors is to invoke a stable model of legitimacy; they are most invoked when legitimacy is most at issue, and the winners are those who succeed in imposing their model of legitimate behaviour on the ancestral past.[7]

As we shall see, this point about the continuous reinvention of tradition applies as closely to the national imagining in recent and contemporary Japan as to ancient Rome. Roman tradition was a miscellany of selective interpretations of a past that was both inherited and continuously manufactured. The inheritance was a matter of record but one open to almost endless permutations. Though there were always competing claims about tradition, some strands became dominant and from time to time, hegemonic. In Rome speakers and writers appealed to the past in three kinds of way. First, they invoked what their own ancestors had done, or allegedly done, so as to claim a present superiority. Second, they appealed to notions of what the whole of 'our ancestors' (*nostri maiores*) had done, or Romans always did, the accepted Roman way (*mos maiorum*), as a continuing norm to be implemented in the present: Cicero was especially prone to use this sort of argument.[8] Third, they contrasted the virtues of the ancestors with a present sorry decline in standards.[9] These forms of reasoning could be employed in conjunction with almost any reading of tradition. Speech in the Forum was continuously remade in the light of contemporary political debate. The flexibility of tradition in the present reflected the oral character of the discussion. 'Memories of the past transmitted by word of mouth survive only to serve the present, and can be constantly discarded, shuffled and adapted to fit changing circumstances.'[10]

But historiographical writing had different conditions of production, being more categorical in form. 'Once recording intervenes to disrupt the continuous adjustments of oral memory, the past emerges as strange and other.'[11] Late Republican antiquarian scholarship just prior to Augustus was especially associated with the notion of a tradition abandoned. This strand of argument gained currency, which provided favourable conditions for a new settlement:

> Roman antiquarianism developed a powerful discourse about the past that relied on scholarly research. But it did so in the context of a period of radical political and social upheaval. It had the effect of unhooking the present, so to speak, from the obligation to follow the recent past. By relocating the legitimizing authority of the ancestors in a remote past, it gave the present a greater freedom to innovate.[12]

> In his radical realignment of the structures of power and authority around his own person, Augustus brought about a sharp hiatus with the traditions of the recent past. Yet he was able to represent this discontinuity as a continuity at a deeper level, a return to older and more authentic Roman traditions, a 'restoration of the *res publica*.'[13]

Augustus' own version of Romanness, drawing on 'a century of debate about what the Roman way should be,' achieved great instrumental authority. It was the source of the narratives about the 'essence' of Rome that underscored his program. It functioned both as a strategy of legitimation and as the language in which the detailed reforms were couched.

> The new order was at once profoundly conservative and revolutionary. In preserving the structures of the city-state of the republic, it gave them new meaning. Augustus' traditionalism, in reaffirming the *mores maiorum*, in morality, religion, social structures and social practices, was not a veil for an alternative reality; it was rather the language in which the alternative reality was formulated.[14]

The *princeps* claimed continuity with the old Roman nobility that had been the backbone of Senate and priesthood, even while he decisively dismantled noble power, which was not fit to run an empire. 'It is the perfect revolution, which in changing everything changes also the perception of what is normal and traditional, and so erases its own revolutionary status.'[15] He stabilized and enlarged the Senate, while quietly chaining it to the principate; he regularized taxation, and overhauled military, juridical and city administration and guaranteed city water and the grain supply. The provinces were divided into those in strategically sensitive locations administered by Augustus and the remainder which stayed in the vote of the Senate. Less successfully he sought to regulate family formation, luxury consumption and public morals. Though innovations occurred in later centuries as the machinery of government grew, military and economic problems increased and social classes evolved, the core principles of Augustan governance were never challenged by his successors. For long the Augustan claims about the maintenance of the *mos maiorum* retained their power to persuade, though the old Roman polity structured by patrician bloodlines had vanished.

If modernization now gains its legitimacy by refusing tradition, the example that provides the best contrast with Rome is not the turnover of differentiated commodities in consumer product markets, nor the ageism and disposable innovations of youth culture. It is Mao's Cultural Revolution of 1966–1969, in which China's leader is said to have stated that he would make of the Chinese people 'a clean sheet of paper' as the starting point for change.[16] The Cultural Revolution with all its human, cultural and economic costs became the platform on which China's astonishing modernization was built in the 1980s and after. (Whether Mao himself had this kind of transformation in mind is another question.) The clean sheeting was so complete that across the whole cultural zone in China, from the arts, scholarship and university policy to official ideology and leaders' statements, we can observe a reflex neo-Confucian rhetoric that gestures back to space of tradition which was so thoroughly emptied out. China wants a tradition, and clutches for it in the mind, like a person who has lost an arm but still feels the limb as if it was there.

Multiplicity

In other respect Rome and China are not opposite but congruent. In both of these pan-nations a strong central polity presided/presides over a complex diversity of provinces, cities, languages and cultural identities. Like Rome and unlike the USA, China does not blend its national diversity in a melting pot, though it exerts central control and expects national character to receive its due. But if anything the Romans were more flexible in the face of multiplicity.

Wallace-Hadrill starts from two assumptions about the nature of culture in the Roman world. First, 'identity' is not simple or bounded. Human agents live within a multiplicity of competing identities: locational, ethnic, social, religious, political.[17] Wallace-Hadrill uses textual and archaeological evidence to demonstrate that much of the Roman world shared this assumption. In the Roman world neither culture nor identity was a zero-sum game. Educated Romans and provincials could be both Roman and 'hellenic' without ceasing to be, say, an Italian from Pompeii or a Gaul from Arelate. Latin was a requirement for civilized life but it did not replace local languages—people were not expected to discard their local roots—and did not perform the same functions as Greek. Roman discussions of identity indicate that triangulation was more or less continuous. The different spaces of action (Roman, Hellenic, Gaul from Arelate, etc.) were each used as reference points for the other. In particular, within the pairing of Roman and Greek vital to the Roman world, Roman and Hellenic mores, habits, designs and artifacts were continually compared with each other.[18] In the increasingly cosmopolitan world of the early Empire identity became understood as a process not a state. It was changeable and under the control of human agents rather than something fixed, although public conventions had to be respected. Both typically Roman and typically Greek characteristics were acquired through education.

The second assumption is that cultural relations were on the whole characterized by 'dialogue and multiple identities rather than fusion.'[19] The main self-formation strategy[20] that was used by human agents was that of multiplicity and movement between cultures, rather than the creation of fully integrated hybrid selves. This is not to say that cultural zones were fixed or did not influence each other, or all hybridity was absent. In public personality Roman leaders often displayed Greek elements, though the Roman elements were dominant (rustic local elements were rarely displayed in public). But it was normal, even essential, to live in more than one cultural zone at the same time and to move deftly between them. The distinctions between cultural zones was vectored by geography, language, religion and institutions. Rome, like globalization today, called up openness and flexibility. Arguing against the notion that cultural relations took the form of hybrid or 'creole' sets, Wallace-Hadrill notes that hybrid identity presupposes the substitution of new identity for old. The notion is zero-sum. No doubt some in the Roman world self-transformed in this manner. In some places oppositional local cultures were forced into sublimation. But for the most part multiple (plural) identities could be sustained. People managed their multiple affiliations through code switching:

> The specific model for 'creole' culture is a linguistic one: a Creole language is an independent language formed from elements of two languages to become something new. But it is not by any means the only possibility. A commoner historical phenomenon is bilingualism, whereby two (or more) languages remain in use alongside each other, often in patterns of oscillation characterised as 'code-switching' whereby the user moves from one language to another not only from sentence to sentence, but from phrase to phrase…The Roman world produces no evidence of Creole languages, but abundant evidence of bilingualism and code-switching, and at all social levels: Latin and Greek, Latin and Italic dialects, Latin and Punic, Latin and Gaelic. While there is clear evidence that Roman rule extended the use of Latin across the Mediterranean, there is little of the suppression of local languages.[21]

Wallace-Hadrill reviews life in the Italian cities in the late Republic. For a long time Rome maintained an antinomy between Romans and non-Romans in the areas it controlled. The towns of Italy varied between those without citizenship, those that had been granted the citizenship as a matter of grace and favour, and colonies of Roman citizens who were often former soldiers. The spread of Roman control was not matched by a drive to spread the Roman way of life and still less to spread an inclusive citizenship. In the growing Republic Roman identity remained rigidly defined. Like everything else in the polity—divided between patricians and plebeians, and still led by the handful of aristocratic families that monopolized the priesthood and appealed to the authority of their ancestors (*maiores*) in the course of every dispute—it was a privilege of birth. If Italians wanted to imitate Roman practices that was a matter for them. There was no attempt to impose Latin on the Italian towns and the Romans made little attempt to know their dialects. Thus a de facto bilingualism was practiced by Italians and tolerated by Rome. This came to support multiplicity of identity. For a time distinctive Italian cultures survived and flourished amid the civil order and material plenty associated with the spread of urban settlement and Rome's international wars. Municipal leaders were adept at one and the same time in the local language, religion and customs; in Latin and Roman practices; and in the Greek world which had long been a major presence in the peninsula. Multiple cultural positions provided flexible means of securing social evolution and personal advantage:

> ...the Oscan who speaks Latin as an Italiote on Delos has the advantage, and in speaking Greek in addition only strengthens the advantage, since Greek enjoys currency without dominance. Should the Oscan-speaking Italiote find himself speaking Greek to a Latin-speaking Italiote, he enjoys an additional advantage, of distance from the language of domination.[22]

A standardized form of Latin emerged during the late Republic. Latin alone was never sufficient as a marker of Roman identity, though its spread was one sign of the expanding Roman world. As we shall see, during the time of Augustus and after Latin increasingly displaced many local dialects in the Western provinces.[23] However, Greek was never displaced by Latin. On the contrary, the world role of that language grew under the Empire. Not only did it remain dominant in the administration and commerce of the East, it became adopted throughout the Western Empire as a second language of use. From time to time this concerned those Romans who believed that Latin ought to be the universal language of rule throughout the Empire or that Greek had corrupted the *mos maiorum* at home. But in the East the communicative motive of Roman administration was to be understood, not to enforce Latin as an act of normalization, and in the West Greek became part of the *mos maiorum* itself. Romanness disseminated the Hellenic.

ROMAN AND HELLENIC

Much of the story of Roman culture under the later Republic and the Empire is the story of the asymmetrical pairing of Latin/Greek in language, and Roman/Hellenic in culture. Throughout their history the Romans were open to Greek currents, especially from Southern Italy. The idea of a pre-200 B.C.E. authentic Roman untouched by Greece was a myth created later for rhetorical purposes. During the Roman conquest of the Eastern Mediterranean there was a wholesale transfer from Greece to Rome of artifacts and human and intellectual resources in sculpture, painting, ceramics and household goods, architecture, theatre, music, literature, rhetoric, philosophy, mathematics, medicine and other areas. Rome gave back its governance and administration, and its organization of city spaces, water supplies, roads and communications. The two modes, Roman and Greek, were not symmetrical or a substitute for one another. Rather there was a division of labour between them. Rome was identified above all by Latin, political systems and the complex pattern of Roman tradition which was continuously remade and interpreted. The Greek was identified by language and Hellenic culture. In the encounter between Greek and Roman elements the Romans never forgot their claim to superiority, but each culture became redefined through its contact with the other. Wallace-Hadrill finds 'the Roman conquest of Greece led not to fusion but reciprocal exchange. The cultures…enter into a vigorous and continuous process of dialogue with one another.' People of both cultures were active players in their self-transformation, and mutual transformation.[24]

Romans and Italians learned to speak Greek and imitate Greek cultural practices without becoming less Roman or Italian or both. While the Greeks defined themselves by the contrast with barbarians, Romanness became more sharply defined by the contrast with Greekness.[25] Roman scholars and statesmen emphasized the virtues of the Roman toga as distinct from the Greek pallium.[26] In architecture, the famous treatise of Vitruvius codified the Roman debt to Greek forms while proclaiming the superiority of both Roman adaptations and innovations, and absorbing Italian architecture outside Rome into the Roman side of the divide.[27]

> Vitruvius' revolution lay in the demonstration that Greek theory could be reconciled with current practice in Italy without compromising identity…the "we" he constructs is remarkable, and the product of a specific moment, an Italy transformed by the trauma of the Social and civil wars and brought together in the new Italo-Roman identity which [was]…a key to the Augustan revolution.[28]

Vitruvius argued that the geometry of the Roman theatre which began with four triangles in a circle was inherently superior to the Greek theatre with its three squares in a circle.[29] Likewise, the male nakedness of the Greek gymnasium was a source of licentious[30] but Roman baths (*thermae*) were healthy. Yet Romanness also annexed Greekness. As the Western provinces and Africa became romanized the Romans brought to them not only Latin Roman life but also Greek and the Hellenic. Both sides were part of the Roman world.

One of the most striking characteristics of Roman culture from the earliest stage—that is, the first waves of Greek colonization in Italy—is the ability to maintain its difference from the Greek while constantly modifying itself in directions assimilable to the Greek. The close contact between the two cultures allows endless possibilities for contamination (call it 'creolization' if preferred), but so long as the Roman constructs itself as different from the Greek, the Greek elements it has borrowed/ imitated/ stolen/ hijacked are romanized by an act of self-redefinition.[31]

Wallace-Hadrill argues that in conquering the East in partnership with its Italian allies, Rome opened itself to the installation of the Hellenic as part of a continuing process of transformation by 'the heart of power at Rome itself.' An analogy for the relation between hellenization and romanization is 'the two phases of the circulation of the blood. If hellenization is the diastolic phase, by which blood is drawn into the centre, romanization is the systolic phase, that pumps the oxygenated blood back to the extremities.' Hellenization and romanization needed 'to alternate constantly, to keep the system alive.'[32] In their education Romans took from Greece its literary and intellectual pursuits, less so its music and plastic arts. They did not see high culture Greek scholarship as defining of Roman identity, which was located in the ancestral tradition and the Roman mores. From the time of Cicero just prior to Augustus, Greek literature and Roman mores became combined in the notion of humanitas, in which the civilized person was distinguished from the barbarian on the basis of high culture, and habits and morals. Apart from its dual origin, what is striking about humanitas is its potential universality. It is accessible to any free person in the Empire. 'Any human being may be humane, though many (the barbarous) tend to bestiality, in their ferocity and lack of education. The concept thus actually creates the possibility of "culture" that is not confined by the local boundaries of a particular community—though in effect you must join the Greco-Roman club to achieve it.'[33]

Openness and Inclusion

Beyond Rome was the world of the 'barbarians.' Here Rome and Greece shared a common sensibility. The totalizing anti-barbarian ideology in Athens emerged during the Persian wars, though there was continued contact and exchange of ideas, despite the official ideology. Likewise Rome's sense of the external Other was fostered in its numerous boundary wars and the recurring threat of invasion by Celts or Germans. Romans distinguished themselves from uncivilized barbarians in two ways: the notion of customary and law-abiding behaviour, and the notion of personal cultivation. (Not surprisingly when the Northern tribes broke into the Western Empire in the fifth century C.E. and sought to imitate the civilization they found there, this included its formed cultural attributes and sometimes the *mores*). But for Romans the dangerous Other also had its attractions, especially as fashion motifs. Subordinated 'barbarians' made glamorous slaves. German auxiliaries often served as imperial bodyguards. Civilizations of the East constituted another kind of Other. Cultures that were non Roman and non Greek were a perpetual source of ideas in art and design. The Roman conquest of Egypt by Augustus opened the city to Egyptian influences in design, painting and funerary monuments. But the city fathers drew the line against values and ideas which they saw as in blatant contradiction of Roman *mores*. The cult of Isis was repeatedly repressed and was forced underground in Rome.[34]

Throughout Roman history the external boundary between nation and Other underwent little change. But the mechanisms of social exclusion/inclusion within the Roman world changed considerably. The main dynamic was the progressive inclusion of the externalized Other, the Italians and the provincials, into the Roman heartland. As noted above this process of inclusion was at the same time political and cultural. (The secondary dynamic was an uneven process of improvement in the position of leading freedmen, former slaves, who at times during the Empire obtained great wealth and power.) Much of the history of the late Republic consisted of a series of armed conflicts in which the largely aristocratic elite in the city was challenged by groups immediately below or outside it who successfully established a claim to belong to the elite. The bloody Social War of 91–89 B.C.E. was triggered by the fact that while Italian cities enjoyed the freedoms of multiple identity, many were shut out of the commanding heights of the polity. The dual structuring of citizens/non-citizens throughout the peninsula came to constitute an increasingly unsatisfactory political settlement. Local Italian elites engaged in monumental building, always a significant investment in identity, creating Roman-style urban centres that were financed by the spoils of conquest in the East gained while fighting in Roman armies.[35] Yet the patricians at the head of the Republic continued to resist their claim for inclusion as citizens with full political rights. To gain those rights the Italian cities fought for them. The Italians lost the Social War but gained the franchise and gradually, a growing number of places in the Senate. The knights (*equites*) also expanded their clout. The story of the final decades of the Republic was the erosion of traditional aristocratic power and the beginning of a more inclusive notion of Romanness. Augustus systematized both of these processes. It was ironic that the democratization of the franchise happened just as the electorate was robbed of its old instrumental power by the ascension of all powerful emperors.[36] Nevertheless inclusion in the polity had an all important cultural meaning as a signifier of inclusion within the national imaginary. Arguably it was exclusion from the status of citizen, not so much the power of voting per se, that had caused the Social War. As in the United States today but more so—because at this stage Roman citizenship was more exclusive—the category of citizen signified an elect, a superior group of people that commanded respect. 'The transformation of citizenship from a reciprocal bundle of rights and obligations to a form of social dignity is basic for Roman cultural identity,' states Wallace-Hadrill. 'Citizenship is no longer expressed through actions (voting, fighting) but through symbols: it becomes more urgent to define culturally what "being Roman" is about when it is reduced to a socio-legal status.'[37]

> Roman cultural identity is vigorously contested in the republican period, so long as the identity of the citizen body, and the distribution of power within it, was also contested. Augustus, in achieving a sort of consensus, one which allowed continuing expansion of the citizen body, and continuing penetration of the elite from the margins, was able to establish a sort of consensus about what Romans were like, how they behaved, what their cities were like, what customs and rituals they followed. To the extent there was a consensus, and a recognizable package of Roman culture could be endorsed, to that extent 'romanization' could spread to the provinces. Precisely because that spread involved more recruitment to the citizen body, and negotiation with new groups with their own cultural background, there was room for fluidity and change, and for a vast range of local difference within what even so could be recognized as 'Roman,' from Hadrian's Wall to Palmyra.[38]

It began to become apparent that Romanness in all senses now lay within anybody's reach—or at least anybody who rose up through the army on merit, succeeded in trade or commerce, or obtained a powerful patron. The national imaginary became populated by an ever-growing number of actual human subjects with a direct investment in that imaginary. Roman law divided the world into Roman citizens and *peregrini*, outsiders. At the end of the Social War in the late Republic there were about one million citizens. By the death of Augustus the number had risen to five million.[39] After Augustus the citizens kept growing at the expense of the *peregrini*, although the status of women and slaves never formally altered. The commanding heights of the polity also expanded in the same elastic fashion. The Senate and the consulship were progressively extended to nearer and then further colonies. Provincials moved from the command of legions to governorships and then to the principate itself. A century after Augustus, Trajan from Spain assumed the purple, followed by his nephew Hadrian. An African, Septimus Severus was the most successful soldier emperor after Trajan. Soon after in 212 C.E., Caracalla extended citizenship to all free persons in the empire.

In fact the net of Roman inclusion was cast wider than the formal polity and again the means of inclusion were cultural. On the periphery of the empire but within the military line which marked the boundary with the barbarian world beyond, local native elites in the provinces were incorporated into the role of devolved rulers on behalf of Rome through the medium of romanization. Their children learned Latin and Greek. They acquired literature and philosophy and floor mosaics and Campanian tableware. They habitually attended gladiatorial contests and the theatre. *Humanitas* was a many-sided tool for creating a universal empire. As Tactius points out when discussing the introduction of Roman culture to the British elite, the instrument of control was 'the more effective because perceived not as a form of enslavement but as value shared by mankind.'[40]

HOMOGENIZATION

Thus the broadening of the polity was joined to the thickening of Roman/ Hellenic cultural practices. And in this process inclusion begins to turn into homogenization. As the imperium settled into the deep groove carved out for it by Augustus, the closer people were to the centre of the power, the more that local difference began to become absorbed into the dominant cultural forms. 'The end result is to provide a common cultural identity to the Italian peninsula associated with Roman citizenship.'[41] Later Narbonese Gaul, Spain, Africa and the more distant provinces followed. The dual political and cultural process in turn had implications for the old forms of multiplicity in Italy and the nearby provinces. Local language and cultural practices became swallowed by the Greco-Roman tide. Local languages began to fall out of use in the face of Latin. Strikingly the reign of Augustus was long enough for dual local/Roman identity to disappear over much of Italy.[42] This was not because multiplicity was suppressed by the state. It was because the Greco-Roman tide proved culturally irresistible.

Correspondingly, the social story of the first two hundred years of Empire—when civil order and economic prosperity were at their height—was the expansion of the middle class and the diffusion of full Romanness, in the form of the lifestyle of the wealthy, to the next layers of the population. Wallace-Hadrill describes how 'the relentless pursuit of fashions by the elite is driven by the hot breath of competition from emergent groups below. Emulation is the counterpart to distinction, the urge to maintain a social distance expressed in the material superiority of luxury.'[43] Here 'the drive is not merely to "ape" social superiors, but to create distance from inferiors.'[44] The signs of luxury consumption spread to the level below, 'sub-luxury.' This was 'the downmarket imitations of luxury which reach a wider diffusion than the true luxuries of the elite, but which nevertheless serve to maintain distinctions at lower levels.' He notes that there was a remarkable proliferation of 'sub-luxury' and a 'close liaison' was maintained between the world of luxury consumption and the world of sub-luxury.[45] They were both part of the same socio-economic system, articulated by the consumption of status goods. Much the same kind of status economy with a progressively inclusive dynamic was apparent in the classical period in the lowland cities of the Maya in Mesoamerica. The increasing circulation of status goods strengthened the stake of the middle social layers in the aristocratic system.[46]

The upward move in status was associated with the acquisition of the yin and yang Romano-Hellenic identity, which was both plural and also integrated as a single system, and the decisive abandonment of rustic identities. This final achievement of Romanness was signaled by consumption and its display. The vertical extension of an elite national imaginary, down the social scale to include all of those who had the money and the learned cultural attributes to carry it off, corresponded to its horizontal extension from the centre at Rome to the provinces. In both processes we can see an incremental homogenization rolling out. The process of upward mobility did not implode the social hierarchy. On the contrary, mobility depended on the existence of the hierarchy. None are so fierce in defending a social hierarchy and its rules of operation as those who have just scrambled to its top. Rome continued to distinguish the elite from the masses, just as it continued to insist on the distinction of Roman from non-Roman: slaves, foreigners and barbarians.

Thus despite the clear-cut hierarchy in the Roman world its mechanisms of inclusion worked even in the lower reaches of the social scale, though stopping short of the slaves. Roman cultural forms that depended on large-scale public infrastructure financed by the emperors or the elite—temples, theatres, baths, amphitheatres, forums and basilica—were open to the whole citizenry and more. Vespasian's Coliseum took in everyone in the city. Another example was the great public baths, the *thermae*. Open, inclusive and immensely popular, the baths stripped every Roman to an elemental nakedness on the ground of the nation. The *thermae* distinguished the clean-smelling urbane citizen from the unwashed barbarian.[47] They manifested the imaginary of a commonness Romanness.

> Such *thermae* acted as a monumental display of the power of the emperors who built them; that power was advertised by the physical mass, by the feats of architecture, and by the capacity to pull crowds. If baths, through purveying pleasure, could display power, whether of the villa-owner, or the provincial city magistrate, or of the Roman emperor, then it was successful as a construction of a social identity that was unmistakeably Roman. In civilization, power and pleasure advance hand in hand...[48]

Following a census of all inhabitants of Rome instigated by Julius Caesar, Augustus exhaustively catalogued the city and reorganized its districts. This allowed him to track potential taxation revenues on a comprehensive basis, maintain public facilities and iconic monuments, render the city safer from recurring fires, and make its precincts more accessible to its inhabitants and also to the outsiders who journeyed there from the four quarters of the empire and beyond. Augustus provided a systematic knowledge of the city to all by mapping it down to the level of individual properties. There had been no Republican street maps. Now detailed maps of the city in marble were erected in prominent places, a visual simulation of the national imaginary. Later emperors continued this practice:

> Lack of maps puts the visitor at a disadvantage, empowering the local knowledge of the inhabitants. The open display by the emperors of a detailed map of their capital was more than a boast of monumental scale. It advertised their own knowledge and control of that dangerous capital, advertised the expertise of the officials, surveyors, census-takers and City Prefects, on whom they relied; and proclaimed to the stranger that the city was open to all citizens, wherever in the empire they came from, and not under the control of the local power-brokers...the maps allowed Roman citizens, strangers in their own city, to recognize who and where they were.[49]

Rome Today

Later societies have been transfixed by the creativity of late Republican Rome in civic affairs (in every political mode except harmony) and also by the magisterial Augustan settlement. In its comprehensive architecture and the depth of its human understanding the Augustan system is akin to J.S. Bach, and achieved a similar kind of pre-modern closure of form. It also created a standard that doomed the later Empire and the subsequent centuries to mediocrity. This in no way has detracted from the power of the idea, and perhaps has reinforced it, while raising the cunning of Augustus to the status of icon. The normative power of the nation recreated by Augustus has been a problem. The Roman imagining of the world was never enough to blueprint later ages. Yet the West could not forget and was long blind to its limitations. Such disparate state-building projects as those of Charlemagne, the Byzantines, the Holy Roman Empire, the Tsar of all the Russias, Napoleon, the Ottomans, not to mention the Church of Rome, drew reflected glory from the Empire of Augustus. In the worlds of art and intellect the Renaissance turned on the appropriation of Rome, as did the neo-classical three centuries later. Too often, the United States reaches back to its ancient forbear to understand itself. What is lost in each of these excursions into antiquarian mimetics is a sense of the specificity and limits of the Roman settlement. The problem is not 'Rome eternal,' it is Rome internal, the Rome in our heads. The Augustan settlement was a well crafted local-national solution to deal a specific set of imperial problems at a time when a solution was possible. It was the product of its circumstances. It was not a system for all times.

HEGEMONY

The limitation of the Roman example lies not so much in the social hierarchy: the brutal life of many slaves, who withered long before their time amid the remarkable affluence, and the empty pomp of later emperors, more magnified and mostly less able than Julius Caesar and Augustus—though Roman slavery and imperial pomp have both exercised a nasty appeal for some in later ages. Rather the limitations of Augustan Rome are twofold. First, because its goal was stasis, it was finally inflexible. The early imperial system provided for an evolving tolerance and inclusiveness and proved elastic for at least the next two centuries. But it did not create continuous innovation. Second, it was unfitted for the global space. Although the Roman handling of nation was very impressive in fluidity and breadth, and in its capacity to sustain and grow into a large imagining, and though there is much about the times of Augustus that speaks to our times, the Romans occupied a space different from our own time in crucial ways. Inclusive as it was within, Rome drew its potent unity also from Othering the barbarian outside. There is no Outside in a world society. We have reached the planet's edge. Moreover, inside its perimeter, Rome's dominance of mental and social forms was complete. Plural as it was, there was only one civilization in the Empire. That is not the world we now inhabit.

Interpretations of Rome differ according to where one sits. For the Romans 'Rome' was the cultural universe. For many Americans, in this regard Rome is analogous to the United States. The United States is the cultural universe, and the rest are inferior imitators, or they just don't get it yet. In other words the nation—not the world as a whole—is seen as the appropriate analogy with Rome. Following this familiar line of thought, imperial Rome and imperial United States are seen to have much in common. For example, as both saw/see it, beyond the margin of the customary world there is a barbarian Other and this is one of the drivers of national-imperial identity. And it is true that one clue to the persistence of the archaic notion of American exceptionalism in an age of advanced globalization and an inter-dependent world is this imagining of a national-imperial dimension with barbarian margin. Carrying the parallel further, the USA also combines the Roman kind of insularity, broad but bordered, with a fecund openness to outsiders. It is possible to make the transition from barbarian to citizen in the USA, as it was in Rome, though it is less easy than in Rome after Caracalla's reform. The analogy between Rome and the United States has been the subject of hundreds and articles and books produced from inside the United States; many of them focused on the later Roman years, the decline and fall of the imperial project. These arguments speak to an insular fear that America itself will 'fall' and American exceptionalism will turn out to be not so exceptional after all. But it all looks different outside the US. To other nations the notion that American civilization is in a state of terminal decline is simply irrelevant. The US is the creative centre of modernity and the overwhelming world leader in many spheres. At the same time, outside the US the premise that the USA (or the West) plays the role of Rome in the contemporary setting is not accepted. And it is inconceivable it will ever be accepted. Most of the world is committed to a different global project, characterized by a plurality not only of cultures but of civilizations—under the sign of a common modernity that most (though not all) seem to accept and embrace, and on the basis of a shared ecology and economy.

This suggests that we need to unlearn the Roman lesson of hegemony, which both its Othering of the barbarian and its claims to unique civilization and exceptional destiny were designed to promote. The striving for imperial hegemony today is a contest without a winner. Even if it could be achieved, the costs of hegemonic dominance by a single power would be too great, in a global setting in which there will soon be no margin of retreat. In a wholly Americanized world there would be no place for a self-determining Africa and Latin America, Europe, China, the middle-sized powers of Southeast Asia, or Japan. The dominance exercised by Rome within its military perimeter was such that it eventually mopped most of the local languages and cultures in the Empire. We need to find a way to world society without relying on universal military occupation by a single political power and a single notion (however rich) of the cultivation of the self. In particular, we need to find a different resolution of the tension between homogenization and diversity to that of the later Roman Empire. From Diocletian onwards Rome could shore itself up temporarily only by mighty and unsustainable efforts of state centralization. Its tradition became hollowed out, and as its economy and civil order began to fragment and Rome reached the limits of the elastic expansion of status— and hence the lifetime value of the citizenship peaked and began to decline— the commitment of its citizens became secured by a taxing bureaucracy, a totalitarian imperium and ineffective absolutism, and always, an unstable military force. By then the human freedoms that began to open up in the late Republic, and were systematized under Augustus, had vanished. Rome, still confronting the barbarian Other, was reduced to the lesser of two evils. The margin thinned. Popular consent to the state dropped away.

The achievements of Rome that dazzle us were not in the later trajectory from Augustus to absolutism, and the final clinging to power as an end in itself. Those achievements were the product of the late Republic and the early Empire, and their wonderful simultaneous evolution of cultural complexity and public space. It was a time when the nation was becoming more than a nation. It reached out to something larger. In doing so it spoke to our global condition.

ROMAN GLONACAL

Rome was profoundly and steeply hierarchical, more so than any modern nation. At the same time it was culturally inclusive and in that respect more like settler states such as the USA, Canada, Australia and Argentina than like Switzerland or Japan. The Roman Empire did not use differences based on place of birth, skin colour or religion to secure either the social hierarchy, or inclusion in the citizenship, or cultural inclusion, or the boundary between the barbarians and the Roman world. In that respect the Augustan settlement broke decisively with the exclusive practices of the Republic. It also differed from many polities that followed, including the modern nation-states that emerged in the nineteenth century and supervised 'their' populations more closely than the predecessor states. In can be argued that in relation to inclusion, the high modern state of nineteenth-century Europe was a regression from Rome. It often divided and ruled its populations, especially its colonial populations, on the basis of supposedly irrevocable differences handed down at birth.[50] And this kind of national imaginary has not yet disappeared. Consider Malaysia, in which the distinction between *bumiputra* Malays who are categorized as necessarily Muslim, and citizens of Chinese and Indian descent, is inscribed in the constitution and associated with differential rights and obligations. And as we shall see, Roman cultural openness differs in another way with Japan.

The Roman plurality of vision and agency is instantly recognizable to us. Free people in Augustan Rome experienced multiple dimensions of identity-formation, much as people do today. The metropolitan Roman was simultaneously Roman, Greek and local. The provincial Italian Roman was at the one time Roman/Greek, Italian and local. People today live in the glonacal setting with its three dimensions of imagining and action (global + national + local). It is very striking that the multiple Roman self-imagining and agency strategy were no lesser in scale and complexity than our imaginings and strategies in the global context today. One difference was that in Rome, in the absence of synchronous communication at a distance, multiplicity was less insistent and simultaneous. One moved between the different roles in physical space as now but not also in virtual space. One was less likely to confront all of the dimensions of life in the same place at once. In a provincial village one could set aside the Roman dimension more easily than people today can set aside the global dimension. This might have rendered code shifting easier to manage. Even so, there would be many situations where at least two of the three sensibilities were required. The Roman example also provides clues as to how the different dimensions of human imagining and action articulate through each other. For example Romanness could be measured against Greekness, in both directions. In language pairings the relations between the two languages are highly complex and variable. In Rome Greek retained cultural authority but Latin was the language of power and cultural interpretation. In China, the national language of Putonghua (Mandarin) is the seat of cultural identity, the function that in Rome was divided between Latin and Greek, yet in some domains English enjoys an instrumental power akin to Latin. In the United States English is overwhelmingly dominant but Spanish may yet become the administrative language in the West and Southwest of the empire, like Greek was in the Roman East. In contrast, in monocultural Japan, English has technical uses, but in the encounter between English and Japanese within Japan, there is never an engagement in the imaginative world of the Other.

Another clue for the present is that Romanness was absorbed into local settings in varying ways and to varying degrees. Likewise Arjun Appaduari comments that in the global setting, global cultural forms that work across the different local settings must become 'domesticated' into local practice.[51] In the same manner globalization also becomes embedded in various ways in the national dimension. Global forms become manifest in varying ways in different nationally-defined systems—for example as when governments or universities borrow policies from the stock of common New Public Management knowledge. Roger King notes the mutual influences at work: 'It is not one-way traffic from the global…While policy internationalism influences the local it does not do so as a form of one-sided domination but is itself also influenced by the local, including by national processes of culture, interpretation and regulation.'[52] In this manner processes of globalization, together with the processes of national and local embedding and adaptation, together expand the global networks.[53] In his history of the making of the modern world Christopher Bayly[54] makes the same argument.

> Processes of convergence will nearly always display national differences as global templates are 'negotiated' with local conditions. Moreover, some forms of national divergence from globalizing models may actually aid transnational policy convergence by allowing acceptance of the key features while preserving adaptability to local pathways in the details. That is, rather than global standards becoming 'adopted,' they are 'interpreted.'[55]

An alternative term for the local 'interpretation' of global standards is 'translation,' which suggests an inner-directed movement between inner and outer zones of language/ knowledge/ culture. This notion of translation is discussed below in relation to Japan. Such processes of interpretation/ translation complicate an already multiple structure. Following Saskia Sassen,[56] King notes that in the national dimension we now find several sets of spaces and relations. Some are traditionally national, some becoming globalized, and some unequivocally global in form already.[57] The same kind of remark can be made about the local dimension of action, which is populated at one and the same time by the irreducibly local, by local elements subject to national colonization, by national elements, by local elements transforming via the global, by global elements, by local elements transforming via globalized national, and so on.

While these notions speak to the process of local adaptation of global standards in the Roman world, at that time the variations in adaptation were more marked, because of the greater autonomy of the local and provincial dimensions. Despite this, with hindsight we can say that in the long run the Roman imperial-national dimension was largely decisive in relation to the provincial and local dimensions. As noted, in much of the Empire local languages and customs eventually weakened. Despite geographical distance and Roman administrative devolution, in many places the Latin language and Roman identity outlasted the fall of the Western Empire better than did local identities (this was less true in outlying provinces such as Britain, where Roman imagining was never as strong as in the heartlands). It remains to be seen whether global imagining will prove as potent in future as imperial Roman imagining was in the past.

The global dimension lacks the support of a potent state apparatus like that of Rome, or the modern nation-state. Yet it is pervasive and it is often irresistible. This is suggestive. Global modernisation has non-state drivers.

There is no global state. Globalization is a world-wide process without a state, though one with many subjects. This suggests two things. First, it confirms that confined notions of Nation—whether monocultural, territorial or imperial—cannot contain the sum of human endeavour. A geo-strategic logic of Nation and a world of mutually exclusive nation-states will not suffice, especially when mapping the global space. Second, it demonstrates that cultures can exist separately from state machinery. It is evident that many cultures are active in the global dimension. This again allows us to distinguish between a nation of people (and their national culture) and the state. For much of the long history of Japan, especially the period since 1600, a strong state played the key role in shaping the nation. But it did so with reference to an inherited civilization of remarkable qualities, that evolved both inside and outside the nation-state. During periods of fragmentation of the polity the Japanese nation and its culture continued to evolve. Thus Nation exists independently of the nation-state, as well as through it. It is to the history of Japan, and to the Japanese nation today and its uneasy relationship with the global setting, that we now turn.

II. Nihonjinron

From Japan the world always appears as an inter-national space. It is never a global space. This is because the world is comprised by bounded nations. Among them Japan itself is unique and all-important. That last ironic universalism is embodied in all national identity. But in Japan, the home to a brilliant civilization unsurpassed in certain of the realms of human creativity, this boundedness and self-referencing are carried to almost the fullest possible extent. The concentrated national imagining served Japan well during the high time of the modern nation-state in the century after 1850, but has led to growing difficulties in the contemporary setting, in which global imagining is now indispensable to action, over the long term the state-created bounds of nations are slowly dissolving, and global strategies will determine which human identities survive and flourish. Whatever happens to nations and national imagining—and they will not simply disappear, especially in the form of national cultures—it is clear that a super-positioning of the national and the global is going on.

In the new Cambrian sea of global vision, imagining and action, it has become essential to manage multiplicity and combine an evolving self-certainty with openness and facility in cross-border engagement. Japan has a profound sense of self but supports it with the old national device of monoculture, and one that is relatively inflexible. Japan has been unable to combine a hegemonic centre with internal space for difference, graded diversity at the periphery and the conversion of the Other, in the manner of Rome or even to the extent of the United States. Internally, social difference is acknowledged and hierarchy is debated, but cultural difference is not so much suppressed as unacknowledged. It does not exist. Externally, Japan is closely aware of foreign developments, for this vigilance defends the nation, but foreign elements are always translated into Japanese and thereby integrated as a kind of subordinated hybrid before they are admitted inside the boundary. It is almost impossible to migrate into Japan. Rome opted for multiplicity, within the terms of Roman dominance. Plurality was one of the key elements in an imperial strategy of growing inclusiveness. Japan opts rather for hybridity on Japanese terms, as the means of sustaining the vital distance. This forces it to deal with the foreign largely via those techniques of engagement that protect separation and distance: economic exchange and (less often and more unhappily) military force. When

Japan reaches out across the border it does so only in terms of its own brand of *mos maiorum*. As we shall see, Japan has sometimes changed deeply, but only so as to continue in isolated splendour. Like Romanness was for the Romans— but with much less curiosity about the rest of the world than in ancient Rome or in the USA today—Japan, the Emperor and Japaneseness are enough. This is the sum of life. Japan's horizon is always itself.

The construction of a deeply satisfying sense of national self, the *Nihonjinron* project, is a major cultural industry in Japan. (Note that in this chapter the term '*Nihonjinron*' is used more broadly than in that conventional meaning where it refers to a set of discourses that assert the uniqueness of Japanese culture and people.[58] In this chapter '*Nihonjinron*' means a larger project of construction of bounded national identity, in which the agencies of the state play a key role, but not the only role). Government is the self-appointed guardian of the *Nihonjinron* project but it permeates also corporate and civil ideologies, not just agencies of the state, but public and private education, civil society and literature, and cultural 'soft goods.'

Through the continuing construction of *Nihonjinron*, what we can call 'Japaneseness'—that is, the inherited tradition of Japan—is likewise remade on a continuing basis—just as the Roman tradition was continually being remade within the Roman polity. Mostly this process of remaking in Japan is slow and incremental. Sometimes it is dramatic and compressed. Always it looks back as much as forward. The abiding objective inherited from the revered and naturalized past is reproduction into the future. Perfect in simplicity, a timeless beauty triumphs over death. Human life is ephemeral. We are leaves scattered by the wind, and all our works are but a dream within a dream. But Japan of the seasons with its long roots, older than the Buddha, is real and it is eternal. More eternal than Rome. Yet Japan is always in peril.

Things cannot go on like this. But the task of transformation is immensely challenging. Bounded Japan is as old as human history in the islands and has older geographic origins.

Bounded Japan

Four themes stand out in the long history of Japan. The first is cultural continuity. The second theme, the main matter of this chapter, is national isolation. The third theme is state building. Japan's national character has continuing roots in the civil order but is also produced by a centralized nation-state of often high calibre that has appointed itself guardian of formalized tradition and as mediator between Japan and the world beyond. The fourth theme is a genius for certain kinds of creativity. This has shown itself not merely in the achievements of Japanese science, which are very considerable, and the creation of technologies, products and distinctive and varied works of art, but in a remarkable capacity for re-imagining and remaking the nation. Japanese history undergoes a kind of punctuated evolution. Gradual economic and social evolutions are accompanied by long periods of cultural and political stasis. At rare moments of crisis the nation re-invents itself. Its national political system is remade, its traditions renovated and its isolation re-set. After the foundation moment of national construction, the Taika reforms in the seventh century C.E., there were two such moments of punctuated evolution, both of which transformed the nation and its relations with the Other outside Japan: the creation of the Tokugawa/Edo regime after 1600, which isolated the nation from almost all foreign influences, and the Meiji 'restoration' of 1868, which strengthened the state and triggered a rapid modernization and catch-up with the West, while sustaining a partial separation from the world that protected Japan's tradition and sense of self.

Japan's history demonstrates a particular genius for patterned creativity. The dating of flint tools suggests that manufacturing *homo sapiens* lived in Japan from about 30 thousand years ago. At that time Japan was not geographically isolated. The sea level was lower, the present islands were all connected and the southern island of Kyushu was joined to Korea. Later, the Korean strait formed and Japan became physically separated. Around twelve thousand years ago after the Last Glacial Maximum and towards the end of the temporary return to extreme cold in the Younger Dryas, the Jomon culture in Japan was producing what seems to be the first pottery in human history. 'Jomon,' which means chord pattern, refers to the design of the vessels. William Burroughs notes that 'what is remarkable is that the Jomon were still a hunting, gathering and fishing society, living in small groups, when they developed this advanced technology.'[59] They also created ceramic figurines. Recent archaeological discoveries are pushing back the breakthrough moments in East Asia. The first evidence for rice cultivation on the marshy banks of the Yangtze River in China has been dated at 13.9 thousand years ago, before the onset of the Younger Dryas.[60] This is almost one thousand years before the earliest evidence of cereal cultivation in the Middle East by Natufian people on the banks of the Euphrates in northern Syria. Rice cultivation and rice cultures in China found their way to Japan from over the sea via Korea. But the point is that Japan, while influenced by China, has long evidenced its own dynamic of creativity.

Japan was the last point eastward in the super-continent, the end of the long line of the flows of people and ideas and techniques. Here geographical isolation was decisive. Japan's bounded continuity has always been facilitated by its island geography. Protected by the Korean strait, Japan could manage and limit passage from Eurasia. With the exception of two moments in the last two centuries, when superior American military power broke in from the East, Japan has always had the choice of receiving foreign influences or ignoring them. Kublai Khan sent two invasion fleets in 1274 and 1281 C.E. but was defeated by armed resistance and a *kamikaze* (divine wind) that that is said to have sunk half of his ships. All other wars on the soil of Japan were civil wars. Under favourable circumstances island nations can develop unique strengths. Japan was further from Korea than Britain was from France, enhancing its freedom of control. After the early cultural flows from China and Korea, the Japanese created a unique pathway for themselves, a mix of indigenous elements, brilliant adaptations, and an unsurpassed precision in making things. For most of its history Japan determined which foreign influences it took in, reshaping them to render them consistent with the evolving traditions of the nation. Indeed, isolation has been seen as necessary to sustain the sense of national self, the essential Japan, rendering the desire for separation from the rest of the world more powerful than any need for cross-border synchrony. Thus cultural continuity and national isolation have enabled and encouraged each other. But it is becoming harder to sustain both Japan's national isolation, and the reproduction of Japan's lovingly maintained traditions, some of which suggest the Neolithic.

Japan still seems closer to the Neolithic than other industrialized societies, though there is artifice about it. Japan manages itself as Neolithic in the way that Singapore manages itself as modern: by design. Japan knows that nature is terrible: this is a land of earthquakes, tsunamis, fires and *kamikazes*—and sudden death is always close at hand. So Japan has made a pet of nature, in its mannered celebration of the seasons and the pine plantations on the hillsides. The Neolithic calendar is more important than elsewhere. The whole country has been planted with cherry blossom trees that flower in April, and maple trees that turn red in late November[61] and everyone is attuned to the rhythm of this studied ritual of natural colour. At cherry blossom time, which is as significant in Japan as Thanksgiving in the USA, though the occasions have little else in common, there are parties all over the nation. Rice farming is still the true Japan. Japan's policies of agricultural protection seem even harder to shift than those provided for wheat farmers in Kansas or cheese-makers in France. Rice is no longer a form of currency in Japan as it once was, and was in much of Asia. But it continues to be central to identity in Japan at a level unmatched in staple crops elsewhere in the industrialized world, though there are older parallels in the role of bread in mediaeval Europe, potatoes in Ireland or maize in Mesoamerica. Likewise, the tea ceremony also connects to the long memory of Japan. The favoured style of ceramics for the tea ceremony has always been rough hewn, deliberately primitive with maker's flaws included. The most valued pieces are those that speak of the most distant past. Further, 'the philosophy behind Japanese food culture appears to be a paradoxical belief that no cooking is the best kind of cooking.'[62] Once, all food was eaten raw. Again the cultural reflex is to acknowledge the ancestors, whose spirits are alive and with us today, by living as they had lived in the distant past. This is the animist essence of Shinto.

In Kyoto, the cultural capital of Japan and seat of the emperor for most of the nation's history, thousands of mediaeval Buddhist temples and Shinto shrines and a smaller number of castles and noble houses are maintained. These are positioned in grounds, gardens and ponds that are closely related to the buildings. Often the founding design has survived, particularly in the gardens. The most visited sites are in pristine condition. Many are staggeringly beautiful. Kyoto is one of the jewels of the Earth. It is as if the Forum of late Republican Rome or the Mayan temples of Palenque in Mexico were open to today's visitors in more or less their original state. Each week many thousands of tourists pass through Kyoto and also the earlier imperial capital of Nara which is one hour away by train. Most visitors are from within Japan, and many of them observe religious forms at the temples and shrines. These sites are not archaeological relics. Astonishingly, they are living parts of today's Japan. In Kyoto the great temple of Kiyomizu-dera, founded in 798 C.E. and rebuilt under the third Tokugawa shogun Iemitsu in 1633, perches on the edge of the mountains in Southern Higashiyama like a sentential watching over the city.[63] Japan's ancient visual icons, such as the vermillion *tori* gates at the entrance to every shrine, and the ubiquitous Mount Fuji, flicker through every facet of popular culture. But the habit of cultural reproduction is deeper than these regular observances suggest. It is manifest at the level of relations and values and runs through almost every field of creative endeavour. The same design motifs and variations continually recur. Likewise institutional forms and social relations recycle, though from time to time they change. Writing on Japanese nationalism and globalization Takashi Inoguchi remarks that:

> Japanese cultural nationalism allows the selective absorption of the global diffusion of foreign ideas, institutions and technologies in a facile and nonchalant fashion, but does not let those penetrate society easily. Japanese culture's deep traditions normally stand in the way of globalization's penetrating processes...Why and how the Japanese nation has kept its cultural identity sufficiently intact despite all the vicissitudes it has experienced throughout the modern century is a matter for serious consideration.[64]

The point applies not just to the modern century but to the last 1500 years. Japan remains astonishing in the extent of its cultural maintenance. It is dif-

ficult for most modern societies, where continuous transformation and the idea
of progress and futures are so determining, to understand the contemporary
role of the traditional in Japan, including the role of the lineage of tribe and
self in identity. Most families still return each year to the place seen as the family seat where the ancestors are located. Yet progress and innovation are also
central motifs in Japan. Industry constantly innovates in areas like urban
design and computerized animation. There is always tension between on one
hand tradition, on the other mobility and modernity. But the balance between
tradition and modernity differs from that found in Western nations, and also
from China where modernization is more exclusive and complete than in
Japan. As Yoshio Sugimoto argues, one reason is the key role of the nation-
state in national identity. 'While changing its form of authority, the state
remains strong and keeps moulding national culture despite the increasing
globalization of the economy and technology.'[65] At the same time, 'the spread
of globalization and the rise of cultural nationalism constitute an interactive
process.'[66] National culture and globalization are mutually transforming and
interpenetrated. This means that human agency in Japan cannot be bound by
the national dimension alone, no matter how determined the state, especially as the global dimension grows in importance.

EARLY NATION: TAIKA

The resistance of Japan to immigration is symptomatic of its isolation.
Immigration is viewed as a loss of control. After all, it has happened at least
once, deep in Japanese pre-history—and the ancestors of the present population were the disturbers of the peace. In the last millennium B.C.E. the Jomon
were progressively displaced and pushed into northern Honshu and Hakkaido
by waves of immigrants later known as the Yayoi, who probably came from the
Korean peninsula. They brought with them bronze and iron technologies and
productive wet-rice farming. Trade and warfare quickened. Dozens of incipient kingdoms were gradually absorbed into a loosely consolidated polity in
the Yamato region of mid Honshu, centred on the Nara area. The Yamato
rulers, some of whom were women, were buried in increasingly monumental
tombs. Erected on the scale of similar structures in much of the ancient
world, these suggest a growing accumulation of wealth. Building techniques,
measurements and furnishings became standardized. External decorative features indicate some Chinese influence but were always distinctively Japanese.
In the fourth century C.E. the interior grave goods suggest rising East Asian
influences. There were several Yamato military interventions in Korea. The first
verifiable Japanese emperor dates from this time.

The next two centuries were the high time of Japan's openness to East

Asia. In the mid-fifth century C.E., Chinese writing was introduced from the Korean kingdom of Paekche. A century later Buddhism followed from the same source. The new religion was promoted by the Yamato rulers as a means of unification. Buddhism was a reforming, modernizing influence that encouraged scholarship, artistic expression and social design. Buddhist temples became repositories of technical knowledge. Many different Buddhist sects were to emerge. Buddhism was welcomed into Japan alongside the traditional animist religion of Shinto, which continued to sustain most of the day-to-day rituals. Shinto, 'the way of the gods' (*kami*), drew on ideas of a ubiquitous spirit world populated by spirits and ancestors. Eventually, in a long process of assimilation, Buddhism and Shinto joined together as the national religion of Japan, sharing many sacred sites while retaining distinctive organizations. It was a heterogeneous pairing, and the relationship began as plural, but it became more hybrid over time.

Thus Shinto tradition and mystery was joined to Buddhist cultural sophistication. The timeless ancestral religion of life in the world, Shinto, was joined to the Buddhist afterlife. The result was a flexible set of ideas that could be put to differing uses. All modes of time were accessible, subject positions were flexible, and almost any strategic position could be accessed—reactionary, conservative, innovative, transformative or transcendent—though some were easier to access than others. The duality of Shinto and Buddhism installed in *Nihonjinron,* constructed Japaneseness, a paradoxical quality, whereby each recreation of old Japan, the changing notions of the essential nation, were mobilized to drive a bold new departure. If Buddhism was the modernizing force, a primary source of ideas for social improvement (later the modernizing function shifted to the *daimyo,* the economy and the state machine), at the same time Shinto allowed the Japanese to embrace new realities—provided they could convince themselves that the novelty was already-existing and sanctioned by the ancestors. Nevertheless the veneration of tradition in the world, that was inherent in Shinto and remained undisturbed by Buddhist notions of the ephemeral present and the afterlife, forced cultural evolution into a punctuated rhythm. A backward-looking approach to tradition meant that changes in human practice were difficult to achieve. But at rare intervals, when the conditions and pressures for change had accumulated sufficiently and the will for change could be installed at the centre of the state, astonishing reinventions of the nation could take place.

The proto-state engineered synthesis of Shinto and Buddhism also established the characteristic Japanese method of dealing with cross-border influences. As noted, the essence of this method was to layer the incoming foreign ideas with essentially Japanese elements. The new ideas were translated into the national context before being absorbed. Once tamed in this manner their contents could be tapped without displacing existing cultural practices or disrupting an autarkic national self-determination. The assimilating-hybrid element became dominant over the initial plurality. It enfolded an asymmetry between national and foreign in which the former never lost control. Today most Japanese people describe themselves as both Shinto and Buddhist, and understand both religions to be essentially Japanese.[67]

Likewise when government was being consolidated Japan's rulers drew on more developed ideas from China but adapted these into Japanese forms. The constitution of 604 C.E. propagated by the regent Prince Shotoku contained a strong Confucian flavour. It emphasized harmony and hard work. This was followed by the Taika reform, the first of the great top-down makings of the Japanese polity. Like the later Edo and Meiji reforms it both created a central state machine and transformed economic, social and cultural life. A code of law was enacted. Through careful, incremental negotiations with the noble families landholdings were nationalized and allocated. Serfdom was abolished and all persons defined as imperial subjects. These changes were achieved on the basis of a cultural consensus that was underpinned by the ideological authority of the emperor. 'Taika period Japan is a singular example of a society attempting to set up a centralized imperial form of government without a strong element of armed force and preliminary conquest.'[68] A centralized bureaucracy was created under the authority of the emperor, with the capacity to raise taxes. However, Japan did not follow the Chinese practice of admitting to high rank scholars who were successful in competitive examination. Birth remained the only determinant of rank. The priesthood was the only way that someone from the lower classes could rise in the world—here Buddhism again showed itself as the modernizer—but the highest places in government remained the preserve of the leading hereditary nobility, which was resident in the imperial court. The lesser aristocracy headed up Japan's five hundred districts. They too were defined as servants of the emperor. In the early eight century the imperial family supported the preparation of historical works which legitimized its power through claims of divine descent.[69]

The outcome was a Confucian polity shaped for Japanese conditions. In 710 C.E. the first permanent capital was created at Nara with a Department of State, a Department of Worship confined to Shinto, and the Buddhist temple of Toda-ji with a huge bronze image of the Buddha, then the largest wooden building in the world. The capital was moved to Kyoto (Heian) in 794. By then the Southern Island of Kyushu had been fully absorbed and Japan was unified into a single nation, except for the Ainu resistance in Northern Honshu. The central government maintained a standing army to guard against possible attack from Korea or a revitalized Tang dynasty China. A serious defeat in Korea in 662 persuaded the Japanese to adopt a solely defensive policy, which persisted for the next 900 years.[70] Cross-border influences weakened. National evolution became more dominated by indigenous agency.

NATIONAL CULTURE

In the Heian period (9th-12th centuries CE) strong central government continued for the first three generations. Gradually, however, the emperors became largely reduced to puppets of the Fujiwara and other leading families. The locally-based nobility enhanced its independence, recruited samauri retainers and focused its creative energies on military innovations and adventures. The role of the bureaucracy and the temples ebbed and flowed. The threat of foreign invasion receded and no large-scale irrigation works were required. These factors diminished the potential role of the state, compared to Egypt, the Middle East, Mesoamerica and Southeast Asia. A desultory national leadership maintained the forms but was mostly unstable, always contested, and episodically fragmented by armed conflict. Nevertheless, much as when the Holy Roman Empire, with its echoes of Augustus, exercised a lopsided authority—instrumentally weak and ideologically powerful—in mediaeval central Europe, in Japan the weakened nation-state was able to maintain some sway over the islands. The notion of a centralized polity had been implanted. The Taika reforms and Nara period had 'laid the foundations of later administrative systems.'[71] And significantly, despite the ebb of centralized national power, agricultural productivity and internal trade grew and it was a flourishing time for national culture. Culture moved more independently and on a higher plane. Buddhism flourished as the centre of learning within an identifiably Japanese civilization. Though art and architecture began by reflecting strong Chinese influences, as in many other fields, 'after 800 a more creative process produced distinctively Japanese styles.'[72] Typical shrine buildings were a crafted synthesis of Shinto and Buddhist forms. In painting, the last century of the Heian period saw the rise of Japanese techniques, which replaced the curved lines and soft colours typical of Chinese temple art with angular lines and more brilliant motifs and applied the new approach to scroll painting. In China scrolls had been chiefly used for panoramic views of landscapes and cities. In Japan they became used for narratives. In music, Korean and Chinese forms were increasingly supplemented by Japanese instruments and composition.

Literature also flourished. In about 900 C.E. a phonetic system was developed that enabled people to write in readily intelligible Japanese, though for some time Chinese remained the language of business and official documents.

Literacy branched between prose works in the Japanese mother-tongue, many of which were composed by upper-class women able to exercise significant social agency, and works in Chinese by men. Surviving prose in Japanese from this period, including the court diaries (*nikki*), exhibit immediacy and a marvelous flexibility in communicating subtle emotion. *The Tale of Genji* written by the court-lady Murasaki Shikibu in about 1004 is regarded as the world's first psychological novel. It is remarkably true to life, drawing closely on the author's life observations, and also broad in social coverage. Thus the move to Japaneseness, the indigenous creation in language form, enabled the new form of literature. Short forms of poetry by both men and women also flourished. The forms were strict and on the face of it, limited. In the tenth century the dominant poetry consisted of five line tanka; later it was three line haiku with their 5–7–5 syllable form and standardized allusions to nature and the seasons. The minimalist and allusive nature of poetry paralleled the later introduction of the zen *karesansui* rock and sand gardens at the centre of temples, designed to facilitate contemplation. The austere regime of zen Buddhism was especially attractive to the samauri (warrior) class. *Karesansui* can be repeatedly viewed without yielding a single meaning.

The minimalism, ambiguity, paradox and naturalized asymmetry abundant in this period still lie at the heart of Japanese aesthetics. Japan's aesthetic tradition ties the distant Neolithic to the ever-changing now in the eye of the beholder. Neither the past nor the present can be exhaustively known. Thus the origins of Japaneseness remain forever shrouded, while at the same time its contents are not static but are left free to evolve over time. Creative cultures benefit from this kind of bounded openness and can also profit from the lack of answers. Minimalism makes room for a soaring imagination. Unlike its aesthetic opposite, which is the abundant European baroque, the zen aesthetic does not prescribe the forms that creativity might take. Creative cultures also gain from the mainstreaming of their principles and the spread of their most elegant designs. The later Heian period 'saw the beginnings of an emphasis in culture on the provinces and commoners, and a movement away from religion as a source of inspiration.'[73] Painting moved from preoccupation with devotional abstractions to life as it was lived in the everyday world. The principles of Heian aesthetics and some of its specific motifs became absorbed into the cultural forms used in commerce and administration.

THE DAIMYO

Beginning with the ascension of Minamoto Yoritomo to the shogunate in 1192, the four centuries until 1600 are characterized as the 'feudal' period of Japanese history. There were continuous innovations in technology, commerce and the arts. The decentralization of power from the Kyoto region encouraged the strengthening of local farming, mining, manufacturing and commerce under the protection of local *daimyo* across much of the country. Trade with China stimulated economic activity in Japan. This period also saw the ripening of the zen-influenced *no* drama[74]—in which the pause without action is as important as action—and the *cha-no-yu* (tea ceremony), and *ikebana* (flower arranging). As in the Mayan zone (chapter five), 'a common cultural life, disseminated by travelers, proved stronger than political divisions.'[75] Yet because cultural commonality and economic dynamism were not associated with political coherence, the material benefits they promised were undermined. The aesthetic principles of the day included *wabi* (subdued taste), *sabi* (elegant simplicity) and *kare* (severe and unadorned).[76] But these principles were negated in the conflicts between the great military houses, in which the motif was not restraint but a grasping at excess.

In the dominance of the *daimyo* aristocracy, paralleling much of mediaeval Europe, the Taika/Nara system reached a final fragmentation. The emperor retained symbolic power and an unquestionable primacy in Japanese hearts—the throne was (and still is) the repository of Japaneseness, which was the whole meaning of life. But Neolithic essence could not power the machinery of state, and an emperor that sought to be powerful in the world, like the mediaeval papacy, ran up against stern resistance. Go-Daigo (1288–1339) attempted unsuccessfully to restore a Nara-like authority to the throne. He was deposed, struggled militarily and returned, and was then marginalized by a rival throne that was occupied by a tame emperor in the familiar role of pawn to the *daimyo*. The real national leadership continued to be exercised by shoguns, but as the regional lords became stronger the shogun's control also deteriorated. The shoguns did not control enough of the levers of power. For example the Hojo shogunate at Kamakura capably organized the national defence against the Mongols, but after Kublai Khan's invasion was withdrawn, the Hojo regime could not pay all of the Japanese troops. Though most expected the Chinese to return, the national army could not be sustained. Hojo authority fell away.

In the fifteenth century the country slipped into a period of continuous civil war that lasted for a hundred years, the Sengoku (Warring States) era. From 1467–1477 the Onin War was fought between two armies contending for control. They were based in different parts of Kyoto and fought each other building by building, completely devastating the city. Kyoto became a 'field of fire.' Few temples survived. Those sites that were not burned were looted. War spread throughout Japan. Central authority vanished. Free to operate as they saw fit, the provincial daimyo learned that distance bred autonomy, while proximity enabled control. They invited their own warrior retainers to live near the main castle of the domain.[77] Meanwhile the larger Buddhist temples maintained armies of their own. Gangs of masterless samurai roamed the countryside. It was almost as destructive as the Thirty Years War of religion in seventeenth-century Europe. That period in Europe triggered a profound shift in common values, towards a more secular culture and the international order based on national sovereignty created by the Peace of Westphalia (1648). Likewise, the agonizing immolation of timeless Japan on the Onin-Sengoku bonfire, lit by egoistic *daimyo* and fanned by *bushido* (the warrior code), was to become the platform for the re-assertion of *Nihonjinron*. The lessons learned from the Sengoku were the resurrection of the nation-state, the taming of the *daimyo* and samurai in the interests of the nation, and the end of war, in the most remarkable of all the makings of Japan.

Punctuated Evolution: Edo

In the 1540s Europeans arrived and saw the possibilities. Civil war provided the Other with opportunities to hijack the path of nationally-controlled evolution. The Portuguese and Spaniards thought they had found a polity ripe for the politics of divide and rule which had just been used to smash the Atzec and Inca empires in the Americas, and a population ripe for conversion to Catholicism. Japan's feuding *daimyo* were more interested in the potentials offered by European guns, though some saw firearms as a breach of *bushido*. Meanwhile the Iberian powers sought to strengthen their position in Japan by managing its silk trade with China. China had suspended direct dealings with Japan because of Japanese pirate activity.[78]

However, in the second half of the sixteenth century the polity in Japan began to transform. Given the growing European presence it was just in time. What changed was the emergence of charismatic leaders able to win at warfare. In Rome before Augustus a succession of leading figures in the Republic achieved personal military ascendancy and temporary political control: Marius, Sulla, Pompey and then Julius Casear. In Japan three successive national unifiers emerged, gathering an ascending authority. The first was Oda Nobunaga, who conquered more than half of the country. Nobunaga was ruthless. He set aside tradition when he needed to. He used firearms as it suited him and broke the power of the independent Buddhist sects. On the hillside of Hieizan in Kyoto Nobunaga burned 3000 buildings of the vast Enryakuji temple complex with thousands of monks and warriors inside. The religious element in Japanese life begins to ebb at this time.[79] Nobunaga promoted the Christians as a counter-weight to the temples. He also began a process of modernization, surveying the land, redistributing territories and standardizing weights and masures. After Nobunaga was trapped and forced to commit suicide by one of his generals in 1582 he was succeeded by another general Toyotomi Hideyoshi, the second unifier. Equally brilliant in the field and a better negotiator than Nobunaga, within a decade Hideyoshi was supreme dictator of Japan.[80] Hideyoshi consolidated his political power by commanding the families of major provincial daimyo to take up residence in his headquarters at Osaka castle, restricting the capacity for rebellion. He continued Nobunaga's early modernization policies. Between 1582 and 1598 the natural and economic resources of the whole nation were surveyed—Japan's Domesday Book moment, enabling an update of the tax base[81]—and instigating religious reforms, temple rebuilding and urban infrastructure. The dictator compulsorily collected all swords and other weapons from the farming caste and began to enforce a firmer social differentiation between farmers and samurai. Hideyoshi himself had risen from a warrior-peasant family. His social reforms were designed to fix the membership of social castes by birth so that the ambiguity and upward mobility that had characterized his own career would become impossible. Increasingly concerned about potential invasion by Spain, Hideyoshi reversed Nobunaga's tolerance of Christians, who had obtained a substantial foothold in the Southern island of Kyushu. However, after a small number of executions persecutions were halted.

On his death Hideyoshi left a five-year-old son as heir. Government by a council of noble regents and five administrative commissioners soon broke down. The strongest daimyo proved to be Tokugawa Ieyasu, the chief vassal of Hideyoshi, whose power base was centered on Edo (present day Tokyo). In 1600 at Sekigahara north of Kyoto Ieyasu defeated a force led by one of the commissioners, Ishida Mitsnari. In Japan this is known as 'the battle for the world.' It was a main turning point in the nation. In 1603, a year in which William Shakespeare was working on versions of *Othello*, *King Lear* and *Macbeth*, Ieyasu, the third unifier of Japan, was granted the title of shogun by the emperor. Twelve years later the remaining Toyotomi forces were destroyed at Osaka Castle. This finally freed Ieyasu to build a stable regime on the base created by Nobunaga and Hideyoshi. The Tokugawa-Edo regime was to last for two hundred and fifty years. Ieyasu, who considered every decision with an eye for the long term, is one of the great figures of human history and the supreme architect of contemporary Japan.

The Tokugawa-Edo settlement implemented systematically by Ieyasu, his obedient son Hidetada and his able grandson Iemitsu, remade Japan just as Augustus remade Rome. The Edo settlement was a pre-industrial modernization as brilliant and remarkable as was the Roman settlement. The Tokugawa objective, which was achieved more completely and last longer than the

Roman settlement, was to transcend the Sengoku by recasting Japan on a secure and stable basis. As with the Augustan settlement, the centerpiece of the Edo settlement was the restoration, renovation and remaking of national tradition. Here the paradoxical duality at the heart of *Nihonjinron* showed itself. The object of the Edo settlement was to fix in place Tokugawa Ieyasu's idea of the eternal Japan by renovating or transforming all of its major sectors. Half a century of accelerated innovation followed. As in Rome the Edo regime did not establish a long-term momentum for modernization and later the balance shifted back towards reproduction and quiescence. There was less sclerosis in the regime and the nation than in the later Roman Empire because Edo Japan did not face military and administrative problems on the Roman scale that drove continuing growth in the state machine; because the pronounced devolution always part of the Tokugawa polity and economy allowed continuing innovations at the grass-roots throughout the period, because the great landowners nevertheless were unable to accumulate as much independent power as in the later Roman Empire when central authority weakened; because the leaders of the Japanese state continued to support a dynamic commercial sector; and because they remained curious about new ideas.

For Ieyasu the first priority was to stabilize central authority, which was both the essential instrument of immediate pacification and the means for remaking the nation. The *shogun* took control of harbours, towns, mines and other areas that were strategic in military or economic terms. Geographical mobility within the country was severely restricted, in a manner that now seems unimaginable—wheeled transport was banned, people wanting to travel required written authority, checkpoints were established, and initially many bridges were destroyed so as to channel passage thorough controlled areas. Ocean-going vessels were closely monitored. The restriction of people movement underlines the pre-industrial nature of the settlement, in which neither unregulated commerce nor unregulated manufacture were seen as sacrosanct. It did not prevent the development of economic production and trade, which were important priorities of the regime, but ensured that precisely because of its intrinsic and political importance, economic life would be closely supervised by the state. *Daimyo* were required to spend every second year at the Tokugawa headquarters in Edo with their families kept there permanently as hostages. As under Hideyoshi but on a larger scale, the regular passage of *daimyo* and their retainers was a major stimulus to economic activity, and it infused in the *daimyo* a dual national/local imagination.[82] *Daimyo* had to seek the permission of the *shogun* to build or extend castles and for the marriage of themselves and their heirs. Over time this transformed the nobility from an independent fighting warrior class into a tamed courtier class. Those *daimyo* who had supported the Tokugawa prior to Sekigahara in 1600 were granted privileges but a feature of the Edo regime was its comprehensive character. As in Rome, aside from the regime's incorrigible opponents all persons were incorporated into the new order.

Continuing the process begun by Hideyoshi, Japanese society was divided conclusively into four social castes: samurai, farmers, artisans and merchants. Social mobility was banned. The samurai, who no longer had wars to fight, became administrators and managers for the *daimyo* and the Edo state machine. The code of *bushido* was modernized to reinforce filial obedience while portraying the samurai as moral exemplars of national values. This tied the warriors more securely to the agenda of the regime while reducing prospects of a military breakout. There samurai were internally differentiated, with the noble families elevated above the rest. In practice the distinctions between farmers, artisans and peasants were difficult to enforce but the line between the sword-wearing samurai and the rest was closely maintained.

Tokugawa ascendancy was facilitated by the quality of the early shoguns after Ieyasu, who followed his written legacy and expanded creatively on it. It was also fortunate in the dynastic stability of the family, in sharp contrast to the Roman experience. Single family regimes and their collective apparatus are rarely reproduced as effectively as this. Nor was there any challenge from the standing army, often the harbinger of political change in Rome. Unlike Rome the Edo regime did not need an army to defend itself against the barbarian. The barbarian Other was an idea with which to strength national identity, as it had been in Rome, but until the arrival of the American fleet in 1853 it was never a practical problem. This meant that the only meaningful challenge to the Edo regime would have been a military challenge from among the *daimyo*—but who would want to return to the Sengoku? Primarily, however, the Tokugawa succeeded because like Augustus they established a stable machine that worked through rather than against other centres of power. In keeping with Japanese tradition the regime sustained considerable devolution of authority to the provincial nobility[83] and the priesthood, a greater extent of devolution than in Rome. At the same time, like Augustus it enmeshed the elite in a complex web of roles, obligations and responsibilities. This stabilized central control, much longer than in Rome.[84] Here the Edo regime also benefited from the larger role played by tradition in *Nihonjinron*, compared to the function of the *mos maiorum* in Rome (which after Augustus became increasingly undermined by the larger inclusion of a diverse Empire). The Edo regime always rested on the authority of the emperor, though it was careful to maintain the throne's state of dependence on the shogunate. Above all, the regime benefited from its ability to draw part of the samurai caste into the *baku-*

fu, the corps of state officials. The samurai, constituting about 5 per cent of the national population, enjoyed relatively high social status. They were characteristically self-disciplined and were often intellectually and aesthetically competent. The *bakufu* functioned on the basis of precedent, deliberation and consensus and longer term bureaucratic interest. They imagined themselves, the regime, the nation and its timeless tradition as one and the same. They were the ideal technicians of *Nihonjinron*. The transition of the military to a caste of educated bureaucrats was completed early, in the first three generations of Tokugawa ascendancy.[85] The most enduring outcome of the Edo period was to be a coherent nation-state machine that saw itself as the guardian of the national character.

Other samurai served the 300 provincial *daimyo* as *han* officials. The *han* directly controlled three quarters of the country, the shogun and *bakufu* the remaining quarter. With the *daimyo* absent for long periods provincial authority passed to locally based councils and officials, some of which fostered modernization initiatives. Both the state and provincial bureaucracies exercised rights of taxation in their own domains and had obligations of care, while the *bakufu* monopolized the strategically important national functions such as religion, monetary policy, relations with the throne in Kyoto, civil peace and foreign contact. The shogun retained the right to intervene directly in an individual *han*. There were too many officials and duplication was inevitable, but over time these plural administrations were closely interwoven in a coherent *baku-han* system. In contrast with the fragmented nature of most of Europe at the time, but consistent with the stronger nation-states that emerged in Europe later, in the nineteenth century, Edo Japan functioned as a single country with one set of laws, though jurisdiction was divided.[86] This sustained provincial autonomy alongside national control within a common political culture devoted to social order and public welfare.[87]

NATIONAL CHARACTER

The Edo settlement enforced conformity to given social and cultural values more effectively and in greater detail than the Augustan settlement in Rome, which was least effective at the level of regulation of family life and personal conduct.[88] The Edo-renovated national values emphasized Confucianism, without naming it as such. Thus they highlighted obedience and education but weakened the freedom and social standing of women. Detailed and differential codes of conduct were applied to all four classes, including the design of homes, clothing and food. Regulation of dress and housing was especially important to the regime because these were signs of status. The Edo regime was more successful than the Roman emperors in controlling status display.[89]

Personal conduct was closely supervised. 'Rude behaviour' was a capital offence, defined as 'acting in an unexpected manner,'[90] a formulation which allowed the authorities to insert deference to national traditions and conventions as a normal requirement. Anti-social conduct was monitored by secret police. Parents and village elders could be made responsible for the conduct of children and subordinates. Edo reinforced the social values of obedience to authority, collective responsibility and public spiritedness, and behaving as expected. These values have outlasted the Edo period. Visitors to Japan testify to the complete conformity to traffic signals and the litter-free urban precincts, 140 years after the end of the Tokugawa regime. These apparently trivial examples suggest that conformity in Japan has deeper cultural roots than a particular authoritarian state, regardless of whether the communal values were originally formed by the state or appeared independently of it. In Japanese the term *seikatsu* refers to the everyday life that people make for themselves, individually and collectively, in which they produce and improve their lot. As human societies develop, their civil capacity for *seikatsu* grows and becomes one of the repositories of custom and innovation.[91] As the Edo period proceeded, evidence began to accumulate of popular detachment from the machinery of the nation-state as the memory of Iyeasu's military victory faded. But there was no evidence of detachment from the national tradition that Edo had renovated, enforced and supported—that abiding sense of what is was to be Japanese that was the Neolithic *raison d'etre* of the regime, even more than was national economic prosperity.

Notwithstanding the depth of state control, the Edo period was dynamic in many areas. The notion that the Tokugawa-Edo regime can be dismissed as a 'feudal' (meaning backward) formation, which was perpetuated by the nineteenth-century Meiji reformers and also by American and European politicians and commentators who wanted to prise open Japan for their own purposes, is far from the truth.[92] Edo Japan was highly urbanized for its time. Within a century of the peace created by Sekigahara the national population had doubled and by 1720 Edo was the world's most populous city, a distinction it still holds today.[93] Trade expanded spectacularly as a result of the social order under Edo. Merchants were supervised less closely than the samurai and the farmers who were tied to the land. Over time merchants accumulated capital by providing goods and services to the *daimyo*, and also loans to the *daimyo*, individual samurai and later to the bureaucracy itself.[94] Internal tolls and customs barriers were scrapped, and the currency, weights and measures received definitive standardization.[95] By linking the administration of Edo, Osaka, Kyoto and Nagasaki the shogunate established a framework of market exchange on a national scale. The money economy spread well into the countryside and became increasingly dynamic. Prosperous farmers drove much of the nation's economic activity. Outside the cities political authority was decentralized but economic life was integrated into a single system. The *bakufu* was able to adapt to and facilitate the growing role of commercial finance:[96] though commerce was regulated politically its economic autonomy was respected. From the seventeenth century onwards, notwithstanding the Edo caste structure, the economy also drove a more complex division of labour. This evolved along with continuous advances of technology and productivity in agriculture and fishing.[97] By the mid-nineteenth century the workforce in Japan had developed as 'disciplined, skilled, educated and mobile.'[98] Living standards rose and the middle class expanded throughout the years of Tokugawa rule.[99] Metallurgy and silk weaving forged ahead. There was an outpouring of ceramics. Both the samurai and merchants led patterns of consumption. Most of the items of daily living that are considered typically Japanese had their origins in the Edo period. Merchants were lightly taxed, though from time to time forced loans were imposed on wealthy individuals. Classically, state revenues were generated mainly by farm production. At the end of the Edo period the regime found itself chronically short of cash. Non-agricultural revenues were expanded, including levies on merchants, but this was not enough, and deficit financing became installed in government, a habit that still persists in public finance.[100]

Urban infrastructure and utilities and public health, which benefited from being managed by the shogun and the Edo *bakufu*, were well ahead of the prevailing provision in Europe and North America. The road network was expanded and improved across the nation. When Japan faced a deforestation crisis in the second half of the seventeenth century, the regime took the far-sighted measures celebrated by Jared Diamond in *Collapse* (2005). It slowed population growth, increased subsistence from fisheries and reduced dependence on rice farming, slowed land clearing, reduced timber harvesting, and started planting. Laws concerning logging were strictly enforced. By 1800 the decline in timber production had been reversed. Today four-fifths of Japan's land area is covered by plantation forest.[101] Education was especially strong in comparative terms. By the end of the Edo period approximately one third of the population of 30 million people were literate, including half of the men, and all samurai children male or female, a rate of literacy much higher than in Western Europe. A broad network of institutions was operating, including 11,000 village schools, a strong starting point for acclerated modernization in the Meiji period that followed.[102] Japanese education was mostly Confucian, but the Edo period saw the emergence of a distinctive school of national learning (*kokugaku-ha*) which was neo-Shinto in temper and focused on Japanese traditions. This lent itself to national exceptionalism and there was a xenophobic tone to some *kokugaku* work. Yet it was more open to innovations in national life, including selective westernizations, than were the Confucian traditions—always providing that the *kami* and the emperor were honoured.[103]

Merchants supported innovations in the performing arts such as the visual and mobile *kabuki* drama, the *bunraku* (puppet theatre) and the performing *geisha*. Novels were further developed, and the allusive and evocative *haiku* was invented by Matsuo Basho (1644–1694). Innovations in indigenous visual arts continued. These included the *ukiyoe* (wood-block prints) in both portrait and landscape modes. The best known by Katsushika Hokusai (1760–1849) and Ando Hiroshige (1797–1858) portrayed views of Mount Fuji and scenes along the Tokaido highway in which iconic national symbols were nested in daily life. The *ukiyoe* were widely disseminated within Japan. Later they excited nineteenth-century European visitors and influenced impressionism and post-impressionism in painting and interior decoration. Monet and van Gough were among those who produced Japanese-influenced works at the time.

NATIONAL CLOSURE

As in the later Heian period and the years that followed, in the Edo period the main sources of its innovations were indigenous to Japan. Unlike the later Heian period this was a matter of conscious choice. The country might have become infused with Europeanization, like most of Asia after 1600. But in seeking to render predictable the relations between Japan and the rest of the world, and manage the impact of foreign knowledge and values within Japan, the Tokugawa took the most simple approach. They blocked cross-border relations and from 1639 onwards implemented the era of *sakoku* (secluded country). Japan was closed to the outside world and vice versa. In doing so Japan adopted an approach which had been favoured by China in the fifteenth century, but unlike the Chinese government the Edo regime was strong enough to enforce almost complete isolation and maintain it. Isolation was introduced by stages. In the first part of the seventeenth century the shogun licensed Japanese traders with Vietnam, the Philippines and Thailand, hoping to circumvent the cultural problems created by foreign traders. Within Japan, the Hideyoshi edicts against the Christians were invoked, missionaries were expelled and after 1618 there was full-scale persecution. By then no *daimyo* were Christian. Christians were forced underground and in the absence of contact with its spiritual home in Europe the religion steadily weakened over time. All contact with Spain was terminated by the *bakufu* in the 1620s. In 1638 there was an uprising by Japanese Christians in southern Kyushu. This was the final trigger for *sakoku*. Overseas travel was banned and all Japanese abroad were forbidden to return. Japanese trade voyages were stopped. Catholic Westerners were banned, a decree directed at the Portuguese. A handful of Protestant Dutch were maintained on an isolated island near Nagasaki to facilitate trade with China and the rest of the world. The conduct of the Dutch was directly regulated by the *bakufu*. The *bakufu* also authorized trade with China and Korea via the islands of Okinawa and Tsushima respectively, and with the Ainu on Hokkaido, which had not yet been fully incorporated into Japan. The Korean trade was the most important. Several hundred Japanese were stationed at the permanent trading station of Pusan in southern Korea with the approval of the *bakufu*.[104] There were frequent diplomatic contacts between Japan and Korea, though not with China.[105]

The small Dutch enclave was important because it became the point of entry for new scientific and medical knowledge from Europe. *Sakoku* largely cut Japan off from European discoveries after 1650. At that time Japan was the technological equal of Europe. Two hundred years later this was no longer the case, conspicuously so in the military field. That was the price that was paid for the maintenance of total Japanese control over the nation's own social, commercial and cultural evolution in the Edo period. The result was that when modernization did occur it took place on Japanese-directed terms but had to be compressed. However, before the Edo regime fell, most highly placed and educated Japanese were aware of the gap between Japan and the West. They were informed by *rangaku*, a distinct field of Japanese-based learning that drew its foundational data from Europe via the Dutch enclave at Nagasaki. Increasingly this provided new insights in medicine, geography, navigation, astronomy and weapons.[106] Another source was Chinese treatises on Western knowledge. The indirect acquisition of Western learning by these methods was belated, slow and partial. Still, dissemination of new knowledge within Japan was effective because of the high literacy level. Christopher Bayly notes that 'as in Europe, there was an interesting conjuncture between print, learning and commerce. Great Japanese firms developed their own systems of commercial reporting and market research and sometimes had the products printed and sold.'[107] In the late Edo period the regime sent delegations to Western Europe and the United States in search of military and industrial techniques.[108] New ideas were tested according to validation methods that had been developed to resolve disputes among Confucian scholars. This entailed an observation-based empirical approach that facilitated the handling of new technologies.[109] Nevertheless, the move in the face of new ideas was always to turn them into Japanese ones.

The ultimate success of the *sakoku* closure was that it was absorbed into the popular and enduring understanding of Japaneseness. Consistent with the sense of national superiority and exceptionalism, it reinforced *Nihonjinron* and became integral to it. Like the late Western Roman emperors, the shoguns lost popular support when they could no longer guarantee the national border. The Tokugawa regime wanted to manage a transition to what it knew was an inevitable foreign engagement but could not prevent the myriad of humiliations meted out to the Japanese in trade conducted on lop-sided terms and enforced by foreign ships and soldiers on Japan's soil. The regime went down to the cry of *sonno joi!* ('revere the emperor and expel the barbarian!'). Thus the new interface with the world under the Meiji regime was opened by a strident rejection of engagement, and the hyper-modernization of the Meiji period was driven by a potent claim for tradition. The paradoxical flexibility of *Nihonjinron* once more revealed itself in the hour of crisis. Japan transformed itself into new, continually changing and of the foreign Other—so as to again assert itself as always separate and forever divine.

Punctuated Evolution: Meiji

The later Tokugawa shoguns ruled as heads of committee rather than by personal fiat. Not all were strong and effective. The reflexive capabilities of the system weakened. The energetic reforming shoguns tended to be those who emphasized national tradition, built state power and restrained entrepreneurial initiative. Those who favoured economic freedoms tended to be more lax in administration and tolerant of corruption. This polarity in the political culture was to outlast the Edo period. As Part III shows, in contemporary Japan it confers on quasi-market New Public Management (NPM) reforms, in sectors such as higher education, a distinctively top-down and conservative character. Moves to devolve authority to universities are nested in an over-regulation in which past practices are reproduced and close state control is retained.

By the mid-nineteenth century, with state reproduction often at cross-purposes with economic and cultural innovations, plus the growing sclerosis of the machine, considerable dissatisfaction with Edo rule had accumulated. A key popular theme was the corruption of officials who had betrayed the emperor's mandate, though the point was mostly made indirectly. 'Samurai and populace criticized the Tokugawa government by comparing it to ideal Japanese or Chinese kingdoms of the past,' states Bayly. Despite the standard Confucian trope 'their criticism concentrated on the abuses, ills, and inefficiencies of the present.'[110] While new critiques are usually expressed in terms of old ideas, the vibrant civil culture of the later Edo period both signifies Japan's cultural resources and underlines the fact that while *Nihonjinron* was (and is) constructed periodically by states, it was more than a tool of states. Installed in personal and national identity, Japaneseness is deeply rooted at the popular level and is generic in relation to public forms. At moments of crisis the debates are often conducted through differing readings of *Nihonjinron*, and a re-imagining of *Nihonjinron* driven by the nation-state is only viable if it resonates with popular perceptions.

It is impossible to say how long the Edo regime would have lasted. It was brought down not by internal implosion but by the sudden breach of *sakoku*. Japan's location in the Northwest Pacific conferred on it a key position in the global shipping system, to which it continued to be oblivious. Foreign crews that landed in Japan were imprisoned or executed. In 1853, and again in 1854, US Commodore Matthew Perry arrived in Edo Bay with a flotilla of warships to demand the opening up of Japan to the provisioning and re-fitting of ships. Later a US consul arrived, followed by the European powers. The Other began to emphasize access to trade. While the notions of an unfettered right of market exchange and the obligations of all nations to open themselves trade from anywhere were peculiar to the USA, the global character of sea transport could not be ignored. Nor could the superior American firepower, and it was essential to head off military invasion and direct colonization. The shogunate was forced to sign trade treaties that gave 'most favoured nation' rights to all the foreign powers. Under these treaties the regime lost the right to impose tariffs on imports, and resident foreigners on Japanese soil were exempted from Japanese legal jurisdiction. This humiliation triggered the *sonno joi* movement, which was centred on outlying Southern Kyushu and Western Honshu. Like the Tokugawa dynasty, which promised the end of civil war, the *sonno joi* slogan met the popular need of the time—the reassertion of Japanese self-determination—so well as to be irresistible. But it was another matter to achieve its goals. The reformers were unable to expel the Western powers immediately. However, they were able to mobilize the authority of the Emperor to displace the shogunate. The coup of 1867–1868 became known as the 'Meiji restoration.'

The term 'restoration' reflected the Meiji group's reliance on the throne as their source of legitimacy. They reasserted 'the ethnic myth of divine monarchy and good rulership.'[111] Amid the new emphasis on the court, archaic forms and titles dating back to Nara were brought back into the centre of the polity. In reality the Emperor Mutsuhito (later known as Meiji[112]) came to follow the time honoured imperial tradition of accepting the advice of the self-appointed and self-perpetuating Meiji government in all matters. 'Restoration' also points again to the characteristic paradox of the Japanese nation. The venerable national tradition was stridently reasserted just at the moment it was remade. Both ends of the argument were mobilized against the Tokugawa regime, which was seen to have by-passed the emperor, while at the same time it had failed the tests of modernization. Remarkably, Meiji *Nihonjinron* coupled a heightened emphasis on tradition, on Japaneseness, with hyper-modernization at the behest of the state.

As its political strategy suggests the Meiji oligarchy proved highly competent. Most of its founding members were inexperienced, and it was oligarchic and self-referential in operation with democratic forms playing a minor role, but it learned quickly, renewed itself effectively and avoided capture by individuals. In these ways its political culture was in continuity with the Edo regime. Above all the Meiji regime was an effective modernizer. In a generation it installed the forms of a modern nation-state and industrial economy parallel to those of Britain and Germany. The first steps were implemented immediately on taking power. The high offices of the Edo *bakufu* were abolished and the Tokugawa land holdings taken. The Emperor was moved to Edo, renamed as Tokyo and confirmed as the seat of government. Though there were eighteenth months of resistance by forces associated with the displaced shogunate, the regime change within the bureaucracy and the nation was less difficult than might have been expected. In the nation the richer merchants and financiers stayed on the sidelines until the polity had settled. In government middle-level officials were promoted to replace the senior ones in eclipse. 'Behind these successes lay *baku-han* pluralism which permitted changes to be made from within the existing structure and its traditions, rather than from outside.'[113] Meanwhile a further round of missions, more extensive than those under the Tokugawa, was sent abroad to observe Western institutions and practices. Western specialists were brought into Japan to advise on everything from banking and finance to mining, industry, transport and armaments. Foreign professors were appointed to the newly established national universities.

Going deeper, the Meiji leaders overhauled the Edo social order in order to encompass the economic and social changes of the preceding period, the need for accelerated modernization, and the construction of a new machinery of state. The four-tier caste system, which had been fragmented by mobility and the more complex division of labour, was abandoned and people were free to choose their occupation and where they lived. The regime forced the *daimyo* to give up their title to the *han* in exchange for provincial governorships or new roles in the state or economy. These new opportunities were substantial. The regime itself established many of the new industries needed in the transition from an agricultural to an industrial economy. Once established by government these industries were sold off cheaply to chosen entrepreneurs.[114] By this method the regime fostered the large combines that came to dominate much of the economy, and maintained members of the *daimyo* and samurai castes in leading social roles. When the army was fully professionalized the remaining samurai lost their military functions and hereditary privileges, including their right to wear the pigtail and the two swords, and later they were stripped of their state pensions as well. Nevertheless:

> Many samurai families successfully negotiated this sharp transition. They staffed the new bureaucracies, the growing army and navy. Some of them cleverly invested their stipends and bonds in new, prospering enterprises, emerging alongside members of merchant firms (*zaibatsu*) as leaders of business. Even if the basis of their power in the social hierarchy had been transformed, people still looked up to the samurai. This was not least because they successfully captured and embodied the sense of national pride which permeated the politics of the Meiji era.[115]

In these changes the samurai completed the long transformation of the cult of *bushido*, from obedience to the feudal master, to serving the national public. Their social status was no longer absolutely guaranteed by birth, and their future roles were at the behest of the reformed and regenerated nation-state. Thus the traditional elites were fragmented and opened for internal restructuring, the state was more completely in control, and the way was cleared for a modernized elite that would be meritocratic to the degree necessary to compete successfully with the West. The element of meritocracy—which had been subordinate not absent in the Edo period—was formalized. In 1882 Japan followed the modern German model in introducing an examination for promotion in the civil service.[116] The Meiji regime did not acknowledge the fact that this was also the ancient Chinese model. It saw the East and Asia as backward.

A new uniform tax system was put in place early in the Meji period, based on the newly centralized land ownership. Later the state finances benefited from revenues gathered from the colonies in Asia. Huge resources were taken out of China after 1895.[117] The Meiji state moved to overhaul the ports and create transport infrastructure. The construction of railways boomed in the last two decades of the century. By 1885 almost the whole country was covered by the electric telegraph.[118] By this time agricultural productivity had been sufficiently intensified so as to free up much of the labour force for manufacturing and establish a global role for Japan in steel and ship-building. Meanwhile the rate of growth of education increased, and the social and vocational participation of women began to broaden. By 1910 there was near universal schooling for all children from the ages of six to twelve years. This paralleled developments in the most advanced societies in Europe.[119] At the turn of the century in Japan research universities were being created almost as quickly as in the USA. Japanese scientists in fields such as seismology, the study of earthquakes, were making path-breaking contributions.

NATIONAL AND MODERN

After taking office the Meiji regime formally confirmed the hated treaties with the European powers, signifying both a desire to be incorporated into the international order, and a realization that Japan would need to modernize before it would be treated on equal terms. The Meiji slogan was *fukoku kyohei* ('rich country, strong army'). The abiding aim was to regain full independence so as to protect and advance Japaneseness as an end in itself. The strategic objectives, the means of insuring against further violations of independence, were to catch up with the West in military, technological and economic terms and become a great international power. Another Meiji slogan was *oitsuke oikose* ('catch up, overtake').[120] At the same time, in utilizing Western concepts and technologies, tradition was protected and the national character remained determining, by using translation. Foreign knowledge was adapted so as to render it Japanese before being disseminated. The strategy was assimilation rather than integration. It was essential to absorb the foreign technical knowledge without adopting the foreign values. Matter inconsistent with Japaneseness was Othered and discarded, without translation. A third slogan of the Meiji era was *wakon yosai* ('Japanese spirit, Western technology').

As Morris Low notes, 'this dualism allows the Japanese to create a space for their own culture and to develop a sense of identity based on the relationship between Western technology and Japanese cultural traditions.'[121] *Wakon yosai* was a new trope in *Nihonjinron*. The depth of the transformation from Edo to Meiji should not be under-stated. Instead of always reading change through the prism of tradition and continuity, as in pre-industrial times, government and people now coupled tradition with modernity. The Meiji imagining of tradition/modernity quickly became emblematic of the nation. It remains so today.[122] It is a sign of the tectonic nature of the trauma induced by Perry and the foreign traders, that this novel antinomy of tradition/modernity became so quickly absorbed into the political culture and aesthetic sensibilities, and on a permanent basis. The tradition/modernity antinomy was expressed sometimes as synthesis, for example in architecture, and sometimes as contradiction, especially in visual arts and literature. At the 1900 exhibition in Paris there was much interest in a Japanese painting of a young girl in a kimono, standing on a bridge and looking into the far distance along the railway lines.[123] This synchronized with the work of European artists who also focused on tensions between industrial modernization and tradition. In both Japan and Western Europe an emphasis on scenes from daily life imbued this tension with a new humanism. Because of their vibrancy and popular orientation at the time of the Meiji restoration, traditional arts of Japan such as painting, lithographs and pottery were able to make an effective transition to global cultural exchange, using both old and new styles.[124]

All the same, it was a difficult pairing to make work. Japan was not equipped for dual identity, or for opening up itself to an uncontrolled disruption from outside. Both would have wholly overturned Edo Japan and thus broken continuity altogether. The Meiji regime had no intention of doing that. Thus for both reasons, Meiji Japan was unable to bring tradition and modernity into an equally weighted antinomy, as nations such as Britain had done. Nothing like the long pairing of Roman and Hellenic was possible in Japan. Japanese policy makers and cultural producers strove towards a synthesized 'Japanese modernization' that they could never quite visualize in the round. The attempt was futile. A fused Japanese tradition-modernization was a chimera. Notwithstanding the flexibility of the Shinto reading of the ancestors, whatever was the notion of time that underpinned Shinto, it was not modernity. But aside from the samurai revolt of the early Meiji period, it was rarely questioned that Japan needed both tradition and modernization. It needed to draw on both the West and itself. Both parts of the antinomy of Japaneseness and Western modernization *had* to be embraced.

The Meiji regime already had a formula for doing this. In the first millennium C.E. Buddhism had been assimilated into a composite national religion of Shinto/Buddhism. In the Meiji era the solution was to include both parts of the traditional/modern dual in the mix, but again within the terms of an over-arching nationally controlled project—in which, in the last analysis, the inner-facing national character of Japan was non-negotiable. In other words, to the extent that the Meiji era achieved a hybrid of Japaneseness and industrial modernity ('Japan's partially self-fashioned modernity' as Christopher Bayly calls it),[125] this hybrid, which was always a domestication-assimilation of the foreign, was therefore incomplete and necessarily subordinated to the national project of bounded Japan. Regardless of the need for selective Westernizations, it was inconceivable the Shinto heart and the emperor system—with their long line to the Neolithic, nested in the enthralling beauty of timeless Japan and pared to a piercing essence by the zen aesthetic—could ever be dethroned from the position of supreme definer of all things in Japan. For example Bayly discusses the political philosophy of Nakae Chomin, the most liberal and anti-authoritarian of the political leaders of the Meiji era. Even for Nakae a polity based on individual rights and agency was always insufficient. He believed that 'the emperor and his ministers would have to remain the ultimate arbiters of the fate of the Japanese people.'[126] Likewise, modernity drove economic markets and the pace of amazing creativity in sectors such as building, clothing and household artifacts, and later electronics and graphics, but the main Japanese imagining never broke free from a self-referential *Nihonjinron*. It still has not broken free. Japan is still Meji Japan. Another Japan is needed.

The strategic risk for the Meiji regime was that in this resolution of tradition and modernity—in which plurality was qualified by the subordination of modern to the national, and the potential for global imagining was obliviated behind the national horizon of vision—would weaken the zeal for modernization and the engagement with worldwide knowledge. Hence the Meiji regime and its successors incessantly promoted the spectre of international competition, the need to know the Other, and the vital task of catch up to protect and advance Japan. As a *waka* (31-syllable poem) by the Emperor Meiji himself stated:

> Yononaka no hito ni okureo torinubeshi
> Susuman toki ni susuma zariseba

> We shall fall behind our fellows in the world
> If, when we should advance, we make no move at all. (127)

The emperor popularized Western dress and other habits to focus his subjects on the need to surmount the international challenge. This constantly forced a version of the global dimension into view but confined Japanese vision of that global dimension through a national lens, in which only some things could become visible. The Meiji perspective was the national-centric equivalent of a geocentric cosmology, the old belief in a universe revolving around the Earth. The world, when it was entertained at all, rotated round Japan. At the same time, the 'emulate and catch-up' reflexivity was so deeply implanted that long after Japan reached or exceeded most industrialized countries, in sectors such as universities and research there was and is a continued assumption that Japanese institutions must be inferior, as if catch-up was/is the only global project. Thus in motivating improvement, the first rhetorical move is always to point to the alleged superiority of the West—often coupled with a wistful regret that Japanese tradition is insufficiently appreciated in the West. Still universalized in contemporary Japan, the Meiji reflex continues to sustain an international rather than a global view of the world.

The Meiji nation-state continued the Edo project of reproducing and shaping national character. At the same time this was a more effective nation-state, like its counterparts in Europe. It managed the population with mono-cultural intensity. The goal was a nation unified by homogeneity. The essentialized Japan proclaimed by Meiji was both a description of reality and an ideal to be achieved. For certain Japanese the norm bore little relation to their lives,[128] but that did not diminish its normative potency, though it detached some people from the state-sponsored *Nihonjinron* project. The regime established the first standardized national language and bore down hard on cultural diversity in peripheral regions, and non-ethnic Japanese such as the Ainu, increasingly moulding them to fit the 'state-defined form.'[129] Education combined a modernized post-Confucian syllabus, in which science was prominent, with the teaching of *kokutai*, a government-led *Nihonjinron* project focused on the distinctive character of Japanese institutions and traditions. *Kokutai* emphasized the emperor and modeled the state as a hierarchically ordered family. Later it was used as a vehicle for the cult of state Shinto.[130] As this suggests, despite successful installation of genuflection to Western modernity, and the habit of borrowing in response to it—both of which remain part of industrialized Japan—the self-referential nation increasingly reasserted itself as the Meiji years proceeded.

The pairing of tradition and modernity can take many different forms. Some in the modernizing West even pretended they could abandon tradition altogether, abolish memory and live solely in the present and future. The example in music was Debussy, for whom on principle the melody was never repeated.[131] But in reality Western Europeans dug deep into their long traditions at every turn. In Japan the resolution of tradition/modernity that became dominant pointed in the opposite direction to the Debussy imagining. Increasingly Meiji Japan found it necessary to explain and justify its modernizations in terms of *Nihonjinron*. As soon as practicable the foreign specialists and professors were replaced by experts from Japan. The messy plurality on the soil of the nation was shut down, which came as a relief. In the 1890s and after, as military and economic goals were reached and the Meiji generation aged, the cultural pendulum swung back to Japanese exceptionalism. The *Nihonjinron* reflex prestructured the evolving national agenda and paved the way for the intensified militarist modernization after World War I. Between the world wars a stridently nationalist *kokutai* became mobilized against leftist and critical work in the arts and literature.[132] The spirit of *kokutai* lives on in the unwillingness of the education ministry to sanction in school history a full account of the drivers and effects of the 1931–1945 period.

INTERNATIONAL COMPETITION

Following Prussian models of the army and British models of the navy, the regime created the strongest military power in Asia. Increasingly the military and the state sustained a notion of a bounded Japan that coupled an outlook almost as autarkic as that of Edo, with an aggressive approach to international competition without regard for the need for a harmonious global order. Japan remained self-referenced, as if the spirit of the *sakoku* closure was still in place, while at the same time intervening freely across borders. It realized Toyotomi Hideyoshi's old dream: to extend the terrain of *Nihonjinron*, constructed Japaneseness, by bringing the Others of East Asia to heel. Japan forced an unequal treaty on Korea in 1876. It manufactured a successful war with China in 1894, gaining Taiwan. It beat Russia in 1904–1905. It annexed the Korean Peninsula in 1910. The unequal trade treaties were rectified. Typically foreign military intervention received strong support from patriots at home. 'The government always had to deal with a public opinion several times more bellicose than it cared to be itself.'[133]

The Taisho period of 1912–1926 saw a temporary softening of approach. A partial democratization of the polity was accompanied by stress on diplomacy in international matters, though there was continued aggression towards China. But Japan was not admitted to multilateral diplomacy on the basis it sought. In 1902 it had signed the Anglo-Japanese Alliance, the first alliance on an equal basis between a Western and non-Western nation. But the global naval settlement at the end of World War I sought to restrain the size of Japan's navy, and when Japan proposed a racial equality clause to the newly formed League of Nations this was rejected. In 1924 the USA introduced race-based immigration policies that appeared to be directed at the Japanese.[134] The nation continued to build its economic and military strength and became more sectional in its international alliances. It allied itself with fascist Germany and Italy and a more strident and xenophobic nationalism became dominant. Cosmopolitans were viewed as traitors. The ultra-nationalists reworked the foundations of the *Nihonjinron*. Continuing a stance with roots in the early Meiji government,[135] Buddhism was defined as a non-Japanese religion and subject to persecution. Solely Shinto shrines were set up in the conquered Asian territories. However, the failure of this effort to suppress Buddhism reinforced the point that *Nihonjinron* was not infinitively plastic in the hands of the state, but depended also on its resonance in autonomous popular culture.

In foreign policy the militarists imagined a Greater East Asian Co-Prosperity Sphere under Japanese control. In 1931 Japan seized control of Manchuria from China and the Soviet Union. When the multilateral League of Nations objected Japan left the League. In 1937 it launched the savage invasion of China, and after striking against the American fleet in Hawaii at Pearl Harbour in December 1940, moved quickly to occupy Southeast Asia. The USA took three years from mid-1942 to roll back the Greater East Asian Co-Prosperity Sphere and force the abandonment of Shinto-fascism and the forward military policy inherited from Meiji. The atomic weapons dropped on Hiroshima and Nagasaki in 1945 were not needed to resolve the war but their use reinforced Japan's national rejection of militarism in the postwar period.

The American Occupation of 1945–1952 was a determined but not always consistent effort to remake Japan along Western lines. Crucially, however, the emperor system was retained, and for the most part the national bureaucracy was left in place.[136] This was not one of the rare Japanese moments of punctuated evolution. The national culture was too resilient to be either displaced by the occupation or become its instrument. Some reforms of the occupation period survived but where Japanese opposition to reform was strong it was resisted successfully or reversed after 1952. *Nihonjinron* then reasserted itself via the business sector, where Keynes' animal spirits were coordinated by state supervised conglomerates. Though the democratic political system introduced by the USA was (and is) chronically shambolic that did not greatly matter. The bureaucracy maintained continuity and the long view. The time horizons of business leadership were also longer than those in the Anglo-American countries.

Within forty years of the wreck of Hiroshima and Nagasaki Japan had become the second largest and strongest economy in the world. The dazzling postwar miracle is too well known to review here. The points that should be emphasized are that bounded Japan remained bounded, a strong state was still the advocate and guardian of *Nihonjinron*, and the Meiji methods of modernization were sustained. The old great power imagining of Hideyoshi and the Meiji was rechanneled into economic competitiveness. The export sector was built across manufacturing and later, 'soft power' cultural goods, while inward cultural flows continued to be mediated by national institutions, though with growing difficulty. Foreign knowledge, ideas and technology were translated into Japanese using the same two-step absorption. Japan needed to know the foreign Other to sustain its place in the world, but there was no desire to achieve synchrony.

Insularity

National insularity, especially when it incorporates national superiority and exceptionalism, precludes the need for cross-border empathy in which people open themselves to relations with the foreign Other. Insularity is a deliberate disjuncture in cross-border relationships. Since the beginning of the imperial line in the first millennium C.E. Japan had opted to maintain its own bordered world, rather than engage freely with other worlds (and now, with the globally accessible world-as-a-whole). Maintaining a world of itself, Japan had no need to imagine another. The brilliance of the Meiji system was that it found a way to sustain *Nihonjinron* while defending Japan and advancing its interests within the world-wide relational system, without the need for cross-border empathy which was reckoned as potentially subversive of Japan.

Realizing that the simple refusal of engagement adopted by the Edo regime was no longer viable, Meiji had to do something more complex. For quite some time it worked. Meiji enabled Japan to stay behind its fence, translate and adapt, and maintain competitive position. *Nihonjinron* remained dominant over the foreign elements and Japan could continue its long-term project, for many endlessly creative and fascinating, of evolving national identity in the arts and literature within a rich monoculture. The fact that Japanese language was not shared in the world, and few Japanese became fluent communicators in the spoken languages of other nations, facilitated the refusal of empathy and increased the height of the wall between nation and Other.

In cross-border matters Meiji installed a regime of limited mobility without empathy in which the aim was not mutual interest or commonality, it was to secure instrumental purposes based on national self-interest. Inter-national relations, as distinct from global relations, can be conducted at an advanced level without empathy or the desire for it. Nations can engage in trade, and one-way information flow, and war, without opening themselves to reciprocal relations, which inevitably have transforming effects at home. Open-ended and reciprocal relations, the kind of effects that flow freely, beyond the control of states, are unpredictable. Without the expedient of prohibition, Meiji sought to maintain the Edo capacity to render cross-border relationships predictable. It perfected the art of drawing benefits from the world, especially in matters of trade and of technology, without becoming vulnerable to it. This refusal of empathy preserved an exclusively Japanese control over self-invention, at the price of the failure of imagining. The long isolated nation-centrism was continued, and this, plus the refusal of empathy that could overcome the isolation, made it difficult to enter the imaginary of another, or to conceive or need the global, which is the multi-centred system of the world, or to understand universal humanism. Or to share Japan deeply with the outsider.

This is not to say that Japanese culture and identity are sustained solely by the nation-state or that bordered Japan has no popular roots. Regardless of the fragmentation of authority or episodic crises at the top of the polity 'Japan seems to sail on serenely,' which indicates the resilience and depth of Japanese cultural practices.[137] The brilliance of *Nihonjinron* is that it rests on the larger cultural infrastructure of national identity even while reproducing it *and* capturing it for the project of excluding the outside world. The project of exclusion is not necessary to Japan. It is not essential to exclude the foreign to remain Japanese. This was clear at different points of history, for example the Nara period, and the century before Edo. But today it is difficult for even globally engaged Japanese professionals to enter the life worlds of Others, a process which is retarded by a nagging sense of 'why does it matter?' So there is bewilderment at the difficulty of 'internationalizing' Japan, or Japanese business, or universities. Something is missing, but no one knows what it is. The lacuna is the desire for cross-border empathy. The inhabitants of a gated estate do not need to commune with those outside it. Not only is the superiority of Japanese life taken for granted, it is also assumed that only a Japanese person can understand it, or would want to share in its benefits. While there are barriers to external engagement in all cultures, borders are inherent in identity, the barriers are higher in Japan. Too often, Japan is nothing less and nothing more than *Nihonjinron*.

EXCLUSIONS

Cross-border flows are inhibited by two factors. First, as noted, there is the inherent suspicion of unassimilated, undomesticated foreign things, and distaste for foreign values. There are many Japanese people who do not share this outlook, but many others, perhaps most, are simply not interested in engaging closely with the outside. For example, among many university professors there is an abiding view (notwithstanding the Meiji reflex that 'Japan must be behind the West') that a PhD from a research university in Japan is better than a foreign degree. Here 'better' means 'more suitable'; and this means not being too Westernized—as if one cannot have multiple affiliations. Second, there is the matter of global language. It is now broadly agreed by educated professionals in Japan that it is essential to read English because it is the global language and a vital source of knowledge. So much is consistent with the Meiji outlook. But it is not widely felt that it is necessary to synchronize with English-speaking people by becoming fluent in English language conversation in real time. It is not necessary to share an inter-subjective space, or form ongoing cross-border work groups that are fully integrated, let alone to make global community. This outlook has even given rise to the belief that Japan should be able to develop its own distinctive form of English as a means of preserving Japaneseness in the traditional way, through a process of transforming the foreign language into something that can be defined as distinctly Japanese. Consider this argument as advanced by the then Vice-President, later President of the University of Tokyo:

> English is a very difficult problem. I think those who speak the native tongue of English should think of the handicap which the non-native tongue people suffer from. This is very important. For example the Japanese speak a different, very characteristic English. We cannot differentiate R from L. This is very famous. Also we have only five vowels like Spanish…(English should not be seen as) the Queen's English…It's not world standard. Japanese English is one of the standards, and Chinese English is, many Chinese Englishes, and Australian English also….it's very important to…keep our traditional way of cultural differentiation. Otherwise the

University of Tokyo will lose its identity. *(Hiroshi Komiyama, Executive Vice-President, University of Tokyo)*

This makes sense from the point of view of national self-determination, defined so as to exclude global relations in the manner of the Meiji state. And there is no reason why the UK or the USA should have a monopoly on the forms of the global language, or that English should be the only global language. But a common global language in itself is a global public good. The argument for differentiation of that language and the maintenance of two-step rather than direct communications makes sense from an exclusively national point of view but is absurd if the objective is global communicability. The notion that national identity can only be preserved by maintaining a barrier of unintelligibility, a one-way window of dark glass, in which Japan understands the world but the world cannot fully understand Japan, is solipsistic. Likewise Japan's capacity to share in the circulating global creations is handicapped if it refuses full engagement and is indifferent to global synchrony. It is not viable to expect others to offer borrowing rights and full transparency, if the nation cannot or will not reciprocate. As in the USA, so in Japan: the price of national exceptionalism is that it robs its proponents of the capacity to imagine the global dimension as a common communicative space.

Concurrent with this diminishing of the external imagining, there are internal barriers. Within Japan many voices are excluded or muted in social life. We have seen that the nineteenth-century nation-state relied on universalizing, often racialized notions of the nation. Meiji was no different to other states in that respect, and Japan has always acknowledged regional cultural differences, which provide the content of much humour in Japan. But Japan has persisted longer with the homogenizing monocultural approach than have most nations. Much difference within the nation is not acknowledged. The position of women in terms of workforce participation, membership of the professions and in positions of leadership is weaker than in most industrialized countries. Little discussed within Japan is the position of the *burakumin*, the untouchable caste, which is numbered in the millions. This group had long roots but was codified in the Edo period. Its members were said to be those who handled butchering and other functions categorized as 'unclean,' but the *burakumin* also served the regime as useful scapegoats for the discontent of the peasantry. Many *burakumin* live together in residential areas and are readily identified, while others have sought to blend with the general population, making the precise calculation of numbers impossible. There is still a stigma attached to *burakumin* status, though this is officially denied. Secret registers are maintained for consultation by prospective employers or fathers-in-law.[138]

It is only recently that the indigenous Ainu in Hokkaido have gained some official recognition. The inhabitants of Okinawa, many of whom who speak non-Japanese languages at home, also report discrimination. Severe difficulties face the Zainichi Koreans, descendants of those brought to Japan as forced labourers in the inter-war period. They numbered 443,000 in 2006. They have rights of permanent residence but only some have gained citizenship and they are treated as second class in much of Japanese society.[139] The monoculture does not prevent members of minority groups from generating innovations, or acts of stellar creativity, but will tend to diminish the incidence of such works. Hierarchical and exclusive societies narrow the points of origin of creative work. All else being equal they also eliminate some opportunities for cross-cultural intellectual triangulation and synthesis. When the inner Other is excluded at the same time as the outer Other, the options are drastically narrowed.

JAPAN AND ROME

Thus while Japan shares much with Rome, in other ways it is in stark contrast with Rome. Both had their foundational settlements, their moment of pre-industrial modernization when their polity, economy, society and culture were recast. They share a similar relationship with an inherited and constructed tradition central to their understanding of themselves and the world. If societies create themselves as Cornelius Castoriadis argues (see chapter 1), both Rome and Japan used an evolving narrative of themselves to give themselves form and shape. There are also differences here. Japan's tradition has had more stamina than Rome's, which faded as the Empire became cosmopolitan, and then lost part of its remaining potency, the part associated with the pagan city-state in Latinium, when in the fourth century C.E. Constantine declared Rome to be Christian. Unlike Rome Japan is not the great power of the day. Perhaps this is why its tradition is reinvented more carefully and protected more fiercely. But this also points to a problem that was transcended more successfully in Rome than in Japan. As Peter Murphy notes, in order to stabilize themselves, self-inventing human societies have to deal with 'the double-edged problem of persistence. This is the problem of how to combine ongoing experimentation in form making with the durability of forms thereby created.' Japan errs on the side of durability. Mostly it is locked into stasis, punctuated by rare shattering transformations at moments of national crisis, akin to the sudden earthquakes that are integral to life in the islands. It is locked into stasis now. Rome found it easier to keep altering for a time, partly because it was more inclusive, continually augmenting itself by drawing on more and more constituencies from within and coopting the barbarians from without. Eventually the flexibility required was too great, the Augustan structures could no longer manage. By then the Roman tradition was no longer 'thick' enough to sustain an Edo or Meiji scale transformation. But Rome's national defence and economy were always more difficult to manage than those of isolated and bounded Japan.

Rome was always clearly bordered and so is Japan today. They both chose to define themselves in contrast to on one hand the barbarian Other without, on the other hand the less-than-full-citizen Other within. In Rome the inner Other was the slaves. In Japan it is the Koreans, the transshipped victims of the Greater East Asian Co-prosperity Sphere. There the similarities end. The approach to national space, openness, multiplicity, inclusion and cross-border initiative could not be more different. The Romans had no need to widen the moat, put up the drawbridge and close the castle gate, but in its relations with the world, through its long history from the Heian era when tradition was set to the present, Japan has done nothing else. The Romans managed difference as plurality. The full range of cultural resources was on the table. The Japanese force the foreign into a Japanese mould, discarding what does not fit the Japanized hybrid. Rome defined itself in contrast and partnership with Greek and the Hellenic life. Japan knows no such cultural and linguistic companion. It seems that Chinese and English are threats to the national identity, not resources for its exercise and evolution. In Rome Latin and provincial diversity were not just tolerated but mobilized for imperial rule. Citizenship was progressively extended to all free persons. In Japan internal cultural difference is unrecognized and an outsider cannot enter the land of the gods. External cultural difference fascinated the Romans. Both nations borrowed cultural motifs from abroad, but Japan is anxious about foreign culture in a way the Romans were not, and tends to block a fuller engagement with it. Thus it is hard for people in Japan to imagine the global. One suspects the Romans would have done better—though they would always have seen a Roman Earth,[140] they were no more likely to imagine the Other as equally worthy of respect than is bounded Japan. All the same, in the era of Empire the Romans set aside the old Republican conceit that no outsider could know Rome, and sought to bring the Roman to the world, and the world to Rome. In Japan it is sincerely felt that no outsider can ever really know Japan. If the language is not a decisive barrier, than a required lifetime of customary behaviour is the other obstacle.

Even when the Outsider lives a whole life in Japan, she or he cannot become truly Japanese, not even in the third or fourth generation. Outsider citizens are few. Migrants are almost unimaginable. How could Japanese people live in harmony with them? So the way into Japan is largely blocked and it will require a mighty cultural shift if the ageing population (see Part III) is to be redressed. Correspondingly, there is no desire within Japan to bring the essence of Japan to the world, to sustain a Japanese theme in the human concert, in the world society now being made. But the desire to make the larger world into a better place is less strongly felt than might be expected of people steeped in social responsibility. The Romans never stopped living in Rome when they ventured out to the world, and in the early Empire romanization became a universal mission. It was never like this in Japan, even in the days of military empire. For the Japanese life at home invokes one set of expectations, life in the world another. The world is full of dangers. This can never be put right. But in Japan there is no need to strive to make the world into a paradise. Paradise is already here at home.

Creativity

The limits formed by insularity also suggest questions about creativity in Japan, in relation to creation in both the innovation and discovery modes. We have seen that creations in the national imagining are rare, vectored by crisis and followed by long periods of stasis. Does the same rhythm of punctuated evolution and the same dependence on top-down motors of creation vector other fields of imagining? Moreover, the growing importance of global creation—creative aesthetics, science and commercial technologies all now emerge in globally networked fields of activity—poses the problem of Japan's leadership role in creative activity. We have seen that creation in Japan is often nationally referenced, not globally referenced, as emphasized by the failure of many creators in this deeply literate culture to become fluent in foreign languages. Moreover, the national need is often for reproduction and refinement of pre-given forms—global fields of creation seem to place a higher premium on novelty and on larger stretches across diversity, the bringing together of previously separated contents, often heterogeneous or opposing, in order to make something new. Is there less of this in Japan?

It is a mixed picture. In the last half century, while the Meiji national imagining has continued to play out and the national/ global problem has been continually postponed, Japan has been an unambiguously major power in business, finance and industry organization, and also in cultural industries. The national strategy is now to emphasize the export of cultural goods, 'soft power.' Japan consistently excels in certain branches of social organization, such as transport systems and waste management. But it has been difficult for the nation to lead in the fields of foreign policy and diplomacy, or modes of government, where it closely tracks Westminster neo-liberalism. Nor has it been highly active in finding solutions to the common and worsening human problems of climate, food, water and energy. Since the 1980s Japan's economic wealth has allowed it to claim shared ownership of global problems. Currents within the nation want to do this, but they have not been dominant. A national imaginary sustained by self-referencing and enclosure will not permit a genuine commitment to making the world. And now the chain of brilliant innovations in economic and industrial forms seems to have petered out. In specifically creative fields, Japan has been a remarkable pioneer in animation. It is second only to the USA (though a long way behind it) as an inventor of new kinds of cultural goods and images for mass commercial dissemination. Japanese designers produce world-exciting work in fashion and architecture and in many branches of the performing, plastic and imagistic arts. Most iconic Japanese products, such as the films of Hayao Miyazaki or the sushi/sashimi bars spreading in city centres in many countries, are sourced directly from Japanese cultural tradition. Japanese communications and marketing are also superior, though better crafted for the Japanese mindset than for the world. There is also a sense that work in most fields follows predictable tracks. In the sciences and philosophy Japan has not been a notable creator of new paradigms and keystone insights—that is, discovery in the sense of chapter 3—though Japanese science is often very creative at the next level.

In Japan certain kinds of creativity are easier than others: those that enact or inhabit traditional cultural forms; those that embody zen principles of simplicity and minaturization; and those nested in thick familial-style relations, such as integrated forms of production (see below). There are also inhibitions. Free-wheeling critical work of the path-breaking kind tends to be stifled, in a setting in which the *yokonarabi* ethos ('do as others do') is strong. The iconoclast does not corner a piece of the market in ideas within a culture full of strident and discordant voices, as in the United States. In parts of the West the tropes of criticism and rejection can be highly functional for creators, facilitating the imagining of opposites while anesthetizing the shock of the leap into the unknown. Shared gestures of criticism and rebellion underpin critical communities, safe houses within which creations are welcomed and nurtured. But in Japan the iconoclast is a social pariah that disturbs the common harmony. In the universities, creative work is nested in institutions confined by the horizon of the Meiji state. Yet research universities everywhere are quintessentially global. National referencing is a handicap when knowledge is more strategically vital than ever, and most ideas are accessed via global flows. This tension is especially difficult in universities in Japan (see Part III).

All of this suggests that Meiji-inspired imitative development and referred innovation has run its course. A culture that combines continuous foreign borrowings with rare punctuated (and bounded) national discovery has its limits. Japan has been a brilliant follower and great innovator on the basis of its adaptations from the common store of knowledge. Where does a successful borrowing culture go when catch-up has been achieved? What is the next step? How does an innovative borrowing culture become a broad-based discovery culture, able to create outside as well as inside its traditions--augmenting the common store of major discoveries, renewing itself, and opening up a range of hitherto untried strategic options for itself and the world? The problem of insular Japan is closely tied to the limits of its discovery culture. Japan's unwillingness to fully embrace the global dimension has cut off its post-Meiji options.

Japan has the deep aesthetic reserves with which to power a major leap forward in many areas but is not tensing itself to make the spring. This raises two questions: that of ability and that of motivation. The question about ability highlights the distinction between innovation and discovery. As we have seen, the Meiji restoration devised a straightforward formula for innovation, sourced from the Nara past. Japan interprets its borrowings from outside via its internal aesthetic tradition, internalizes the resulting hybrid, and often makes the innovation better in the process, which is the advantage of the second mover. Creative work always requires a second self. With borrowing and innovation, the internal self borrows a second self from outside and then absorbs it. But discovery works conversely. In the case of discovery, the internal self has to imagine its own second self—produced by the inner self but fashioned as external to it. This imagined second self is the one that does the previously unimaginable, it pulls together the two irreconcilable parts of the paradox, which is the motor of creativity. Thus discovery requires a capacity to work with plural identity, in which self-referencing is combined with a second self for whom the conventions are suspended long enough for the new idea to emerge. (The parallel of this move in personal identity formation is the sojourning student in the foreign environment, who maintains the old national self while at the same time developing a second self in the country of education).[141] But not only is it difficult to suspend convention in Japan, more importantly, plural identity itself is mostly a bridge too far. In the case of innovation this is not a constraint. The process of innovation suppresses the borrowed second self as soon as possible, turning it into something Japanese. But in discovery, the second self must be imagined, welcomed and nurtured. The development of a capacity to work with multiplicity—like the confident and flexible Romans with their second Hellenic selves—might be a key to unlocking a larger discovery sensibility in Japan.

Bounded Japan is singular Japan and vice versa. It cannot deal effectively with the second self which is both inside and outside. An open and plural Japan could become something else. An open and plural Japan would not abandon its traditions. These would continue to provide ways of appropriating the world, and feed into the drivers of changing identity. But its traditions would be drawn into a continuing productive antinomy with the succession of second selves, from without and within, that are posed by modernity. This pairing of national tradition and an increasingly global modernity is a feature of contemporary creative cultures. It is likely that in Japan the first pairing of Buddhism with Shinto took something like this form, powering the remarkable Taika reforms and the Nara period, before the two religions became hybridized-assimilated by the national project of *Nihonjinron*. As we have seen, early Buddhism in Japan was a modernizing force. Contemporary China is in the throes of a modernization that may release the creative antinomy of national tradition/modernity on a gigantic scale. Time will tell whether that great project is successful. (As suggested, one of the questions yet to be resolved here is about the forms of its tradition that are now accessible to China: the ongoing potentials of its sense of national self).

But multiplicity requires not just a desire to imagine the Other, conspicuously absent in most of Japan, but also a facility in doing so—an instinctive capacity to enter into diverse and opposing mindsets. This is where the stranger factor, and the paradox of familiarity with strangers, comes into play. Active synchronous participation in the global setting can build the necessary sensibilities. This is where the question of motivation comes in. Whether it is personal change or national change that is in question, great transformations above all rest on agency, on the will to change. Japan in 1600 had the will for national peace. Japan in 1868 had the will for national independence. Japan now needs to create the will for global engagement, or that will not happen. The key to moving forward is the will to imagine; the will to synchronize with the Other, to know the stranger; the will to multiplicity and to make the second self; and hence the will to discovery, including self creation. In Japan the question that matters is—is it *necessary* to discover? Or does *Nihonjinron* provide the answers to all questions, by referring them back to its Neolithic essence, or pushing them off into the void? As long as self-referencing is an end in itself, so that a kind of cultural narcissism prevails, then Japan will miss the opportunity to build a discovery culture in the front line of creation, which is its place in the world. And in doing so remake the world and remake itself.

INDUSTRY

In 2006 the World Bank Institute published a report on *Japan: Moving toward an advanced knowledge economy*.[142] This was largely authored by Japanese nationals and located in Japan's policy history and workplace sociology, free of the Anglo-American ideological strictures that in the work of the Bank often serve as a substitute for grounded analysis. The report focused on the comparative global capacity of industry and the question of barriers to creativity.

In the 1980s the Japanese model of production was superior. It was widely imitated outside Japan in the early 1990s. Its strengths are those of large-firm integration based on cultural cohesion, firm loyalty and the free sharing of tacit knowledge and information across divisions and hierarchies. The model encourages accumulation of shop-floor-based knowledge and firm-specific skills acquired through purpose-oriented in-house training. Relations with suppliers are also integrated and over time all of those involved in the production process come to know each other well. Production can be continually tuned, saving time, reducing costs and lifting quality. In the 1970s and 1980s Japanese firms made significant productivity gains by applying the principle of *kaizen* (continuous improvement). The Japanese business philosophy of 'Total Quality Control,' which developed out of this model of production, became universally adopted the world over. Another imitated prototype was 'Just in Time' inventory practices, which depend on internal information transfer at speed. At the same time, in this model of production there is a firm boundary between the firm and other firms. In that respect the model company, a stand-alone 'silo' within the business environment, reproduces the structure of the bounded Japanese nation within the world setting. The downside of the model is that firms patterned according to this design are better at utilizing internal networks, firm loyalty and tacit knowledge, and less good at external communication and at tapping into labour and supplier mobility and the full range of available technologies, which requires facility in explicit rather than tacit knowledge. 'This was reflected in a not-invented-here (NIH) mentality that disregarded technologies developed outside the company.'[143] Again we find that what is missing is the capacity to work with the second self, the stranger, the Other.

Japan continues to exercise world leadership in many branches of industry, including automobiles, cameras, robotics, pollution prevention equipment, solar energy, ceramic condensers, small electric motors, optic technology, and bicycle components. It has been a pioneer in mobile phone technology. Nevertheless, while the utility of the 1970s/1980s model varies by industry sector, it no longer provides the overall edge it once did. When the world began to emulate its production and management techniques Japan's competitive advantage was narrowed. More seriously, the model was poorly equipped to manage production of ICTs (information and communications technologies)—a key industry in its own right and the main driver of productivity gains across all sectors in the global era. 'The 1990s is often called the lost decade for Japan, and it was the electronics industry that mostly lost its way. Within electronics, it was information and communication technology that was most affected.'[144]

> In the 1990s, it was realized that some types of final products, primarily in electronics, can use a different model. In particular, subassemblies and components can be built to common, usually open, standards. This means each part can have multiple suppliers and multiple final assemblers. The idea of interchangeable parts moved beyond screws and capacitors to disk drives and monitors. This is often called modularization. Competition among component makers can lead to more rapid improvement than is usually the case when development is done in-house or by a closely related company. This is often called the Silicon Valley model....In IT markets since at least the early 1990s, creativity and nimbleness have counted. The open-standards modularization approach of the Silicon Valley model gave many U.S. firms an edge over competitors using proprietary standards and the integral approach. In such an environment, tacit knowledge may be of relatively less importance than before.[145]

The modular approach encourages suppliers to innovate using their own R&D resources. Rather than having to imagine all innovations itself, the firm can tap into a network of other firms with an incentive to innovate.[146] Thus ICTs launched a networked information economy in which 'silo' firms were placed at an increasing disadvantage. ICTs operate on the basis of explicit, codified and common approaches to knowledge and information, not localized implicit knowledge. In the 1990s information flowed more efficiently than before and confidential networks could be created. Increasingly, firms moved forward on the basis of information sharing and exchange with selected outside agents. 'The result is a network-based model of management that creates win-win situations and offers comparative advantage.'[147] The loose ties of a networked economy also lend themselves to continuous shopping around among suppliers, partners and potential R&D producers in order to optimize innovation capacity, production process and cost. In this world long-term partnerships and dependence on in-house R&D can be too confining. ICTs place a premium on speed of response to the opportunities emerging in the open and common information setting; in the ICT environment innovations can be sourced from anywhere. 'The flow of publicly available information via the Internet is growing much faster than the flow of internal company information...information relating to unannounced products and technologies, for example, and know-how related to a company's unique management techniques.'[148] On the ICT industry Nezu states:

> The new paradigm is called 'open innovation.' This refers in part to the availability and use of external resources—especially technology provided from outside the firm. The key point here is that most successful firms in the global IT sector, including even the larger ones, have moved away from an NIH attitude and instead

seek technology where and how they can find it.[149]

But Japanese firms in ICT and elsewhere are never as comfortable with openness as their American counterparts. Openness carries 'an aura of disloyalty to the firm.'[150]

The networked setting also encourages firms to partner research universities as potential sources of creative breakthroughs. Though prior to the 1980s relations between US firms and universities were under-developed, that decade saw the rise of Silicon Valley, linked to Stanford and the University of California campuses, and the Boston Corridor near MIT. In Japan links between firms and creative personnel in universities were still low key, informal, and inhibited by state regulation of the universities and by the openness of universities to all comers and their primary reliance on explicit rather than tacit knowledge.[151] But a further and fundamental limit of the 1970s/1980s model is that it underplays the role of discovery in business competition. Focusing on predictable incremental improvement, the safe option for investors, it is poorly placed to deal with the punctuated, discontinuous, risky, unpredictable pattern of ICTs-related innovations and the continuous re-imagining of business problems.

> Company sophistication comes about in two ways. The first is operational effectiveness, which is the extent to which companies approach world best practices in areas such as production processes, technologies, marketing methods, and management techniques. The other, which is more fundamental to success in an advanced economy, is the degree to which companies have distinctive strategies.[152]

Japanese industry made its great gains using the first approach rather than the second. It set the world standard in operational effectiveness. In relation to strategies, Japan relied (and relies) more on intelligent borrowing and decision-making than on its own creativity. A large part of the potential offered by the imagination is thereby taken out of the picture altogether.

As we have seen, national boundedness is closely tied to the lacuna in creation. The limitations of the 1970s/1980s Japanese production model are linked to the limitations of global imagining in Japan. ICTs confer economic advantages on those firms highly competent in global English, able to make full use of English-language templates—the more so because digitalization of processes using Japanese creates a complex problem of double coding—and able and prepared to partner with firms and inventors and source innovations located anywhere in the world. Within Japan, industry has become divided into firms able to operate with global freedom and fluidity, partnering effectively abroad; and a larger hinterland that is more confined to the 1970s/1980s model of production and national singularity. Rather than being joined together in a productive antinomy of the global and the national/local, these differing groups of firms are separated, with one operating at the cutting edge and the other remaining nation bound. This situation is unlikely to change quickly, because the hinterland is protected by *Nihonjinron* and its refusal to imagine the global. As Yonezawa and Kosugi conclude in their chapter of *Japan: Moving toward an advanced knowledge economy:*

> Our observations suggest that existing labor and industrial customs are not likely to change drastically. This means that for the time being, Japanese society will experience the coexistence of its traditional systems and a globalized system.[153]

AESTHETIC WORK

Japanese innovation faces another economic barrier that has cultural roots. Stellar creativity does not always transfer into efficient business practice. Artists can be indifferent to the market. This the whole world knows. But perhaps this problem has a larger reach in Japan, affecting not just creative work but most work. There is a highly developed aesthetic quality and politeness at the heart of day-to-day tasking. This extracts its rents. One of the curiosities of Japanese capitalism is that it is not, after all, capitalism—or not wholly or consistently so. The classical capitalist incentive is to maximize the average profit per unit of commodity sold. Typically, capitalist mass markets are most effectively serviced by medium quality production in which costs not essential to making and selling the product are taken out. But in Japan this cuts across the profound commitment to traditional social and aesthetic values that have roots in other than business culture. Production according to aesthetic principles means providing goods or services designed and executed at the highest level of quality. Social values mean doing the right thing by others according to the conventions of politeness and collective well-being.

Many digital communications, cameras and electronic goods are offered at a higher level in Japan than elsewhere. Often they have more functions than most consumers want. Picture and sound quality are habitually superior. But these same goods are priced at a disadvantage in world markets, being more expensive than competitor products. Likewise, many of the ordinary items in department stores are minor exquisites of form and design. There is also a commitment to diversity in which all the variations of the product form are on offer, drawing on the wide range of traditional design motifs. This commitment to best possible work extends to the wonderful care and cleanliness of public places in many towns and suburbs, and the regular gardening and hedge trimming of public highways by workers in uniform equipped with the latest in spotless machinery. It goes to the careful checking of every form that is filled in. It shows itself above all in the advanced awareness and extensive protocols in people services, in which the slow, detailed forms of Japanese synchrony are practised with meticulous care in some of the world's fastest cities. Despite the high levels of efficiency in production in Japan, which is often brilliantly designed for simplicity of form, rationality of function and optimum management of time—qualities with long antecedents in Japanese aesthetic and intellectual practices, preceding capitalism—the commitments to social values and aesthetic quality add labour time at every stage. Though these behaviours augment employment, they are non-competitive in the capitalist sense. Nor do they necessarily meet the felt needs of consumers. This is industrial production practiced with the mentality of the plastic or performing artist. It is also something else, more collective in character: a sense of the fitness and rightness of things, and belonging, and proper public display. This is life practiced as a long sequence of tea ceremonies great and small. The pride of every person lies in following the long ritual of choreography that a nation drenched in politeness demands, so that from infancy until the last breath, every move is executed with perfect clarity and grace.

III. Universities in Japan

Japan has one of the strongest higher education systems in the world, if strength is measured by the number of first degree and graduate students, the rate of participation of young people in higher education, the volume of research outputs, and the number, range and prestige of institutions. We could expect this to be the case, given the size and economic power of Japan, the nation's long history of high literacy rates and scientific and civil scholarship, and 140 years of accelerated modernization policy. In general terms the Meiji ambition of 'catch up' with Europe was achieved more than two decades ago though like other national higher education systems Japan has not caught up to the USA. Japan is the third largest investor in R&D in the world and it spends more on universities than any other country except the United States—though the US spends seven times as much as Japan[154]—and possibly also China. But it is doubtful that Japan has the second or third most successful and influential university system, whether comparing stand-alone national performance (that is, a height comparison of national university systems on a silo-to-silo basis), or the effect of the different nations in shaping the global dimension of knowledge and education. The UK outdoes Japan on all research indicators except aggregate size and has 11 institutions in the Shanghai Jiao Tong table of the world's top 100 research universities, including two of the top 10, Cambridge and Oxford. Japan has five universities in the top 100 including Tokyo in twentieth place. This is the same number of leading universities as Germany and one more than Canada. In the next decade Japan might be passed by Germany, which since 2007 has stepped up investment in its research universities.[155] Using the Leiden University research indicators, which identify comparative research quality in terms of citation per faculty, the leading universities in Switzerland, the Netherlands, Sweden and Denmark appear stronger than those of Japan.[156]

The Japanese 'idea of a university' has no global resonance. The modern research university has been shaped by German and American models. The UK and to some extent France have exercised influence, as did the Soviet model prior to 1990. Japan has been a follower not a leader in university design. It has made little contribution to the new university strategies developed in the global era (see chapter five). Although Japan has the strongest research universities and along with Korea the highest student participation rates in Asia, the Asian universities that excite attention are in Singapore and China, not in Japan. Here Japanese higher education is a puzzle. In any industrialized nation universities, and especially their research institutes, are expected to harbour creative cultures. They are meant to encourage innovation, and at best, discovery. Why does Japan sustain world leading design cultures in spheres such as architecture, urban systems, transport, household goods, and new cultural goods; yet fail to be a significant innovator in system design and institutional strategy in higher education, let alone a maker of intellectual paradigms with global salience? And despite the outstanding quality of the best research in Japan, does research under-perform overall? Also, active global engagement has become compulsory for research universities. Why are leading universities in Japan more insular than their counterparts in most (but not all) other parts of the world?

Universities in Japan as in most nations are creatures of the nation-state and the state-building strategies of the twentieth century. The state is the largest single paymaster in research universities in Japan as in most nations. Universities are also organs of civil society, leading families, professions, border-hopping academia and emerging global communities. These stakeholders are becoming more important. But the state is still the fattest yellow carp in the pond. In Japan the discursive and instrumental power of the state is strong in the nation and in the universities. The state in Japan is not a big spender. It follows the UK/Australian example in using scarcity of funds to control higher education, rather than using additional investments to motivate and enable it. But the state in Japan is a close regulator and more inclined than most nation-states to intervene in matters of culture, values and behaviours, in continuity with its Edo and Meiji predecessors. As discussed in Part II the state is also the chief protagonist of *Nihonjinron*, constructed Japaneseness. It always reads university policy through the lenses of national preservation and state interest—not the liberal formation of individuals, the augmentation of human knowledge, or global synchrony as an end in itself. Among other functions, the historic task of *Nihonjinron* is to manage, control and assimilate foreign elements as they enter Japan; to tame them as required, borrow what is useful for national purposes, and jettison that which is seen as incompatible with national tradition. The state sees the universities as an annex of itself, part of the state machine, and a primary organ of *Nihonjinron* in translating/ assimilating foreign ideas and technologies. This function is particular to Japan, though something like it plays out less systematically in other parts of East and Southeast Asia and in the Middle East.

The modern state-university relationship in Japan has ancient roots. It reaches back via Meiji, and the state centralization and international closure of the Edo period, to the state cooption of Buddhist scholars in the Nara period. The *Nihonjinron*-managed balance between modernism and tradition prevailing in Japan's universities differs from the balance in some other sectors in Japan. For example in urban planning and transport systems, technological and economic developments have positioned modernism in the driver's seat. In finance, it is unquestionable that the yardsticks of performance are global. But though research universities in Japan, like those everywhere in the world, like to see themselves as the humming and whirring future of modernization, in Japan the tradition-bearing and national sanitization roles of universities often seem to be dominant. This is apparent not in the knowledge content of curricula and research, but in the place of the universities in policy and regulation, the weakness of much university executive leadership, and the subordination of global relations to national functions. Alongside these specific factors in Japan's history that tie state and university closely together, the modern universities are cobbled to the state in a second and more familiar sense. The Japanese government sees the universities as potential instruments of national economic development and competitiveness, that should be more effectively harnessed to national industry. In this regard the state in Japan has the same attitude to the universities, and frustrations with them, as its counterpart states in all modernizing countries.

Now the logic of the global research university, and the logic of open creativity, both demand that the universities engage freely and go global without restraint. As we have seen, national-global tensions are inherent in the research university today, in Japan as in all nations (chapter five). Nevertheless, the point is that universities are doubly entangled with state agendas in Japan. *Nihonjinron* brings the dilemmas common to all university systems to a head in Japan. At the same time *Nihonjinron* casts an ideological blanket over Japan's universities that makes it hard for them to grasp their own national-global problem. Because the conventional vision of higher education is nation-centric and nation-bound—much more so than Singapore and more so than the UK, Western Europe and China, for example—it is difficult to envision higher education as a global space. But this constraint on the imagination created by *Nihonjinron* is accepted as normal. It is a sign of the depth of the difficulties facing the research university in Japan that on one hand there is widespread criticism of what is seen as undue state supervision of the public universities, but on the other hand the expected national function of the universities is little discussed and indeed is taken for granted. Like the nation itself, the national role of the universities is a matter of unquestioning pride—even though the policy expectations of the universities are closely tied to the problem of over-regulation, and if the universities were reset these expectations would need to be renegotiated. Nor is the global role and impact of Japan's universities a general matter of concern among professors, though global standing and impact are primary issues for many in the universities of China and Europe. The universities become globally referenced only in the standard comparisons of research performance. There the Meiji reflex of *oitsuke oikose*, which is never far from the surface of thinking, comes into play.[157] Thus attitudes oscillate between a deep complacency that Japan's universities must be best because they are Japan's, and the standard Meiji trope of 'catch up, overtake,' we are behind and we must improve. Neither attitude has a solid grounding in reality. And the global engagement of Japan's universities is understood and measured not in terms of their cross-border relationships, or the flow of ideas or effects, or the contribution of those universities to the world, but in terms of their stand-alone firepower. Not global effectiveness, inter-national effectiveness.

National System

The first seven national research universities were designated as Imperial Universities to distinguish them from other higher education institutions, and founded on the model of the German research university, beginning with the University of Tokyo (*Todai*) in 1877. They were primary instruments of the Meiji *oitsuke oikose* catch-up agenda. Jun Oba notes:

> One of the paramount missions of the imperial universities was to import advanced knowledge from Europe and the USA, and to develop human resources and to found a research base for the purpose of modernizing the country as rapidly as possible.[158]

Akiyoshi Kawaguchi and Denis Lander refer to the role of the Meiji universities in 'providing a window on the world which permitted modernization through the assimilation of Western science and culture'[159], which captures the controlled nature of the process. In the 1930s universities other than the imperial group were permitted.[160] After World War II a single system of four year degree-granting institutions was created, plus a second sector of junior colleges attended mostly by women, as continues today.[161] Local national and 'public' research universities were added. In addition to the seven comprehensive research universities in the imperial group there are now 40 comprehensives and 40 specialists. The imperial group have been integrated into the university system but retain a leading position. The funding system favours institutions with doctoral programs,[162] and older research universities readily reproduce historical advantages of prestige, size and human resources.[163]

More than three-quarters of young people (76 per cent) enter tertiary education in Japan, above the OECD average of 71 per cent[164] In 2007 there were 3.165 million students in Japanese higher education, 24.3 per cent in the public sector. Of these 0.262 million students were enrolled at doctoral level, 58.7 per cent in public institutions. In 2007 there were 1254 higher education institutions in Japan, including 756 universities. The mission of universities is to conduct teaching and research programs and 'develop intellectual, moral and practical abilities.'[165] There are also 598 two-year junior colleges with a vocational, practical and pastoral emphasis, nearly all in the private sector. The two-year college programs are nested in a four-year framework with opportunities to progress to university. There are 64 colleges of technology (*kosen*), mostly in the public sector, with lower entrance standards and five-year vocational training.[166] There are also almost 2800 professional training colleges in the private sector with a diverse range of functions including general education in the community. These are largely outside the framework of ministerial regulation. In this group the *senmon gakko* emphasize employability skills, and are growing in importance.[167] Thus higher education in Japan is diverse and also ordered according to a hierarchy of institutions with both different kinds of roles and different levels of status, reproducing the ancient and universal idea of a population ranked by function. The hierarchy of institutions is deeply entrenched and is universally understood,[168] much like the grades of status in the samurai caste in the Edo period. 'There is fierce competition to enter the most prestigious universities, public and private' as these offer routes into the elite professions.[169] For example Tokyo University often supplies leaders of government departments and major corporations. The competition at point of entry is akin to universities in the USA and China and fiercer than in most other countries. But the leading national research universities struggle to sustain the American Ivy League performance to which they aspire. Total public and private investment in universities as a proportion of GDP is only half that of the United States. There is also indifference towards problems of undergraduate teaching, despite widely reported problems of student under-engagement.[170] As in the UK, amid scarcity research tends to take priority over teaching.

The private sector of higher education, consisting of both elite and low prestige institutions, has played a key role in the growth of mass higher education. It includes 75.7 per cent of all students and 78.2 per cent of all institutions, including 76.7 per cent of universities, making it larger than in any other industrialized country. Public funding provided 12.3 per cent of the revenue of private institutions in 2006. The private sector charges tuition fees at close to full cost level. In Japan the role of households and other private sources of higher education funding is high by world standards: 1.0 per cent of GDP compared to public funding of 0.5 per cent.[171] As its size suggests, the private sector is heterogeneous. It includes elite institutions such as Keio and Waseda Universities in Tokyo. When the Liberal-Democratic Party is in power Keio has educated much of the cabinet. Both of these private universities are in the world's top 400 for research,[172] though nearly all research support in Japan goes to public universities. The private sector also contains a large number of local institutions of lesser status than public universities. These institutions are strongly affected by declining student demand in the wake of a demographically induced fall in the school leaver age group. 'It is estimated that in 2008 alone, nearly half of all private institutions had difficulty meeting their student quotas.'[173]

All universities, including private institutions, must meet the standards set down in the 'School Education Law.' Established universities are regularly re-accredited. The state also determines new institutions.[174] It is never far away, but government regulation and policy are focused primarily on the public institutions, which include most of the high status teaching institutions and nearly all research activity, and where its capacity to regulate is concentrated. But the state is better at stopping others from taking decisions than it is in solving problems.

GRADUATE EDUCATION AND RESEARCH

One of those problems is non-research graduate education. Masters-level professional training is not as well populated as in comparable countries, except in engineering. In 2007 the number of graduate students per 1000 population was half the level of the USA, UK and France, and one-third of Korea with respect to full-time students.[175] There is a history of reports that propose an upgrading or expansion of graduate education.[176] Their tone has acquired a new urgency since total student numbers started falling. But there continues to be poor support for graduate degrees in the labour market and this dampens down student demand for Masters-level degrees. Some scholars argue that in the Japanese relationship between education and society, the sorting role of higher education predominates over its role in forming human capital attributes such as productivity and creativity.[177] Social sorting is accomplished primarily in the fierce competition at the end of schooling for entry into first degree programs. It is believed that after many students tend to coast to completion of the degree, as employers sort graduate applications for positions on the basis of the reputation of the first degree university rather than grades at university. In many industries advanced second degree education is irrelevant or even harmful to career prospects. The 2009 OECD review of tertiary education in Japan notes 'Japanese employers have not rewarded graduate study,' 'In many instances it is viewed with disfavour, since it may actually impair adaptation to the firm's corporate culture.'[178] Doctoral education is in a healthier condition. However, the widespread use of Japanese as the primary language of examination—more appropriate in the humanities than science or most social-science—excludes much doctoral research from global circulation.

Japan is well resourced for creative research, spending 3.18 per cent of GDP on R&D (2004) compared to 2.57 per cent in the USA (2006).[179] There were 830,000 persons involved in mandated R&D activity in 2007, though only some were involved in 'innovation' activities in the sense used in this book, and only a tiny handful were engaged in 'discovery.' In all 58.5 per cent were located in business organizations and 36.6 per cent in higher education. Just 13.8 per cent of all research expenditure was for 'basic research.'[180] Because Japan is third largest investor in R&D this still constitutes a large pool of knowledge. According to the US National Science Bureau in 2005 Japanese researchers published 55,471 science and technology papers, 7.8 per cent of world output, second to the United States at 28.9 per cent.[181] However, in some respects the structure and culture of higher education narrows the base for discovery work. A significant national weakness is the low inclusion of women in the professoriate. In 2004, 6.1 per cent of full professors in national universities were women, compared to 18 per cent in the USA and 22 per cent in Finland.[182] Further, the old imperial universities and a handful of others dominate measured research outputs. This does not in itself militate against discovery research (though it may narrow the potential for innovations) as in all countries discovery research mostly takes place in institutions where leading researchers and scholars congregate. Though Japan's stratification is intensive, competition between the leading institutions is not as intense as in the USA. Top research universities are guaranteed social prestige regardless of their records in discovery research. Those universities are also primary instruments of national policy and closely regulated by the state, unlike their American counterparts, and associated with academic cultures more conservative and less open to newcomers than in the USA. This combination of conditions—high stratification, close regulation, moderate inter-institutional and meritocratic pressures, conservative faculty–is unlikely to be optimal for discovery.

NATIONAL REGULATION

In its review of tertiary education in Japan, conducted in 2006 but contested by the Japanese Ministry of Education (MEXT) and not released publicly until 2009, the OECD reflects on 'the traditionally close control of the sector by government—not just of the public, but also of the private institutions.' The other body with substantial influence is the professoriate, which tends to resist change.[183] Successive reforms to higher education have purported to move the universities away from their historic location as a department of state. But as in many other countries, the systems of state control have been modernized rather than weakened. They have been shifted from direct micro-ordering, to part devolution and steering from a distance. Japan has adopted features of neo-liberal system organization and New Public Management (NPM) practices in which higher education is modeled like a business and the national system is framed as a competitive market (albeit one vectored by the old hierarchy), and the semi-independence of the professoriate is weakened. In 2005 the government stated that its role should change from 'stipulating and regulating higher education policies' to 'presenting a vision of future higher education and "guiding" autonomous institutions.' This new role was to be executed by 'presenting the direction of future development' and 'setting or revising the framework' of the national system' and also 'focusing on financial support.'[184] But the history of *Nihonjinron*-inspired policy suggests that 'presenting a direction' would be prescriptive and normative and backed by controls ensuring the 'direction' is implemented, such as conditions attached to 'financial support' and requirements for reporting and evaluation. So it has proved. What distinguishes the case of Japan in the neo-liberal era is that the influence of the state continues especially powerful, the autonomous personalities of the universities are weak, and there are more detailed controls than in the English-speaking world or Northwest Europe.

Neo-liberal reforms allow the nation-state to become more effective in implementing a Meiji agenda whereby the universities are positioned as instruments of *oitsuke oikose* and *Nihonjinron*. But the Meiji catch-up objective does not extend to introducing US or European forms of liberalization in governance and organizational culture. There is no end in sight to close control, whatever rules, systems, regulatory instruments and funding allocations are used to achieve it. As one former MEXT official puts it, reflecting on recent policy history:

> Through these actions the national universities learned to be more responsive to
> the various policies initiated by government. Their responsiveness greatly changed
> the relationship between government and the universities. The Ministry of
> Education has begun to see the universities more as schools than as centres of
> learning. This means that universities are now regarded as requiring administra-
> tion rather than consideration as respected sacred academic centres. The more the
> universities become school-like institutions, the less they are able to resist gov-
> ernmental initiatives.[185]

The main neo-liberal reform was the 'corporatization' initiative of 2004 in the
national universities. The reform package was promoted with reference to the
Meiji reflex, the assumption that Japan was behind the international competition and needed catch up:

> Though regarded with some hostility within the universities themselves, there was
> a widespread political and public sentiment that reform was overdue and that, in
> comparison with the higher education systems among Japan's traditional peers in
> North America, Australasia and Europe, Japanese universities were falling
> behind.[186]

Prior to 2004 faculty employed by the national universities were civil servants
in the legal sense, and the number of staff for each unit was 'meticulously fixed
by the government.' Universities could not modify these quotas, establish new
units or restructure existing units without authorization.[187] The reform established national universities as legally independent corporations[188] able to
employ their own staff. Within the universities more power was given to institutional governing bodies, with a majority of members from outside the institution. Within the universities the autonomy of faculty assemblies was reduced,
to strengthen the central executive and governance.[189] The president of each
university was made chief executive and given strong formal powers. Line item
budgets were replaced by block grant funding, and institutions given permission to generate and retain private revenues, providing them with greater financial autonomy and flexibility.[190]The universities were also given more freedom
to design and implement curricula according to their missions, goals and
objectives, and offered scope to introduce internal competition between academic units, and vary conditions of work and pay levels. These were all significant changes that were consistent with the capacity of the universities to
operate on their own behalf in the global context.

But at the same time, the new self-determining agency of the national universities was nested in continued top-down controls. First, quality assurance
procedures were ordered so as to use quality assurance as a mechanism for
supervising institutional activities and priorities from outside. Universities

were expected to introduce internal quality assurance mechanisms to encourage a continuing culture of reflexive improvement. This might have supported self-management, but it was nested in the framework of regular quality evaluation by an external agency accredited by MEXT. It was also locked in to the funding system,[191] as government budgetary allocations are informed by the external evaluation reports and self-reports by institutions. This encourages timidity, imitative behaviours and self-censorship. It inhibits the institutions from risk taking or new initiatives that might take time to deliver benefits, which might be looked on with disfavour by the external agency and/or the Ministry. Second, planning mechanisms require the universities to negotiate the detail of their activities with the ministry. They must develop six year forward plans negotiated with MEXT and submit reports to government on an annual basis in relation to fulfillment of those plans. The six year plans does not go to issues of mission or strategy or internal structural reform. Instead the plans lock in the status quo, in detail,[192] creating inflexibility and inhibiting new initiatives. Thus the institutions are regulated both prospectively and also retrospectively,[193] and subjected to accountability for the detail of their activities at both stages, a remarkable extent of surveillance. In effect they are also subjected to annual budgeting,[194] inhibiting the capacity for autonomous action unless funded from non-government revenues, and controlled by resource scarcity. Corporatization reform included an annual reduction in government funding of 1 per cent. The state can drive activities and priorities by applying incremental funds, for example via competitive schemes.

Corporatization led to the changes in the pattern of finance desired by the ministries. At the end of the 1990s, ongoing government funding of the national universities was 66 per cent of their total revenues, with another one quarter derived from teaching hospitals. The reforms allowed the universities to raise private monies and from 2007 onwards to adjust tuition within a 20 per cent cap, and increased research support in the form of separate competitive grants. In 2006 just over 40 per cent of total university revenues took the form of ongoing state support, which was relatively low compared to most of OECD Europe, though not the USA and Australia.[195] But in the outcome corporatization has resulted in less change in practices than many expected. This is due to four factors. First, the reluctance of MEXT to abandon close control of national universities, and hence the limited character of the reforms, and continued weakness of institutional autonomy. Second, institutional conservatism and academic resistance. Third, within the universities the weakness of autonomous executive agency, strategic thinking, and internal management of budgets and university cultures.[196] Fourth, the failure to include a global dimension, by using cross-border activities and opportunities as a driver of internal change, as some other nations have done. These factors reinforce each other.

The MEXT retains key controls that inhibit free executive decision-making. Not only are there caps on the number of enrolled students and maximum tuition charges, and controls on borrowing, the ministry has final say in relation to 'the majority of academic reorganizations at the departmental or program level.'[197] At the same time many universities have not yet taken advantage of the new framework. Between 2006 and 2009 the proportion of staff employed on fixed term contracts rose from under 10 per cent to 18 per cent,[198] and some universities vary wages and terms of employment on a case-by-case basis, but many do not.[199] Some have increased private incomes substantially, many have not. The leading universities remain highly risk averse. This is consistent with the outlook of the state itself, which in the words of the OECD wants 'dynamism without risk.'[200] The reforms have had little impact on educational priorities, teaching and research cultures.[201] Despite the reform focus on executive presidents, some are still not full time, and in many universities election processes still play a role in selection.[202] Though governing bodies do not have to adopt the choices of staff electorates, the presidency is still being shaped by criteria other than capability as manager-leader, which works against reform: 'In universities where the voting system is maintained, several presidents (known as reformers for their audacious managerial innovations) have been defeated at the polls.'[203] There is also a lack of executive administrative capacity below the presidency. Many leaders at vice-president and dean level have no background in managing.[204] Under the pre-2004 regime senior administrators were appointed by the MEXT,[205] locking the day-to-day running of national universities into the state. The state has cut the tie but some universities are still groping for the old security of departmental guidance. 'Japanese universities do not yet have a pool of academic administrators with extensive management and financial experience to take on the strategic management of more autonomous and entrepreneurial university institutions.'[206] These factors limit the capacity of the universities to objectively observe the national political economy, and the global map of research universities, and to position their global and national operations in relation to each other. In turn this lacuna limits their capacity to imagine, implement and alter strategy.

The OECD has characterized the outcome of the reforms as 'not so much the introduction of total autonomy as a shift from control to supervision...the rhetoric of change has been accompanied by the reality of conservatism.' The universities have less independence than those in the USA, UK and the Netherlands, in reallocating resources internally, raising loans or exploiting possible investment opportunities.[207] The 2004 reforms 'represent a necessary but not a sufficient condition for the Japanese tertiary system to become internationally competitive and to allow the multiplication of sustainable world class universities.'[208] The role of the state in Japanese universities is closer to that in China, Taiwan China, Malaysia, Korea and Singapore, than in the bulk of the OECD countries. However, reform in Japan has been less through-going than in China and Singapore. Nor has the state stepped back as far as it has done in Singapore. China and Singapore place greater emphasis on building proactive executive leaderships inside the universities, that are able to imagine their operating environment as a field of action, strategize, and take national and especially global initiatives.

Boundedness

INSULARITY

The strengths and limitations of bounded Japan play out in the university setting. The apparent completeness of national ways of seeing and doing and widespread acceptance of the nation-state as both the necessary and the sufficient arbiter of relations with the world. Strong internal networks coupled with under-developed external relations. A sophisticated monoculture coupled with the inability or unwillingness to work with plural identity. Self-sufficiency and ignorance of the larger field of action, except as a place of barbarians and dangers, or as the medium of the Meiji desire for self-improvement. An inability to imagine the global setting, and indifference to global synchrony and proactivity. The under-development of global visibility, communications, engagement, mobility and accessibility, all of which can be measured and show up in cross-country comparisons and national trend lines. Though some can glimpse these problems and a few see them in sharp relief, there is widespread doubt about whether such issues really matter and little conviction that a decisive change in perspective and behaviour is required, including new patterns of external engagement.

It was inevitable that the main line of evolution of relations between Japan and the world, through the *sakoku* era under Edo to the Meij-instigated process of two-step translation and absorption of the foreign into the Japanese, would stunt the potential global engagement of Japanese higher education and research. The problem is entrenched more deeply by the characteristic Japanese pattern of strong clan-like internal networks within organizations, in which personnel within a single community are closely engaged with each other and develop strong systems of tacit information and in-house training and socialization, but external relations are weak and there is indifference to other kinds of thought. This is a problem within the national university system, where intra-institutional relations are stronger than inter-university ones. This happens in most countries, but it is a larger problem in Japan than, say, the USA, because of low faculty mobility. However, the silo approach is a greater weakness in relation to global relations—where bounded Japan as a whole operates in the manner of the silo organization on the larger stage. And the problem of national self-sufficiency also goes deeper than this, to the ontology of the university. Is this an institution whose circumference is that of humanity and the world, if not the whole universe? Or is eternal Japan sufficient in itself, the sum of life, and thus the sum of the Japanese university?

One suspects that for most university personnel it is it is enough for the Japanese university to be Japanese. It is true that in most university systems the global imagination is not a property of the majority—Singapore is exceptional in that regard, as is Bologna-affected Northwest Europe. Nevertheless, in the university systems of most industrialized nations, there are significant parts of the academic community that exhibit a curiosity about foreign others, strong desires for global synchrony, and excitement in global action. Part of the excitement of global relations lies in the encounter with sameness in other settings, the discovery of kindred spirits. Part of it derives from the engagement with diverse mindsets and intellectual forms. Universities in many nations are junction stations for cultural encounters. But these attitudes are less evident in Japan. Because Japanese identity is mostly understood in monocultural terms, cross-cultural experience is not strongly valued, while plural identity among Japanese themselves is suspect. Neither educational nor employment systems recognize the benefits of cross-cultural experience and imagining. Most companies do not value the foreign experience of graduates at the point of hiring.[209] Within universities themselves, remarks Horie: 'Traditional Japanese systems are not suitable to assess knowledge, including mental growth, obtained through students' intercultural experiences.'[210]

From bounded Japan the world's universities and national systems appear as a phalanx of competitors facing the nation. From this perspective it is impossible to envision global higher education as a common field of action in which Japan is one player and its effectiveness depends on an acute understanding of its global position, potentials and strategies. In a paper entitled *Why is Japan invisible in global higher education?* Fujio Ohmri argues:

> Japan and its higher education need to adapt to global knowledge society, where borderless mobility, visible knowledge, and strategic management, with visible decision-making and rules, are the most important norms.[211]

To 'adapt to global knowledge society' it is essential to understand the global setting as it *actually is*, not how one would like it to be, or how it was in

1868. When the Japanese universities look outwards they mostly see the traditional comparators identified at the Meiji moment, the United States and Western Europe/UK. They do not see East Asia and China so clearly, though there is fear of China in Japanese universities. Japan is as ambivalent about its inclusion in Asia as the British are about their inclusion in Europe. Both believe, wrongly, that because they have imagined a larger project (in Britain that project is the old Empire with America in tow, in Japan it is Japan!) they can escape the logic of geographical proximity. The Meiji impulse was to dismiss China, Taiwan China and Korea as backward nations and potential victims. The Meiji regime believed that modernizing Japan had to transcend the East. If necessary, it had to secure the respect of the West by claiming regional dominance by force. This world view was shattered by events after 1940 and especially after 1985. It is painfully obsolescent. But no replacement world view has been devised. The result is that in relation to East and Southeast Asia Japan is curiously mute.

Yet global geo-strategy suggests that the *main* priority for Japanese universities is to forge closer relationships with universities in East Asia. The region is emerging as the third great domain of the knowledge economy, next to North American and Europe. China, Korea and Japan are culturally united by written language. For this reason, in all three countries the main part of the foreign student population is sourced from each other.[212] Grass-roots regional educational blending has begun. This will further mobility between the professional labour markets. The OECD remarks on the growing cross-border movement of students within East Asia. It adds that 'the framework for regional integration does not yet extend, as it does in Europe, to the recognition of qualifications, the quality and status of higher education institutions, and the comparability of curricula.'[213] It is a telling indicator of the limitations of bounded Japan, and the force-freeze locked in by the Meiji moment, that universities and policy makers are still indifferent to the momentous potentials offering in East Asia. A comparison of Chinese and Japanese universities in relation to their approaches to internationalization suggests there is greater openness in China.[214] East Asia offers Japan the opportunity to build a greater global presence in higher education and research, though proximate alliances and the formation of an East Asian region to parallel the Bologna developments in Europe. For the moment Japan still has the strongest system of research universities in the region. This constitutes a strategic advantage. But the state is chronically unable to decisively address the historical legacy and move on to new regional relations. Japan's universities could move ahead of government—if *Nihonjinron* was weaker inside the universities, the regulatory stranglehold was looser and the executive was stronger. Like the state, Japan's universities so far have been unable to find the moral courage to make peace with their counterparts in Korea and China and move towards regional university integration.

DISENGAGEMENT

Some universities and some university presidents in Japan openly talk about the need to be proactive across the border: to form alliances, move students and staff in both directions and accumulate experience. One is Waseda University. Waseda has established joint degrees with leading foreign partners, and opened premises in Singapore. But in most institutions global activity is marginal and internationalization policy is a low priority, as the OECD review observes.[215] Futao Huang compares the outcomes of two similar surveys of the academic profession in Japan, in 1992 and 2007. This shows that the level of international activity had increased in the national universities but had decreased in the private sector. Further, the proportion of staff who favoured an increase in international activity declined.[216] The last finding would be duplicated in few other countries. In most national systems there has been an increase in research collaborations and academic visits since the early 1990s. [217] In Japan a lesser proportion of faculty go abroad for short visits or 6–12 month stays, compared to faculty in most other countries. Here the pattern in Japan is closer to that of the USA than Europe.

> Q. Has there been an increase in foreign influence, more interchange, more watching the universities of the world?
>
> A. Not so much, I think. (*Toshiro Tanaka, Vice-President Keio University, interviewed in 2004*)
>
> The 'inward globalization' is very very slow. (*Vice-President Waseda University, Ken-ichi Enatsu, interviewed in 2004*).

Global work is also limited to the inter-national view of the world. Because they are unwilling or unable to glimpse the global dimension in larger view, universities instinctively fall back on the old national version of the cross-border 'problem.' Japanese universities have experienced more than two decades of government-sponsored 'internationalization' programs. There is little clarity about the meaning of the term.[218] Though there is broad in-principle commitment to *kokusiaka*, meaning self-change or self-reform in response to international influences, this reflexivity is focused on international competitiveness and awareness, more effective global positioning, and enhancement of the inward flow of foreign students, who are expected to help local students to improve their knowledge of foreigners without the cultural risks entailed in going abroad.[219] Within the terms of Meiji the Japanese self does not change in the course of inter-national relations, except to acquire new knowledge which is assimilated into Japanese knowledge, and new skills. As long as 'internationalization' stops there, the status quo will not be disturbed, however much 'internationalization' funding is applied to it.

There is no quick fix. It is deeply difficult for universities in Japan to 'internationalize' because of the *Nihonjinron*-fostered indifference to global synchrony and engagement. This indifference shows itself at every turn. It is as if the trilobites (chapter four) decided that they were not going to use those new eyes, they were just not going to look, and if they saw something strange in the newly visible Cambrian sea, they were not going to let it disturb their daily routines. Most Japanese universities do not signal a clear desire for global connectivity. They do not reach out vigorously. They seem uninterested in global display, virtual or real, though this is a primary signifier of global universities. Commonly, the websites of leading universities in Japan lack depth of information in English, though they provide a mine of information in the national language. Futao Huang notes that one distinguishing character of academic faculty in Japan is that on average they tend to be more research active than faculty in most nations. This might suggest the life of the imagination is more active in Japan. However, faculty in Japan are also less mobile than their counterparts in many other countries. Their knowledge and their imaginings are more nationally bounded.

> The other distinguishing quality of the Japanese faculty is that there has been less mobility in their academic life than is the case in any of the other countries [in a 2007 comparative international survey]. In terms of international mobility, according to a government survey, as of 2009, though only 66.1 per cent of Japanese researchers had had the experience of going abroad, only 10.6 per cent of them had worked in foreign countries and just 2.0 per cent of Japanese researchers were considering conducting research in other countries in the near future.[220]

The proportion of faculty in Japanese universities with foreign degrees is low by OECD standards—7 percent in 2007. This indicates both that few Japanese-born faculty complete PhDs abroad; and that few jobs are occupied by the foreign born. Both suggest a lack of engagement with other national systems, and a lack diversity of academic personality within Japan. The proportion of foreign trained faculty is higher in the leading private universities, which offer some classes in English, and in the small number of universities that specialize in international education or English-language approaches, than in the national universities. But the national universities house the research system. Arguably, such universities require a mix of locally reproduced and overseas trained faculty. The first group helps to sustain the national capacity in basic research across all fields. The second, internationally experienced group maintains foreign academic links after graduation and acquires multiple or hybrid characteristics. It provides bridge and portal functions, integrating the national universities into the global circuits of knowledge and the evolving cross-border networks; facilitates access to foreign-generated ideas, often prior to publication; and increases the visibility of the national universities and the transparency of their research strengths.

A key to the retarding effects of *Nihonjinron* is its impact on language use. Language is at the core of communicability and identity. Universities that borrow and adapt from foreigners need to learn their written language, but if there is no need for synchrony or deep collaboration, spoken language does not matter. This is the perspective of a nineteenth-century university system, not a twenty-first-century one—a system that ignores the transformation in intersubjectivity engendered by communicative globalization.

> So we can read, or we can write, but very few are good in communicating. Therefore Japanese basically know what people say, but not open to express their own opinion. *(Ken-ichi Enatsu, Vice-President Waseda University, interviewed 2004).*

> Japan is protected by the sea and the Japanese language. Those are two main barriers to the free movement of people. *(Toshiro Tanaka, Vice-President Keio University, interviewed in 2004)*

The lack of direct communicative capacity in global English conditions other problems: the low level of engagement of Japanese faculty abroad, the largely closed nature of Japanese universities to outsider faculty, the difficulty of attracting foreign graduate students, and the inability to conduct inclusive programs and activities in the global language:

> The problem is language. Japanese is a high barrier to overcome. If we had many [graduate] programs that use English we could easily invite world class professors to give lectures for a short period. At the moment the audience are not so good at understanding English. We cannot invite the foreign professors. *(Hiromitsu Ishi, President Hitotsubashi University, interviewed 2004)*

Japan is not the only country where the monocultural and the monolingual are combined. The English-speaking nations impose the same limitation on themselves. However, English- speaking nations open themselves in other ways, through collaboration and the inward movement of foreigners, and they already have global English. Universities whose mother tongue is not shared with the world have no choice but to become bilingual in the skills of collaboration and mobility, even before their nations have made that transition. But Japan's universities face a larger challenge than overcoming their aversion to the Trojan horse of English. They also need to speak Chinese. The way forward is to combine first degree programs in Japanese, in which English and Chinese are taught subjects, with graduate research programs in English. By this strategy national language maintenance would be ensured, a new capacity in multiple identity would be created, regional cooperation would be furthered, and Japanese universities would enlarge their contribution to the global conversation in knowledge.

The OECD review notes that the proportion of foreign faculty in the national universities is very small.[221] A survey reported by Aki Yonezawa and colleagues found that 97.3 per cent of faculty in national universities support the employment of foreign faculty in principle, to augment Japan's research talent. The same group provided 100 per cent support for the Meiji objective of making the universities 'more internationally competitive.'[222] But there is no groundswell of support for opening permanent positions to foreigners or employing them as full professors, and little discussion of reforms to the career structure overall. The government has set an ambitious target of 300,000 international students,[223] but skirts around the key question of the language of instruction in doctoral education. Given the decline in domestic student demand in many private universities, first degree foreign students are seen as a major source of student numbers and revenues. The more important issue for Japan, which receives less attention, is how to build the international graduate student intake in order to better connect Japan's universities to the global knowledge economy.

CREATIVITY

In the universities the lack of communicative power in English (and Chinese) is joined to the inability to manage plural identity and the second self. We have seen that communicative globalization calls up facility in the kind of commitments formed in electronic networks: stop-start relations, multiple allegiances, loose and changeable ties. The social sinews of the global dimension are not the same as home base with its long time horizons, intensive loyalties and tacit knowledge transfer. Facility in the global university setting does not mean replacing strong ties with weak ties. The global research university does *both*. It takes its centred self out into the world, where it pursues its locally nested agenda. This requires a facility to combine two modes of relationship, two forms of identity. But as we have seen, the polyphonic capacity to move freely between identities and relations often seems lacking in Japan, and the missing element is multiplicity. The global dimension is a world of second selves. This is precisely what creates its fecund possibilities for universities. It is stocked with resources for imagining and creating—and making and doing. But in order to work its many possibilities, a capacity to imagine the plural,

the second self, is needed. It is precisely this which seems to be so difficult in
Japan. This is the legacy of bounded Japan. Is it unbreakable? What is the key
to unlocking the chicken-and-egg problem? If Japanese universities cannot go
out into the world with ease, if they cannot yet become proactive in all parts
of the world, they need to populate their mental landscapes with second
selves by bringing the world into Japan. They need to bring into Japan foreign professors and foreign doctoral students, in numbers.

The other question about universities and creativity is about their capacity to recreate themselves. Japan's genius in self-invention is a matter of
record. That same record suggests that major changes are possible only at
moments of crisis, and are dependent on top-down intervention by the state.
In the United States the leading research universities periodically recreate
themselves. The creation of self-evolving universities capable of exercising
global leadership has not been tried in Japan. However, a major crisis of
reproduction is looming, and this might enable the universities and much else
to be remade.

If present demographic trends continue, by 2050 the Japanese population
will be 25 percent lower and much older than at present. There will be a massive decline in the population of working age and an unsustainable ratio of
dependents to workforce. Enrolments in higher education are already declining. The only remedy is large-scale migration. One figure canvassed in government is 6–8 million people. But Japan has no history of planned migration
at scale. This would challenge national tradition at the core, in relation to issues
of insularity/inclusion. Is it possible for immigrants to become 'truly Japanese'?
How long would the process take? What are the criteria? And how would the
continuing transformative effects of a large new population of 'non-Japanese
Japanese' be managed? Very difficult issues, but this is also a case of crisis-as-
opportunity. The influx of a large migrant population could energize Japan by
enabling issues of national identity and plurality, and relations between citizens
and strangers, to be reworked. The encounter between tradition and Others
could be a mighty fillip, providing ways of rethinking traditional practices and
stimulating many innovations. Such changes also offer to make Japan more
competent in global relations.

It is a rare opportunity indeed—especially if it can be grasped in the manner of 1615 or 1848. The issues posed by large-scale migration are impossible to address within the present political culture. The universities could play
a vital role here: in changing the policy and civil cultures, in research, and in
the design of infrastructure and social institutions. For the universities to play
a socially transformative role here would require as great a change in their internal cultures and organization as required in Japanese society as a whole. They

could make fuller use of their intellectual resources if they developed sufficient agency as institutions to contribute independently without continuous state intervention. The paradox is that unless the nation-state makes a change in the universities sufficient to enable and encourage them to become self-evolving, this the universities will not be able to play this role. In the Meiji state, government is the first and only point of leverage, even when the task is to engineer the move beyond Meiji.

National and Global

In *The Birth of the Modern World* (2004) Christopher Bayly remarks that the history of modern globalization has usually been written in terms of 'the rise of the West' and notions of American or Western exceptionalism. Nevertheless, while Europe and its American colonies enjoyed certain advantages and were more dynamic than the rest of the world in 1750, so that they were able to move to a position of global dominance in the nineteenth century, globalization has always been 'multicentric' in character.[224] The Western nations secured dominance in the military sphere, by building more potent nation-states, by their exploitation of the development of production and consumption at home and aboard, in the sphere of the world religions, and through the capacity to create and utilize ideas and knowledge, including science, ideologies and the rationalities of nation-states. But the advantage enjoyed by Western Europe and America was not as great as was suggested by their premier position in the winner-takes-all military sphere, and that advantage eroded in the twentieth century, with Japan leading the way. Moreover, at the highpoint of Western dominance by no means all significant change was initiated from Europe and America. As Bayly remarks, we now know that events in apparently peripheral zones such as the Balkans, Indochina or Afghanistan can be decisive. [225] Throughout the last two hundred years, nations everywhere from Cairo to Delhi to Beijing to Edo/Tokyo grappled with problems of global modernity similar to those facing Los Angeles, Toronto, Stockholm and Vienna. 'The origins of change in world history remained multi-centred throughout. We need not so much to reorient world history as to decentralize it.'[226]

It is therefore essential to bring Asia, the Middle East, Africa and Latin America fully into the picture. The briefest glance at the history of the twentieth century underlines the weight of Japan, a driving force in global economic and military affairs, though as a matter of deliberate policy Japan has held its national culture largely separated from global intercourse. This is not to argue that the pendulum of world history is now swinging from West to East—the idea of 'the decline of the West' is as simplistic and culturally centric as

'Western exceptionalism.' In fact if present trajectories continue, Japan might lose ground within the world, though other East Asian nations will not.

Much of the story of modernity is the story of the rise of the nation-state. Japan benefited from the unusual coherence of its nation-state, supported by *Nihonjinron* which drew on the long tradition of Japan to mobilize a singular national identity and a state instrumentality as potent as those of Britain and Germany. The world is now in a post-Meiji era. But Japan is not. The nineteenth-century nation-state has been relativized by communicative globalization. This has reset the strategic options. Globalization places a premium on communicative competence, and working with multiplicity; on global imagining and strategy; and on actions that are at the one time economic, political and cultural. Cities, societies and cultures that will be the most effective in future will combine bounded identity with openness to the stranger and thick global traffic and engagement. But Japan still protects itself from the new reality. This is manifest in the regulation of Japanese universities. The universities are still understood exclusively as creatures of the state and its Meiji project, not for what they are—institutions with one foot in the nation and the other in the expanding global dimension. Japan's strategy since 1600 has been to secure bounded identity, timeless Japan, by closely limiting international engagement. But self-isolation is now self-negating, in all spheres. Cultures with no resonance in the larger human family will become marginalized even at home. The Meiji approach has growing opportunity costs for Japan's universities, and hence for Japan. The university offers Japan a medium for global connections and flows, for remaking national culture and bringing Japan to the world. If Japan is to make the transition from a primarily borrowing culture to a fully-fledged discovery culture, the university is vital. The university could be the engine of the continuous renewal of national tradition—breaking free of the limitations created by Japan's reliance on stasis combined with punctuated renewal at long intervals. This would strengthen national self-determination. Continuous modernisation would have an internal driver as well as an external one. But *Nihonjinron* still turns the Japanese imagination inwards, filters out the global, banishes the second self and locks the universities into the old national stasis.

Meiji fostered power of a high modern kind, in which merit and mobility were fixed within a firm social hierarchy and national border. In the global setting, money matters as much as before but authority is more diffuse. Hierarchies are loosened. Civil society, which spills over national borders almost as readily as knowledge, gains ground viz a viz the state. Nation-states are not disappearing, but in future national identity and agency will be less bound by the limits of the nation-state. Civil and cultural forms of national and locational identity will loom larger. The spread of diasporic national cultures illustrates this. Here the university, despite its sometimes archaic forms, is flexible. It is as readily turned to looser global connections, diasporas and strangers as it is to directed national projects. This indicates the national/ global ambiguity of the university. This ambiguity is one of its defining characteristics. This ambiguity enables it to function as a learning medium in which the nation becomes more worldly, while at the same time it brings a global cosmopolitanism to bear on the nation. As Matthews and Sidhu state, 'a cosmopolitanism which extends the capacity to mediate between and within national cultures is positive if it creates possibilities for dialogue with the traditions and discourses of others and if it widens the horizons of one's own framework of meaning.'[227] They also remark that global convergence and communication alone 'do not automatically give rise to globally oriented and supra-territorial forms of subjectivity.'[228] Cross-border systems and flows do not necessarily generate cosmopolitan relations with Others, based on openness towards them, nor a sense of the world as a whole. As studies of cross-cultural relations show, sometimes increased contact is associated with heightened tension and reinforced insularity.[229] Still, global connectedness is a necessary condition for the formation of a diverse global human society even if it is not sufficient. Equally important is the desire for cross-border synchrony, grounded in sympathy with the Other. At their best universities are especially good at fostering the desire for synchrony.

Paradoxically, unless the university is in some measure 'disloyal' to the nation, in the sense that it places the global good and especially the maintenance of a global space *above and if necessary against* the felt interests of the nation, the university cannot give the nation what it needs. And the university can only do all this when it seamlessly networks inside the global dimension with other nations and universities. But it cannot operate such direct global connections while using the Meiji technique of two-step translation of the foreign into the national. This slows effective communication, inhibits networking and blocks cross-border synchrony. In an Internet era it is no longer possible to hold the world at arms length. And this is a serious problem for Japan because since Nara it has *always* held the world at arms length. With the old Meiji scaffolding stripped away, monocultural Japan finds itself counterposed to the global without a means of mediation. To operate globally, Japan must become global and itself at the same time. The same is true for the Japanese university. In short, nationality must remake itself in glonacal form if it is to remain effective. It is difficult to achieve this. How does national modernization remake itself in a more global era, opening itself up to global flows while pursuing its global project? All nation-states face this strategic problem and must work hard to remake and re-position themselves. In Japan the problem is acute. The national enclosure of vision is especially complete and compelling. It is sculpted with high aesthetics. When walking in the fifteenth-century garden of Ginkaku-ji in Kyoto, or looking across the water at Kinkaku-ji, the Temple of the Golden Pavilion first built in 1397, as it sparkles in the sun, it is easy to never know that a new kind of global Japan is needed—a deep shift in the national imagining, greater than those of Edo in 1600–1640 and Meiji in 1868–1890.

The need to supplement Japan's demography with large-scale migration poses a very difficult challenge. But this is the crisis-as-opportunity that could enable the transformation of identity and cross-border relations on an historic scale. Settler societies such as the United States and Australia benefit from their on-going diversity, in which the stranger is continually made familiar, and vice versa. As we have seen this facilitates the imagining of the second self, the conjunction of heterogeneous pairings that is at the core of creativity. For example, most break-though discoveries seem to originate from persons who live in two (or more) worlds, and somehow manage to weld together the contradictory potentials of both. Settler states include many people like this. With its internal regional diversity India has parallel potentials. Historically Japan chose to eliminate the scope for multiplicity. From Nara onwards it opted for a rich assimilating monoculture that future generations would continually deepen with their respect for the past. Demographic engineering is a one-off opportunity to bring the amazing culture of Japan into conjunction with differing identities. Japan has an advantage here. It has discarded less of its traditional cultural resources than have other industrialized nations, including China with which it shares part of its heritage. A core question about universities in Japan is how they can contribute to the migration project and its social and cultural evolution.

Beyond the question of how to be Japanese in the era of communicative globalization, lies the second and ultimate question about Nation: How to be proactive on the global plane? How to contribute to the evolution of global society, where Japanese cultural forms and themes at best would be one of a number of main strands? The conversation about global society is messy. A Japanese sense of pattern and order is continually violated .The outcomes are difficult to predict and harder to control. To share that global conversation Japan needs vestibules where it can negotiate relations with the larger world, where reciprocal reflexivity is possible, not just the controlled adaptation sanctioned by Meiji—where there is scope for the second self and for heightened creativity in national imagining and global organization. The university in Japan is one such vestibule. It can connect to similar vestibules in other nations.

Aki Yonezawa and Hugo Horta remark that Japan provides a test case of what a non-English language nation university system can achieve in the global setting.[230] Of course to undergo that test, universities in Japan will need to become English language universities in some respects, particularly in relation to research and graduate education. In turn this poses the strategic possibility that in the longer run Japan and Japanese universities might enfold the Japanese-English pairing into the cultural evolution and identity of the nation—roughly like (for such analogies are never exact) the pairing of Latin and Greek in Ancient Rome, or Saxon and Norman French in mediaeval England, or Spanish and English in California and the Southwest of the United States today. All of these pairings are different—particularly in the relations of power between the two parts—but they share in common a fecund interchange, the potential for hybrid cultural forms, and a dual reflexivity, whereby each is visioned through the lens of the other. (We can note in passing that the best research work in comparative education also takes this form.[231]) The pairing of Japanese and English would also be a glonacal pairing of national and global language, which would create strategic flexibility.

Alternatively Japan has the option of evolving a pairing between Japanese and Chinese. The pairing between Japan- Korea is more ready to hand, but lacks the power of Japan-China. At the root, Japan and China have more in common than Japan and the English-speaking world. And the long-term geo-strategic payoffs of part-integration in East Asia are apparent. The political obstacles are formidable. Many people in Japan believe that Japan will be swallowed if it moves 'too close' to China, either because of China's sheer size or because Japan opens the door too wide. This kind of fear and its corollary, which is a lack of confidence in the learned global capacity of the nation, paralyzes any possibility of a forward move and an escape from the Meiji dilemmas. Looking at the problem constructively, Japan has something special to offer. International synergies are normally negotiated in terms of assets such as trade. Japan also has a traditional East Asian Buddhist/national culture more intact than any other. This could speak to the lacuna in tradition in post-Mao China. Many Chinese and Korean visitors are immediately impressed by the Japanese aesthetic, underlining the potentials for ease of empathy.

Another prospect is for Japan as a three-way cosmopolitan zone, where Japanese, Chinese and English are all important strands within the nation and its global relations. But until the sea-change takes place, the decision to open up and engage, none of these options are possible.

The Global Imagination

In a world in which we can see to the edge there are still ways to be national.

It is inconceivable that contrasting strands of human culture will disappear. Some will survive, others will not. Some will give rise to hybrids and successor species. New species will emerge. Nation-states and national cultures often depend on each other, and tend to produce each other, but they are not the same thing as each other. Not all nation-states are sustained by a main culture. Some bridge many cultures. Some national cultures seem dependent on a machinery of state and would wither without it. The flow of others runs deep and sustained, wherever their agents go in the world, and whether they are sheltered within a bordered state or not.

The first president of post-colonial Vietnam was Ho Chi Minh, a great cosmopolitan who was soaked in the love of country. He integrated a range of influences into his thinking. At the beginning there was Confucianism and a millennium of Vietnamese scholarship. There were the ideas of liberty and equality from the French revolution that was close to his heart, and led him to always hope for better from the French, who seemed to confine their ideals to France; English liberalism and the American declaration of independence, which provided part of the text for the proclamation of the first constitution in Hanoi in 1945; Marx and Lenin, whom he engaged with all his life; the early Soviet model, which he lived at first hand; the Chinese road and the peasantry; and the novels of Tolstoy and Anatole France and much more, for Ho Chi Minh wrote poetry and theatre as well as social and economic analysis and political tracts.[232] One suspects that he would have been especially well equipped for the challenges of piloting a disadvantaged but confident and connected nation, and its institutions of learning and cultural identity, through the currents and shoals of a more global era. It was an era he was ready for.

There are very few stories of national identity older than the Viet in the Red River Valley in the north of Vietnam, though Japan is as old and China is even older. The history of the Viet is one of continuing struggle for national self-determination, shared by the whole people regardless of the state regime in power. One after another all of the occupying or invading powers have been seen off by the Viet—the French, the Japanese, the Americans and the Chinese. The Chinese invaded Vietnam a dozen times over 1500 years, the last in 1979. Ho Chi Minh said that 'nothing is more precious than independence and freedom.' This quote embodied the national spirit so well that it is placed above the entrance to his mausoleum in the Vietnamese capital. Bac Ho was right about independence and freedom. This is the idea of human agency, and it rises about every sterile account of socio-economic determinism and the 'inevitable laws of history.' And so it became possible to free Vietnam from the invader. But Ho might have added that only under certain circumstances is the combination of freedom with independence the optimal one. When national independence is tightly bound in Edo/Meiji fashion this does no harm to negative freedom, the freedom from coercion that was famously privileged by F. A. Hayek. But it diminishes the freedom of humans to imagine and act. Independence plus identity, combined with openness and engagement, serve a nation better.

Global convergence shapes human imagining, just as it shapes the limits and prospects of nations. Most accounts of globalization talk of how 'it' is changing the human mentality. This account has focused on the manner in which, at the same time, globalization is 'us,' and the global space of action is being generated by human imagining and actions, in the continuous exchange of object and subject. And once our capacity to create the World reflexively is fully accepted, the stakes are lifted. The challenge for Nation (chapter 6) and University (chapter 5), whether operating within or outside the nation state inherited from the nineteenth century, is how to share the making of World (chapter 4). Nation, University and World: these are constituents of the global imagination, which began to emerge with the evolution of vision among the proto-trilobites at the beginning of the Cambrian era. The creation of the global imagination is the history of the Earth.

Notes

1. The example of Indonesia springs to mind. With more than 17,000 islands, 300 language groups and a huge range of human economies and societies, the nation is sustained by little more than Islam, state military power, an often desultory state bureaucratic machine with partial reach across the nation, and the national language. Along with Islam in most of the nation, the language is the element that provides cultural coherence. The language has been lifted from minority to majority status by its inculcation through basic education since independence in 1945, i.e. through state building strategies.
2. Virgil, 1916.
3. Wallace-Hadrill, 2008, xix.
4. *ibid*, 32.
5. *ibid*, 13.
6. *ibid*, 34 & 215ff.
7. *ibid*, 217.
8. *ibid*, 225 & 227.
9. *ibid*, 218.
10. *ibid*, 231.
11. *ibid*, 232.
12. *ibid*, 232.
13. *ibid*, 239.
14. *ibid*, 453.
15. *ibid*, 258.
16. 'A clean sheet of paper has no blotches, and so the newest and most beautiful pic-

tures can be painted on it'—quote attributed to Mao Zedong in 1958. See Macfarquhar & Schoenhals, 2006, p. 2.

17. Wallace-Hadrill, 2008, 9.
18. *ibid*, 5–6.
19. *ibid*, 6.
20. Marginson, 2009b.
21. Wallace-Hadrill, 2008, 13.
22. *ibid*, 28.
23. Albeit a Latin influenced by Greek linguistic theory and structures- *ibid*, 57–68.
24. *ibid*, 163.
25. *ibid*, 23–24 & 41.
26. *ibid*, 41
27. *ibid*, 144ff.
28. *ibid*, 209.
29. *ibid*, 144–145.
30. *ibid*, 184.
31. *ibid*, 28.
32. *ibid*, 27.
33. *ibid*, 35.
34. *ibid*, 357–359.
35. *ibid*, 103 & 133–137.
36. 'If what the Italian allies wanted was the vote, it may seem paradoxical that their moment of "triumph" under Augustus should lead to its abandonment. But if what they wanted was the dignity and protection that came with the vote, this is what Augustus ensured that they had'—*ibid*, 451–452.
37. *ibid*, 452.
38. *ibid*, 453–454.
39. *ibid*, 444.
40. *ibid*, 35.
41. *ibid*, 98.
42. *ibid*, 81–86.
43. *ibid*, 98.
44. *ibid*, 436.
45. *ibid*, 370.
46. Demarest, 2004.
47. Wallace-Hadrill, 2008, 188–189.
48. *ibid*, 189.
49. *ibid*, 312.
50. Bayly, 2004.
51. Appadurai, 1996.
52. King, 2009, 8 & 13–14.
53. *ibid*, 13.
54. Bayly, 2004. See Part III of chapter five.
55. King, 2009, 7.
56. Sassen, 2006 ,42–43.
57. King, 2009, 3.
58. Befu, 2009, 25.
59. Burroughs, 2005, p. 121. The Jomon people appear to have been the ancestors of

the Ainu, the long repressed minority people confined to the northernmost island of Hokkaido.

60. Burroughs, 2005, p. 192. 'The exploitation of rice may have pre-dated the Younger Dryas in East China. Fossil phytoliths have been identified from late glacial to Holocene sediments in the East China Sea that were probably transported by the Yangtze River from its middle or lower reaches. The phytoliths appeared first in the sequence at about 13.9 thousand years ago and disappeared during the period of 13–10 thousand years ago, which includes the Younger Dryas.' (Phytoliths are small particles from the cell walls of certain plants such as rice). In the Middle East the cultivation of wheat, barley and other grains has been dated as early as 13 thousand years ago, soon after the beginning of the Younger Dryas. In the Americas squash were being domesticated on the tropical coast of Ecuador at least 10 thousand years ago. It maybe that the Younger Dryas foregrounded the potential of agriculture in temperate and tropical areas, despite creating additional obstacles to its practice which stopped it temporarily on the Yangtze, because the great cold altered the regular global migration patterns of big game, rendering alternative food sources essential—Burroughs, 2005, pp. 192–193. It is also very significant that once learned in the Yangtze basin, the cultivation of rice returned despite the interruption caused by the millennium long reversion to extreme cold conditions.

61. At least these are the seasons in the Kansai, that zone of the island of Honshu including Kyoto and Osaka which is the cultural heart of the nation, and in the adjacent Edo (Tokyo) zone which has been the political and economic hub since 1600. The cherry blossoms earlier in the South of the islands and later in the North.

62. Ishige, 2009, 302.

63. Thank you to Richard James for this insight.

64. Inoguchi, 2009, 349–350 & 340.

65. Sugimoto, 2009, 16.

66. *ibid*, 16.

67. The emblematic pairing of Shinto and Buddhism was formally broken by the Meiji regime in 1870, and the two religions—to the extent they could be distinguished in practice—were set against each other by the Shinto-fascist regime of World War II (see below), but the pairing continued in the popular imagining.

68. Mason & Caiger, 1997, 44.

69. *ibid*, 25–51; Henshall, 2007, 36.

70. Mason & Caiger, 1997, 46–47.

71. *ibid*, 50.

72. *ibid*, 110.

73. *ibid*, 110.

74. '*No* has been built on zen techniques of suggestion and stylistic implication. But unlike the tea ceremony, *no* did not grow out of zen alone.' The classical *no* plays drew on the whole gamut of cultural elements of the day. They 'are striking testimony to the ability of Japanese culture to assimilate not only foreign ideas and discoveries but also elements from its own past into a new and exciting synthesis. It is a culture which relies heavily on established traditions, yet in its great moments, and in response to new developments and influences, it can reshape traditions in a satisfying way'—*ibid*, 152–153.

75. *ibid*, 148.

76. Henshall, 2007, 40.

77. Mason & Caiger, 1997, 146–147.
78. *ibid*, 188.
79. *ibid*, 173.
80. Hideyoshi also instigated two invasions of Korea, as a preliminary to a planned invasion of China. The first expedition began well but Korea and China together beat off the Japanese. The invasions ruined Korea and were very costly for both Ming China and Japan.
81. *ibid*, 178.
82. David Landes comments on the energizing impact of the practice of *sankin kotai* (alternate residence) on economic creativity. 'The movement of several hundred *daimyo* and their families from provincial han to Edo and back made for constant stir, an exposure to strange places, and new commodities…' Landes, 1999, 365.
83. Inoguchi, 2009, 170.
84. Mason & Caiger, 1997, 193.
85. *ibid*, 212.
86. Diamond, 2005, 303.
87. *ibid*, 196–212.
88. Wallace-Hadrill, 2008.
89. In Rome unbridled displays of wealth by freedmen was a continuing concern for imperial administrations, which sought to regulate the smaller luxury goods in detail. Paradoxically, this only reinforced the status inducing role of consumption—Wallace-Hadrill, 2008, 325. Japan, like China, focused on regulating larger items such as houses and the rules governing interior furnishings according to caste, and was more successful.
90. Henshall, 2007, 42.
91. Sugimoto, 2009b, 7.
92. Bayly, 2004, 79.
93. Diamond, 2005, 295.
94. Mason & Caiger, 1997, 246.
95. Diamond, 2005, 295.
96. Mason & Caiger, 1997, 218.
97. Diamond, 2005, 295 & 299.
98. Bayly, 2004, 181.
99. *ibid*, 56.
100. In 2006 the Japanese Ministry of Finance reported that 22.4 per cent of annual public expenditures are absorbed in national debt repayment, which is a very high ratio by OECD standards—Newby, 2009, 42.
101. Diamond, 2005, 294–306 .
102. Henshall, 2007, 43.
103. Mason & Caiger, 1997, 246.
104. Mason & Caiger, 1997, 207–208.
105. In this period neither Japan nor Korea sought to reduce the other to vassal status. This respect for national sovereignty was in contrast with later Japanese policy towards Korea, and with the approach then taken by China to other Asian nations. Edo Japan refused to conduct diplomatic relations with China on vassal terms.
106. Bayly, 2004; 318–319; Mason & Caiger, 1997, 246.
107. Bayly, 2004, 79.
108. *ibid*, 181.

109. *ibid*, 319.
110. Bayly, 2004, 79. See also 288–289.
111. *ibid*, 288.
112. 'Meiji' meant 'enlightened rule.'
113. Mason & Caiger, 1997, 260.
114. Mason & Caiger, 1997, 278.
115. Bayly, 2004, 423. See also Mason & Caiger, 1997, 271.
116. Bayly, 2004, 276.
117. *ibid*, 270.
118. Mason & Caiger, 1997, 272.
119. *ibid*, 301.
120. Henshall, 2007, 44.
121. Low, 2009, 130.
122. Morris Low refers to 'the Japanese embrace of modernity, and the concomitant confidence of the Japanese people in themselves and at times their traditions'—Low, 2009, 130.
123. Bayly, 2004, 382.
124. *ibid*, 382–383.
125. Bayly, 2004, 12.
126. *ibid*, 305.
127. Distributed at the Meiji Shrine in Tokyo.
128. Befu, 2009, 27.
129. *ibid*, 23.
130. Mason & Caiger, 1997, 294–296, 302 & 322.
131. Copland, 2009/1939, 172.
132. *ibid*, 318.
133. Mason & Caiger, 1997, 269.
134. Henshall, 2007, 45; Bayly, 2004, 461.
135. Bayly, 2004, 334 & 337.
136. Itoh, 2002, 12.
137. Inoguchi, 2009, 174 & 177.
138. Aoki, 2009, 182–198.
139. *ibid*, 183–184.
140. A novel by Sophia McDougall (2005) imagines exactly that.
141. Tellingly, students from China often find it more easy to do this than students from Japan. For more discussion of issues of self-formation in cross-border education, see Marginson & Sawir, forthcoming. Thank you to Peter Murphy for his insights in relation to the problem of discovery in Japan.
142. Shibata, 2006a.
143. Nezu, 2006, 83.
144. Shibata, 2006b, 7.
145. Shibata, 2006b, 6.
146. Nezu, 2006, 81–82.
147. *ibid*, 100–101.
148. *ibid*, 100.
149. *ibid*, 83.
150. *ibid*, 83.
151. *ibid*, 83.

152. Takeuchi, 2006, 40.
153. Yonezawa & Kosugi, 2006, 123.
154. Marginson, 2010.
155. SJTUGSE, 2009.
156. CWTS, Leiden University, 2009.
157. The Meiji notion of catch-up incorporates the private sector as well as the public sector. For example interviewed by the author in 2004 the then Vice-President of Waseda University, one of the leading two private universities in Japan, stated that 'compared with Western countries or Western education institutions we are very far behind.' However, in an interview conducted in the same month at the University of Tokyo the Executive Vice-President stated that Japan had caught up with West in science and technology by the 1970s. The notion of Japan being 'behind' has more obvious merit in relation to organizational design and global links (where some countries are clearly more advanced and better innovators) than in relation to research achievements.
158. Oba, 2008, 629.
159. Kawaguchi & Lander, 1997, 103.
160. Itoh, 2002, 9.
161. Huang, 2009a, 4.
162. Oba, 2008, 630.
163. Yonezawa, 2003, 12.
164. OECD, 2009, 59.
165. Newby, 2009, 13.
166. Huang, 2009a, 4.
167. Newby, 2009, 13.
168. Itoh, 2002, 8.
169. Newby, 2009, 26.
170. Masters, 2008.
171. OECD, 2009, 221.
172. SJTUGSE, 2009.
173. Huang, 2009a, 8.
174. Newby, 2009, 15 & 17.
175. Maruyama, 2008, 100.
176. Itoh, 2002, 21–22; Teichler, 1997, 295–296; Yonezawa & Horta, 2009, 6. If the selecting/sorting function of higher education tends to exceed and displace its role in forming human capital, this is true in all nations and not just Japan. The point is rather that Japan is the only country where this is widely acknowledged in the sociology of higher education. For more on the theoretical issue see Marginson, 1993.
177. Teichler, 1997, 285, 288–290.
178. Newby, 2009, 64 & 96.
179. NSB, 2009. Most recent available data.
180. Huang, 2009a, 9–10.
181. NSB, 2009. Includes social sciences.
182. Newby, 2009, 55–56.
183. *ibid*, 9.
184. Huang, 2009a, 12.
185. Yamamoto, 2007, 82.

186. Newby, 2009, 11.
187. Oba, 2007b, 294.
188. This idea was first proposed in a 1971 report by the Central Council for Education in 1971 but was shelved amid negative responses. There has been a long history of attempts to render higher education more 'flexible'—Itoh, 2002, 17–19.
189. Prior to the 2004 reform: 'For the bulk of institutions, however, all academic decisions had rested with the professors' councils in each faculty and while financial decisions could be made by the university's board, in practice the professors' councils had huge powers of veto, without being responsible for the financial and strategic consequences of their decisions. Indeed, since decisions of any significance were normally only arrived at after a consensus had been received, the system of checks and balances tended to operate in a reactive, even negative, way, rather than in a positive and proactive manner'—Newby, 2009, 32.
190. Oba, 2007a, 15–16.
191. Huang, 2009a, 6–7.
192. Newby, 2009, 36.
193. Huang, 2009a, 7.
194. Newby, 2009, 35. National universities were also subjected to 1 per cent annual funding cuts.
195. For the international comparison see OECD, 2009. See Huang, 2009a, 5. The government encouraged the growth of reliance on private effort in another way. Since 2004, seven company-formed universities have been approved by MEXT—Huang, 2009a, 2. This is a shadow play of education-as-a-business, from the neo-liberal policy textbook. These institutions remain marginal to Japanese higher education overall.
196. Ohmri, 2009, 2.
197. Newby, 2009, 17 & 35. The first three controls are common to many national higher education systems but the last is unsual.
198. Huang, 2009a, 12.
199. Newby, 2009, 19.
200. *ibid*, 27.
201. Oba, 2007a, 33; Huang, 2009a, 14.
202. *ibid*, 19.
203. Oba, 2007b, 292.
204. Oba, 2007a, 20.
205. Oba, 2007b, 294–295.
206. Newby, 2009, 20.
207. *ibid*, 19.
208. *ibid*, 18–19.
209. Yonezawa & Horta, 2009, 6.
210. Horie, 2002, 75.
211. Ohmri, 2009, 2.
212. Yonezawa & Horta, 2009, 10–11.
213. Newby, 2009, 85.
214. Huang, 2007.
215. Newby, 2009, 85.
216. Huang, 2009b, 147–149.

217. Marginson, 2009a.
218. Yonezawa et al., 2009, 129.
219. Horie, 2002, 65; Yonezawa, et al., 2009, 128–131. .
220. Huang, 2009a, 11.
221. Newby, 2009, 84.
222. Yonezawa et al., 2009, 138–139.
223. Ninomiya, et al., 2009, 122.
224. Bayly, 2004, 470.
225. *ibid*, 470–479.
226. *ibid*, 470
227. Matthews & Sidhu, 2005, 55.
228. *ibid*, 49.
229. Marginson & Sawir, forthcoming.
230. Yonezawa & Horta, 2009, 4.
231. Marginson & Mollis, 2001.
232. Broucheux, 2007.

References

Aoki, Hideo (2009). *Buraku* culture. In Yoshio Sugimoto (ed.), *The Cambridge Companion to Modern Japanese Culture*, 182–198. Cambridge: Cambridge University Press.

Appadurai, Arjun (1996). *Modernity at Large: Cultural dimensions of globalisation*. Minneapolis: University of Minnesota Press.

Bayly, Christopher A. (2004). *The Birth of the Modern World 1780–1914. Global connections and comparisons*. Oxford: Blackwell.

Befu, Harumi (2009). In Yoshio Sugimoto (ed.), *The Cambridge Companion to Modern Japanese Culture*, 21–37. Cambridge: Cambridge University Press.

Broucheux, Pierre (2007). *Ho Chi Minh: A biography*. Transl. Claire Duiker. Cambridge: Cambridge University Press.

Burroughs, William J. (2005). *Climate Change in Prehistory: The end of the reign of chaos*. Cambridge: Cambridge University Press.

Centre for Science and Technology Studies, Leiden University, CWTS Leiden (2009). *The Leiden Ranking*. Accessed 31 August 2009 at: http://www.cwts.nl/cwts/LeidenRankingWebSite.html

Copland. Aaron (2009 [1939]). *What to Listen for in Music*. New York: New American Library.

Demarest, Arthur A. (2004). *Ancient Maya: The rise and fall of a rainforest civilization*. Cambridge: Cambridge University Press.

Diamond, Jared (2005). *Collapse: How societies choose to fail or survive*. London: Penguin.

Henshall, Kenneth, University of Canterbury (2007). History. In Chris Rowthorn (coordinating author) *Japan*, 35–49. Melbourne: Lonely Planet.

Horie, Miki (2002). The internationalization of higher education in Japan in the 1990s. *Higher Education*, 43, 65–84.

Huang, Futao (2007). Internationalization of higher education in the era of globalization: What have been its implications in China and Japan? *Higher Education Management and Policy*, 19 (1), 47–61.

Huang, Futao (2009a). *The Case Study of Japan*. Unpublished paper. Hiroshima: Hiroshima

University.

Huang, Futao (2009b). The internationalization of the academic profession in Japan: A quantitative perspective. *Journal of Studies in International Education*, 13 (2), 143–158

Inoguchi, Takashi (2009). Globalization and cultural nationalism. In Yoshio Sugimoto (ed.), *The Cambridge Companion to Modern Japanese Culture*, 336–351. Cambridge: Cambridge University Press.

Ishige, Naomichi (2009). Food culture. In Yoshio Sugimoto (ed.), *The Cambridge Companion to Modern Japanese Culture*, 300–316. Cambridge: Cambridge University Press.

Itoh, Akihiro (2002). Higher education reform in perspective: The Japanese experience. *Higher Education*, 43, 7–25.

Kawaguchi, Akiyoshi & Lander, Denis (1997). Internationalization in practice in Japanese universities. *Higher Education Policy*, 10 (2), 103–110.

King, Roger (2009). Policy internationalism, national variety and networks: Global models and power in higher education states. Draft paper.

Landes, David (1999). *The Wealth and Poverty of Nations*. London: Abacus.

Low, Morris (2009). Technological culture. In Yoshio Sugimoto (ed.), *The Cambridge Companion to Modern Japanese Culture*, 130–146. Cambridge: Cambridge University Press.

Macfarquhar, Roderick & Schoenhals, Michael (2006). *Mao's Last Revolution*. Cambridge: Belknap Press of Harvard University Press.

Marginson, Simon (1993). *Education and Public Policy in Australia*. Cambridge: Cambridge University Press.

Marginson, Simon (2009a). The academic professions in the global era. In Jurgen Enders and Egbert de Weert (eds.), *The Academic Profession and the Modernization of Higher Education: Analytical and comparative perspectives*, 96–113. Dordrecht: Springer.

Marginson, Simon (2009b). Sojourning students and creative cosmopolitans. In Michael Peters, Simon Marginson & Peter Murphy, *Creativity in the Global Knowledge Economy*, 217–255. New York: Peter Lang.

Marginson, Simon (2010). Higher education as a global field. In Simon Marginson, Peter Murphy & Michael A. Peters, *Global Creation: Space, mobility and synchrony in the age of the knowledge economy*, 201–228. New York: Peter Lang.

Marginson, Simon & Mollis, Marcela (2001). 'The door opens and the tiger leaps': Theories and reflexivities of comparative education for a global millenium. *Comparative Education Review*, 45 (4), 581–615.

Marginson, Simon & Sawir, Erlenawati (forthcoming). *Ideas for Intercultural Education*. In production.

Maruyama, Fumihiro (2008). The development and quality assurance of graduate education in Japan. *Higher Education Forum*, 5, March, 99–112.

Mason, R.H.P. & Caiger, J.G. (1997). *A History of Japan*. Revised edition. Tokyo: Tuttle Publishing.

Masters, Coco (2008). Class dismissed. *Time*, 6 March.

Matthews, Julie & Sidhu, Ravinder (2005). Desperately seeking the global subject: International education, citizenship and cosmoplitanism. *Globalisation, Societies and Education*, 3 (1), 49–66.

McDougall, Sophia (2005). *Romanitas*. London: Orion.

National Science Board, NSB (2010) *Science and Engineering Indicators*. Accessed on 3

January at: http://www.nsf.gov/statistics

Newby, Howard, Weko, Thomas, Breneman, David, Johanneson, Thomas & Maassen, Peter (20009). *OECD Reviews of Tertiary Education: Japan.* Paris: OECD.

Nezu, Risaburo (2006). Information infrastructure. In Tsutomu Shibata (ed.) *Japan: Moving toward a more advanced knowledge economy. Assessment and lessons,* 67–88. Washington: World Bank Institute.

Ninomiya, Akira, Knight, Jane & Watanabe, Aya (2009). The past, present and future of internationalization in Japan. In *Journal of Studies in International Education,* 13 (2), 117–124.

Oba, Jun (2007a). Incorporation of national universities in Japan and its impact upon institutional governance. In Research Institute for Higher Education (RIHE) (ed.), *Changing Governance in Higher Education: Incorpration, marketisation and other reforms—A comparative study,* 15–36. Hiroshima: RIHE.

Oba, Jun (2007b). Incporporation of national universities in Japan. *Asia Pacific Journal of Education,* 27 (3), 291–303.

Oba, Jun (2008). Creating world class universities in Japan: Policy and initiatives. *Policy Futures in Education,* 6 (5), 629–640.

Ohmri, Fujio (2009). *Why is Japan invisible in global higher education?* Unpublished paper. Kumamoto: Kumamoto University.

Organization for Economic Cooperation and Development, OECD (2009). *Education at a Glance.* Paris: OECD.

Sassen, Saskia (2006). *Cities in a World Economy.* Third edition. Thousand Oaks: Pine Forge Press.

Shanghai Jiao Tong University Graduate School of Education, SJTUGSE (2009). *Academic Ranking of World Universities—2009.* Accessed 31 December at: http://www. arwu.org/ARWU2009.jsp.

Shibata, Tsutomu (ed.) (2006a). *Japan: Moving toward a more advanced knowledge economy. Assessment and lessons.* Washington: World Bank Institute.

Shibata, Tsutomu (ed.) (2006b). Introduction. In Tsutomu Shibata (ed.) *Japan: Moving toward a more advanced knowledge economy. Assessment and lessons,* 1–10. Washington: World Bank Institute.

Sugimoto, Yoshio (2009b). 'Japanese culture': An overview. In Yoshio Sugimoto (ed.), *The Cambridge Companion to Modern Japanese Culture,* 1–20. Cambridge: Cambridge University Press.

Takeuchi, Hirotaka (2006). The competitiveness of Japanese industry and firms. In Tsutomu Shibata (ed.) *Japan: Moving toward a more advanced knowledge economy. Assessment and lessons,* 35–48. Washington: World Bank Institute.

Teichler, Ulrich (1997). Higher education in Japan: A view from outside. *Higher Education,* 34, 275–298.

Wallace-Hadrill, Andrew (2008). *Rome's Cultural Revolution.* Cambridge: Cambridge University Press

Yamomoto, Shinichi (2007). The incorporation of national universities and its impact on higher education in Japan. *Higher Education Forum,* 4, February, 79–85.

Yonezawa, Akiyoshi (2003). Making 'World-Class Universities': Japan's experiment. *Higher Education Management and Policy,* 15 (2), 9–24.

Yonezawa, Akiyoshi, Akiba, Hiroko Akiba and Hirouch, Daisuke (2009**).** Japanese university leaders' perceptions of internationalization: The role of government in review and support. *Journal of Studies in International Education*, 13 (2), 125–142.

Yonezawa, Akiyoshi & Horta, Hugo (2009). *Reconsidering the realities of the international student market: A perspective from Japan and East Asia.* Prepared for the 22nd conference of the Consortium of higher Education Researchers, Porto, Portugal. Sendai: Tohuku University.

Yonezawa, Akiyoshi & Kosugi, Reiko (2006). Education, training and human resources: meeting skill requirements. In Tsutomu Shibata (ed.) *Japan: Moving toward a more advanced knowledge economy. Assessment and lessons,* 105–126. Washington: World Bank Institute.

MODEL THREE:

Re-Imagining Education

7. *Thinking*

MICHAEL A. PETERS

> 'A *picture* held us captive.'
> —LUDWIG WITTGENSTEIN, *PHILOSOPHICAL INVESTIGATIONS*, #115.

> 'What is given to thinking to think is not some deeply hidden underlying
> meaning, but rather something lying near, that which lies nearest, which
> because it is only this, we have therefore always already passed over.'
> —MARTIN HEIDEGGER, 'NIETZSCHE'S WORD: GOD IS DEAD,' *THE QUESTION
> CONCERNING TECHNOLOGY*, 111.

Why the Present Emphasis on Thinking?

There is no more central issue to education than thinking. Certainly, such an emphasis chimes with the rationalist and cognitive deep structure of the Western educational tradition. The contemporary tendency reinforced by first-generation cognitive psychology was to treat thinking ahistorically and aculturally as though physiology, brain structure and human evolution are all there is to say about thinking that is worthwhile or educationally significant. Harré and Gillet (1994) provide a brief account of the shift from what they call 'the Old Paradigm' of behaviorism and experimentalism, based on an outdated philosophical theory of science and metaphysics, towards psychology as a cognitive science in its first and second waves. The impetus for change from the Old Paradigm they suggest came from two sources: the 'new' social psychology which took its start from G.H. Mead and, more importantly, the 'new' cognitive psychology that developed out of the work of Jerome Bruner and G.A. Miller and P.N. Johnson-Laird. They maintain that the second cognitive revolution began under the influence of the writings of the later Wittgenstein (1953), which gave a central place to language and discourse and attempted to overcome the Cartesian picture of mental activity as a set of inner processes. The main principles of the second revolution pointed to how psychological phenomena should be treated as features of discourse, and thus as a public and social activity. Hence: 'Individual and private uses of symbolic systems, which in this view constitute thinking, are derived from interpersonal discursive processes…' (Harré & Gillet, 1994, p. 27). The production of psychological phenomena, including emotions and attitudes, are seen to depend upon the actors' skills, their 'positionality' and the story lines they develop (Howie & Peters, 1996; Peters & Appel, 1996). The third 'revolution,' also utilizing Wittgenstein (among other theorists), was advanced by social psychologists such as John Shotter (e.g., 1993) and Kenneth Gergen (1985, 1991). These views also emphasized a social construction rather than an individualist cognitivist construction. Gergen (2001) acknowledges the sociology of knowledge tradition and maintains that once knowledge became denaturalized and re-enculturated the terms passed more broadly into the discourses of the human sciences.[1]

The movement of critical thinking also tends to treat thinking ahistorically, focusing on universal processes of logic and reasoning.[2] Against this trend and against the scientific spirit of the age this chapter presents a historical and philosophical picture of thinking. By contrast with dominant cognitive and logical models, the chapter emphasizes *kinds of thinking* and *styles of reasoning*. The chapter grows out of interests primarily in the work of Nietzsche (Peters, 2000; Peters et al., 2001), Heidegger (Peters, 2002) and Wittgenstein (Peters & Marshall, 1999; Peters, 2000, 2001, 2002), and in its extension and development in Critical Theory (Peters et al., 2003a, b) and French poststructuralist philosophy (e.g., Peters, 2003a, b, c). The paper draws directly on some of this work to argue for the recognition of different *kinds of thinking*, which are explored by reference to Heidegger, and also the significance of *styles of reasoning*, which are explored by reference to Wittgenstein and to Ian Hacking.

I begin with the admonition, 'Always historicize! Always pluralize!' for Reason also has a history. The narrative of critical reason has five 'chapters' beginning, first, with Kant; followed by, second, its bifurcation with Horkheimer and Adorno into theoretical and practical reason; third, its separation into three by Habermas (1987) according to knowledge interests—technical, practical and emancipatory; and, finally, its pluralization in the material conditions of discourses (Wittgenstein, Foucault, Lyotard). The fifth chapter is in a sense a postscript—a working out of the consequences of accepting that reason, like knowledge and the value of knowledge, is rooted in social relations. In some forms this is both a naturalization and a pluralization of Kant: not one reason, but many. It is clear that the history of reason is the history of philosophy itself, and as history, both revisable and open to interpretation.

To talk of 'thinking skills'—a concept that dominates contemporary educational discourse—is already to adopt a particular view of thinking, that is, thinking as a kind of technology. This view of thinking is a reductive concept of thinking as a means-ends instrumentality, a series of techniques that can move us from one space to another. In the so-called knowledge economy emphasis in the curriculum has passed from the knowledge and understanding of traditional subjects and disciplines to generic, *transferable skills* that allegedly equip learners with the means by which they can learn. These are often described in psychological language as meta-cognitive skills, that is, learning how to learn, and are now squared off against information-processing skills, knowledge management skills, entrepreneurial skills, and social skills like team-building.

In part, this reductive notion of thinking receives an impetus from both cognitive psychology and neoclassical economics. The work of the first-wave cognitivists, especially Jean Piaget, conceptualized thinking in terms of developmental stages and mental *operations*. He was among the first to operationalize thinking and to define it according to stages of children's development.[3] Second-wave cognitivists, picking up on the information-processing model of the mind, initiated by Claude Shannon's work in information theory, began to model the mind on the brain by way of a strict analogy with the computer. This has led, in the third wave, to the study of thinking and the mind in terms of brain states, pursued in different ways by Howard Gardner (1983), who talks of 'multiple intelligences,' and the Churchlands (1989, 1995), who talk of 'neural nets' (connectionism) and devise naturalized epistemologies.[4]

In neoclassical economics, at least since the early 1960s, the notion of human capital theory has focused on human competences, which are taken to be both observable and measurable. First developed by Theodor Schultz (1971), an agricultural economist, and then taken up by Gary Becker (1962), the notion of human capital was theorized as key competences that were measurable for economic purposes. Becker himself indicates that when he first introduced the term in the 1960s there was near universal condemnation of it, and only 20 to 30 years later two US presidents, Reagan and Clinton, from opposing political parties, used the term as though it was a bipartisan affair. As the marketization of education proceeded during the 1980s the emphasis on human and social capital grew, as did the emphasis on the related concepts of entrepreneurship and enterprise.

First-generation cognitive psychology and human capital theory shaped 'thinking' as a reductive concept, analyzing it as stages, or as a set of intelligences, behaviors, know-hows or skills. This approach, historically, might be usefully indexed and explained in part by reference to prevailing political economy—not only a strong emphasis on national competitiveness and on the 'core' generic skills of 'flexible workers' for the new global networked economy, but also the flourishing of a range of new educational technologies and therapies focusing on 'accelerated learning,' 'giftedness,' 'multiple intelligences' and the like.

Kinds of Thinking

In a strong sense philosophy has entertained a special relationship to thinking and reasoning: I suggested earlier that the history of reason is the history of philosophy itself. Kant defines philosophy as 'the science of the relation of all knowledge to the essential ends of human reason' or as 'the love which the reasonable being has for the supreme ends of human reason' (cited in Deleuze, 1984: 1). As Deleuze (1984: 1) himself reminds us, 'The supreme ends of Reason form the system of *Culture*; in these definitions we can already identify a struggle on two fronts: against empiricism and against dogmatic rationalism.'

Heidegger (1968: 3) begins his course of lectures, delivered during 1951 and 1952, with the following: 'We come to know what it means to think when we ourselves try to think. If the attempt is to be successful, we must be ready to learn thinking.' [5] Learning, in other words, is central to understanding thinking. Yet, while there is an interest in philosophy, there is, he suggests, no 'readiness' to think. The fact is that, even though we live in the most thought-provoking age, 'we are still not thinking' (4). In *What is Called Thinking?*, Heidegger is immediately concerned with learning and construes the learner on the model of the apprentice, emphasizing the notion of 'relatedness'—of the cabinet-maker's apprentice to the different kinds of wood that sustain the craft. The learner, by analogy, needs to learn different kinds of thinking.

In his Introduction to *Poetry, Language and Thought* (Heidegger, 1971) Albert Hofstadter refers to the language of Heidegger's thinking:

> It has created its own style, as always happens with an original thinker. Often a sentence or two is all that is necessary to distinguish Heidegger from, say, Wittgenstein, Russell or Whitehead. *The style is the thinking itself* (xvi, emphasis added).

We should remember in passing that the later Heidegger in *Contributions to Philosophy* leads us to a post-philosophical project of 'thinking' where it is taken to mean precisely not that which defined the essence of the Western scientific tradition. Heidegger recognizes different kinds of thinking that have been defined by philosophers within the Western tradition. More importantly for our purposes here, in *What is Called Thinking?* Heidegger advances what we might take as a tentative typology of conceptions of thinking, before discussing his own conception. I have simply listed his suggestions and added Heidegger's own conceptions as well.

1. Thinking as *doxa*: forming an opinion or having an idea (opining).
2. Thinking as '*vorstellen*': representing a state of affairs (representing).
3. Thinking as *rationcination*: developing a chain of premises leading to a valid conclusion (reasoning).
4. Thinking as *problem-solving*: scientific thinking (problem-solving).
5. Thinking as '*beriff*' (Hegel): conceptual or systematic thinking (conceiving).
6. Thinking as *understanding or interpreting the particular* case in terms of the universal (practical judgment).
7. Thinking as a *revealing* of what is concealed (the meaning of Being) (Heidegger's thinking).
8. Thinking as *letting be* (the later Heidegger's post-metaphysical 'thinking').

We do not need to follow the entangled, mystical and poetic thought of the later Heidegger to understand that he usefully distinguishes different kinds of thinking that have defined the Western metaphysical tradition. All I need for my argument at this stage is the recognition of the historical fact of the diversity of notions of thinking: that there have in fact been dominant and prevailing notions of 'thinking' and that these have changed over time, although not in a progression of philosophical sophistication. We might, provocatively, add others to this list. I think we could usefully talk of various forms of cognitive modeling and computer simulation or information-processing as contemporary and technological views of thinking, although this might be considered a category mistake. Or we might, more productively, embrace the different views of Lyotard or Deleuze:

1. Thinking as *information-processing* (cognitive psychology).
2. Thinking as *suspicion of metanarratives*: narratology critique (Lyotard).
3. Thinking as *creating concepts*: philosophizing (Deleuze).

This is not yet to naturalize thinking but simply to establish the case for different kinds of thinking—to pluralize it and to recognize its plurality, a range of different kinds, advanced by different philosophers at different points in the history of philosophy. From kinds of thinking to styles of reasoning, from Heidegger to Wittgenstein—this is the transition that we must now make.

Wittgenstein on Thinking

The work of the later Wittgenstein represents a break with the analytic tradition that is evidenced in Wittgenstein's rejection of both nominalism and the doctrine of external relations, and in Wittgenstein's view of philosophy as an activity—a pursuit separate from science, neither a second-order discipline nor foundational—which is unable to be characterized in terms of a distinctive method. Wittgenstein's liberation of grammar from logic, his rejection of any extra-linguistic justification for language and knowledge, and the 'semantic holism' of the *Investigations* (Wittgenstein, 1953) and *On Certainty* (Wittgenstein, 1979), simply collapses and renders impossible the set of distinctions (e.g., analytic/synthetic, scheme/content) upon which the legitimacy of analytic philosophy depends. For Wittgenstein there is no fundamental cleavage either between propositions that stand fast for us and those that do not, or between logical and empirical propositions. The whole enterprise of modern analytic philosophy rested on the fundamental 'Kantian' duality between scheme and content. Rorty (1980: 169) has moreover stressed the indispensability of the Kantian framework for modern analytic philosophy when he refers to the way distinctions between what is 'given' and what is 'added by the mind,' or the distinction between the 'contingent' and the 'necessary' are required for a 'rational reconstruction' of our knowledge.

Rather than view Wittgenstein solely as a place-holder in the analytic tradition, it is philosophically and historically instructive to position him in terms of his Viennese origins and the general continental milieu that constituted his immediate intellectual and cultural background. Indeed, this rather obvious insight is, in large part, the basis for cultural, historical and literary readings of Wittgenstein and the significance of both the man and his work for education and pedagogy (see Peters & Marshall, 1999).

I have explored elsewhere the importance of style to philosophy through a study of Wittgenstein's *writings*: what I have called Wittgenstein's *styles of thinking*. I want to highlight the fact that the question of style remained an obsession of Wittgenstein's throughout his career—I have argued that it is inseparable from his practice of philosophy. In terms more fully explored elsewhere (Peters & Marshall, 1999), I have argued that Wittgenstein's 'style' is, in a crucial sense, *pedagogical*. By this I mean that appreciating his style is essential to understanding the purpose and intent of his philosophy, especially his later philosophy. In the context of the culture of Viennese modernism, I interpret Wittgenstein's philosophical style as related to his double crisis of identity concerning his Jewish origins and his sexuality, both inseparable from his concern for ethics and aesthetics and from his personal life. With Jim Marshall and Nick Burbules I have explored how these concerns are manifested in his work and his way of doing philosophy, and how Wittgenstein's style may be seen as deeply pedagogical.

More analytically, we can say that the early Wittgenstein of the *Tractatus* moves away from both mentalism, where thoughts are understood as psychic entities in the minds of individuals, and the Platonism of Frege and Russell, which was anti-psychologistic. The early Wittgenstein uses the concept *Gedanke*, or thought, in two related ways: as signifying a proposition (*Satz*), where it is taken to provide a 'logical picture of facts,' and as a mental entity that stands in a relation to reality in much the same way as words stand to a propositional sign. Wittgenstein understood thinking to be a kind of language. Later he contended that the language of thought faced a dilemma, as Hans-Johann Glock (1996: 358) notes:

> On the one hand, thought must be intrinsically representational....On the other hand, this means that the psychic elements do not stand in the same sort of relation to reality as words. More generally, Wittgenstein criticized the view that thinking is a mental process, which accompanies speech and endows it with meaning.

Glock (1996: 359) suggests that Wittgenstein's mature position is to jettison both mentalism and his own lingualism of the *Investigations* to treat 'thinking' as 'a widely ramified concept' which has four major uses:

(a) thinking about or meaning something;
(b) reflecting on a problem;
(c) believing or opining that;
(d) occurrent thoughts which cross one's mind at a particular moment.

Not only does Wittgenstein reject all forms of mentalism, but he links the notion of thinking to behavior, suggesting that thinking is a mental *activity*: it is a *doing*, which is most often expressed in language. As a way of proceeding I suggest that we adopt Wittgenstein's notion of language games as a basis for understanding different kinds of thinking, based on making discursive 'moves' which we can represent in the following form:

1. Learning the rules of the game.
2. Learning to follow a rule by making 'moves' in the game (i.e., practical reason; *practice*).
3. Inventing a new 'move' in the game using existing rules.
4. Inventing a related series of moves (a new 'tactic' or 'strategy').
5. Inventing a new rule in the game.
6. Inventing a series of new rules, permitting new moves, tactics or strategies.
7. Inventing a new game.

Each one of these 'stages' is subsumed by the next level and, clearly, there is a hierarchy that operates. While this notion of thinking recognizes *kinds of thinking*, it does so in a way that naturalizes thinking to *playing* language games; in short, to the material conditions of discourse and to the mastery of its rules, tactics and strategies through use and practice.

One of the consequences of this typology is that it enables a historicization of reason to its material bases in discourses and discursive institutions in ways that have been adopted by discursive psychology and discourse theorists, following Wittgenstein and Foucault. This approach may permit us to investigate the history of reason and reasoning: for instance, the bifurcation of reason with Horkheimer into instrumental and practical reason; its typification as three under Habermas, with the development of critical reason; and finally, its multiplication in discourse use with Lyotard and Foucault. But these observations are only speculations aimed at an approach to the history of reason and styles of reasoning. It is a thought that I wish to pursue more systematically and in an exposition of the recent work of Ian Hacking.

Styles of Reasoning

In his Inaugural Lecture as the Chair of Philosophy and History of Scientific Concepts at the Collège de France (2001), Hacking chose to develop the idea of *styles of reasoning*, which he credits to Ludwik Fleck. A Polish physician and epistemologist, Fleck developed highly original ideas on science in the 1920s and 1930s that were rediscovered in the 1960s and 1970s by Thomas Kuhn (1962) in his *The Structure of Scientific Revolutions*. Fleck basically suggested that 'scientific facts' are constructed by groups of scientists that he calls 'thought collectives.' These thought collectives are said to elaborate a 'thought style' containing norms, concepts and practices (cf. Kuhn's 'paradigms'). Thus, new members of the community become socialized into a specific *thought style* which shapes 'scientific facts' that may be 'incommensurable' with facts produced by other collectives. This incommensurability is seen by Fleck as an important source of innovation. Hacking argues that a style of reasoning introduces new ways of finding out the truth and also determines the truth conditions appropriate to the domains to which it applies. He writes:

> In the sciences we may use many styles of reasoning. Even within mathematics there is still something powerfully right about the distinction between arithmetic and geometry, or, we might better say, between algorithmic and combinatorial styles of reasoning, on the one hand, and on the other what we may loosely call the spatial style, be it geometrical, topological or making heavy use of symmetries. Undoubtedly the most powerful style of reasoning, that which has made possible the modern world, that which has permanently changed the world, large

and small, that which is altering and engineering the world at this moment, is what I call the laboratory style, which was emerging four centuries ago (Hacking, 2002: 2–3).

He offers the caution that 'there are many more styles of reasoning' (2002: 3), emphasizing by way of example his own interest and work on the statistical style, and, by quoting Bourdieu, proceeds to defend a historical argument for the history of reason:

> We have to acknowledge that reason did not fall from heaven as a mysterious and forever inexplicable gift, and that it is therefore historical through and through; but we are not forced to conclude, as is often supposed, that it is reducible to history. It is in history, and in history alone, that we must seek the principle of the relative independence of reasons from the history of which it is a product; or, more precisely, in the strictly historical, but entirely specific logic through which the exceptional universes in which the singular history of reason is fulfilled were established (cited in Hacking, 2002: 3).

Hacking himself, picking up on Bourdieu's lead, argues that each style has its own proof and demonstration criteria, and it own truth conditions. For Hacking, then, a style of reasoning actually creates the truth criteria in a self-authenticating way. He argues (2002: 4):

> Each scientific style of reasoning introduces a new domain of objects to study. Each style introduces a new class of objects, and on the side generates, for each new class of entities, a new realism/anti-realism debate. To stick to the most familiar examples, think of the reality of mathematical objects, with—in the extreme—the opposition between Platonism and mathematical constructivism.

He emphasizes classification as 'the essence of one style of scientific reasoning, and also something needed for thought itself' and considers some fundamental distinctions between classifications in the social and the natural sciences. He acknowledges that 'classification is at the core of the taxonomic sciences, of systematic botany and zoology' (2002: 6), but asks which taxa are real. He discusses Duhem as someone 'committed to the idea of stable, growing and persistent natural classifications' (2002: 7), putting him alongside Nietzsche in *The Gay Science*, whom he cites as follows:

> The fame, name and appearance of a thing, what it counts as, its customary measure and weight—which in the beginning is an arbitrary error for the most part, thrown over things like a garment and alien to their essence, even to their skin— due to the continuous growth of belief in it from generation to generation, gradually grows, as it were, onto and into the thing, and turns into its very body (cited in Hacking, 2002: 7).

Hacking continues his exposition of Nietzsche by reminding us that naming is an historical activity that takes place in particular sites at particular times. As he says, 'Objects come into being,' and, signaling his own intellectual debt to Foucault—whose ontology was both creative and historical—Hacking (2002) mentions his book *Historical Ontology*, which is both a reflection on the uses of history in philosophy and an interpretation of the work of Foucault. In that work Hacking (2000) entertains the concept of historical ontology by explaining how his work (and Foucault's) exemplify it. He also distinguishes it from 'historical epistemology' and 'historical meta-epistemology.' Drawing on the work of A.C. Crombie and what he calls 'styles of reasoning,' Hacking advocates a conception of reason that is neither subjective nor constructivist. Many statements, he argues, including 'the maligned category of observation sentences,' are independent of any given method of proof, and much of our scientific knowledge acquires determinate meaning in relation to specific styles of demonstration such as experimental, axiomatic, and analogical-comparative techniques. Styles of reasoning relativize what is knowable: they constitute a set of techniques both linguistic and material that make statements *candidates* for truth in the first place, and are therefore akin to Foucault's 'discourses.'

Hacking draws largely on Nelson Goodman's (1978) *Ways of Worldmaking* to articulate a theory of 'kind-making.' He credits Goodman with an original discovery with respect to the riddle of induction, which shows that

> whenever we reach any general conclusion on the basis of evidence about its instances, we could, using the same rules of inference, but with different classifications, reach an opposite conclusion (Hacking, 2000: 128).

Goodman's conclusion, then, is the basis for Hacking's claim that we can and do inhabit many different worlds; he quotes Goodman to good effect:

> Without the organization and the selection of relevant kinds—effected by evolving tradition—there is no rightness or wrongness of categorization, no validity or invalidity of inductive inference, no fair or unfair sampling, and no uniformity or disparity among samples (cited in Hacking, 2000: 129).

He summarizes Goodman thus: 'The selection and organization of kinds determines…what we call the world' and kinds come into being through a 'fit with practice…effected by an evolving tradition' (2000: 129). As for kinds, so analogically for classifications and names: as Hacking argues,

> Names work on us. They change us, they change how we experience our lives and how we choose our futures….They work in an immense world of practices, institutions, authorities, connotations, stories, analogies, memories, fantasies…An analysis of classifications of human beings is an analysis of classificatory words in the sites in which they are used, of the relations between speaker and hearer, of external descriptions and internal sensibilities (2002: 9).

Thus, the human and the social sciences do not differ from natural ones only because they socially construct their subjects, or because they require *Verstehen* rather than explanation. 'They differ because there is a dynamical interaction between the classifications developed in the social sciences, and the individuals or behavior classified' (2002, p. 10).

If there is a payoff from Hacking's analysis that ought to be taken on board by educationalists, it is a kind of strong *interactive* classification that he refers to as *looping effects* in order to describe the fact that people who become aware of their classification have changed and can change themselves. He explains the notion of 'looping effects,' which work by recursive feedback, by reference to the history of childhood. He suggests that in the wake of Philippe Ariès's famous *Centuries of Childhood* (1973), childhood has been called a social construct.

> Some people mean that the idea of childhood (and all that it implies) has been constructed. Others mean that a certain state of a person, or even a period in the life of a human being, an actual span of time, has been constructed. Some thinkers may even mean that children, as they exist today, are constructed. Children are conscious, self-conscious, very aware of their social environment, less articulate than many adults, perhaps, but, in a word, aware. People, including children, are agents, they act, as the philosophers say, under descriptions. The courses of action that they choose, and indeed their ways of being, are by no means independent of the available descriptions under which they may act. Likewise we experience ourselves in the world as being persons of various classifications....What was known about people classified in a certain way may become false because people so classified have changed in virtue of how they have been classified, what they believe about themselves, or because of how they have been treated as so classified (10–11).

Interactive classifications are a very common kind in education. Indeed, the literature abounds with interactive kinds—'accelerated learner,' contrasted with 'slow learner' and 'recalcitrant learner'—all to do with the *speed* of learning, as though it characterizes a *kind* of learner. Yet this takes us further away from the second leg of the argument: styles of reasoning—not only *kinds* of thinking, but also *styles* of reasoning.

Such an interpretation and argument establishes the importance of philosophical accounts of thinking and reasoning and their assumed centrality to education, at least within the Western philosophical tradition. I have presented these accounts as both historical and pluralist. They introduce theoretical contestability into accounts of thinking that take us away from the pure realms of cognitive science and logic towards views that are historical, temporal, spatial, cultural, and, therefore, also empirical. We may recognize both *kinds of thinking* and *styles of reasoning*. If we do then a way is open to also recognizing that new kinds of thinking and styles of reasoning come into existence and

are developed and refined over time. This does not diminish their force or efficacy. In the same way that the double bind experiment came into being at a
particular time; that in a short duration it demonstrated a certain kind of efficacy in 'testing' that has not been surpassed; and, that the double bind experiment now represents a standard scientific practice; so too, with thinking and
reasoning and their histories. The acceptance of this historical approach and
plurality might serve as an antidote to the aggrandizement of one dominant
form of thinking and reasoning in the field of education; it might also encourage a greater sensitivity to issues of discourse (or language games), their material conditions, and the rules that constitute them not only within and across
the disciplines but also in their increasingly hybrid profusion.

This theoretical statement of *kinds of thinking* and *styles of reasoning* may
be seen as recognition that the sources of rationality are many and cannot be
reduced to one conception, model or method. It is a philosophical historicist
and materialist conception that grows out of the work of Wittgenstein and
Heidegger and is sympathetic to forms of discourse theory especially as it has
been developed from the thought of Michel Foucault, enabling us to understand how new discourses, 'language games,' and associated ways of thinking
and styles of reasoning develop over time and are part of the evolving moral
and technological order which include new forms of communication and
media.

If conceptions of thinking and styles of reasoning are in some way tied to
the underlying deep logic of different forms of media we must also anticipate
what the significant shifts in media are. Anticipating the argument in the following chapter we can talk about the shift in the style of reasoning from the
model of industrial or mass media based upon a broadcast and one-way transmission logic and cinematic style of reasoning to a model of social media epitomized in the growth of highly decentralized P2P systems that demand
participation, collaboration and creation on the part of the user as a condition
of entry. The term 'social media' only emerged in the mid-2000s when commentators recognized that people's (and especially youth's desire) to connect
was enabled by an emerging collection of interrelated P2P interactive technologies and architectures. Social media are distinct from the old industrial
media of mass communication, such as newspapers, television, and film. As
compared with industrial media, social media are both inexpensive and provide easily accessible tools that enable anyone to publish or access information—that is, to become 'content creators.' These interactive technologies that
comprised the new participatory media embodied a principle of decentralization underlying the idea of the Internet as a whole and was expressed ideologically by the term 'Web 2.0' that allowed for the creation and exchange of

user-created content (UCC). Three trends—people's desire to connect, new interactive technologies, and the economics of online activity—have created a new phenomenon and the new interactive technologies and peer-to-peer architectures have democratized writing and viewing, transforming conditions for creativity in the process, and enabling anyone with access to a computer to become a creator of digital content. We are witnessing a fundamental shift from the age of information to the age of interaction where user-creators by generating digital content are in effect continually recreating themselves in the process. No longer do we go on the Web simply to read static content; rather, we go on the Web to create and share our own ideas and creations through social networking, blogging, wikis and other user-generated media. The ability to create Web content by simply typing words and pointing and clicking, without having to know *anything* about computer programming is the essence of a new age of collective imagination based on 'collective intelligence,' 'crowd-sourcing' and 'socialized knowledge production.' The rise of what has been referred to as user-created content and media has been hailed as being truly groundbreaking in nature, permanently altering the landscape and direction of the knowledge economy, especially in relation to open science, education and learning systems (Peters & Roberts, 2010). With Web 2.0, there is a transformation of thinking and reasoning—a deep technological and moral socialization of thinking and reasoning where the Web has become a truly *participatory* media based on nonlinear dynamic collective communicative processes that are able to harness and personalize the creative talents of individuals.

Notes

1. In his *The Culture of Education* Bruner (1996) distinguishes the *culturalist theory of mind* from the computational theory, based on a model of information processing: 'Culture, then, though itself man-made, both forms and makes possible the workings of a distinctively human mind. On this view, learning and thinking are always situated in a cultural setting and always dependent upon the utilization of cultural resources' (Bruner, 1996, p. 4). He goes on to highlight the contrast between the culturalist and computational theory of mind in terms of a conception that embraces the tenets of *perspectivism* (the meaning of a statement is relative to its perspective), *constraints* (forms of meaning are constrained by our 'native endowment' and the nature of language), *constructivism* ('The 'reality' we impute to 'worlds' we inhabit is a constructed one' p. 19), *interaction* (intersubjectivity or the problem of knowing other minds), *externalisation* (the production of *oeuvres* or works), *instrumentalism* (the political context, e.g., education for skills), *institutionalism* (that education in the developed world takes place in institutions), *identity and self-esteem* (as he says, 'perhaps the most universal thing about human experience is the phenomenon of 'Self,' and we know that education is crucial for its formation' p. 35), and *narrative*

(narrative as a mode of thought).

2. See the website http://www.criticalthinking.org/. On review and critique, see Biesta and Stams (2001), Weinstein at http://www.chss.montclair.edu/inquiry /fall95/weinste.html, Burbules and Park at http://faculty.ed.uiuc.edu/bur-bules/papers/critical.html and Hatcher at http://www.bakeru.edu/crit/litera-ture/dlh_ct_critique.htm.

3. There is now a growing literature on 'post-formal thinking,' which Ken Wilbur (1995) configures as *postmodern* (which is radically contextual) and postulates in terms of the evolution of holistic thinking (which is integrative). Formal operations are said to overemphasize the power of pure logic in problem solving and underemphasize the pragmatic quality of real life cognitive activity. By contrast, post-formal thought emphasizes 'shifting gears,' multiple causality, multiple solutions, pragmatism and awareness of paradox. See Labouvie-Vief (1980), Sinnott (1998) and Marchland (2001).

4. Neural networks are simplified models of the brain that measure the strength of con-nections between neurons. Against the classical view that human cognition is anal-ogous to symbolic computation in digital computers, the connectionist claims that information is stored non-symbolically in the strength of connections between the units of a neural net. Gardner defines intelligence as 'the capacity to solve problems or to fashion products that are valued in one or more cultural setting' (Gardner & Hatch, 1989). Using biological as well as cultural research, he formulated a list of seven intelligences: logical-mathematical, linguistic, spatial, musical, bodily-kinesthetic, intra- and inter-personal, and naturalist. The notion of 'styles of think-ing' also has been used as a predictor of academic performance and discussed in terms of multiple intelligences. Various integrative models have been proposed: Curry's (1983) personality model; Miller's (1987) model of cognitive processes; Riding and Cheema's (1991) model of cognitive styles; and Sternberg's (1997) model as a the-ory of mental self-government, which delineates thirteen styles.

5. This section, which refers to *What is Called Thinking?*, draws on Peters (2002).

References

Becker, G. (1994). *Human Capital: A Theoretical and Empirical Analysis with Special Reference to Education*, Chicago; London: University of Chicago Press.

Biesta, G. & Stams, G. (2001). 'Critical Thinking and the Question of Critique: Some Lessons from Deconstruction,' *Studies in Philosophy and Education*, 20 (1): 74–92.

Bruner, J. (1996). *The Culture of Education*. Harvard: Harvard University Press.

Churchland, P. S. (1989). *A Neurocomputational Perspective: The Nature of Mind and the Structure of Science*, Cambridge, MA: MIT Press.

Churchland, P. M. (1995). *The Engine of Reason, the Seat of the Soul: a Philosophical Journey into the Brain*, Cambridge, MA: MIT Press.

Curry, L. (1983). 'An organization of learning styles theory and constructs,' ERIC Document 235, 185.

Deleuze, G. (1984). *Kant's Critical Philosophy: The Doctrine of the Faculties* Trans. H. Tomlinson and B. Habberjam, Minneapolis: University of Minnesota Press.

Gardner, H. (1983). *Frames of Mind: The Theory of Multiple Intelligences*. New York: Basic Books.

Gergen, K. (1985). 'The Social Constructionist Movement in Modern Psychology,' *American Psychologist*, 40: 266–75.

Gergen, K. (1991). *The Saturated Self: Dilemmas of Identity in Contemporary Life*. New York, Basic Books.

Gergen, K. (2001). *Social Construction in Context*. London & Thousand Oaks: Sage.

Goodman, N. (1978). *Ways of Worldmaking*, Indianapolis: Hackett.

Habermas, J. (1987). *Knowledge & Human Interest*, (orig. 1968) Trans. J. Shapiro, London: Polity Press.

Hacking, I. (2000). *The social construction of what?* Harvard: Harvard University Press.

Hacking, I. (2002). *Historical Ontology*, Harvard: Harvard University Press.

Hacking, I. (2002). Inaugural lecture: chair of philosophy and history of scientific concepts at the Collège de France, 16 January 2001, *Economy and Society*, 31 (1): 1–14.

Hanfling, O. (2001). Thinking, in Han-Johann Glock (Ed.) *Wittgenstein: a critical reader*, Oxford: Blackwells.

Harré, R. & Gillet, G. (1994). *The Discursive Mind*. Thousand Oaks, Calif. London: Sage Publications.

Heidegger, M. (1966). *Discourse on thinking*. A Translation of *Gelassenheit* by John M. Anderson and E. Han Freund, with an Introduction by John M. Anderson, New York: Harper Torchbooks.

Howie, D. & Peters, M.A. (1996). 'Positioning Theory: Vygotsky, Wittgenstein and Social Constructionist Psychology,' *Journal for the Theory of Social Behaviour*, 26, 1: 51–64.

Kuhn, T. (1962). *The Structure of Scientific Revolutions*, Chicago: University of Chicago Press.Labouvie-Vief, G. (1980). 'Beyond formal operations: Uses and limits of pure logic in lifespan development,' *Human Development*, 23, 114–146.

Marchland, H. (2001). 'Some Reflections On PostFormal Thought,' *The Genetic Epistemologist*, 29(3) at http://www.piaget.org/GE/2001/GE-29–3.html.

Miller, A. (1987). 'Cognitive styles: An integrated model,' *Educational Psychology*, 7, 251–268.

Peters, M. A. (2000). *Pós-estruturalismo e filosofia da diferença Uma introdução*, Belo Horizonte, Autêntica Editora. (*Poststructuralism and the philosophy of difference: an introduction*) Trans. into Portuguese by Tomaz Tadeu Da Silva.

Peters, M. A. (2003). 'The university and the new humanities: professing with Derrida,' *Arts and Humanities in Higher Education* 3(1): 41–57.

Peters, M.A. & Appel, S. (1996). 'Positioning Theory: Discourse, the Subject and the Problem of Desire,' *Social Analysis*, 40, September: 120–145.

Peters, M.A. & Marshall, J.D. (1999). *Wittgenstein: philosophy, postmodernism, pedagogy*, Westport, CT. & London: Bergin & Garvey.

Peters, M.A. (2000). 'Writing the self: Wittgenstein, confession and pedagogy,' *Journal of Philosophy of Education*, 34(2), May: 353–368.

Peters, M.A. (2001). 'Philosophy As pedagogy: Wittgenstein's styles of thinking.' *Radical Pedagogy*. 3, 3 (http://www.icaap.org/iuicode?2.3.3.4).

Peters, M.A. (2001). 'Wittgensteinian pedagogics: Cavell on the figure of the child in the *Investigations*,' *Studies in Philosophy and Education*, 20: 125–138.

Peters, M.A. (2002). (Ed.) *Heidegger, education and modernity*, Lanham, Boulder, NY, Oxford: Rowman & Littlefield.

Peters, M.A. (2002). Nietzsche's legacy for education revisited, *Studies in Philosophy and Education* forthcoming

Peters, M.A. (2002). Wittgenstein, education and the philosophy of mathematics, *Theory and Science*, 3(3) (http://theoryandfscience.icaap.rorg/).

Peters, M.A. (2003). 'Truth-telling as an educational practice of the self: Foucault, *parrhesia* and the ethics of subjectivity,' *Oxford Review of Education*, 29(2) 207–223.

Peters, M.A. (2003). Geofilosophia, educação e pedagogia do conceito, *Educação & Realidade*, 27(2) July-December 2002: 77–88. Trans. Portuguese, Tomaz Tadeu Da Silva.

Peters, M.A., Lankshear, C. and Olssen, M. (eds) (2003). *Critical theory: founders and praxis*, New York, Peter Lang.

Peters, M.A., Lankshear, C. and Olssen, M. (eds) (2003). *Futures of critical theory: dreams of difference*, Lanham, Boulder, NY, Oxford: Rowman & Littlefield.

Peters, M.A., Marshall, J.D., Smeyers, P. (2001). (eds) *Nietzsche's legacy for education: past and present values*, Westport, CT. & London: Bergin & Garvey.

Peters, Michael A. & Roberts, Peters (2010). *The Virtues of Openness: Education, Science and Scholarship in the Digital Age*, Boulder, Paradigm Press.

Riding, R. J., & Cheema, I. (1991). 'Cognitive styles—An overview and integration,' *Educational Psychology*, 11(3 & 4): 193–215.

Schultz, T. (1971). *Investment in Human Capital: The Role of Education and of Research*, New York: Free Press.

Shotter, J. (1993). 'Harré, Vygotsky, Bakhtin, Vico, Wittgenstein; Academic discourses and conversational realities,' *Journal for the Theory of Social Behaviour*, 23: 459–82.

Sinnott, J.D. (1998). *The development of logic in adulthood: Postformal thought and its applications*, New York: Plenum.

Sternberg, R. J. (1997). *Thinking styles*. New York: Cambridge University Press.

Wilbur, K. (1995). *Sex, Ecology, Spirituality*, Boston: Shambhala.

Wittgenstein, L. (1953). *Philosophical investigations*. Trans. G. E. M. Anscombe, Oxford: Blackwell.

Wittgenstein, L. (1979). *On certainty*. Edited by G.E.M. Anscombe And G.H. Von Wright, Oxford: Blackwell.

8. Image

MICHAEL A. PETERS

> An historical epoch dominated by Greek ocular metaphors may . . . yield to
> one in which the philosophical vocabulary incorporating these metaphors
> seems quaint as the animistic vocabulary of pre-classical times.
> —RICHARD RORTY (1980) PHILOSOPHY AND THE MIRROR OF NATURE, P. 11

> Publicity is the life of this culture—in so far as without publicity capitalism
> could not survive—and at the same time publicity is its dream.
> —JOHN BERGER, WAYS OF SEEING

Introduction

We now live in a world of 'visual cultures,' in a world of *remediation* and *cross-mediation* in which experience of content both appears in multiple forms and migrates from one media form to another (Bolter, 2001). If reality is mediated so too must be social relations. The language of the new social media is easily programmable given its algorithmic character and its numerical coding allows for the automation of many of its functions including media creation. New media are variable and interactive and no longer tied to technologies of exact reproduction such as copying (Manovitch, 2000). They are part of a wider paradigm and system that Castells (2000) calls 'informational capitalism' which is a new technological paradigm and mode of development characterized by information generation, processing, and transmission that have become the fundamental sources of productivity and power. More and more of this information that is the raw material of knowledge capitalism is increasingly either image-based or comes to us in the form of images. We now live in a socially networked universe in which the material conditions for the formation, circulation, and utilization of knowledge and learning are rapidly changing from an industrial to information and media-based economy.

Increasingly the emphasis has fallen on knowledge, learning and media systems and networks that depend upon the acquisition of new skills of image manipulation and understanding as a central aspect of development considered in personal, community, regional, national and global contexts.

These mega-trends signal both changes in the production and consumption of symbolic visual goods and also associated changes in their contexts of use. The radical concordance of image, text and sound, and development of new information and knowledge infrastructures have encouraged the emergence of global media networks linked with telecommunications that signal the emergence of a Euro-American consumer culture based on the rise of edutainment media and a set of information utility conglomerates. What new subjectivities are constituted through social media and what role does image control play in this process? What new possibilities do the new media afford students for educational autonomy? What distinctive forms of immaterial labor and affect do social and image-based media create? And what is the transformational potential of new image-based and social media that link education to its radical historical mission?

The ubiquity of the image in an age of film, video and digital multimedia emphasizes both the ocularcentrism of the twenty-first century and the hegemony of the image that drowns us in an overflow and repetition of images. Is this the 'society of the spectacle' (Debord, 1967) that prefers the sign than the thing itself? Is it a society dominated by 'the violence of the image' (Baudrillard, 1998) of simulacra and simulations that demonstrate a suspicion of vision and the hegemony of vision (Jay, 1993) and points to the ultimate collapse at the end of modernism of the relation between image and reality? Remember Baudrillard's (1998) four-act drama: first, a simulacrum 'is the reflection of a profound reality,' which corresponds to representation; second, 'it masks and denatures a profound reality'; third, 'it masks the absence of a profound reality'; and, fourth 'it has no relation to any reality whatsoever; it is its own pure simulation.'

In *The Future of the Image* Jacques Rancière (2008) suggests that there are two prevailing views about image and reality: the first, exemplified by Baudrillard, maintains that nothing is real anymore, because all of reality has become virtual, a parade of simulacra and images without any true substance; the second believes that there are no more images, because an 'image' is a thing clearly distanced or separate from reality and as we have lost this distance we are no longer able to discern between images and reality, and thus, the image, as a category, no longer exists.

With the increasing dominance of images over text can visual culture deliver on its promises of a pedagogy that exposes the deep bias of images and their inherently ambiguous nature? Can 'visual literacy'—a set of 'vision-competencies' (Debes, 1969)—really deliver on the promise of a critical approach equal to the moment? And is visual literacy really co-present with linguistic literacy comprising a set interacting and interlacing modalities which complement one another in the meaning-making process?

The epistemology of the eye (as opposed to the ear) is central to the philosophical debate revolving around the primacy of vision in Occidental culture and the domination of the gaze that has interested French theory since Bataille and received extensive theoretical treatment by Sartre, Lacan and Foucault among many others. 'The look,' 'the gaze,' 'le regard,' in the hands of these theorists becomes alternately a theory of subjectivity, a map of the existence of others, a form of development of consciousness, and a scientific means of governance and control.

This chapter consists in a series of notes and suggestions towards a critical education. There are pedagogies of the image in the understandings of each aspect of these theoretical developments. This chapter provides the conceptual basis for pedagogies of the image. First, it traces the history of gaze briefly examining the work of Sartre, Lacan and Foucault. Second, and from a different angle, it foregrounds John Berger's *Ways of Seeing* and its relation to the field of visual culture. Third, I focus on Guy Debord's *Society of the Spectacle* and Jean Baudrillard's simulacra. Finally, I discuss Deleuze on the cinema. Each of these approaches I suggest provides the basis for pedagogies of the image—a sort of collective repertoire of tools for analysis.

Pedagogies of the Gaze

'The look' as Sartre terms it constitutes section four of Chapter 1 'The Existence of Others' in Part Three of *Being and Nothingness* that is devoted to 'Being-for-Others.' The Introduction is called 'The Pursuit of Being,' Part One deals with 'The Problem of Nothingness' and Part Two is entitled 'Being-for-Itself.' Part Four includes 'Having, Doing, and Being' which is followed by a Conclusion. 'The look' is part of the examination by Sartre of avoiding deep Cartesian problems of solipsism that originate from a standpoint devoted entirely to the *cogito* or the thinking subject. Sartre argues that we need the Other in order to realize our own being and in the chapter on the existence of others he starts with an account of 'the reef of solipsism' based on an exposition of Husserl, Hegel and Heidegger to arrive at the following conclusion:

> We have learned that the Other's existence was experienced with evidence in and through the fact of my objectivity. We have seen also that my reaction to my own alienation for the Other was expressed in my grasping the Other as an object. In short, the Other can exist for us in two forms: if I experience him with evidence,

I fail to know him; if I know him, if I act upon him, I only reach his being-as-object and his probable existence in the midst of the world (400).

Sartre is led on through the force of his argument to consider the body, both my body and the body of the Other, and the relation of the body to consciousness. Then Sartre proceeds to unpack the three ontological dimensions of the body before discussing concrete relations with others: love, language and masochism; indifference, desire, hate and sadism; and the notion of 'being-with' and the 'we.'

Sartre's account of the look and the Other as someone who must be encountered is a highly influential theory of subjectivity and the emotions. It defines an ontology defining consciousness as a negation aimed fundamentally at freedom formed through the choices we make. I become aware of the Other as a subjectivity and being-for-itself under whose gaze I am transformed into an object. 'The look' in Sartre's philosophy brings into play an intersubjective world and, indeed, the realm of interpersonal relations. Although Sartre emphasizes vision in his initial characterization of our being for-others—and in his continuing talk of 'The Look'—he is keen to point out that vision is by no means necessary. Sartre claims that conflict is the source of meaning of being-for-others which means that 'the look' is objectifying and alienating, where the Other fails to recognize my freedom.

Jacques Lacan develops his view of 'the gaze' from a first encounter with Sartre's *Being and Nothingness* in the mid-1950s and then distinguishes his own view of 'the gaze' from Sartre's the Look in 1964: the Lacanian *gaze* is not *the act of looking*, but *the object of the act of looking*. The Lacanian theory of the gaze undermines Cartesian theories of optics that have always dominated modern theories of perception and made visual perception the paradigm of knowing. For Lacan, seeing is not believing. He develops his position on the Gaze in relation to the notion of the 'mirror stage' where the child achieves a sense of mastery by seeing himself as ideal ego. In this way the child enters into culture and language establishing his own subjectivity narcissistically through the mirror image. Later Lacan differentiates between the eye's look and the Gaze, an uncanny sense that the object of our eye's look is looking back at us. Thus, Lacan's writings on the Gaze and visuality theorize the importance of seeing in the formation of the child-subject through the mirror-self which is an ideal self. He defines the Gaze at one point as the presence of others and then focuses on the function of seeing per se which constitutes 'the manifestation of the symbolic within the field of vision' (Silverman, 168). Finally Lacan likens the gaze to the camera whose only function is to put us in the picture, so to speak. Lacan's views have been influential, not only in psychoanalysis but also in the development of film theory (Mcgowan, 2008), and thus provide a preparatory critical pedagogy of the image.

In *The Birth of the Clinic: An Archaeology of Medical Perception* (*Naissance de la clinique: une archéologie du regard médical*) Foucault focuses on the power of the clinical or medical gaze to explain the creation of a field of knowledge of the body and the way it leads to a radical separation of the body from the person. Foucault describes how he became interested in how the medical gaze was institutionalized, that is, how this new form of the hospital was at once the effect and the support of a new type of gaze. In the essay 'The eye of power' from the collection *Power/Knowledge* Foucault (1980) famously writes of the Panopticum beginning with observations concerning certain architectural projects following the second fire at the Hotel-Dieu in 1772 and the ways in which they revolved around the principles of centralized surveillance designed to solve the 'problem of visibility of bodies.' This problem which was both global and individualizing in terms of the surveillance of space Foucault discovers was not specific to eighteenth-century medicine and its beliefs.

> Then while studying the problems of the penal system, I noticed that all the great projects for re-organizing the prisons (which date, incidentally, from a slightly later period, the first half of the nineteenth century) take up this same theme, but accompanied this time by the almost invariable reference to Bentham. There was scarcely a text or a proposal about the prisons which didn't mention Bentham's 'device'—the 'Panopticon.' (147)

Later in the same essay he theorizes the relation between the gaze and interiorization:

> We are talking about two things here: the gaze and interiorization. And isn't it basically the problem of the cost of power? In reality power is only exercised at a cost. Obviously, there is an economic cost, and Bentham talks about this. How many overseers will the Panopticon need? How much will the machine then cost to run? But there is also a specifically political cost. If you are too violent, you risk provoking revolts…In contrast to that you have the system of surveillance, which on the contrary involves very little expense. There is no need for arms, physical violence, material constraints. Just a gaze. An inspecting gaze—a gaze that each individual under its weight will end by interiorization to the point that he is his own overseer, each individual thus exercising this surveillance over, and against, himself. A superb formula: power exercised continuously and for what turns out to be minimal cost (154).

The gaze becomes the central principle of a series of public architectures, an organization of the enclosed spaces of institutions and the basis not only for low cost, low maintenance infrastructure in clinics, prisons, factories and schools but also the basis of the rise of disciplines and discourses based on systematic observation of the inmates of these institutions. With this development

Foucault provides us with a critical pedagogy of educational disciplines ('architectures') that developed in the eighteenth and nineteenth centuries designed to govern the child, to enhance its autonomy (in the liberal subjects) and to study the dimensions of the child's stages of physical growth and cognitive development.

Pedagogies as Ways of Seeing

Ways of Seeing is the title of a 1972 BBC television series and later book of the same name that questions the deep cultural bias in Western aesthetics based on the phenomenology of perception and the paradigm of seeing. Berger is interested in revealing the ideologies of the visual and in particular the ways in which art in capitalist society has become a commodity. To this extent Berger draws on the discussion of the history of art and art criticism utilizing Benjamin's seminal book *The Work of Art in the Age of Mechanical Reproduction*. The medium is a complex system of rules that allows certain combination and permutations and prohibits others. In effect, it constitutes a language: 'The special qualities of oil painting lent themselves to a special system of conventions for representing the visible. The sum total of these conventions is the way of seeing invented by oil painting' (108).

The question of the image and ways of seeing are unquestionably tied up with the art philosophy and criticism and in particular the experience of the avant-garde whose best-known representatives—the poets Arthur Rimbaud, Paul Verlaine, Stephane Mallarmé and Charles Baudelaire as well as leading artists of the major art revolutionary movements—sought new kinds of art and new forms of artistic expression (i.e., new ways of seeing) that opposed the traditional (bourgeois) institution of art that had been largely captured by industrial capitalism. The industrial (and digital) reproduction of images has permanently changed the visual arts; images have become our deeply immersible cultural environment and can be owned, manipulated and manufactured. They define us and our identities and the struggle over their control serve to construct certain narratives, dramas, tableaux, scenarios and views at the expense of others.

Berger, critically aware of these movements and debates, and operating from a position that is informed by a critique of capitalism and antagonistic to mainstream culture, defines looking as a *practice,* 'much like speaking, writing or signing. Looking involves learning to interpret and, like other practices, looking involves relationships of power' (Berger, 1972: 10). As Berger argues: 'Perspective makes the single eye the centre of the visible world. Everything converges on to the eye as to the vanishing point of infinity' (16). Modern technologies like photography and the motion picture change the perspectival centrality of the image 'What you saw was relative to your position in time and space. It was no longer possible to imagine everything converging on the human eye as on the vanishing point of infinity' (18). As Berger explains the meaning of a photographic image as compared to a prior painted image, becomes both decentered and diffuse and it also develops allusion to other images in systems of images. Berger focuses on the distortions in capitalist consumer culture that are systematically generated through publicity as a particular system of image and image exploitation closely related to freedom of choice and of enterprise that conditions social relations through the glamour of the image. Publicity and advertising creates a society that depends upon an uncritical 'average spectator-buyer'.

The fact is that we are not born knowing how to see either physiologically or culturally. The great biologist J. Z. Young taught us that the human infant learns to see, to focus, to hold perspective, and to master the basics of seeing in a biological sense. But seeing is not acultural, asocial, or ahistorical. Seeing and looking (learning to look) is also learned socially and culturally as part of the production of differences (semiotically) and through various representational technologies that reinforce the repertoire and banks of images that comprise visual culture. In this sense, vision and its physio-social technologies of seeing and looking are less a mirror of truth than instruments of power—less faithful and accurate depictions of the world than actual constituent analytical schemas of visual intelligibility. On the basis of this model the ways we picture ourselves ('self-image') and see others are part of our history of seeing and learning to see just as much as is the way we understand and picture the world. These stable traditions of seeing that involve interpreting the meaning of images and the relations between seeing and being seen also are constituted through perspectives of power that emphasize certain received, 'natural' and acceptable visual discriminations of body, sex, age, gender, class and culture over others. These traditions gel, overlap and are reinforced by the complex relations between images, word, and sound (Sturken & Cartwright, 2001; Schirato & Webb, 2004; Mirozoeff, 2000). Berger provides the now-standard example: 'according to usage and conventions which are at last being questioned but have by no means been overcome—men act and women appear. Men look at women. Women watch themselves being looked at' (Berger 1972, 45, 47). Berger argues that in European art from the Renaissance onwards women were depicted as being 'aware of being seen by a [male] spectator' (ibid, 49).

Others, influenced by Sartre, Foucault, and a line of criticism dating back to Baudelaire and Benjamin, have sought to make the historical connections between vision and modernity evident. Jonathan Crary (1990), for example, has examined *Techniques of the Observer* and the complex relations between vision and modernity in the nineteenth century. He emphasizes the ways in which vision is located in history and links nineteenth-century interest in the physiology of vision to demands of industrialization (81, 85), linking vision and visuality to the changing perceptions of human subjectivity and identity. Like others before him Crary finds that the observer is changed by technological developments, becoming 'the site of certain practices, techniques, institutions, and procedures of subjectification' (5). Each technological device creates a different kind of observer: stereoscopic vision is replaced by photography and its 'illusion of reference' (133). The stereoscope creates a fragmented observer whereas the camera creates an assumed unity in the viewer. The nineteenth century inaugurates 'the visual culture of modernity' which coincides with new 'techniques of the observer' (96) first alluded to by Baudelaire's 'flaneur' a new urban observer/subject who is the 'mobile consumer of a ceaseless succession of illusory commodity-like images' (21).

Pedagogies of visual culture would seek to understand both the meaning of images, the way in which they comprise a language and help us to analyze vision as a social, cultural and historical process. It would examine the history of changing technologies that are involved in the production, circulation and reception of images as well as the exploration of theories of seeing and looking as social and cultural practices.[1]

Debord and Baudrillard

La Société du Spectacle was first published in 1967 with the first English translation in 1970, revised in 1977. The work is a series of two hundred and twenty-one short theses (about a paragraph each), divided into nine chapters. It is a path-breaking text that provides a Marxian interpretation of contemporary mass media with a focus on commodity fetishism before the notion of globalization was used extensively. Guy Debord, for instance, writes:

(1)   In societies where modern conditions of production prevail, all of life presents itself as an immense accumulation of spectacles. Everything that was directly lived has moved away into a representation.

(4)   The spectacle is not a collection of images, but a social relation among people, mediated by images.

(6)   The spectacle grasped in its totality is both the result and the project of the existing mode of production. It is not a supplement to the real world, an additional decoration. It is the heart of the unrealism of the real society.

(147)   The time of production, commodity-time, is an infinite accumulation of equivalent intervals. It is the abstraction of irreversible time, all of whose segments must prove on the chronometer their merely quantitative equality. This time is in reality exactly what it is in its exchangeable character. In this social domination by

commodity-time, 'time is everything, man is nothing; he is at most the carcass of time' (Poverty of Philosophy). This is time devalued, the complete inversion of time as 'the field of human development.'[2]

Commenting on *The Society of the Spectacle* in 1988 Guy Debord said that he had tried to show that the modern spectacle was already 'the autocratic reign of the market economy' that had acceded to an 'irresponsible sovereignty' based on 'the totality of new techniques of government that accompanied this reign.'[3] Debord suggests that he distinguished two rival forms of spectacular power, the concentrated and the diffuse—the former a dictatorial ideology characteristic of Nazi and Stalinist regimes, the latter Americanization of the world dedicated to maintaining traditional forms of bourgeois democracy. The combination of the two (the integrated spectacular) had since imposed itself globally. He also explains how the notion of the spectacular had originated with the Situationists that was influenced by the avant-garde movements Dada, Surrealism and Lettrism which sought to transform art into everyday life in order to overcome the ways that creativity of the people had become crippled and stifled under modern capitalism.

Baudrillard argues that a simulacrum is not a copy of the real, but becomes truth in its own right: the hyperreal. Where Plato saw two steps of reproduction—faithful and right. Where Plato sees basically two aspects the genuine thing and its copy (simulacrum) Baudrillard sees four: (1) basic reflection of reality; (2) perversion of reality; (3) pretence of reality (where there is no model); and (4) simulacrum, which bears no relation to any reality whatsoever. He argues that ours is a postmodern society that has become so reliant on models and maps that we have lost all contact with the real world that preceded the map.

He argues that we have lost all ability to make sense of the distinction between nature and artifice. Baudrillard postulates three 'orders of simulacra': in the first order of simulacra associated with the pre-modern period, the image is a counterfeit of the real; in the second order of simulacra that Baudrillard associates with the industrial revolution, the distinctions between the image and the representation begin to blur because of the mass production and the proliferation of copies; in the third order of simulacra, that Baudrillard associates with the postmodern age, we are confronted with a *precession* of simulacra where the representation *precedes* and *determines* the real and the distinction between reality and its representation disappears entirely. As he reformulates in a piece called 'Simulacra and Science Fiction',[4] there are three orders of simulacra:

(1) Natural, naturalistic simulacra: based on image, imitation, and counterfeiting. They are harmonious, optimistic, and aim at the reconsti-

tution, or the ideal institution, of a nature in God's image.

(2) Productive, productionist simulacra: based on energy and force, materialized by the machine and the entire system of production. Their aim is Promethean: world-wide application, continuous expansion, liberation of indeterminate energy (desire is part of the utopias belonging to this order of simulacra).

(3) Simulation simulacra: based on information, the model, cybernetic play. Their aim is maximum operationality, hyperreality, total control.

He goes on to state:

> There is no real and no imaginary except at a certain distance. What happens when this distance, even the one separating the real from the imaginary, begins to disappear and to be absorbed by the model alone? Currently, from one order of simulacra to the next, we are witnessing the reduction and absorption of this distance, of this separation which permits a space for ideal or critical projection.

Baudrillard's twin concepts of 'hyperreality' and 'simulation' refer to the virtual or unreal nature of contemporary culture in an age of mass communication and mass consumption, a world dominated by simulated experience and feelings, which has robbed us of the capacity to comprehend reality as it really exists. As he indicates simulation begins from the radical negation of the sign as value, and envelops 'the edifice of representation as itself a simulacrum'. This would be the successive phases of the image:

- It is the reflection of a basic reality.
- It masks and perverts a basic reality.
- It masks the absence of a basic reality.
- It bears no relation to any reality whatever: it is its own pure simulacrum (Baudrillard, 1993: 194).

Doug Kellner (1995) suggests that Baudrillard's post-1970s work can be as science fiction that anticipates the future by exaggerating present tendencies that provides early warnings about what might happen if present trends continue. In an assessment of Baudrillard, Kellner (2007) writes:

> In retrospect, Baudrillard's early critical explorations of the system of objects and consumer society contain some of his most important contributions to contemporary social theory. His mid-1970s analysis of a dramatic mutation occurring within contemporary societies and rise of a new mode of simulation, which sketched out the effects of media and information on society as a whole, is also original and important. But at this stage of his work, Baudrillard falls prey to a technological determinism and semiological idealism which posits an autonomous technology and play of signs generating a society of simulation which creates a

postmodern break and the proliferation of signs, spectacles, and simulacra. Baudrillard erases autonomous and differentiated spheres of the economy, polity, society, and culture posited by classical social theory in favor of an implosive theory that also crosses disciplinary boundaries, thus mixing philosophy and social theory into a broader form of social diagnosis and philosophical play.

Deleuze on Cinema[5]

Deleuze makes a classification of three specific kinds of power: sovereign power, disciplinary power and 'control' of communication and views the third kind of power as becoming hegemonic, a form of domination that, paradoxically, is both more total than any previous form, extending even to speech and imagination. Deleuze suggests that it was William Burroughs who first used the term *control* to describe a new form of power and he mentions the way modern institutions of confinement and their principles of enclosure are breaking down. New open spatial forms—open systems rather than closed systems—interconnected, flexible and networked 'architectures' are supplanting the older enclosures. New open institutional forms of punishment, education and health are being introduced without a critical understanding what is happening. As he writes in 'Postscript on Societies of Control'

> We're definitely moving toward 'control' societies that are no longer disciplinary. Foucault's often taken as the theorist of disciplinary societies and of their principal technology, *confinement* (not just in hospitals and schools but in schools, factories, and barracks). We're moving toward control societies that no longer operate by confining people but through continuous control and instant communication.

And he provides the following education example:

> One can envisage education becoming less and less a closed site differentiated from the workplace as another closed site, but both disappearing and giving way to frightful continual training, to continual monitoring of worker-schoolkids or bureaucrat-students (Deleuze, 1995a: 174–175).

Forms of 'lifelong education,' 'distance education' and 'continuous training' have been conceived as part of a new educational 'architecture' designed to support the global 'knowledge economy.' Deleuze warns of what he calls 'ceaseless control in open sites' and the quest for 'universals of communication.' Yet he argues that, even before control societies have been established, already forms of delinquency and resistance—computer piracy and viruses—have appeared and instead of resistance to control societies he suggests 'creating has always been something different from communicating' (175). The notion of 'control' is a political term Deleuze inherits from William Burroughs which is best illustrated in relation to Deleuze's discussion and history of cinema.

Deleuze (1995b) provides an analysis of the cinematic image according to a threefold periodization: What is there to see behind the image? What is there to see on the surface of the image? And, what can we see at all when the background of any image is always another image? (See also Deleuze 1989a,b). Corresponding to each question is a stage of cinema based upon the changing function of the image. The first period characterized by the art of *montage* ascribes a depth to the image in a universal scenography, where filmmakers in the critical tradition, still buoyed by a metaphysical optimism of the new medium, sought to forge a link between the new Art and a new Thought that was capable of providing an *encyclopedia of the world*. In the second age, characterized by the 'sequence shot' and new forms of composition, the new function of the image was a *pedagogy of perception*, taking the place of an *encyclopedia of the world* that had 'fallen apart' (70). As Deleuze notes 'Depth was condemned as 'deceptive,' and the image took on the flatness of a 'surface without depth' (60–70); and:

> Images were no longer linked in an unambiguous order of cuts and continuities but became subject to relinkings, constantly revised and reworked across cuts and false continuities (70).

The emergence of the third period reflects a change in the function of the image and a third set of relations where

> it is no longer what is there to see behind the image, nor how we can see the image itself—it's how we can find a way into it, how we can slip in, because each image now slips across other images, 'the background in any image is always another image,' and the vacant gaze is a contact lens (71).

Deleuze mentions two different factors in the new relation between images. The internal development of cinema which seeks new audio-visual combinations and pedagogies, and the internal development of television which takes on a social function and, therefore, operates on a different level. Just as the critical impulse of the first great age of cinema was manipulated by the authoritarian power of fascism, so too 'the new social power of the postwar period, one of surveillance or control, threatened to kill the second form of cinema' (71). The threat this time comes from 'the way that all images present the single image of my vacant gaze contacting a non-nature, a privileged spectator allowed into the wings, in contact with the image, entering into the image' (72).

Thus, the studio audience is one of the most highly rated forms of entertainment and the zoom has become television's standard technique. As

Deleuze argues:

> The encyclopedia of the world and the pedagogy of perception collapse to make room for a professional training of the eye, a world of controllers and controlled communing in their admiration for technology, mere technology. The contact lens everywhere. This is where your critical optimism turns into critical pessimism (72).

Television threatens the second death of critical cinema because it is 'the form in which the new powers of 'control' become immediate and direct' (75). Deleuze continues:

> To get to the heart of the confrontation you'd almost have to ask whether this control might be reversed, harnessed by the supplementary function opposed to power; whether one could develop an art of control that would be a kind of new form of resistance. Taking the battle to the heart of cinema, making cinema see it as its problem instead of coming upon it from the outside; that's what Burroughs did in literature, by substituting the viewpoint of control and controllers for that of authors and authority (75).

There is not space here for a full account of Deleuze on the development of cinema or the set of concepts he works up from Peirce's semiology and Bergson to describe the shift to time and movement. According to Deleuze, we now live in a universe that could be described as metacinematic and his classification of images implies a new kind of camera consciousness that determines our subjectivities and perception selves. We live in a visual culture that is always moving and changing and each image is always connected to an assemblage of affects and forces. There are three types of cinematic movement-images: *perception images* (that focus on what is seen), *affection images* (that focus on expressions of feeling) and *action images* (that focus on the duration of action), each type associated with long shots, close-ups and medium shots. Deleuze's work on cinema is not a history of cinema but rather a taxonomy, an attempt at the classifications of images and signs by means of Bergson and Peirce.

From Cinematic to Social Media Modes of Production

To be sure, as Jonathan Beller (2003) has argued cinema marks a profound shift in the relation between image and text—'the watershed of the subjugation of language by image.' Inspired by Deleuze and early Critical Theory Beller theorizes that 'cinema as an innovative shift in both industrial capitalism and cultural practice marks, therefore, the restructuring of language function in accord with the changing protocols of techno-capitalism.' He summarizes his argument:

> As a precursor for TV and computing and Internet, cinema transacts value trans-

fer across the image utilizing a production process that can be grasped as founded under the rubric of what I call 'the attention theory of value.' The deterritorialized factory, that is the contemporary image, is an essential component of globalization, neo-imperialism, and militarization, organizing, as it were, the consent (ignorance of) and indeed desire for these latter processes. Thus 'cinema,' as a paradigm for image-mediated social production, implies a cultural turn for political economics. It also implies that it is the interstitial, informal activities that transpire across the entire surface of the socius as well as in the vicissitudes of the psyche and experience that are the new (un-theorized) production sites for global capital—and therefore among the significant sites for the waging of the next revolution (91).

And Beller (2003: 105) concludes:

> When appearance itself is production, the ostensible immediacy of the world always already passes through the production-system. Cinema is a deterritorialized factory which extends the working day in space and time while introjecting the systems language of capital into the sensorium. Cinema means a fully-mediated *mise-en-scene* which, like the magician's forced deal, structures human choice by providing the contexts and options for responses that are productive for capital. Yet we must remember that it is humanity who made the cinema, despite the masters of global appearance's claims to the contrary. The star is not out there, but s/he is of ourselves. Cinema is the secularization of a world historical revolution in human interaction that contains in *potentia* the material realization of a universal disaffection with capitalist domination and oppression.

Beller (2006) argues that cinema and other media formations including the internet as media platform, are deterritorialized factories in which spectators work or perform value-productive labor. The cinematic mode of production (CMP) is an exploitation of the sociality that characterizes a spectator economy. The question is whether we have already moved beyond spectatorship and the spectator economy to one now centered on new social media and a social mode of production that requires collaboration and co-creation as a matter of participation and entry.

Social media are different from industrial media in that they are designed to be disseminated through social interaction using highly accessible and scalable publishing techniques. Using Internet- and web-based technologies to transform broadcast media monologues (one-to-many) into interactive and participatory dialogues (many-to-many) results in the democratization of knowledge and information—and transforms participants from spectator-consumers into content producers. There is reason to think that the CMP is closely tied to the principles of industrial media and industrial capital while social media operates on different principles reflecting the logic of free software. As Christopher M. Kelty (2008: 2) argues:

> Free Software is a set of practices for the distributed collaborative creation of software source code that is then made openly and freely available through a clever, unconventional use of copyright law. But it is much more: Free Software exemplifies a considerable reorientation of knowledge and power in contemporary society—a reorientation of power with respect to the creation, dissemination, and authorization of knowledge in the era of the Internet.

When he writes of the *cultural* significance of Free Software he means

> an ongoing experimental system, a space of modification and modulation, of figuring out and testing; culture is an experiment that is hard to keep an eye on, one that changes quickly and sometimes starkly. Culture as an experimental system crosses economies and governments, networked social spheres, and the infrastructure of knowledge and power within which our world functions today—or fails to.

The logic of free software as it underwrites social media has breathed new life into new facets of culture from music to politics, engendering what Kelty calls a recursive public—one that is '*vitally concerned with the material and practical maintenance and modification of the technical, legal, practical, and conceptual means of its own existence as a public*' (3). In this new social media culture the individual imagination is harnessed in forms of hypertextual forms of multi-creation that ties the expressive to politics and to democratic action, transforming and reshaping the deterritorialized community as one, a global polis with shifting and temporary alliances mobilized for particular causes and social movements and political events. In this way social media becomes a re-imagination machine and education based upon it in both public and personalized forms moves from pedagogies of the image and economies of the gaze to pedagogies of creative P2P collaboration and economies of the imagination.

Notes

1. This description is based on various visual pedagogy website including Viz. Visual Culture: Rhetoric: Pedagogy at http://viz.cwrl.utexas.edu/, Visual Studies Initiative at Duke University at http://visualstudies.duke.edu/, Visual Culture Collective at http://visualculturecollective.googlepages.com/home, Visual Studies program at the University of Houston at http://www.visualstudies.uh.edu/, and Visual Studies at the University of California at Irvine at http://www.humanities.uci.edu/visual-studies/.
2. These selections are based on The Society of the Spectacle at http://library.nothingness.org/articles/SI/en/pub_contents/4.
3. This commentary appears at http://www.notbored.org/commentaires.html.
4. See http://www.depauw.edu/sfs/backissues/55/baudrillard55art.htm.
5. Part of this section on Deleuze is based on material taken from Peters (2009).

References

Ann, M. & Moxley, K. (2002). *Art History, Aesthetics, Visual Studies.* Massachusetts: Clark Institute & Yale University Press.

Baudrillard, J. (1983). *Simulations.* New York: Semiotext(e).

Baudrillard, J. (1993). The Evil Demon of Images and the Precession of Simulacra, in Thomas Docherty (ed.), *Postmodernism: A Reader.* New York: Columbia University Press.

Baudrillard, J. (1994). *Simulacra and Simulation.* Ann Arbor: The University of Michigan Press.

Baudrillard, J. (1998). Simulacra and Simulations *Jean Baudrillard, Selected Writings*, ed. Mark Poster, Stanford: Stanford University Press, 1988, pp. 166–184.

Beller, J. (2003). The Cinematic Mode of Production: Towards a Political Economy of the Postmodern, *Culture, Theory & Critique*, 2003, 44(1), 91–106.

Beller, J. (2006). *The Cinematic Mode of Production.* Dartmouth: University Press of New England.

Berger, J. (1977). *Ways of Seeing.* London: Penguin.

Debord, G. (1977). *The Society of the Spectacle.* London: Black & Red [1967] at http://www.marxists.org/reference/archive/debord/society.htm.

Deleuze, G. (1989). *Cinema: The Movement Image*, trans. Hugh Tomlinson and Barbera Habberjam, Minnesota: University of Minnesota Press.

Deleuze, G. (1989). *The Time Image*, trans. Hugh Tomlinson and Robert Galeta, Minnesota: University of Minnesota Press.

Deleuze, G. (1995a). Postscript on Control Societies, in *Negotiations, 1972–1990*, trans. M. Joughin, New York: Columbia University Press, 177–182.

Deleuze, G. (1995b). Letter to Serge Daney: Optimism, Pessimism, and Travel. In *Negotiations, 1972–1990*, trans. M. Joughin, New York: Columbia University Press: 68–80.

Dikovitskaya, M. (2006). *Visual Culture: The Study of the Visual after the Cultural Turn.* Cambridge, MA: The MIT Press.

Ewen, S. (1999). *All Consuming Images: The Politics of Style in Contemporary Culture* (1st ed.). New York, NY: Basic Books.

Fuery, K. & Fuery, P. (2003). *Visual Culture and Critical Theory.* London: Arnold.

Jay, M. (1993). *Downcast Eyes: The Denigration of Vision in 20th-Century French Thought.* Berkeley: University of California Press

Jay, M. (2005). (Ed.) 'The State of Visual Culture Studies,' themed issue of *Journal of Visual Culture*, 4:2, August.

Crary, J. (1990). *Techniques of the Observer: On Vision and Modernity in the Nineteenth Century.* Cambridge, MA: MIT Press, 1990.

Kellner, D. (1995). *Media Culture. Cultural Studies, Identity and Politics Between the Modern and the Postmodern*, London and New York: Routledge.

Kellner, D. (2007). Jean Baudrillard, *Stanford Encyclopaedia of Philosophy* at http://plato.stanford.edu/entries/baudrillard/.

Kelty, C.M. (2008). *Two Bits: The Cultural Significance of Software.* Durham, NC, Duke University Press, at http://twobits.net/.

Lacan, J. (1988). *The Seminar. Book I. Freud's Papers on Technique, 1953–54.* Trans. John Forrester. New York: Norton; Cambridge: Cambridge University Press.

Mcgowan, T. (2008). *Film Theory After Lacan.* New York: State University of New York

Press.

Morizoeff, N. (1999). *An Introduction to Visual Culture.* London: Routledge.

Peters, M. A. (2009). Education and 'Societies of Control'; From Disciplinary Pedagogy to Perpetual Training. In: *Bildung der Kontrollgesellschaft. Analyse und Kritik pädagogischer Vereinnahmungen* [*Education of the society of control: critical andragogy and educational theory*]. Carsten Bünger, Ralf Mayer, Astrid Messerschmidt, Olga Zitzelsberger (Eds.), Schöningh, Paderborn.

Sartre, J.P. (1958). *Being and Nothingness: An Essay on Phenomenological Ontology*, trans. Hazel E. Barnes, London, Methuen [1943].

Schirato, T. & J. Webb. (2004). *Understanding the Visual.* Singapore: Allen & Unwin.

Sturken, M. & L. Cartwright. (2001). *Practices of Looking: An Introduction to Visual Culture.* USA: Oxford University Press.

9. *Practice*

MICHAEL A. PETERS

Introduction

In the previous chapter I argued that advent of social media heralded a re-imagination of the public means for education and scholarship involving a shift away from passive consumption of text and image, away from pedagogies of the image and economies of the gaze to pedagogies of creative P2P collaboration where the 'user' becomes a creator of digital content and digital media. This shift I suggested was related to a significant re-positing of economies of the imagination—new open systems of peer knowledge production, learning and education that permit and enable the creation of digital content. In this present chapter, I pick up on this theme to argue for the notion of 'personalization' as a consequence of open communication and knowledge systems. Personalization in effect becomes a principle of autonomy promoting and permitting a new responsibilization of individuals as the basis for a raft of reforms that guides the ship of state away from welfare state politics and simple neoliberal market deregulation and privatization to a new society of 'we-think' and 'we-creation' based on the co-production of symbolic public goods.

Personalization

Personalized learning has emerged in the last decade as a special instance of a more generalized response to the problem of the *reorganization of the State* in response to globalization and the end of the effectiveness of the industrial mass production model in the delivery of public services.[1] The massively centralized, overburdened, 'big,' paternalistic and unresponsive welfare State is no longer considered neither morally or economically desirable, nor efficient or effective. Personalization is held to provide an overall solution to the problem of the bureaucratic State and the future answer for the provision and an ever-increasing demand for public services that depend upon the active participation of the citizen. Policy advocates argue that personalization will encourage a form of self-responsibilization and citizen empowerment within a more 'open architecture' of government permitting both greater choice and the co-production or co-creation of public goods. It is argued that personalization enables greater customization of public services, niche marketing and the tailoring and targeting of public services in accordance with the different and specific needs of various client or constituent groups. As a generalized policy response to the reorganization of the State personalization rides on the back of the revolution in open government made possible by the revolution in communication and information technologies that provide new architectures of citizen participation and collaboration.

Yet personalization is only the latest response to a series of policy strategies in the post-war years to the problem of the bureaucratic State—its remoteness, lack of transparency, its over-regulation, and its paternalism. Personalization developed in response to the twin problems of globalization and the second industrial divide. Its conception, implementation and ultimate success or failure will be determined in part by the landscape of past policies and, in particular, the policies of the neoliberal era focusing on privatization, the emphasis on the quasi-market and the emulation of private sector management styles in government. To a large extent, the neoliberal reform of the public sector rested on principles of 'new public management' based on promotion of market-like arrangements, elements of rational choice theory, and in the later stages its combination with performance measurement and management. Aspects of personalization are conceived in sympathy with the radical disaggregation of State monopolies, decentralization of decision-making, and the promotion of consumer choice as a public service principle. Indeed, one might argue that new open architectures of citizen participation and collaboration that characterize new Web 2.0 platform technologies and affordances enable governments today to take advantage of and enact a related set of notions, rights, and principles underlying social movements that were first raised and have been promoted progressively since World War II.

This chapter reviews these initiatives laying out the policy landscape and focus on related problems and strategies designed to solve the problem of the unresponsive State. It itemizes eight overall policy strategies that have prevailed since World War II which together have shifted the ethos and mode of delivery of public services away from large centralized unresponsive State bureaucracies in favor of the consumer or client, often blurring the lines between the concepts of 'citizen' and 'consumer' and sometimes doing so deliberately (see Peters, 2004a,b). The chapter outlines the main policy strategies that have been pursued since World War II with the aim of shifting the ethos and mode of delivery away from large centralized unresponsive State bureaucracies in favor of citizen-, consumer- or client-systems based on the 'citizen-consumer.' It also profiles the rise of the concept of personalization in the United Kingdom's public policy as a major new philosophy of public service and emphasizes the significance of personalized learning as the pilot, flagship and 'guinea pig' of the larger public policy experiment.

The personalization of public services is an idea whose time has come or so it seems. The United Kingdom New Labour government under Tony Blair and more recently, Gordon Brown, has systematically introduced personalization as a basis for social reform in an age of mass collaboration. In less than a decade from its introduction in the late 1990s, personalization has come to define a major change in British political philosophy and a shift in the underlying principles of the organization of social policy. It also represents the adoption of a new style of *molecular* government that implies a radically decentralized social democratic relationship between the individual and the State. In essence, this shift can be viewed in part as a strategy for modernizing social democracy in the face of increasing globalization, the decline of the mode of mass production, and a response to a new model of 'openness' exemplified in open source and e-government characterized by the digitalization of society.

With the increasing demands for better and more transparent democracy, for greater citizen participation, and for delivery systems of public goods to be tailored to the needs of individuals, personalization is an over-arching policy idea, strategy and philosophy that will increase its influence as its implementation is refined and developed. A stunning example of this kind of development is the advent of personalized medicine that moves away from generic drug and medical treatments to forms of treatment that focus on the genetic makeup and inheritance, and the age-related, gender-related, and ethnicity-related specificity of the 'patient' who now becomes responsible for his or her health and records (history) in ways previously unthought of a generation ago. The notion of personalization also has been a strong thrust in realm of education policy especially in the United Kingdom which is explored later in the chapter.

Strategies for Overcoming the Bureaucratic State

Postwar strategies adopted by many western governments to overcome the problems of an overly complex and centralized bureaucratic State have involved a range of initiatives from both the Left and the Right. I mention here only the main ones and briefly describe them without commenting on their complexity or overlapping characteristics (see Fig. 1 below). These are so to speak pen-nail sketches of policy strategies and movements that originate in diverse sources both within and also outside government that aim at redefining the relationship between the individual and the State often for reasons concerning the changing nature of democracy and the encouragement and enhancement of democratic virtues of transparency, openness, access, equal distribution, choice, voice, participation and so on. Looked at in this sense one could easily mount a case for a view of *personalization* as a theory of direct democracy even though many of the technological affordances and the thinking behind them come from the disciplines of manufacturing systems, engineering, marketing and business management.

(i)	Deinstitutionalization
(ii)	Accountability and the Critique of the Professions
(iii)	Rise of the New Social Movements
(iv)	Community Development and Official Empowerment Ideologies
(v)	The Movement for Open Government
(vi)	Devolution
(vii)	Neoliberalism and the Crisis of the Welfare State
(viii)	New Public Management

Figure 1. Strategies for overcoming the bureaucratic state

(i.) Deinstitutionalization

In one sense the model of personalization emerges from the critique of the bureaucratic welfare state based on the old style industrial mass production response to demand for public services. This critique builds on criticisms of the bureaucratic welfare state that originated first on the Left by those such as Ivan Illich (1971, 1973, 1975) in the late 1960s who criticized forms of institutional State paternalism because it created institutional victims or dependent cultures robbing the individual of their own vitality, self-responsibility and autonomy. For Illich and others on the Left that picked up on this State 'totalitarianism' the answer was a form of 'deinstitutionalization,' especially in medicine and education. Schooling has little to do with education, Illich maintained, because it fostered a kind of psychological impotence, crippling its incumbents and making them more dependent on the institution and seeking ever-more forms of advanced 'treatment,' rather than independence or personal autonomy. Illich's model of deschooling was championed by those who in preference to State mass schooling chose small, private community schools or embraced home schooling and distance education possibilities.

The same logic was applied in the treatment of mental illness where 'de-institutionalization' became a general response to the failure of large bureaucratic State institutions. It became a reality in the 1970s and 1980s when new wonder drugs self-administered seemed to promise a form of independence which was accompanied by a new welfare ideology of 'empowerment' and emerging forms of 'community care.' These innovations at least in theory were to permit the disassembly of expensive, large, centralized State institutions and the move to more flexible decentralized local care by community workers. The de-institutionalization critique was also wedded to a critique of professionals and professionalism. Illich (1978) argued that professionals had arrogated powers to themselves often at the expense of their clients or the people they were supposed to help.

(ii.) Accountability and the Critique of the Professions

After World War II and the postwar settlement many critics increasingly came to see the welfare state as 'big,' top-heavy with bureaucrats and administrators, over-regulated, over-centralized, complex, expensive and unresponsive to the very groups it was notionally designed to serve. The central claim was that State bureaucrats were more interested in increasing their own power or preserving their own position or capturing benefits for themselves ('professional capture') than in serving their constituents or improving the quality of the services they were offering. It is not clear empirically how true this claim of professional self-interest—or 'bureaucratic welfare capture'—was of various professionals groups comprising the public sector such as nurses, teachers, doctors, dentists, and State servants. Certainly, the critique chimed with a growing demystification of the professions as doctors and lawyers began to lose their aura of authority and expertise.

In a series of public scandals many different professionals had been exposed as those who had abused their position and privilege. There were numerous cases, for instance, of male doctors who had exploited female patients or male professors and teachers who had taken advantage of those in their charge. State-funded professions in the immediate postwar period had unchecked power, often clocked in State secrecy and/or anonymity. The increasing perception was that professionals had little accountability and often exercised their power against the very client groups they were supposed to help and serve. The criticism of the lack of professional accountability focused discussion on the notion of 'professionalism' and on developing codes of ethics and of practice not only to encourage better practice but also as much to indemnify and insure themselves against plaintive damages.

(iii.) Rise of the New Social Movements

The growth of the new social movements during the 1970s added a strong feminist and cultural set of criticisms to the generalized critique of professionals deepening claims and criticisms about abuses of power and lack of professional and research ethics. Many of the specific criticisms of the abuse of State power were gender-related in origin or focused on the differential and unfair treatment of minority groups, whether indigenous or immigrant. These ethical issues were highlighted in medical trials where in high publicity trials women were denied medication as part of a control group experimentation where informed consent was absent or ignored. The abuses were, in essence, a denial of citizen's and/or patient rights. The 1970s and 1980s in part as a result of these abuses and growing 'conscientization' of new social movements that developed group solidarity on the back of civil rights saw the development in the public service of new demands for professional and bureaucratic accountability. The analysis of formal relationships between State professionals and employees and their clients became more sensitive to the rights of individuals and various social and cultural groups. The accountability movement which took many different forms for the first time paid some attention to *reciprocal* rights and responsibilities among professionals and their client groups.

(iv.) Community Development and Official Empowerment Ideologies

Community development also became a popular form of decentralized government assistance especially in poorer or developing countries. It also became associated with the benefits of increased participation of various groups in their own 'community development.' It was often seen as a means of enhancing the decision-making capacities of individuals and local organizations. Empowerment that developed during the civil rights era and became refined as a form of group assertiveness especially within the women's movement during the 1970s and 1980s was harnessed by State agencies as a means to emphasize change through choice-making and enhancing one's positive self-image to overcome stigma and provide skills for developing a personal sense of agency and self-efficacy. This political process that enabled others to gain power and authority quickly became part of 'personal growth' theory, and other change mantras were adopted first by participatory-oriented social sciences and social services including action research models. They quickly became part of official empowerment ideologies associated with everyday management language. In this way empowerment was seen as providing a solution to Taylorism, the mass production model and bureaucratic workplaces. Essentially it was seen as a strategy for creativity and avoiding problems of worker alienation through concepts of worker participation in management and other forms of 'self-management.'

(v.) The Movement for Open Government

The movement for open government has its origins in the passing of legislation concerning freedom of information beginning in the 1960s with the establishment of the Ombudsman office and the limitation of State secrecy. Since the U.S. passed its Freedom of Information Act in 1966 other western countries have followed suit—Denmark and Norway in 1970, France and the Netherlands in 1978, Australia, Canada and New Zealand in 1982, Hungary in 1992, Ireland and Thailand in 1997, South Korea in 1998, United Kingdom in 2000, Japan and Mexico in 2002, and Germany in 2005.[2]

Freedom of information grew out of a long-standing attack on State secrecy that was made by Enlightenment philosophers and also associated with various freedoms, including freedom of the press. In this sense freedom of information is emblematic of both political transparency and administrative accountability and an essential part of the theoretical background to personalization as the movement concerned with access to personal information recorded by the State.

(vi.) Devolution

Devolution really has its home in democratic theory and needs to be distinguished from the other D's that dominated public sector provision of the 1980s—deregulation, decentralization, and dezoning (in education)—all of which were often employed in the attempt to stimulate market-like conditions for the production of public goods and services. In terms of democratic theory devolution is the granting of statutory powers by central government to sub-national level be it state, regional or local. Often devolution refers to the financial arena permitting state and regional governments to levy taxes or collect revenue in order to dispense or provide services. It can also mean a constitutional arrangement that enables a form of 'home rule' for regions beyond the merely financial arena enabling local government bodies to make decisions and/or pass legislation. Devolution can take three forms: administrative, executive and legislative (see House of Commons, 2003).

(vi.) Neoliberalism and the Crisis of the Welfare State

In the western world during the 1980s a distinctive strand of neo-liberalism emerged as the dominant paradigm of public policy. Citizens were redefined as individual consumers of newly competitive public services, and citizen rights were re-defined as consumer rights. The public sector itself in many administrations underwent considerable 'downsizing' as successive government have pursued the privatization agenda. Government often began by selling off state assets and adopting the quasi-market in public services. Public management was delegated or devolved while executive power often became concentrated even more at the center which now decided on the new rules of the game. Nowhere was this shift more evident than in social welfare and education. There was a clear shift away from universality to a 'modest safety net' in the United Kingdom, Canada, New Zealand and Australia. The old welfare goals of participation and belonging were abolished or drastically rewritten. User-charges for social services and education were introduced across the board. Substantial cuts in benefits and other forms of income support were introduced and eligibility criteria were also tightened up. Targeting of social assistance became the new social philosophy and there was a greater policing of welfare recipients aimed at reducing benefit fraud and closely monitoring levels of welfare assistance. The stated goal of neo-liberals has been to free citizens from the dependence on state welfare. The old welfare policies, allegedly, discouraged effort and self-reliance and, in the eyes of neo-liberals, can be held responsible for *producing* young illiterates, juvenile delinquents, alcoholics, substance abusers, school truants, 'dysfunctional families' and drug addicts. At all levels the notion of market solutions have been embraced as a means of responding to the crisis of the welfare state and the problems of declining revenues, rising taxes and ageing populations.

(vii.) New Public Management

Most entrepreneurial governments promote *competition* between service providers. They *empower* citizens by pushing control out of the bureaucracy, into the community. They measure the performance of their agencies, focusing not on inputs but on *outcomes*. They are driven by their goals—their *missions*—not by their rules and regulations. They redefine their clients as *customers* and offer them choices....They *prevent* problems before they emerge, rather than simply offering services afterward. They put their energies into *earning* money, not simply spending it. They *decentralize* authority, embracing participatory management. They prefer *market* mechanisms to bureaucratic mechanisms. And they focus not simply on providing public services, but on *catalyzing* all sectors—public, private, and voluntary—into action to solve their community problems (Osborne and Gaebler, 1993: 19–20). *New Public Management* (NPM) is the name for a group of strategies that OECD countries adopted in the 1980s that emerged as a new paradigm involving the devolution of authority from the center in an effort to strengthen steering mechanisms, encourage greater flexibility by optimizing information technology, and to ensure better performance, control and accountability. This NPM model and ethos was also interested in improving the management of human resources and better more responsive government through developing the quasi-market and emphasizing both competition and choice as a means for improving the quality of regulation.

All of these post-war strategies for reducing the size of the State and for overcoming what are seen to be intractable difficulties of the bureaucratic welfare state center rest upon some mixture of empowerment of the citizen through self-responsibilization, choice and self-help combined with efforts to decenter, devolve and decentralize the State, often through the introduction of stricter accountability regimes that provide universal goals, targets, and annual performance reviews. The old nineteenth-century liberal administrative State that was embodied in central government and departments gave way to the welfare and post-welfare States that were modeled on mass production service management aimed at providing universal public services. The neoliberal models and ideals seriously questioned the universality ethos and introduced the quasi-market as a means of *customizing* public services through a series of performance indicators, contracting out, and accountability regimes focusing on principal-agency relationships. This culture of public sector management, now more than often performance-based, seeks to emulate private sector management styles and to introduce all the trappings of modernized management styling that is open to development and sensitive to the new fashions of business practice and strategy.

Mass Customization

The term 'mass customization' originated in the areas of marketing, manufacturing and management as a means of providing custom output through the use of flexible computer-aided manufacturing systems that combine the low unit costs of mass production with individual customization. The term was first coined and defined by Davis (1987) in *Future Perfect* as a strategy for involving customers in the development process of a product or service in order to address individual needs. Essentially, mass customization emerged in the last decade as a solution for addressing the new market complexities while still enabling firms to capture the efficiency advantages of mass-production, especially in view of the differentiation of markets and the changing demands and characteristics of consumers. Davis, who coined the term, refers to mass customization when 'the same large number of customers can be reached as in mass markets of the industrial economy, and simultaneously they can be treated individually as in the customized markets of pre-industrial economies' (Davis 1987: 169). For Tseng and Jiao (2001) the objective of mass customization is 'to deliver goods and services that meet individual customers' needs with near mass production efficiency.' Frank Pillar (n.d.) identifies four levels of mass customization and goes on to define it as a vision to develop a truly customer-centric ethos.

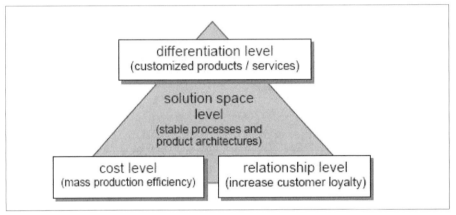

Figure 2. The four levels of mass customization.

As Kumar (2007) argues:

> Initial definitions of MC were rather broad and envisioned businesses delivering individualized product to each customer quickly and affordably as a result of integrating flexible and agile processes efficiently....Subsequent definitions of MC are narrower and more practical. These envisage deployment of IT capabilities (for customer co-design), flexible processes, agile manufacturing systems, and MC specific organizational/supply chain structures to deliver customized (as opposed to individualized or personalized) products with wide but limited options to customers....A distillation of these definitions leads to the following: MC is essentially a business strategy that permits building high customization levels into a product at low prices typically associated with mass production of those products. It has three distinct elements through which low price mechanisms spring forth: (1) modular product design, (2) finite solution space, and (3) customer co-design. Each of these serves to improve the customization level of the product, while also reducing cost and/or improving profits.

Kumar also notes that mass customization has taken off in the area of social networking. The most noticeable developments underscoring the strategic initiatives aimed at personalization, however, have occurred in the industries that provide services that support or promote human creativity, self-expression, social networking, and/or pursuit of hobbies. Picaboo (customizing digital pictures and albums), LuLu (customizing, publishing and marketing manuscripts), CeWe (customized digital photo books, albums), Blurb (bookmaking software), and Moo (greeting cards, postcards) are just a few companies that have moved to the forefront of the personalization movement, each registering impressive sales growths (14%) in 2007. Perhaps the leader of such companies is Mark Zukerberg's Facebook, which allows friends and families to upload their photos, exchange ideas, and upload other electronic files. It expanded its clientele to 62 million members of friends and families in a span of 3 years and was estimated to cross the 100 million mark at the end of 2007. The other companies that have helped the cause of personalization at a trailblazing speed are YouTube and MySpace. Not surprisingly, these three companies share the top five web traffic rankings determined by Alexa. To the extent volume of web traffic directly correlates with sales, these companies are living proofs of the success of personalization strategy.

It is the confluence of mass customization over the last decade especially in social networking and social media that has led some to focus on its application to the delivery of social or public goods and to emphasize the features of co-production and co-design, reimagining and reengineering the contribution that citizens might make to the co-production, co-design, and co-delivery of public goods. Mass customization seems to provide a means that captures many of the decentralization and empowerment strategies advanced as a way of overcoming the difficulties of the central State and the problem of 'one size fits all.'

Personalization in the United Kingdom

The personalization of public services emerged in the 2000s as a new basis and platform for social reform under New Labour in the United Kingdom. It can be seen as a new political economy of welfare that is a response to globalization and the post-industrial divide in an age of mass collaboration. It is an approach that institutes and supports 'molecular' government, that is, a new decentralized social democratic relationship between the individual and the State. As such it represents a major change in British political philosophy as well as social policy. It is also clear that personalization quickly became New Labour's new 'big idea' for the third term under Tony Blair and Gordon Brown. The term was first introduced into policy discourse in the United

Kingdom by New Labour's *Modernising Government* (1999) that outlined the Government's program of renewal and reform based on personalization and the promise of information technology to offer a 24/7 more responsive, inclusive, integrated, 'joined-up' government. In a sense this report was based on an understanding of the shortcomings of the bureaucratic State and the requirement to tailor services to the needs of the individual citizen.

The term surfaced and was strongly profiled by Tony Blair and the Education Minister Estelle Morris in reference to the end of 'one size fits all' comprehensive schooling. In a speech to the Labour Party Conference in 2002 Tony Blair extended the theme of modernizing government speaking about a new contract between the citizen and the 'Enabling' State which empowers citizens rather than trying to control them and individualizes services according to their needs. As he remarks: 'Out goes the Big State. In comes the Enabling State. Out goes a culture of benefits and entitlements. In comes a partnership of rights and responsibilities.' He applies this notion to education in the following way: 'In education, we need to move to the post-comprehensive era, where schools keep the comprehensive principle of equality of opportunity but where we open up the system to new and different ways of education, built round the needs of the individual child.'[3] At the same conference Estelle Morris advanced personalization as a rationale and means for ending 'one size fits all' comprehensive schooling to launch the model of City Academies.[4] In 2004–2005 David Miliband, the new Minister, took on the role of defining and refining the vision of personalized schooling, taking his lead from Charles Leadbeater (2004: 18) from the Demos think-tank, who proclaimed 'Personalization is a very potent but highly contested and ambiguous idea that could be as influential as privatization was in the 1980s and 1990s in reshaping public provision.' In 2007–2008 Gordon Brown defended and endorsed the personalization vision, extending its provisions and elaborating a notion of the 'citizen-consumer' consistent with personalization.

The idea of personalization was brokered and advocated by three associates of Demos[5] which advertises itself as 'the think tank of everyday democracy':

- **Charles Leadbeater**—Management thinker and expert on creativity & innovation; Demos Associate
  - *Personalization through Participation: A New Script for Public Services* (2004)
  http://www.demos.co.uk/files/PersonalisationThroughParticipati on.pdf
  - *The Shape of Things to Come: Personalization and Collaboration in Education* (2005)—http://www.standards.dfes.gov.uk/sie/docu-

ments/shape.pdf

- **Tom Bentley**—Executive Director for Policy and Cabinet for the Premier of Victoria (Australia); Demos Associate
  - *The Adaptive State: Strategies for personalizing the public realm* (2003)—http://www.demos.co.uk/files/HPAPft.pdf
- **David Hargreaves**—Associate Director for Development and Research, Specialist Schools and Academies Trust; Demos Associate
  - *Personalising Learning* (2004–6) 1–6 http://www.schoolsnetwork.org.uk/uploads/documents/6492.pdf
  - 6 iNet Publications focusing on personalizing learning and leadership.

These three policy advocates drew on the language of 'mass customization' and followed the shift from 'mass customization' to the notion of mass personalization in business strategy that focused on serving a market for one. As Kumar (2007) indicates the underlying factors allowing the shift from mass customization to mass personalization in business strategy are

1. development of information technologies such as peer to peer (P2P), business to consumer (B2C), and Web 2.0,
2. near-universal availability of the Internet,
3. customer willingness and preparedness to be integrated into the process of product co-design and co-creation,
4. modern manufacturing systems, such as flexible manufacturing,
5. mass customization tools such as modularity and delayed differentiation, which help reduce manufacturing cost and cycle times and
6. deployment of customer-satisfaction-specific software called customer relationship management (CRM) to engender customer retention.

Kumar (2007) goes on to comment:

> If mass customization was considered a contradiction in terms, mass personalization is even more so. Mass personalization is a limiting case of mass customization. Whereas both of these strategies are guided by the criterion of product affordability consistent with mass production efficiencies, the former (mass personalization) aims at a market segment of one while the latter (mass customization) at a market segment of few.

Leadbeater (2004) observed 'Personalization could have a similar impact and reach because it could provide a new organizing logic for public provision, linking initiatives…(for) more personalized public services, to initiatives…creating the public good from within society' (18). He defined 'personalization' as 'putting users at the heart of services, enabling them to become participants

in the design and delivery, services will be more effective by mobilizing millions of people as co-producers of the public goods they value' (19), and indicated that 'Personalization has the potential to reorganize the way we create
public goods and deliver public services' (19). For Leadbeater (2004) deep personalization 'could mean promoting greater capacity for self-management
and self-organization' (19). Leadbeater (2004) usefully outlines five meanings
of personalization moving from the simple to the more complex and more
radical:

- Personalization could mean providing people with a more customer-friendly interface
  with existing services.
- Personalization could also mean giving users more say in navigating their way through
  services once they have got access to them.
- Personalization could mean giving users more direct say over how money is spent.
- Personalization could mean users are not just consumers but co-designers and
  coproducers of a service.
- Personalization could mean self-organization.

Figure 3. Five meanings of Personalization

Leadbeater acknowledges that while consumer choice has moral and practical limits in provision of public services, personalization through participation
enables a connection between the individual and the collective by allowing
users a more direct, informed and creative voice designing, planning, deliver-
ing and evaluating the service they use. It allows for both 'choice' and 'voice'
and thus empowers the 'citizen-consumer.' This is the operating principle of
the self-organizing society. As Leadbeater (2004: 88) argues

> The chief challenge facing government in a liberal, open society is how to help
> create public goods—such as a well educated population, with an appetite to
> learn—in a society with a democratic ethos, which prizes individual freedom and
> wants to be self-organizing and 'bottom-up.'

And he goes on to argue:

> In an open, self-organizing society, government has to become molecular: it has
> to get into the bloodstream of society, not impose change or deliver solutions from
> without (Leadbeater, 2004: 88).

Leadbeater is adamant that personalized learning does not apply market thinking to education. He maintains that it is not designed to turn children and parents into consumers of education; rather 'the aim is to promote personal
development through self-realization, self-enhancement and self-development.'

He envisages a form of decentered education where 'The child/learner should be seen as active, responsible and self-motivated, a co-author of the script [service] which determines how education is delivered.' And he concludes 'A mass, personalized learning service would be a revolutionary goal. By giving the learner a growing voice, their aspirations and ambitions would become central to the way services are organized' (88).

Personalizing Learning and Public Sector Reform

The then UK Labour Minister of Education, David Miliband (2003) picked up the idea of personalization and sought to define it as a major part of the social democratic settlement in education and a response to the conundrum of 'how to ensure that a universal service responded to the particular needs of individual students.' In *Opportunity for All*, Miliband outlines 'personalized learning' as a means for targeting social disadvantage and the unique power to contribute to equality of opportunity, using the advantage of universal service in terms of scale, diverse practice, alternative strategies 'to help tailor education to the individual needs of students.'

'Personalizing Education: The Future of Public Sector Reform' is the title of a paper by Miliband (2004) where he again follows the theme of a social democratic settlement that aspires to make universal the life chances of the most fortunate by responding to the three great challenges facing social democracy: 'the challenge of equity and excellence; the challenge of flexibility and accountability; and the challenge of universality and personalization.' It is here that Miliband (2004) refers to Piore and Sabel's (1994) *Second Industrial Divide* as the text where he learned that the era of mass production would be superseded in the advanced economies by the age of flexible specialization. Under this new regime of regulation ('flexible specialization') products previously produced for a mass market are now tailored to personal need. (See my discussion above under Mass Customization). Thus, personalization provides 'a new choice for those who are not satisfied to rely solely on the state or the market.' Miliband (2004) then proceeds to define five components of personalized learning based around assessment for learning, effective teaching and learning strategies, curriculum entitlement and choice, school organization, and building a strong partnership beyond the school.

When Miliband argued that personalized education is the future of public sector reform he treated it as an experiment that in its early stages had all the promise of a utopian idea. Yet in a sense not recognized by Miliband or other advocates of personalization, *personalized learning is the presupposition of personalization in all other forms of personalization* not only in the cultural and evolutionary sense of bootstrapping future generations and educating them what and how to personalize public services and complex matters such as their own health, social security and retirement planning but also in terms of the learning necessary in order to be able to take advantage of personalization per se and to be able to learn the art of personalization which demands some level of computer literacy and information technology sophistication.

1. A personalized offer in education depends on really knowing the strengths and weaknesses of individual students. So the biggest driver for change is assessment for learning and the use of data and dialogue to diagnose every student's learning needs.

2. Personalized learning demands that we develop the competence and confidence of each learner through teaching and learning strategies that build on individual needs. This requires strategies that actively engage and stretch all students; that creatively deploy teachers, support staff and new technologies to extend learning opportunities; and that accommodate different paces and styles of learning.

3. Curriculum choice engages and respects students. So personalized learning means every student enjoying curriculum choice, a breadth of study and personal relevance, with clear pathways through the system.

4. Personalized learning demands a radical approach to school organization. It means the starting point for class organization is always student progress, with opportunities for in-depth, intensive teaching and learning, combined with flexible deployment of support staff.

5. Personalized learning means the community, local institutions and social services supporting schools to drive forward progress in the classroom.

Figure 4. Five components of personalized learning

Personalization: The History of a Policy Idea

The notion of personalization did not receive much attention or discussion by policy or education communities. Given its touted status as an idea as 'big' as privatization personalization received very little analytical or robust discussion in academic circles. Personalized learning received some attention and opposition. In 2004 The Learning and Skills Development Agency (LSDA) cast doubt on the validity of work on different learning styles which was seen to underlie the notion of personalized learning. In Scotland and England teachers unions warned of extra workload fears surrounding 'personal learning plans' but the then Scottish Minister, Peter Peacock pressed ahead with personal learning planning anyway. The National Confederation of Parent Teacher Associations warned that personalized learning confuses parents. In March 2005 Blair and Kelly introduced personalized tuition, extra lessons in small groups to stretch the brightest and help struggling pupils to catch up. The Minister Ruth Kelly, taking up her new appointment, began by dismissing the term as 'jargon' only to revoke her dismissal later and to embrace its principles wholeheartedly. In 2005, the theory of individual learning styles, reflecting Department of Education and Skill's emphasis on 'choice' was effectively debunked by Frank Coffield's team, especially the MRI based hereditary studies. In the same year, Schools Minister Jacqui Smith introduced 'leaders of personalization' to oversee individual learning for every 14 to 19-year-olds and in 2006 the Labor Government pledged £1.3 billion investment in personalized learning. Later in 2007, Christine Gilbert (Ofsted) in the 2020 review called for personalization and remarked that schools had reached 'a plateau on improvement' and indicated that traditional solutions are no longer working. In the period following Gordon Brown's assumption of the office of prime minister, he heartily endorsed the notion and philosophy of personalization of public services and of personalized learning, having tied it to the creation and promotion of citizen-consumers in a speech to the Social Market Foundation.

It might be argued that personalization is an idea whose time has come. In a very short period of time personalization came to define the British Labour Government's political philosophy, social policy, and new style of molecular government. This shift was a response to modernizing social democracy in the face of increasing globalization and a new 'openness' characterized by digitalization of society. And it made something about arguments concerning complexity on the one hand and principles for self-organization on the other.

Criticisms have been made of personalization as a generalized strategy and also as it applies to learning per se. Cutler et al. (2007) have questioned whether personalization really does involve a critique of State and professional paternalism. They also note ambiguities with different kinds of personalization (on Leadbeater's spectrum) and ask for a clarification of 'choice' in relation to personalization: does it imply more competition, quasi-market and more performance measures, they ask? They also suggest that personalization is at odds with Labour's policy of quantitative educational targets, obligatory testing of pupils, and publication of test results.

Campbell et al. (2007) suggests that personalization is a collective activity and that it provides a common framework within which individuals develop their learning. They remark that personalized pedagogy is not new and that it originates out of Vygotsky's work into what is called 'the transacted cur-riculum' or constructivist learning and they question the extent to which this pedagogy is generalizable across different subjects. Most importantly, they use-fully raise issues concerning age, ability and class and the extent to which per-sonalized learning is generalizable across these variables. In particular, they inquire whether constructivist learning is effective with all age groups, includ-ing the very young, and whether the aim of co-producing knowledge in the classroom is appropriate for all ability levels. These are substantial points and well justified even if their attribution of personalized learning is possibly astray and does not recognize the ways in which the idea of personalization grows out of discourses concerned with manufacturing systems, engineering and man-agement and how it took root first in forms of social networking and social media. It may be the case that personalized learning is consonant with certain claims made by proponents of various kinds of individualized learning, includ-ing those that emphasize individual learning styles but to make this connec-tion and to seek to explain the development of personalized learning in terms of its educational history alone is to make a mistake concerning its politics and political economy. Whether personalized learning is a pedagogic theory or a coherent set of teaching methods remains to be seen, but certainly it is the case that the concept and practice, however variable it might be in actuality, will radically alter the role of the teacher and also the parent, especially if there is to be an emphasis on the co-production, co-design, and co-evaluation of public knowledge goods, especially at the higher levels.

Ultimately, personalization does imply the adoption of a wider political phi-losophy that redefines the question of responsibility for education from the school with increasing participation and collaboration by parents and children. The question remains to what extent it is possible to ask children to partici-pate in and take personal responsibility for shaping their own education.

Personalization brings together three elements as a generalized solution to provision of public services:

1. It makes use of new open technologies and forms of social media (*the technological imperative*).

2. To devise architectures of citizen participation and collaboration in 'prosumer' open governance systems with an emphasis on co-production of public goods (*the social democratic imperative*).

3. That harnesses high levels of individual motivation through use of social networking and utilizes rational choice making with the aim of promoting personal identity and autonomy (*the psychological imperative*).

Figure 5. Personalization as a generalized solution

The public policy democratic experiment in the United Kingdom needs careful evaluation and discussion especially of the ways in which these three imperatives can and might be brought together into some alignment that enhances the possibilities of democracy and citizenship active participation in the general welfare. This is a political and philosophical question that also demands a public airing and debate given that personalization is rapidly emerging not only as an innovation business strategy but also a political democratic experiment that avails itself of technological developments of social media and brings together the political, technological and the social. Personalization (together with customization and individualization) provides an important basis both as a generalized solution to problems of public service delivery but also as a means of realizing the aims of liberal learning theory: at one and the same time it provides the participatory and collaborative architecture for education and democracy.

Notes

1. This paper is based on the keynote presentation 'Personalization, Molecular Government and the Reform of Social Policy' to the iClass Symposium, *When the Virtual Meets Virtue: From e-Learning to e-Education*, 26–27 May, Brussels, 2008. iClass was one of the largest EU integrated projects funded under Framework 6, running for almost five years involving 17 major stakeholders and ending in June 2007. iClass is an e-Learning platform designed to empower learners through the enhancement of self-regulated personalisation of the learning process (SRPL), where personalisation is defined as adaptation of the learning process and its content to the personal characteristics and preferences of the learner.
2. The list is taken from the Wikipedia entry on 'Open government' http://en.wikipedia.org/wiki/Open_government which in turn acknowledges Alasdair Roberts (2006) *Blacked Out: Government Secrecy in the Information Age* (Cambridge, CUP).
3. The speech is available at http://www.staff.city.ac.uk/p.willetts/IRAQ/TB011002.HTM.
4. For the full text of her speech see http://www.guardian.co.uk/politics/2002/oct/02/labourconference.labour5.
5. See the Demos website at http://www.demos.co.uk/.

References

Bentley, T. (2003). *The Adaptive State: Strategies for personalizing the public realm*, at http://www.demos.co.uk/files/HPAPft.pdf.

Blair, T. (1999). *Modernising Government*. Presented to Parliament by the Prime Minister and the Minister for the Cabinet Office by Command of Her Majesty. At http://www.archive.official-documents.co.uk/document/cm43/4310/4310.htm.

Campbell, R.J. et al. (2007). Personalized Learning: Ambiguities in Theory and Practice,

British Journal of Educational Studies, 55(2), June: 135–154.

Cutler, T., Waine, B. & Brehony, K. (2007). A New Epoch of Individualization? Problems with the personalization of Public Services, *Public Administration*, 85(3): 847–855.

Davis, S. M. (1987). *Future perfect*. New York, NY: Addison-Wesley.

Hargreaves, D. (2004–6). *Personalising Learning* (2004–6) Volumes 1–6, http://www.schoolsnetwork.org.uk/uploads/documents/6492.pdf.

House of Commons (2003). An introduction to devolution in the UK. House of Commons, Research Paper 03/84, 17 November 2003. At http://www.parliament.uk/commons/lib/research/rp2003/rp03–084.pdf.

Illich, I. (1971). *Deschooling Society*. Harmondsworth, UK: Penguin.

Illich, I. (1973). *Tools for Conviviality*. London: Boyers and Cooper.

Illich, I. (1975). *Medical Nemesis*. Harmondsworth, NY: Penguin.

Illich, I. (1978). *Disabling Professions*. NY: Marion Boyars Publishers.

Kumar A. (2007). From mass customization to mass personalization: a strategic transformation. *International Journal of Flexible Manufacturing Systems* 19(4b):533–547.

Kumar, A., Gattoufi, S. & Reisman, A. (2008). Mass customization research: trends, directions, diffusion intensity, and taxonomic frameworks. *International Journal of Flexible Manufacturing Systems* (2007) 19:637–665. Published online: 21 May, 2008.

Leadbeater , C. (2004). *Personalization through Participation: A New Script for Public Services*, at http://www.demos.co.uk/files/PersonalisationThroughParticipation.pdf.

Leadbeater , C. (2005). *The Shape of Things to Come: Personalization and Collaboration in Education*, at http://www.standards.dfes.gov.uk/sie/documents/shape.pdf.

Osborne, D. and Gaebler, T. (1993). Reinventing Government: How the Entrepreneurial Spirit is Transforming the Public Sector. New York: Penguin.

Peters, M.A. (2004a). Citizen-Consumers, Social markets and the Reform of the Public Service, *Policy Futures in Education*, 2(3 & 4): 621–32.

Peters, M.A. (2004b). Rights to Education and the Learning Citizen in European Democracy, *Kwartalnik Pedagogiczny*, University of Warsaw, 194(4): 93–102.

Piller, F. (2003). *Mass Customisation*, 3rd edition, Wiesbaden: Gabler.

Piller, F. (n.d.). MC definition discussion—A focused view on the term at http://www.configurator-database.com/definitions/mass-customisation/mc-definition-discussion.

Piller, F. T. (2008). Observations on the present and future of mass customization. *International Journal of Flexible Manufacturing Systems* (2007) 19:630–636. Published online: 2 April 2008.

Tseng, M.M. and Jiao, J. (2001). Mass Customisation, in G. Salvendy (Ed.) *Handbook of Industrial Engineering*, 3rd edition, New York: Wiley, 2001, pp. 684–709.

ABOUT THE AUTHORS

SIMON MARGINSON is Professor of Higher Education in the Graduate School of Education at the University of Melbourne, Australia, where he works in that University's Centre for the Study of Higher Education. He has held continuous Australian Research Council project funding since 1995, was elected as Fellow of the Academy of Social Sciences, Australia in 2000, designated an Australian Research Council Australian Professorial Fellow in 2002, and an Honorary Fellow of the Society for Research in Higher Education UK in 2005.

He was awarded the Outstanding Publications Award of the American Educational Research Association Division J, for 2001 (with Mark Considine) and the George Z. F. Bereday award for the best journal article of 2001, Comparative and International Education Society, in 2002 (with Marcela Mollis) and the Woodward Medal at the University of Melbourne as the outstanding scholar in the humanities and social sciences (2008). He works on problems of higher education and education policy, comparative and international education, studies of globalization, and the knowledge economy and creativity. Simon is active in scholarly circles in the Asia-Pacific, Europe, and North America and Mexico; has provided advice on higher education and globalization for the governments of Australia, Malaysia, Hong Kong, Vietnam and New Zealand, and several policy papers for OECD; is frequently called on to provide papers on university comparison and ranking; and is active in media commentary on higher education.

He is a member of the Editorial Board of *Times Higher Education* and also *Educational Researcher*, the *Journal of Higher Education*, *Higher Education*, *Higher Education Quarterly*, *Thesis Eleven*, the *ASHE Reader on Comparative Education*, *Critical Studies in Education*, *Higher Education Policy*, the *Journal of Education and Work*, *Journal of South East Asian Education*, *Asia-Pacific Journal of Education* and the *Journal of Higher*

Education. He edited the *Australian Journal of Education* from 1995–2000. Simon has published about 200 scholarly articles, reviews and chapters; and three edited books and 11 sole authored or jointly authored books, including *Markets in Education* (1997), *The Enterprise University* (with Mark Considine, 2000), *Prospects of Higher Education* (2007), *Creativity in the Global Knowledge Economy* (with Michael Peters and Peter Murphy, published by Peter Lang 2009), *Global Creation: Space, mobility and synchrony in the age of the knowledge economy* (with Peter Murphy and Michael Peters, Peter Lang, 2010) and *International Student Security* (with Chris Nyland, Erlenawati Sawir and Helen Forbes-Mewett, Cambridge University Press, 2010).

Five of his books have been published in China including an original collection of papers on higher education and globalization (translated by Li Mei, Peking University Press, forthcoming).

PETER MURPHY is Associate Professor of Communications and Director of the Social Aesthetics Research Unit at Monash University, Australia. He is co-author of *Global Creation* (Peter Lang, 2009), *Creativity and the Global Knowledge Economy* (Peter Lang, 2009), *Dialectic of Romanticism: A Critique of Modernism* (Continuum, 2004), and author of *Civic Justice: From Greek Antiquity to the Modern World* (Prometheus/Humanity Books, 2001). He has co-edited *Philosophical and Cultural Theories of Music* (Brill, forthcoming), *Agon, Logos, Polis* (Franz Steiner, 2000) and *The Left in Search of a Center* (University of Illinois Press, 1996) and is the editor of special issues of *Empedocles: European Journal for the Philosophy of Communication* on Paradox (Intellect, forthcoming) and *South Atlantic Quarterly* on Friendship (Duke University Press, 1998).

His body of work includes more than seventy journal articles and chapters in edited collections. He has been research fellow and visiting professor of philosophy in the Graduate Faculty of the New School for Social Research in New York City; visiting scholar in the Hellenic language and literatures programme at the Ohio State University; visiting scholar at Panteion University in Athens, Greece; visiting professor in political science at Baylor University, Texas; director of the master of communications programme at Victoria University of Wellington, New Zealand; visiting research fellow in philosophy at Ateneo de Manila University in the Philippines; and visiting professor in communications and media studies at Seoul National University, South Korea, and in the Department of Arts and Cultural Studies at the University of Copenhagen, Denmark.

He is coordinating editor of *Thesis Eleven: Critical Theory and Historical Sociology* (Sage), and from 1998 to 2001 he worked in senior editorial roles for Australia's most successful Internet start-up company, Looksmart.

MICHAEL A. PETERS is Professor of Education in the Department of Educational Policy Studies at the University of Illinois at Urbana-Champaign and holds a position as Adjunct Professor at the Royal Melbourne Institute of Technology in the School of Art and at Guangzhou University, China. He held joint professorial positions at the Universities of Auckland (NZ) and Glasgow (UK) during 2000–2005. He was elected Academic Vice-President of the New Zealand Association of University Teachers, elected an inaugural Fellow of the New Zealand Academy of Humanities, awarded Senior Scholar at the University of Illinois and elected a member of the Royal Society of New Zealand.

He is the executive editor of *Educational Philosophy and Theory* (Wiley-Blackwell) and editor of two international ejournals, *Policy Futures in Education* and *E-Learning* (Symposium). His interests focus broadly on education, philosophy, and social theory and he has written some forty books and many academic papers, including most recently: *Creativity and the Global Knowledge Economy* and *Global Creation* (Peter Lang, 2009) with Simon Marginson and Peter Murphy; *Showing and Doing: Wittgenstein as a Pedagogical Philosopher* (Paradigm, 2008) with Nick Burbules and Paul Smeyers; *Global Knowledge Cultures* (Sense) with Cushla Kapitzke; *Subjectivity and Truth: Foucault, Education, and The Culture of Self* (Peter Lang, 2008) (AESA Book Prize, 2009), *Why Foucault? New Directions in Educational Research* (Peter Lang, 2007), and *Building Knowledge Cultures: Educational and Development in the Age of KnowledgeCapitalism* (Rowman & Littlefield, 2006), all with Tina Besley.

Index